Collected Writings of
JOHN MURRAY

Collected Writings of

JOHN MURRAY

PROFESSOR OF SYSTEMATIC THEOLOGY
WESTMINSTER THEOLOGICAL SEMINARY
PHILADELPHIA, PENNSYLVANIA
1937–1966

Volume two
SELECT LECTURES IN
SYSTEMATIC THEOLOGY

The Banner of Truth Trust

THE BANNER OF TRUTH TRUST
3 Murrayfield Road, Edinburgh EH12 6EL
PO Box 621, Carlisle, Pennsylvania 17013, USA

© 1977 Valerie Murray

This collection first published (Volume 2) 1977
ISBN 0 85151 242 9

Printed in Great Britain
by W & J Mackay Limited, Chatham

Contents

Preface   vii

I
_____

1 The Origin of Man   3
2 The Nature of Man   14
3 Trichotomy   23
4 Man in the Image of God   34
5 The Adamic Administration   47
6 Free Agency   60
7 The Fall of Man   67
8 The Nature of Sin   77
9 Inability   83

II
_____

10 Common Grace   93

III
_____

11 The Plan of Salvation   123
12 The Person of Christ   132
13 The Atonement   142
14 The Obedience of Christ   151

Contents

IV

15 The Call   161
16 Regeneration   167
17 Justification   202
18 Adoption   223
19 Faith   235
20 The Assurance of Faith   264

V

21 Definitive Sanctification   277
22 The Agency in Definitive Sanctification   285
23 Progressive Sanctification   294
24 The Pattern of Sanctification   305
25 The Goal of Sanctification   313

VI

26 The Nature and Unity of the Church   321
27 The Government of the Church   336
28 The Form of Government   345
29 Arguments against Term Eldership   351
30 Office in the Church   357
31 The Sacraments   366
32 Baptism   370
33 The Lord's Supper   376
34 Restricted Communion   381

VII

35 The Interadventual Period and the Advent:
   Matthew 24 and 25   387
36 The Last Things   401

Preface

IT was never John Murray's intention to produce a Systematic Theology and in so far as this volume follows, to a limited extent, the form of a Systematic Theology, the responsibility belongs to the publishers and not the author. The material here presented was not written consecutively: it was prepared at different periods in Professor Murray's life and for different purposes. Some chapters are class lectures at Westminster Seminary, others are addresses given at public meetings, and a few are articles for publication. There is therefore an inevitable unevenness in the presentation which would have been eliminated if the author himself had prepared this work for the press.

John Murray consistently resisted appeals that his comprehensive class lectures on Systematic Theology should be published, even though he had the full manuscripts. His chief reason appears to have been that his work as a whole was so representative of the volumes of systematic theology already available that the printing of his own lectures would be unwarranted. But this is not to say that he thought reformed theology had reached definitive conclusions on all biblical subjects. On the contrary, he judged it to be the constant business of the Church to seek a larger knowledge of Scripture for, as he writes in a characteristic sentence, 'We are but touching the fringes of the mystery of God's will . . . Here we have unsearchable wisdom, facets of revelation that pertain to ways past finding out.' His self-judgment on his long teaching ministry was that it had been given to him to make some contribution to the understanding of Scripture on relatively few subjects. It was *these* subjects, rather than Systematic Theology as a whole, which received most of his attention in the latter part of his life and happily they figure prominently in the manuscripts which he prepared in what he considered to be a more finished form than his class lectures. These manuscripts were, for the greater part, in the hands of the publishers at the time of his death, and others were found among his papers. This material supplies a considerable part of the present volume, namely, 'The Origin of Man'; 'The Nature of Man'; 'Trichotomy'; 'Man in the Image of God'; 'The Adamic Administration'; 'Free Agency'; 'The Plan of Salvation'; 'The Person of Christ'; 'The Atonement'; 'The Obedience of Christ'; 'The Call' (chapters 1 to 6, 11 to 15) and the five chapters on Sanctification (21 to 25). The two chapters—'The Nature and Unity of the Church', and 'The Government of the Church' (26 and 27)—are addresses he gave at the Leicester Ministers Conference in 1964. They contain his mature thought on aspects of ecclesiology and, on at least one important point, reflect an advance on traditional presbyterianism. It was our impression that he wished to revise these two addresses before they were published in permanent form—perhaps to enlarge or simplify his argument in places—but this was not to be.

As far as is known to us the only chapters in this volume which have already appeared in print are as follows: 'The Origin of Man', a chapter in *The Law and The Prophets*, edited by John H. Skilton and published by Presbyterian and Reformed Publishing Co. in 1973; 'Common Grace', an article in *The Westminster Theological Journal*; 'Definitive Sanctification' and 'The Agency in Definitive Sanctification', published in the *Calvin Theological Journal*; 'Arguments against Term Eldership', in the *Presbyterian Guardian*; 'The Form of Government' published by the Evangelical Presbyterian Fellowship, London; and 'The Last Things', printed as a Supplement to the *Acts of The Reformed Ecumenical Synod*, 1963. To these publishers gratitude is expressed for permission to reprint the articles in their present form.

The remaining material in this volume has been taken from the manuscripts of his class lectures or from manuscripts which, based on his original class lectures, he had prepared for addresses on various occasions. An interesting and typical example of the way he worked can be seen by comparing the chapter on Regeneration (taken directly from class lectures) with his treatment of same subject in his published volume, *Redemption—Accomplished and Applied*. In the latter volume the chapter on Regeneration is clearly based on his class lectures; it contains the same elements of thought, lucidly presented, but it lacks the detailed exegesis which he considered necessary for students. In general the content of his class lectures is more demanding than the same material when it had passed under his hand for publication. For example, he expected his students to have a working knowledge of Latin and gave quotations from Latin authors without any translation in class lectures.[1]

Possibly another reason why John Murray did not want his class lectures to be printed as delivered was that he had the highest regard for brevity and an economy of words in all published material. He exhibited this quality magnificently in his *Commentary on Romans* and it will be seen most prominently in this volume in those chapters which he had himself prepared for printing.

John Murray was called to serve the church of Christ in a day when, for the most part, adherence to Scripture and to the doctrines of historic Christianity was in eclipse. The twentieth century may be remembered by the church of the future as an age in which theology and Christianity, learning and piety, had parted company, save in the testimony of a few. Prominent among the few was the author of these pages and we do not doubt that they will be read with deep enrichment by the redeemed until the Advent of the Saviour.

IAIN H. MURRAY
Edinburgh, April 1977

[1] Where this occurred in the contents of this volume translations have been supplied.

I

1

The Origin of Man[1]

For our knowledge of man's origin we are mainly dependent upon the first two chapters of Genesis (cf. also Matt. 19:4, 5; Mark 10:6, 7; Luke 3:38; 1 Cor. 11:8, 9; 1 Tim. 2:13). In these chapters in Genesis there are three leading emphases:

First, the universe had a beginning; it is not eternal (Gen. 1:1, 31; 2:1; cf. John 1:1, 3; Col. 1:16, 17; Heb. 11:3). Only of God can eternity be predicated, and all that is distinct from God came to be by his will and word (cf. Psalm 33:6, 9). The data mentioned in Genesis 1:1, for example, are basic to all Christian thought of God, of reality distinct from God, and of God's relation to this reality.

Second, in the production of the heavens and the earth there is sequence and progression. They did not come to be by a single all-embracing fiat. There is ordered process moving to the climax of man's formation, to man as the crown of God's handiwork. The platform of life for man is prepared by successive steps and life itself appears to an appreciable extent in an ascending scale until it reaches its apex in man.

Third, at each stage in this progression God speaks and gives his command. We read repeatedly, 'And God said' (Gen. 1:3, 6, 9, 11, 14, 20, 24, 26, 29). No *single* grand fiat endowed created reality with potencies which spontaneously by energies intrinsic to them produced the various forms of life. We are advised of the significance of God's *word* and of the efficacy belonging to it (cf. especially Gen. 1:3, 11, 12; Psalm 33:9).

It is within the framework of these emphases that we must interpret

[1] Published in *The Law and the Prophets*, edited by John H. Skilton, Presbyterian & Reformed Publishing Co., 1973.

the account of man's origin and appreciate the distinguishing features as the indexes to the distinctiveness of his origin.

DISTINCTIVENESS ARISING FROM THE UNIQUE ENGAGEMENT OF GOD'S COUNSEL

'And God said, Let us make man' (Gen. 1:26). These terms have no parallel elsewhere. The uniqueness does not reside in the fact that God spoke, but in what he said: 'Let us make'. The formula is not that of simple fiat as in the case of light (Gen. 1:3). Nor is it that of command in reference to existing entities—'let the earth bring forth tender herb' (Gen. 1:11); 'let the waters swarm swarm[1] of living creature' (Gen. 1:20); 'let the earth bring forth living creature' (Gen. 1:24). The terms 'let us make' indicate that there is unique engagement of divine thought and counsel, and bespeak the fact that something correspondingly unique is about to take place. This formula of itself implies that there is distinguishing character to that which is contemplated because there is distinguishing preoccupation with the event. According to the Bible's account, man is not in any aspect of his origin on a parity with other creatures; the distinctiveness appears in the counsel of which his origin is the effect.

DISTINCTIVENESS ARISING FROM THE NATURE WITH WHICH MAN IS ENDOWED

'Let us make man in our image, after our likeness' (Gen. 1:26). The sequence in which this occurs is eloquent of the contrast between man and all other forms of life, animate and inanimate. The latter were made after their kind (cf. vss. 11, 12, 21). The reiteration in verses 24, 25 points up the contrast most forcefully. 'And God said, Let the earth bring forth the living creature after its kind, cattle, and creeping thing, and beast of the earth after its kind: and it was so. And God made the beast of the earth after its kind, and the cattle after its kind, and every creeping thing of the ground after its kind: and God saw that it was good.' On five occasions this formula 'after its kind' or 'to its kind' occurs. Then in verse 26 the abrupt change from 'to its kind' to 'in our image, after our likeness' draws our attention to radical differentiation

[1] Here and elsewhere John Murray employed his own translation to bring out the precise force of the original.

4

between the pattern to which other forms of life conform and the exemplar which is the model for man. In the former case there is indeed the pattern established by the Creator. But there is no suggestion of a heavenly exemplar. 'To its kind' implies no more than a fixed pattern in accord with God's design. In the case of man there is also the divine design. But there is incomparably more. The pattern designed and determined is the exemplar provided by the character of God himself. God *willed* that man's identity should consist in God's own image and likeness. But the exemplar itself was not something willed to be; it is that which belongs to God himself intrinsically. Intelligent response to this datum of revelation is one of amazement, and we exclaim: 'What is man, that thou art mindful of him!' (Psa. 8:4). Man's origin is not only the unique subject of God's counsel; man is from the outset the recipient of unique endowment and dignity.

DISTINCTIVENESS ARISING FROM THE LORDSHIP WITH WHICH MAN IS INVESTED

'And let them have dominion over the fish of the sea, and over the fowl of the heaven, and over the cattle, and over all the earth, and over every creeping thing that creepeth upon the earth' (Gen. 1:26). That man's creation is the last in the series, we may regard as correlative with this lordship. The prerogative rests, however, not on the sequence but upon the nature with which man is endowed. He is in the image of God. Since God is sovereign, man's likeness to God involves the exercise of a sovereignty that is correspondent. He is God's viceregent because he is like God.

The demarcation between man and the other animate creatures that stand in the closest relation to him (cf. vss. 24, 25) is hereby exemplified in unmistakable terms, and it becomes impossible to conceive of man as in any respect on a parity with other animate beings, not to speak of the inanimate. The scope of the investiture indicated in that quoted above shows the distinctiveness belonging to man in the totality of his relationships.

DISTINCTIVENESS OF GOD'S PROCEDURE IN THE FORMATION OF MAN

'And the Lord God formed the man dust from the ground, and breathed in his nostrils breath of life, and man became living creature' (Gen. 2:7).

There are differences between Genesis 1:1–2:3 and Genesis 2:4–25. In the former passage man appears in his place in the creative process as a whole and in relation to creation as a whole, particularly in his relation to the earth on which he lives. The panorama is inclusive and all-embracive. But in Genesis 2:4–25 we have a more detailed account of the mode of action in forming both the man and the woman, and man appears in his more immediate relations and environment. Genesis 2:7 is consonant with this purpose and it is concerned with the origin of Adam as distinct from Eve. This distinction is not intimated in Genesis 1:27. For there we are simply told that God created them 'male and female'. We do not have divergent accounts of creation. Genesis 2 is supplementary, and obviously furnishing details that would not be in accord with the structure and design of Genesis 1.

In dealing with Genesis 2:7 and with the distinctive features it sets forth we must take account of the various elements.

1.   *Formation*. 'The Lord God formed the man dust from the ground.' 'Dust from the ground' informs us that matter, previously created by God and taken from the earth, entered into the composition of man's being from the outset. When Adam was made in accordance with the design and resolve of Genesis 1:26 it was not by simple fiat, by what has been called *creatio ex nihilo*. In making man, the word of God, and the action corresponding to it, operated upon existing substance, and this substance of material character was subjected to formative action on God's part, action prior to any other action. 'Dust from the ground' belongs to man's constitution from the outset; it is not an appendage or accident. This is confirmed later, when God said to Adam: 'Dust thou art' (Gen. 3:19); it belongs to his person.

There are necessary corollaries:

(i) Man has affinity with his non-animate environment, with the ground on which he walks and from which, to a large extent, he derives his sustenance, the ground which it is his task to till, dress, and subdue. There is congruity between man and his environment. And for this there is a necessity. If it were not so there would be a discrepancy between man and his habitat, between man and his task, an incompatibility that would have negated the verdict: 'God saw everything that he had made, and, behold, it was very good' (Gen. 1:31).

6

(ii) Man has affinity with other animate beings on this earth. There is a striking similarity between Genesis 2:7 and 2:19. In the latter we read: 'And the Lord God formed from the ground every beast of the field and every fowl of the heaven'. There is affinity in respect of constitutive element, even though there may be an important difference between 'dust from the ground' and 'the ground'. There is also affinity in the formative action. So we fail to appreciate the witness the Bible bears to man's affinity with his environment if we overlook these data.

We must not emphasize the similarity of Genesis 2:7 and 2:19 so as to eliminate the distinctiveness of the former. Genesis 2:19 must be taken in conjunction with Genesis 1:24, 25. In the latter the results are prefaced by the command: 'Let the earth bring forth living creature' and the thought is permissible that there were potencies deposited by God in the earth that were to put forth their energies at the divine behest (cf. also Gen. 1:20). Genesis 2:7 must be co-ordinated with Genesis 1:26, and nowhere is there in the case of man any formula that approaches that of Genesis 1:20, 24, 25. We need only repeat the formulae concerned in the respective cases to detect the difference. And yet the difference must not be allowed to obscure for us the all-important lessons of affinity implicit in the consideration that God formed the man dust from the ground.

2. *Impartation.* 'Breathed in his nostrils breath of life, and man became living creature.' It is here we find the chief differentia as far as Genesis 2:7 is concerned. If the first part of the verse points to affinities with the rest of creation, the second part has no analogy. In no other instance do we find any suggestion of similar action. Man alone owes his origin to the kind of action here expressed. There are several observations:

(i) *Inbreathing.* We may not know the precise nature of the action denoted by 'breathed in his nostrils'. But the terms must represent communication from without and cannot be interpreted as evolution of potencies resident in 'dust from the ground', nor even in terms of potencies belonging to the resultant of the formative action to which dust from the ground had been subjected. Inbreathing stands for interposition on God's part, by special action, for the communication of the breath of life. From this act life, identified as breathing, and manifested in breathing, had been derived.

(ii) *Living Creature.* 'And man became living creature.' The term rendered 'living creature' means animate being, creature with the breath of life. *In itself* this predicate does not express anything distinctive of man as compared with other animate beings. The designation is generic and is applied to other creatures (cf. Gen. 1:21, 24, 30). It is all-important to observe this fact. For it means that it was by the act of impartation, the act of communication from God denoted by inbreathing, that the entity formed from the dust of the ground came to belong to the category of animate being. To state the matter negatively, man did not become animate by any process short of the action specified as inbreathing. If 'man' were previously animate, and the inbreathing constituted him man as distinct from and superior to other animate creatures, then it could not be said that by the inbreathing he became 'living creature'. The inbreathing was not an action superimposed upon an already existing animate being.

(iii) *Man.* We have just noted that it was the inbreathing that constituted this being animate creature. But we must with comparable emphasis assert that by this same action Adam was constituted specifically man. Genesis 2:7 does not refer to any supposed animate progenitor of man. This conclusion is derived from two considerations:

(a) The definition of man is already provided in the preceding context (Gen. 1:26). Hence no other than man thus identified can be in view when we read in Genesis 2:7: 'And the Lord God formed the man'. It is the formation of man, measuring up to the character and status of Genesis 1:26, that is contemplated, not of some animate progenitor of man, not of savage man, but of man whose denotation and connotation are determined for us by the preceding context.

(b) Any lower form of animate life would not only be incompatible with the definition of Genesis 1:26 but also with the rôle accorded to man in the more immediate context (Gen. 2:4–25). The man of Genesis 2:7 is the man to whom God speaks, who receives commandments that are to be intelligently obeyed, and who finds no counterpart among other creatures. It would be exegetical violence to introduce a concept of man alien to every note found in the context.

The upshot of these various considerations pertinent to Genesis 2:7 is, therefore, as follows:

It was the divine inbreathing that constituted man animate creature. It was this same inbreathing that constituted man specifically man. So that which constituted man animate creature was that also which constituted him man, and that which constituted him specifically man is that also which constituted him animate creature. Man's animation in any form or at any time cannot be differentiated from the animation that belongs to him in his specific identity as man made in the image of God. Man did not appear in two stages of animate development, and we may not think of man as possessing an animate life common to him and other beings, and then in addition an animate life distinct from other beings. The animation that is his is the animation that belongs to his distinguishing identity.

CORROBORATION

These foregoing distinctive features are corroborated by various other data:

1. Adam found no counterpart among the creatures of his environment over which he exercised dominion. There was no helpmate answering to him. No consideration could more conclusively demonstrate his uniqueness. A helpmate had to be provided by special action on God's part.

2. The action by which God provided a helpmate differs from the action by which Adam was made. But it differs as radically from the mode of activity in making other creatures as does the action by which Adam was made. In its specific character it is as special and distinguishing as the breathing into Adam's nostrils the breath of life. In these respects the making of Eve as Adam's helpmate is confirmatory of special action in the case of Adam himself. For if the provision of a helpmate for Adam required the special actions described in Genesis 2:21, 22, it was only because correspondingly special action constituted Adam what he was in that distinctiveness to which only Eve could answer.

3. Adam's distinguishing identity and office are shown by his naming the other animate creatures (Gen. 2:19, 20). It is significant that, as the sequel to this function, we read: 'And as for Adam he found no helpmate answering to him' (Gen. 2:20b). Then, after Eve was given, the naming of her as woman because she was taken out of man (Gen. 2:23),

and Eve because she was the mother of all living (Gen. 3:20), indicates
that these names are expressive of origin and function. In like manner the
names given by Adam to the other beings, we would suspect, if not
infer, were not arbitrary symbols, but names chosen with a discrimination that only intelligent perception and observation could furnish. In
any case Adam's dominion over the creatures and the intelligence
necessary for its exercise are clearly evidenced by this prerogative—
'Whatever Adam called any living creature that was its name'
(Gen. 2:19).

4. The sacredness of human life, so clearly stated later on (Gen. 9:5, 6),
is manifested in the condemnation of Cain and the curse inflicted upon
him for the slaying of his brother (Gen. 4:10–14). The differentiation
between man and animals in this respect is certified by the clothing of
Adam and Eve with coats of skins (Gen. 3:21), and even more eloquently by the acceptance of Abel's offering 'of the firstlings of his
flock and of the fat thereof' (Gen. 4:4). The sanctity of human life by
way of contrast is illustrated by the pronouncement by which even the
murderer's life was guarded from wanton assault: 'Therefore whosoever
slayeth Cain, vengeance shall be taken on him sevenfold' (Gen. 4:15).
The only explanation of the sanctity belonging to human life is the
distinctiveness to which Genesis 1:26 and 2:7 bear witness.

5. God placed man on probation and gave commands that were to be
consciously and intelligently fulfilled (cf. Gen. 2:15–17). Between God
and man there is the ethico-religious bond, a relationship not hinted in
the case of the other creatures. For man there is the cultural mandate
(cf. Gen. 1:28) co-ordinate with the dominion bestowed upon him.
The implications of this mandate make its relevance inconceivable on
any lower level than that pertaining to man as defined in Genesis 1:26.
And the mandate is given, not as an undertaking to be fulfilled after he
has attained a future stage of development, but it is his from the outset.
All the powers necessary for the task are conceived of as belonging to
him in virtue of his creation in God's image and likeness.

6. New Testament references to man's origin are distinctly allusions
to the accounts given in Genesis 1 and 2, especially the latter. In our
Lord's teaching, Matthew 19:4 and Mark 10:6 refer unmistakably to
Genesis 1:27 and 5:2; Matthew 19:5 and Mark 10:7 to Genesis 2:24.

In accord with the uniform pattern of his appeal to the Old Testament our Lord thus sets the seal of his authority upon the Genesis narrative and does not recognize or allow for any discrepancy between the concepts that were valid for Old Testament times and those valid for the fulness of the time when he spoke to his disciples and still speaks to us. When Paul writes: 'The first man Adam was made living soul' (1 Cor. 15:45) the Scripture to which appeal is made is Genesis 2:7. For Paul, Adam was the first man. But most significant in this instance of appeal to Genesis 2:7 is the way in which all that follows in the ensuing argument is built upon the truth derived from this text. What belongs to the essence of Paul's soteriology rests upon the parallel and contrast between Adam, the first man, made 'living soul', and Christ, the second man and last Adam, made 'life-giving spirit'. This exemplifies the peril of questioning the veracity or relevance of any detail in the Scriptures concerned. We have not only Paul's imprimatur; we are given to see the implications for what is ultimate in soteriology. Again, in this same epistle, Paul alludes to Genesis 2:21–23 (1 Cor. 11:8, 9, 12) and shows the same regard for its veracity and relevance. The appeal to Genesis 2:7, 21–23 is patently expressed in 1 Timothy 2:13: 'For Adam was first formed, then Eve'. The distinctiveness of Adam as to origin is indicated in Luke 3:38. The genealogy extends from Jesus to Adam. In every other instance the human paternity is stated and the absence of human paternity in the case of Adam is noted by the substitution 'of God', with the implication that only a special act of God explains his coming to be. Earlier in our study we found that generation from any lower form of animate life is excluded. Now we are expressly advised of what is equally implied in Genesis 2:7, that human parentage played no part in Adam's origin.

This witness of the New Testament is, therefore, confirmatory of what we find in the Old Testament and shows that no other conception than that derived from Genesis 1:26, 27; 2:7, 21–23; 5:1, 2 is entertained by our Lord and the New Testament writers.

CONCLUSIONS

The cumulative effect of all the data derived from the early chapters of Genesis is to institute a radical cleavage between man and all other forms of animate life. The crux of the question as it is posed for us by the theory of evolution is: can the portrayal given us in the Bible, and particularly in Genesis 1 and 2, be interpreted as compatible with a theory that man as we know him and, for that matter, man as represented in Genesis, came to be by a process of evolution from lower forms of animate life? It matters not what particular form of evolutionary theory is in view, and it would be extraneous to this study to deal with the various evolutionary theories, even with those of most recent vintage. The issue is the same. As applied to man, is an evolutionary view of his origin compatible with the biblical representation? There are several considerations that demand a negative answer.

1. Man's identity consists in the image and likeness of God. This is man's differentia from the beginning (Gen. 1:26; 5:1; cf. 9:6); he was *made* in this image and likeness and therefore cannot be conceived of on any lower level. When we ponder the stupendous import of this characterization and of the implications for the cleavage between man and all other orders of being in this world, then we are compelled to conclude that no action or process such as would account for the other forms of life would be sufficient for the order to which man belongs. It is only when we fail to assess the significance of the image and likeness of God that we could offer entertainment to a theory that posits continuity with other orders or species of animate life in this world. In other words, to suppose that a process of evolution by forces resident in an order of things incalculably lower in the scale of being could account for man's origin, involves an incongruity once we appreciate the identity of likeness to God.

2. Genesis 2:7 cannot be reconciled with the evolutionary hypothesis, and it confirms the conclusions derived from Genesis 1:26; 5:1; 9:6. It was by *ab extra* impartation, communication from God described as inbreathing, that man became animate creature as well as man in his specific identity. In no respect, therefore, could man be regarded as animate being by evolutionary process. The postulate of evolutionary theory is to the opposite effect. It must maintain that the ancestors of *homo-sapiens* were animate. So in the one text which delineates for us the mode of God's action in making man there is explicit contradiction of the evolutionary postulate. From this contradiction there is no

escape, unless we do violence to the elementary requirements of biblical interpretation.

3. Genesis 2:7, as we found, shows that man has affinity with the material stuff of the earth and with the animate creation as well. There is likeness and for that reason congruity. So we should expect resemblances of various kinds. If there were complete disparity, how incongruous would be man's habitat and vocation. We see the wisdom and goodness of the Creator in these likenesses. No evolutionary hypothesis is necessary to explain them; they are required by the relationships man sustains to his environment.

Man has also likeness to God and, as repeatedly stated, this is his differentia; it is his definition. We may not say that in forming man from the dust of the ground (Gen. 2:7a) the distinguishing and specific character of man was not exemplified. The likeness to God is impressed upon man in his totality and thus upon his bodily constitution. Man's affinities with the rest of creation are correlative with the distinctiveness that is his. We can speak of the affinities only as we keep in view his specific character as the image and likeness of God. Yet we must recognize that in Genesis 2:7 we are apprised of the two factors in man's origin which provide for the twofold likeness. When we read: 'And the Lord God formed the man dust from the ground' we are pointed to man's affinity with his earthly environment and to the action which constituted it. When we read: 'and breathed in his nostrils breath of life' we are advised of the factor which, most specifically, constituted likeness to God and equipped man with the endowments necessary to his vocation.

2

The Nature of Man

THE biblical data (cf. Gen. 2:7; 3:19) show that from the outset there is a material aspect to man's constitution. Man is bodily, and, therefore, the scriptural way of expressing this truth is not that man has a body but that man *is* body. So, first of all, in dealing with the nature of man, we have body.

BODY

Scripture does not represent the soul or spirit of man as created first and then put into a body. The opposite is the case—'The Lord God formed the man dust from the ground' (Gen. 2:7). The bodily is not an appendage. The notion that the body is the prison-house of the soul and that the soul is incarcerated in the body is pagan in origin and anti-biblical; it is Platonic, and has no resemblance to the biblical conception. The Bible throughout represents the dissolution of the body and separation of body and spirit as an evil, as the retribution and wages of sin, and, therefore, as a disruption of that integrity which God established at creation. We must observe the corollaries:

1. The body is intrinsically good. It is not the source of sin, nor is it inherently degrading. No dishonour belongs to man because of the material aspect of his person. The body can become the avenue of solicitation to sin, but sin had and has its genesis in the spirit of man. The dignity of the body is advertised by the fact that of man made in the image of God we read: 'And the Lord God formed the man dust from the ground'.

2. Man is not naturally mortal. Death is not the debt of nature; it is the debt of what violated man's nature, namely, sin.

3. Body and spirit are not antithetical. They are diverse in metaphysical constitution but there is no native or necessary conflict. In unity and concord they constitute the unique personality that man is, made in the image of God.

Genesis 3:19—'dust thou art, and to dust thou shalt return'—in no way contradicts these corollaries. These words occur in the curse upon Adam because of sin and they have relevance only in that context. The meaning is that the penalty takes this way of executing itself in the case of man. Death addresses itself to his personality and takes account of the unique composition of his personality. Hence his return to dust. If he were not dust, he could not return to dust. But the reason for return to dust is not that he is dust, but that he has sinned (Gen. 2:17; 3:17).

In the insistence upon the intrinsic goodness of body, we need not maintain that the body, as created, was endowed with all the qualities with which it would subsequently have been equipped if Adam had been confirmed in integrity and blessedness. It is one thing to say that no evil resided in or necessarily proceeded from the body, it is another thing to say that additional qualities of excellence could have been or would have been imparted. Inherent goodness is quite compatible with development and enrichment of that goodness. The case is parallel to that which applies in general. Man was created in knowledge, righteousness, and holiness. But confirmation of these is a much higher state of blessedness. Confirmation adds to what is good; it does not presuppose evil, the opposite of good.

The implications of the above doctrine have an important bearing on many other aspects of Scripture:

1. *Sin*. Though not the seat of sin, the body becomes depraved. It becomes the agent of sin and its members instruments of unrighteousness unto sin. The body is a sinful body and thus the body of sin (Rom. 6:6). We are too ready to underestimate the gravity of the sensuous manifestations of sin. This tendency is frequently bound up with the notion that the body does not belong to the integrity of personality, and is something alien to it, and incompatible with the highest attainments of spirituality. Thus sensuous lust is shrugged off as something

that belongs to what is not intrinsic to our true nature. Since man is body, he is, as respects responsibility and guilt, as closely identified with the depravity of the body as he is with that of his spirit.

2. *Death.* Even in death the body that is laid in the tomb is not simply a body. It is the body of the person. More properly, it is the person as respects the body. It is the person who is buried or laid in the tomb. How eloquent of this is the usage respecting our Lord. He was buried. He rose from the dead. In reference to Jesus the angel said: 'Come see the place where he lay'. Jesus also said: 'All that are in the graves will hear his voice', and to Lazarus he said: 'Lazarus, come forth'. Believers are dead in Christ, they sleep through Jesus. So what is laid in the grave is still integral to the person who died. In and during death the person is identified with the dissolved material entity. This underlies the gravity of death and the return to dust. 'To dust *thou* shalt return', as also 'Dust *thou* art'.

3. *The Incarnation.* Our Lord's human nature was body and spirit. His body was composed of the material elements which characterize other human beings. Since he took human nature into his person, he was human, and, therefore, he was body and spirit. The mode of his generation was supernatural; he was begotten by the Holy Spirit. But his incarnation was not superhuman or superphysical. He was made of a woman, made of the seed of David according to the flesh (cf. Gal. 4:4; Rom. 1:3). It was some form of docetism that John was called upon to combat when he wrote: 'In this ye know the Spirit of God: every spirit that confesseth Jesus Christ come in the flesh is of God, and every spirit that does not confess Jesus is not of God' (I John 4:2, 3). The import of this is, that the name Jesus is so bound up with the manifestation in the flesh, that the confession of Jesus is confession of his bodily identity. To deny the reality of the flesh of Jesus both prior to and after the resurrection is to overthrow the faith of Jesus.

The bias at work in what John indicts as antichrist (I John 4:3b) was gnostic and associated with the doctrine that material substance is inherently evil. This pattern of thought appears in various forms, and it is a kindred bias that manifests itself in indifference to physical fact and experience, an attitude alien to the Christian faith. The Christian faith has profound concern for facts that transpired in the realm of the phenomenal and historical, in the realm of sensuous fact, of physical experience. No New Testament writer is more jealous for the transcendent and superhistorical aspects of our Lord's person (cf. John 1:1; 1 John 1:2). But it is John who insists that the revelation of the eternal Word and of the eternal life who was with the Father is given through sense experience. It is this insistence we encounter at the outset in his first Epistle: 'That which was from the beginning, which we have heard, which we have seen with our eyes, which we have looked upon and our hands have handled, concerning the Word of life' (1 John 1:1). And lest we should miss this emphasis he reiterates: 'That which we have seen and heard declare we unto you' (1 John 1:3). There is the twofold insistence: first, the reality of the physical manifestation of 'the eternal life who was with the Father' (vs. 2) and, second, that through the medium of sensuous contact with him in seeing, hearing, and handling, they, the witnesses, entered into the fellowship of the Father and the Son, into the fellowship of the Father of whom John affirms in his Gospel: 'No man hath seen God at any time' (John 1:18).

It is true that living faith required more than the sense experience. The inward illumination was necessary to the perception of the meaning of the experiences registered through the senses. But the inward illumination was directed to the interpretation of the significance of the sensuous manifestation and the corresponding experiences, and had no relevance apart from what transpired in the realm of sense. It is also true that we today do not have sense experiences. But our faith today, and the fellowship resulting, rest indispensably upon the witness of those who did see, hear, and handle. The only difference is that our faith rests upon accredited testimony to these facts of physical manifestation, while the faith of the apostles was elicited by direct experience of the same manifestation. 'That which we have seen and heard declare we unto you also, in order that ye also may have fellowship with us' (vs. 3). Hence the highest reaches of true spirituality are dependent upon events that occurred in the realm of the physical and sensuous. A religion that can be indifferent to the bodily, to the physical, to the phenomenal, has no affinity with the Christian faith; it is a spurious religiosity that does not warrant the name 'spirituality'. We can see how intimately bound up with the first principles of our holy faith is the doctrine that man is body. For only then can the redemptive revelation given in and through the *man* Christ Jesus have actuality.

4. *The Resurrection.* Without the empty tomb, and the living again of Jesus' dead and buried body, there was no resurrection. To deny the physical character of the resurrection is to deny the resurrection itself. And in respect of identity and continuity, our Lord has in heaven the same body as suffered on the cross, was laid in the tomb, and lived again on the third day. The resurrection, thus conceived, provides the pattern for the resurrection of believers (cf. Rom. 8:11; Phil. 3:21). And the glory that will be bestowed at the resurrection will consist to a large extent in what could only be true in the realm of sense experience. Christ will then be manifested in the body of his glory. He will be *seen* the second time (Heb. 9:28). This emphasis upon his being seen is profoundly significant. It assures us that the physical occupies a central place in the consummation of salvation, in the attainment of glory. All the demands of the physical will be fully realized and satisfied in the *vision* of his manifested glory. Here is exemplified and vindicated the significance of the body in that which is the pole-star of the believer's hope. Of this we have eloquent corroboration in the believer's groaning and longing: 'We ourselves also, who have the firstfruits of the Spirit, even we ourselves groan within ourselves, waiting for the adoption, the redemption of our body' (Rom. 8:23; cf. 2 Cor. 5:2–4; Phil. 3:21).

5. *The Judgment.* We are to be judged according to the things which we have done 'through the body' (2 Cor. 5:10). Embodied life is the criterion of judgment and destiny. This indicates that no reversal of state and condition takes place in the disembodied period. Hebrews 9:27 is eloquent of the fact that there is a finality to death. 'It is appointed unto men once to die, and after this judgment.' Death and judgment are brought into conjunction as if they were in immediate sequence. The intermediate state falls into the shadow and has no determinative character for the judgment to be executed.

SPIRIT OR SOUL

Even in death the person is identified with the corpse that is laid in the tomb. The relation to the physical is not dissolved even in death. But if the person is identified with what is lifeless, there must be another aspect to the person not subject to the kind of decease that befalls the body. In other words, there must be an entity on the basis of which personality survives. The Scripture provides us with copious evidence to establish the thesis that there belongs to man a subsistence or entity distinguished from the body and characterized by qualities in virtue of which it does not undergo the dissolution that befalls the body in death. The Scripture designates this as spirit or soul.

Our Lord taught: 'Fear not them that kill the body but are not able to kill the soul' (Matt. 10:28). It is obvious that 'soul' is used here in a metaphysical sense. Our Lord is basing his exhortation and consolation upon the differentiating properties and relationships of the two entities. The soul is not subject to the destructive assault that may be brought to bear upon the body. In this case 'soul' does not mean life constituted in a body, for when used in that sense it can be spoken of as laid down (*tithēmi, paradidōmi,* and *didōmi*—Matt. 20:28; Mark 10:45; John 10:11, 15; Acts 15:26; 1 John 3:16) as killed or destroyed (*apothnēskō* and *apollumi*—Matt. 16:25; Mark 3:4; Luke 6:9; John 12:24), as sought after to be taken away (*zēteō*—Matt. 2:20; Rom. 11:3). In Matt. 10:28 it is construed as untouchable in contrast with the body.

In Matthew 26:41—'the spirit truly is willing but the flesh is weak' —there is contrast between flesh and spirit. When 'flesh' is used in the ethical sense (cf. John 3:6; Rom. 7:18; 8:3, 6, 7, 8; Gal. 5:19), it includes the spirit of man as well as the body; it is human nature directed by sin. But in this instance the spirit is excluded from the flesh as weak. In this word of Jesus there is more of extenuation than of reproof. Although 'flesh' may not be taken as synonymous with 'body', yet there is reflection upon the weakness associated with the physical in contrast with the willingness of the spirit as non-physical.

There is also the word of our Lord to the disciples: 'A spirit hath not flesh and bones as ye see me having' (Luke 24:39), again verifying the differentiation in metaphysical quality.

In 1 Corinthians 2:11 Paul says: 'who of men knows the things of the man save the spirit of the man which is in him?' Two observations are relevant: (1) There is in man what is called 'spirit' and (2) of the spirit is predicated knowledge, that is, intelligent apprehension inaccessible to any other man (cf. Rom. 8:16).

The unmarried woman and virgin, Paul says, cares for the things of the Lord 'that she may be holy both in the body and the spirit' (1 Cor. 7:34). This is intended to express sanctification of the whole person, and is, therefore, an inclusive designation, but the distinction between body and spirit is implied in the terms 'both in the body and the spirit'.

Sanctification is defined in its negative aspect as cleansing ourselves 'from all filthiness of flesh and spirit' (2 Cor. 7:1). Again the inclusiveness is apparent but the distinction is implied, and comes close to, if it is not identical with, that of body and spirit in the preceding reference.

The distinction between the bodily and the psychical in human personality is clear in 1 Thessalonians 5:23; 'May your spirit and soul and body be kept entire'.

In James 2:26: 'the body without a spirit is dead', there is enunciation of the distinction and also the assertion that the spirit is the animating principle.

That which is separated from the body at death is called the spirit (Matt. 27:50—'he dismissed the spirit'; Luke 23:46—'Father, into thy hands I commit my spirit'; John 19:30—'he gave up the spirit'; Acts 7:59—'Lord Jesus, receive my spirit').

Scripture calls disembodied persons spirits (Heb. 12:23; 1 Pet. 3:19) and portrays the disembodied state as one of consciousness and awareness of personal identity (Luke 9:30, 31; Luke 16:19–31; Luke 23:43; 2 Cor. 5:1–10; Phil. 1:22, 23). When Paul says: 'We are of good courage and are willing rather to be absent from the body and to be present with the Lord' (2 Cor. 5:8), and says that he had the 'desire to depart and to be with Christ, for it is far better' (Phil. 1:23), what he desired is inconceivable apart from the retention of personal identity, the intelligent exercise of the functions of personality, and communion with the Saviour in the fullest exercise of these attributes.

On the basis of these biblical data we must conclude that man is spirit or soul, as well as body. There is an aspect to his person distinct from the body. There belongs to his identity as man an entity metaphysically differentiated from the body, and endowed with properties and qualities in virtue of which it is not subject to the dissolution which the body undergoes at death. This entity retains its identity and differentiating character after death. More properly, in virtue of spirit the person retains his identity, and continues to exist and be active in a realm and mode of existence consonant with and adapted to the disembodied state. The highest exercises of man as a rational, moral, religious being are predicable of man by reason of this aspect. All that we are most characteristically as beings created in the image of God, has its seat, unity, and abiding meaning in this entity. There is an 'ego', spiritual in nature, indivisible and indestructible, continuously subsistent and active through all the changes of life in this world, in the disembodied state, and in the resurrected life in the age to come.

We must not suppose, however, that the term 'soul' as it occurs in Scripture always refers to this distinct and differentiated aspect of human personality. 'Soul' has various applications even when used of man. In numerous cases it refers simply to life (cf. Matt. 6:25; 10:39; 16:25, 26; 20:28; Luke 14:26; John 10:11–18; Acts 15:26; 20:10; Phil. 2:30; 1 John 3:16), life constituted in the body. 'Soul' is frequently the synonym of person and can stand for the personal pronoun (cf. Matt. 12:18; Luke 12:19; Acts 2:27, 41, 43; 3:23; Rom. 2:9; 13:1; Heb. 10:38; James 1:21; 5:20; 1 Pet. 1:9; 2:25). The thesis is simply that, with sufficient frequency, 'soul' as 'spirit' is used to designate the distinguishing component in the human person.

CONCLUSION

The biblical doctrine is then to the effect that there are two aspects to man. Using the word 'entity' to denote that which has distinctness of being, we can say that there are two entities in man's constitution, diverse in nature and origin, the one derived from the earth, material, corporeal, phenomenal, divisible, the other derived from a distinct action of God, immaterial and ordinarily not phenomenal, indivisible and indestructible. These two entities form one organic unit without disharmony or conflict. In the integral person they are interdependent. They coact and interact. The modes of coaction and interaction are largely hid from us. The union is intimate and intricate and we are not able to define its mode, nor can we discover the relations they sustain to each other. 'The union of soul and body which makes man is not external and extensive, but internal and intensive'.[1]

[1] John Macpherson: *Dogmatics*, p. 194; cf. Calvin: *Inst.* I, xv, 2, and also H. Dooyeweerd: *A New Critique of Theoretical Thought*, III, p. 89: 'The human body is man himself in the structural whole of his temporal appearance. And the human soul, in the pregnant religious sense, is man himself in the radical unity of his spiritual existence, which transcends all temporal structures'. In this definition I would say that 'temporal appearance' is too restrictive and may not do justice to the permanence of the body in the integrity of human life. But with the main thought that the human body and the human soul are 'man himself' I am in complete agreement.

3

Trichotomy

SCRIPTURE usage in respect of the terms 'soul' and 'spirit' does afford plausibility to the contention that man's nature is trichotomic rather than dichotomic, that there are three components, body, soul, and spirit rather than two, body and spirit. Hence scholars of different shades of theological belief, particularly in the last century and a half, have maintained that this usage provides a basis for trichotomy. A classification is scarcely possible and will not be attempted.

C. J. Ellicott, for example, in commenting on 1 Thessalonians 5:23, says that here there is a 'distinct enunciation of the three component parts . . . the *pneuma*, the higher of the two united immaterial parts, being the "*vis superior, agens, imperans in homine*" (Olshausen), the *psuche*, the "*vis inferior quae agitur, movetur*" (ibid.), the sphere of the will and the affections, and the true centre of the personality'. And to assert that the apostle attached 'no distinct thought to each of these words' (Jowett) is 'to set aside all sound rules of scriptural exegesis'.

Franz Delitzsch maintains realistic duality, matter and spirit, but also insists that the Bible represents the supersensuous as consisting of two constituent elements.[1] On Hebrews 4:12 he says that soul and spirit designate the supersensuous, joints and marrow the sensuous. And as joints and marrow are separable constituents so must soul and spirit be regarded. The word of God dissects the whole into its several parts.

The spirit proceeds immediately from God and bears the divine image. Since the fall it has retired into itself and become as it were extinguished. Here the operations of grace begin. The heavenly

[1] Franz Delitzsch: *A System of Biblical Psychology*, pp. 110f., 113.

nature reappears. The soul is the life emanating from the spirit when united with a body. Through sin it has become an 'unfree and licentious disharmony of energies and passions, and a powerless plaything in the hands of material and demonic influences'. The word of God exposes the breach between soul and spirit and the abnormal condition of the soul in itself.

J. B. Heard develops the thesis that the revelation of man's tripartite nature was progressive and parallel to the revelation of God's trinity.[1] In the Old Testament the doctrine of the Holy Spirit was latent, not patent. So with man's spirit. It is in the epistles of the New Testament that the human spirit appears as the divine and regenerate nature quickened by the Holy Spirit and created in the image of God, contrasted not only with flesh but also with soul.

In summary, Heard's position is as follows. The *soul* is the life of man in its widest sense, including all the faculties and energies that are natural to man and necessary to a definition of human nature. The spirit is the faculty or organ of God-consciousness, the presence chamber of God. God is a spirit and can be known and worshipped only through our spirit. Reason, the faculty of the soul, has only a representative knowledge of God, spirit alone has a presentative. Spirit is the sanctuary where God makes himself known; it is the organ of spiritual-mindedness.

Since the fall the spirit is not active in the natural man; it is dead or, at least, dormant. Man is not born with a depraved spirit but with a dead or dormant one. In regeneration the spirit is awakened from dormancy or made alive from death. Regeneration controls the animal in man, purifies the intellectual, but its primary action is to quicken the spiritual. The presence chamber of God is restored and our thought is lost in wonder, love, and praise.

In dealing with this view, we may examine, first of all, the usage of Scripture, then the passages alleged to offer support to the tripartite construction, and then present a resolution of the usage we find in the Scripture.

THE USAGE OF SCRIPTURE

1. *The Person of Man.* Sometimes the whole person is described in

[1] J. B. Heard: *The Tripartite Nature of Man.*

terms of body and soul, at other times in terms of body or flesh and spirit (Matt. 6:25; 10:28—body and soul; 1 Cor. 7:34; 2 Cor. 7:1—body [flesh] and spirit).

These texts are surely intended to be an inclusive description or, preferably, specification of the elements of human personality. If it were otherwise the whole purpose would be defeated. In the case of Matt. 10:28 the completeness of penal destruction is the main lesson, and in 1 Cor. 7:34 and 2 Cor. 7:1 it is the completeness of sanctification that is envisioned. But in the one case body and soul are deemed a sufficient specification, in the other body and spirit. If an integral component were omitted, the completeness would be negated.

James 2:26: This is relevant because it represents the spirit as the principle or condition of life in the body, a position that would not obtain if the spirit is dead or dormant in the natural man. On trichotomic premises, a body without a spirit is not dead; the soul comprises all that is necessary to the survival of the body as a living entity.

1 Corinthians 5:5: Here 'flesh' is used in an ethical sense and the thought is the destruction of that which is sinfully fleshly. But the sin was, in this instance, the sin particularly associated with the body (cf. 1 Cor. 6:18). Thus 'flesh' here does reflect upon the bodily aspect of the human person. If 'flesh' were used in the more embracive ethical sense, that is, as human nature dominated by sin, the spirit would be included as well as the body. So obliquely there is in this text some reflection upon the inclusiveness of the specifications 'flesh and spirit'.

It would be strange that, when occasions arise for describing personality in its entirety, sometimes body and soul have this purpose and sometimes body and spirit, if body, soul, and spirit are the constitutive components of human nature.

2. *The Seat of Spiritual Exercise.* The highest devotional exercises are ascribed to both soul and spirit.

(i) *Sorrow.* In terms of our Lord's undertaking in the days of his flesh and of his vicarious commitment, nothing had deeper significance than his sufferings (cf. Heb. 2:9, 10; 5:7, 8). And it is noteworthy that the grief entailed is predicated of soul as well as of spirit. Nothing engaged his human spirit with greater intensity and effect than the agonies of Gethsemane and Calvary. But it was on the eve of these agonies that he said: 'Now is my soul troubled' (John 12:27), and it was in Geth-semane he said: 'My soul is exceedingly sorrowful unto death' (Matt. 26:38). The form in both cases would not have the pointed relevance to our present topic, or the cogency by way of evidence, were it not so that on other occasions, even when his grief did not have the same poignancy, the spirit is referred to as the seat (Mark 8:12; John 13:21). If the soul is the outer sanctuary, it would scarcely be appropriate to use the term 'soul' when the cup of woe came to its bitterest experience.

It may be that in John 12:27 and Mattthew 26:38 the expression 'my soul' is a Hebraic way of saying 'I am troubled' and 'I am exceed-ingly sorrowful'. But in that event these expressions would still be pertinent to our subject, for they would show that the word 'soul' could be used to designate his person in the experience of its deepest exercises. It would not comport with the distinction trichotomy makes, to use the term 'soul' in connection with the most significant of our Lord's experiences, when the word 'spirit' is used in other instances. The same kind of variation in the use of terms appears in the case of mere men (Acts 17:16—spirit; 2 Pet. 2:8—soul). Grief or sorrow of the most deeply religious character is referred to the soul as well as to the spirit, and this is inconsistent with the trichotomic conception of the soul as *vis inferior*, and with the depreciatory estimate of soul in distinc-tion from spirit.

(ii) *Joy*. The highest spiritual exercises are ascribed to the soul as well as to the spirit (cf. for 'soul' Psalm 42:1–6; 63:5; 103:1, 2; 116:7; 130:6; Isa. 26:9; for 'spirit' Psalm 32:2; 34:18; 51:10, 12, 17; Prov. 11:13; 16:19; Isa. 57:15; Ezek. 11:19; 18:31; 36:26). If it should be averred that the Old Testament usage is irrelevant because the distinction between soul and spirit had not yet been made, yet the distinction obtained though not revealed, and the sustained use of both terms would create a presumption, to say the least, that inspiration was not aware of the radical difference that existed, a supposition incompatible with the Holy Spirit's theopneustic operation in Old Testament Scripture. In the earliest period of New Testament revelation we have the same parallelism in the song of Mary (Luke 1:46, 47; cf. 1 Cor. 14:14–16; 16:18; 2 Cor. 7:13—spirit; Heb. 6:18, 19—soul).

(iii) *Devotion*. In Mark 12:30, for example, we have a statement of the sum of devotion to God. The four terms used are, heart, soul, mind (*dianoia*), and strength (*ischus*). If the spirit is the organ of God-consciousness, it must surely be enlisted in the highest reaches of devotion to God. It would not be consistent with this alleged primacy to omit the spirit in such an enumeration of the aspects of personality.

In like manner various passages refer to community of interest and purpose in the kingdom of God and to wholehearted dedication in the fulfilment of the demands of the Christian vocation. This devotion is expressed in terms of the soul as well as of the spirit (cf. Acts 4:32; 14:2, 22; Eph. 6:6; Phil. 1:27; 2:2, 19, 20). 'One spirit' and 'one soul' are, at least, parallel if not synonymous (Phil. 1:27). To do anything wholeheartedly is to do it from 'the soul' (Eph. 6:6). One soul is equivalent to one heart (Acts 4:32).

The conclusion is inescapable that the centre of devotion and the seat of the most characteristic exercises of the regenerate person is the soul as well as the heart and the spirit. The evidence cannot be adjusted to the supposition that the soul is the outer chamber, and that it is the spirit that is the organ of God-consciousness and the centre of spiritual-mindedness.

3. *The Contrast between Natural and Spiritual.* According to trichotomy the natural man (*anthrōpos psuchikos*) is man whose spirit is dead or dormant, and the spiritual man (*anthrōpos pneumatikos*) is the man whose spirit is revived and attains to hegemony in the human person. The only instances of *psuchikos* in the New Testament are 1 Cor. 2:14; 15:44, 46; James 3:15; Jude 19. *Pneumatikos* occurs frequently. The reasonable procedure is to study the latter and discover its import and application. This will, in turn, indicate the meaning of the contrasted epithet (*psuchikos*). Several instances may be examined:

Romans 1:11—'spiritual gift' (*charisma*). 1 Cor. 12:1–12 is the most instructive index to the meaning, for Paul begins with the words: 'But concerning the spiritual gifts' (*pneumatikōn*), and the succeeding context provides the answer to the reference in this term 'spiritual'. On nine occasions we have reference to the Holy Spirit—vss. 3(2), 4, 7, 8(2), 9(2), and 11. Hence the spiritual gifts are those derived from the Holy Spirit and exercised in the Holy Spirit. Hebrews 2:4 is confirmatory. There we have the expression, 'distributions of the Holy

Spirit'. So a spiritual gift is one derived from and bestowed by the Holy Spirit.

Romans 7:14—If 'spiritual' here had reference to the human spirit, the proposition would be strangely contrary to the premises of trichotomy, for on these the law is addressed particularly to the soul as the sphere of moral decision and judgment. The thought is simply that the law is of divine origin and character; it is of the Holy Spirit.

1 Corinthians 2:13—'combining spiritual things with spiritual'. The meaning is established by the preceding clause, 'but in words taught of the Spirit', namely, 'combining spiritual things with spiritual words'. And 'taught of the Spirit' determines the meaning of the term 'spiritual'. As in the preceding clause the agent is the Holy Spirit (cf. vss. 10–12). So 'spiritual' means taught by the Holy Spirit, indited by the Spirit. Reference to the human spirit as that from which 'spiritual' is derived is rendered exegetically impossible. The same meaning applies to 'spiritually' (vs. 14) and 'spiritual' (vs. 15). As will be observed later, the meaning of *psuchikos* (vs. 14) is fixed by the contrast to 'spiritual'. In 1 Corinthians 10:3, 4, the 'spiritual rock' is said to be Christ and could not be a rock that derives its quality or reference from the human spirit.

1 Corinthians 15:44 (cf. Rom. 8:11)—Here again the contrast appears in application to body (*sōma*). On tripartite premises *sōma psuchikon* would be body governed by soul, as distinct from spirit, and *sōma pneumatikon*, body governed by the human spirit. It is apparent how inconsistent this interpretation would be with trichotomic premises. Paul is dealing with the death and resurrection of *believers* and they are 'spiritual' prior to and at death. Of them it could not be said, even on tripartite premises, that they die as *psuchikoi*. It is surely significant that in the two cases where the contrast expressly occurs, the view in question fails to provide a meaning that is consonant with the contexts. What Paul is emphasizing in 1 Corinthians 15:44 is that the resurrection body is so conditioned by the resurrection power of Christ as 'life-giving Spirit' (vs. 45), that it is no longer mortal and corruptible; it is body belonging to the realm constituted by Jesus' resurrection; it is pneumatically conditioned.

When Paul says that 'flesh and blood shall not inherit the kingdom of

God' (1 Cor. 15:50), he is not denying the physical composition of the resurrection body. It is still body (*sōma*) and therefore physical. What he is saying is that human nature characterized by mortality, corruptibility, weakness, shall not inherit the kingdom of God (cf. vss. 52–54). And the term 'spiritual' draws at least some of its warrant and complexion from the agency and efficacy of the Holy Spirit in the resurrection, as Paul states in Romans 8:11: God 'will make alive your mortal bodies through his Spirit who dwells in you'.

Other passages demonstrating the meaning of 'spiritual' are: Ephesians, 1:3; 5:19; Colossians 3:16; 1 Peter 2:5.

These instances show plainly that 'spiritual', when applied to things, means derived from, or indited by, the Holy Spirit; and when applied to persons, indwelt, directed, and governed by the Holy Spirit. And the contrast instituted between *psuchikos* and *pneumatikos* is not derived from any contrast between the soul and spirit in man, but between man as he is in and of himself; actuated, directed, and governed by his own self; that is, between man as self-controlled, on the one hand, and man indwelt, actuated, directed, and controlled by the Holy Spirit, on the other. The contrast is not that of any duality that exists within man himself, or of any antithesis deriving its definition from the component parts of human nature, but between man in his entirety as self-governed, and man in his entirety as God-governed; between man himself and the Holy Spirit as the governing agent. This apostolic contrast is to the same effect as our Lord's word: 'If any man wills to come after me, let him deny himself' (Matt. 16:24). It is that we offer to self the denial of its demand, namely, hegemony.

4. *Corruption Predicated of Man's Spirit.* Psalm 78:8; Proverbs 14:29; 16:18; 25:28; Ecclesiastes 7:8; Isaiah 29:24; also by implication Psalm 51:10; Ezekiel 11:19; 18:31; 36:26; Malachi 2:16; 2 Corinthians 7:1 (cf. 1 Cor. 2:12).

PASSAGES ALLEGED TO SUPPORT TRICHOTOMY

1. *Hebrews 4:12.* In dealing with this passage we may focus attention upon the terms relevant to our present interest.

(i) '*Joints and marrow*'. These have been interpreted as figurative in this verse, denoting man's immaterial nature. There is no warrant for this view. The body comes under the scrutiny of the Word of God because it is integral to our personality. In accord with the leading thought of the passage, it would be not only appropriate but necessary to mention the most occult parts of our physical frame in order to show that no aspect of our being is impervious to the penetrating scrutiny of the Word of God.

(ii) *'Dividing asunder'* (*merismos*). It is too readily assumed that this term means 'division between', and indicates the distinction between soul and spirit, joints and marrow. This Delitzsch plainly asserts. 'The Divine "Logos" not only penetrates to a man's inmost being, but also divides it into its component parts. . . . The word of God . . . marks out and separates the *pneuma* in him' (*ad* Heb. 4:12). This interpretation is not borne out by the usage of Scripture nor by the verse in question. Usage points rather to the meaning 'division of', 'cleaving', 'dividing within'. It is not the dividing between one thing in its distinct identity and another thing in its distinct identity, but the dividing, sundering, or distributing of a thing in itself. 'Division between' implies two things, 'division within' can apply to one thing; it can be rent asunder.

Hebrews 2:4 is the only other New Testament instance of *merismos*, and the meaning is the distributions of the Holy Spirit, with the accent upon these as sovereignly bestowed. The thought is far removed from that of division or separation of two things; it is that of impartation, dividing out.

The verb occurs, however, frequently, some 14 times (*merizō*). In some cases it means 'to distribute' or 'impart', as the substantive in Hebrews 2:4 (cf. Rom. 12:3; I Cor. 7:17; 2 Cor. 10:13). In some instances the thought of division appears, as when a kingdom is divided against itself, or when an inheritance is divided, or when a married person is divided in the care and concern entertained (cf. Matt. 12:25, 26; Mark 3:24–26; Luke 12:13; I Cor. 1:13; 7:33). In each case the thought is remote from that of separation of one entity from another. It is that of sundering apart, dividing up, distributing.

A compound substantive (*diamerismos*) occurs once (Luke 12:51–53), and the corresponding verb some 11 times. The same import appears, namely, that of an entity being rent asunder and not that of distinguishing one thing from another (cf. Luke 11:17, 18; Matt. 27:35; Mark

15:24; Luke 23:34; 22:17; John 19:24; Acts 2:45). In Acts 2:3 the verb occurs, but the idea is that of distributing, parting asunder and not of separating one thing from another.

Thus there is no instance in which the idea of distinguishing or separating two things is apparent, and the thought of cleaving within is abundantly attested. How does this idea apply to Hebrews 4:12? The relevance is obvious. The Word penetrates to the inmost parts of our being and like a sharp sword can rend them asunder. The Word cleaves soul, spirit, joints, marrow.

Confirmation of this meaning is derived from the anatomy of joints and marrow. These are not adjacent so as to require a sharp sword to get in between to separate. The text does not speak of bones and marrow. So, obviously, the thought is not that of getting in between to separate, but that these are the most inaccessible parts of our physical frame and illustrate the piercing power of the Word when, by a metaphor, it is said to be sharper than a two-edged sword.

(iii) If we were to press the premises of trichotomy, we should find more than trichotomy. The text speaks of the thoughts and intents of the *heart*. If there is the distinction posited between soul and spirit, why not also between soul and spirit and heart?

The lesson of the text is well summed up by Plummer to the effect that joints and marrow represent the most occult parts of our physical frame, soul and spirit our inmost spiritual being, and thoughts and intents of the heart our inmost mental activities. The Word searches all. All is naked and open to God. The Word of God confronts us, and of the Word is predicated the judgment which belongs to God in his omniscience. There is no discrepancy between the judgment of God and that of his Word.

2. *1 Thessalonians 5:23*. It is in accord with the usage of Scripture to employ an accumulation of terms to express completeness (cf. Mark 12:30; Heb. 4:12). It would be in line with this usage to express the entirety of sanctification and of preservation by the terms of the passage concerned, and it would be unwarranted to assume that it is intended to provide us with a definition of the component elements of human nature. This would no more follow in this instance than in the instance of Mark 12:30; Hebrews 4:12.

31

CONCLUSION

The evidence does not support the tripartite construction. We need not suppose, however, that soul and spirit are always synonymous and are interchangeable. The entity denoted by soul and by spirit is to be viewed from different aspects. When one aspect is in view, the term 'spirit' is the appropriate designation, and when another aspect is in view the term 'soul'. For example, dying is represented as giving up of the spirit but as laying down of the soul (life), with different terms in different instances (cf. Eccl. 12:7; Matt. 20:28; 27:50; Mark 10:45; Luke 23:46; John 10:17, 18; Acts 7:59; Heb. 12:23). The variant usage has reference to the distinct aspects from which death may be viewed. Again, the disembodied entity is usually called 'spirit' (Eccl. 12:7; Heb. 12:23; 1 Pet. 3:19) whereas persons embodied are frequently called 'souls', so much so that 'soul' is a virtual synonym for person (cf. Psa. 16:10; Acts 2:27, 31, 41, 43). In such cases it can be seen how inappropriate it would be to substitute the term 'spirit'.

It may be impossible to define precisely the distinction that lies back of the variant usage. There is no hard and fast line of distinction. But it would appear that, in certain cases, 'spirit' views the principle of life as derived from God and returning to him on the event of death, whereas 'soul' views the animating entity as life constituted in a body, and finds its prototype in Genesis 2:7. It is man in his entirety who is called 'living soul'.

It should not surprise us that such a distinction should obtain. We find distinction in respect of the terms 'body' and 'flesh', when, obviously, the same metaphysical entity is contemplated. They cannot be always used interchangeably (cf. Matt. 26:41; 1 Cor. 5:5; 15:39, 44). 'Flesh' often reflects on the weakness of human nature.

Hence, in passages like 1 Thessalonians 5:23; Hebrews 4:12, it is appropriate that both terms should be used for the purpose of emphasizing that the psychical aspect of man, from whatever angle it may be viewed, comes under the sanctifying operations of the God of peace (1 Thess. 5:23) and under the searching scrutiny of the Word of God. And we are at the same time advised that distinct component parts are not thereby denoted because the usage elsewhere can not be adjusted to this construction.

To conclude, the inference would have to be that the spirit or soul is the substrate, centre, and seat of human personality. The unique identity of man is that he is a psychosomatic being with the most intimate correlation, co-ordination, and integration of constituent elements, so that he is equipped to exercise the dominion with which he has been invested. The duality belonging to man's being provides the basis for the duality of relationship, relationship to what is above and to what is below. It is, however, in the unity and integrity of his being that he sustains these relationships. As body alone he could not exercise dominion and it is in his totality that he owes subjection to God. The components of his being may never be viewed in abstraction. It is as psychosomatic being he is made in the image of God, and as such he sustains and exercises all relationships.

4

Man in the Image of God

'GOD said, Let us make man in our image after our likeness . . . And God created the man in his image, in the image of God created he him, male and female created he them' (Gen. 1:26, 27; cf. Gen. 5:1-3; 9:6; 1 Cor. 11:7; Eph. 4:24; Col. 3:10; James 3:9). It would not be reasonable to draw an anthropological distinction between image and likeness. In Genesis 1:26 the words 'according to our likeness' are so co-ordinated with the words 'in our image' that we should take them as explanatory or definitive rather than supplementary. In Genesis 5:1, the term 'likeness' alone is used. But the parallelism of Genesis 1:26, 27 and Genesis 5:1, 2 is apparent and, therefore, the word 'likeness' in the latter is surely intended to express what is involved in both terms in Genesis 1:26. Besides, in Genesis 1:27 'image' alone is used and the proximity to 1:26 would require us not to regard 'image' as synonymous with the double formula of 1:26. Again, in Genesis 5:3 Adam is said to have begotten Seth 'in his likeness according to his image', a reversal of the order and construction followed in 1:26, but again suggesting definition rather than addition. This does not mean that image and likeness can always be used interchangeably, especially in the New Testament. For example, Christ is called the image of God (2 Cor. 4:4; Col. 1:15), but not the likeness (*homoiōsis* or *homoiōma*). But he is made in the likeness (*homoiōma*) of men (Phil. 2:7) and of sinful flesh (Rom. 8:3). Cf. also Hebrews 2:17 in the use of the verb (*kata panta tois adelphois homoiōthēnai*).

The question is: What is this image of God in which man was created and made? On this question much difference has arisen and still continues. The question can be focused thus: Is it something that man lost

34

by the fall, or is it something that belongs inalienably to man and constitutes his definition? Does the Scripture itself throw light on this issue? There are four passages that are relevant at the outset of the discussion.

Genesis 5:3: 'And Adam lived one hundred and thirty years and begat a son in his likeness, according to his image'. It could be argued that a contrast is intended between the image in which Adam begat Seth (vs. 3) and the likeness in which Adam was created (vs. 1), or at least that there is no necessary identification of the likeness of verse 3 with that of verse 1, that the emphasis in verse 3 falls on *Adam's* likeness, but in verse 1 on *God's* likeness, and that, after the pattern of Ezekiel 1:5, all that verse 3 means is that Adam begat a son who resembled himself. There are objections to this view.

(i) Genesis 5:1 harks back to Genesis 1:26. There is no hint that a different conception of likeness and image is introduced at verse 3, and since chapter 5 deals with the book of the generations of Adam, every consideration would suggest that the purpose of reference to likeness and image in verse 3, in connection with the begetting of Seth, is to show that Adam's progeny was to be defined in the same terms as those of Adam himself; in other words, that the identity characterized by the image of God was maintained in Adam's offspring.

(ii) In respect of image and likeness as predicated of man, there is no evidence in Scripture that this predication has any other reference than that of God's image and likeness. Nowhere is there the distinction drawn between the image of God and the image of man by way of contrast and differentiation. To import such a contrast here would be contrary to biblical patterns. 1 Corinthians 15:49 may not be pleaded to the contrary. The contrast is not between the image of God and the image of man in contradistinction, but between the image of Adam as the first man and the image of Christ the second man and last Adam as life-giving spirit, the contrast between what Adam was as living soul (vs. 45; cf. Gen. 2:7) and what Christ was in the power of his resurrection.

(iii) As we shall find later, man in his fallen state is regarded as in the image of God and so there is no reason to posit a differentiation between the likeness and image of verse 3 and the likeness of verse 1.

Genesis 9:6: 'By man his blood shall be shed, for in the image of God made he the man'. This law was instituted for man as fallen, and, there-fore, has relevance for man as such. In this verse there are three considerations: (1) the gravity of the offence of murder; (2) the gravity of the penalty; and (3) the reason for the latter's infliction. If man in his fallen state is not in the image of God, if this identity no longer applies to him, then this fact that he was made in the image of God cannot be the reason for the gravity of the penalty nor of the offence. But it is precisely his being made in the image of God that is given as the reason for the penalty and, by implication, for the gravity of the offence. The thought is that assault upon the life of man is a particularly heinous offence because it is an assault upon the image of God and for that reason merits capital punishment. The assumption is negated if man thus assaulted is not in the divine image.

1 Corinthians 11:7: The man is 'the image and glory of God.' In this passage Paul is dealing with the decorum in respect of head gear to be observed by men and women in the exercises of praying and prophesy-ing. Thus, presupposed is the Christian status of those concerned (cf. vs. 3 also). It might be argued, therefore, that this passage has no rele-vance to the question at issue, namely, man in his unredeemed state.

We must recognize, however, that implied in what governs the Christian relationship and, more specifically, the exercises of worship, is a more basic economy, that 'the man is the head of the woman' (vs. 3), that 'the man is not of the woman, but the woman of the man' (vs. 8), that 'the man was not created for the woman, but the woman for the man' (vs. 9). Paul is applying this basic order to the decorum to be followed in specifically Christian activities. The creation ordinances are not abrogated in the state of sin nor suspended in the Christian economy. So what underlies Paul's injunctions respecting worship has relevance to man in all states, and the assertion that the man is 'the image and glory of God' must likewise pertain to this basic economy that governs the relationships of the man and the woman.

'Image' as predicated of man here is used in a more specialized sense, the image of God that the man is as distinguished from the woman. But it applies to our discussion in this way: if, in the specialized sense, the man is the image and glory of God by reason of the unabrogated order of creation, then man's being in the image of God in the more generic sense, inclusive of the woman (Gen. 1:27b; 5:1, 2) as well as the man, must likewise hold true as the basis of the more specialized predication.

James 3:9: 'Therewith bless we the Lord and Father, and therewith curse we the men who are made after the similitude of God'. This refers to the tongue and occurs in an indictment of the tongue as 'an unruly evil full of deadly poison' (vs. 8). Surely this applies to all vilification of which the human tongue is the organ, and thus the indiscriminate cursing with the tongue is in view. If so, then the statement 'therewith curse we the men who are made after the similitude of God' applies to men generally. In that event men without distinction are said to be made after the likeness of God. In view of the inclusive scope of the indictment it would be arbitrary to interpret the clause 'who are made after the likeness of God' restrictively as referring to the men who are made after the image of God, that is, the godly, in distinction from others, the ungodly, who are not made after God's likeness.

These passages, though not all with equal clarity, are based on the assumption that man as man is made in the divine image, and that as men are propagated there is the perpetuation of that identity expressed in Genesis 1:26; 5:1. There is also the consideration derived from the context of Genesis 1:26. The origin and nature of man are sharply distinguished from other animate beings as made after their kind (Gen. 1:24, 25), and man as made after the likeness and image of God. The basic differentiation resides in this eloquent contrast. The divine image defines the distinct identity of man. The fall does not obliterate this radical differentiation, nor does it destroy man's distinguishing identity. The inference is compelling that, since the differentiation is maintained, the character so expressly stated as the differentiating quality, must also be continued. This conclusion accords with what is true in the case of the creation ordinances. These are not abrogated; neither is man's identity as made in the divine image taken away. This consideration, derived from Genesis 1:26, is the most weighty of all, and in the total structure of the biblical revelation it is borne out by the statements in which man in the image of God is assumed as the premise of our thought respecting man even as fallen.

If we take this position that God's image defines man in his specific character and identity, it would appear to be proper to analyse that in which this identity consists.[1] Man is a person and, therefore, a self-conscious, rational, free, moral, and religious agent. We may focus attention upon the last two characterizations, moral and religious. The term 'moral' in this discussion refers to responsibility. Man lives and moves and has his being in the realm of 'ought', of duty, of obligation to be consciously and freely fulfilled. In this respect he is never non-moral. He is under obligation to obey the will of God in every moment of his life. Conscience, by which he accuses or excuses, is the proof of obligation reflecting itself in his consciousness. This responsibility is based upon what God is. God is justice (cf. Deut. 32:4; 1 John 1:5). This is reflected in the being of man. The ultimate criterion of obligation for man is likeness to God. The law of God which regulates man's conduct is God's perfection coming to expression for the regulation of man's thought, word, and action consonant with that perfection. If the criterion of behaviour is likeness to God, it is because to man belongs a likeness to God that makes it possible for him to have his life and conduct patterned after the exemplar which the attitude and actions of God provide, that is, an intrinsic affinity, depraved and perverted by the fall, yet not obliterated, because it is the ground of obligation. To sum up, it is the metaphysical likeness to God that grounds obligation, and the fulfilment of obligation consists in conformity to the image of God. The term 'religious' in this definition points to the most intimate relation which he sustains to God. Only in God can he find satisfaction; only in the fellowship of God can the aspirations of his soul be realized.

It has been felt that to posit man, as fallen, to be in the image of God impinges upon the doctrine of total depravity, that it supposes the retention by fallen man of what is intrinsically good, a good that needs no more than to be fanned into exercise. It appears to me that thinking should proceed in the opposite direction. If our analysis is correct that the divine image defines man in his specific character as man, then sin is intensified in its heinousness for the very reason that his identity is to be defined in such dignified terms. The higher is our conception of man in his intrinsic essence, the greater must be the gravity of his offence in rebellion and enmity against God. If we think of depravity as enmity against God, the more aggravated must be that enmity when it

[1] cf. Calvin: *Inst.* I, xv, 3 and 4.

is man in the image of God who vents it. And the more total must be that depravity when a being of such character is the subject of it. In a word, the greater is the potentiality for sin, the more aggravated and virulent will be its exercise. Man conceived of as in the image of God, so far from toning down the doctrine of total depravity, points rather to its gravity, intensity, and irreversibility. Finally, it is the fact that man is in the image of God that constitutes the unspeakable horror of eternal perdition.

When we conceive of the image of God as inalienable, we are not to underestimate the impairment resulting from the fall. Man's personality is distorted and he is depraved in his whole being. A person is never in the proper exercise of those attributes that define personality except as he exercises those attributes in the whole-souled love and service of God. Man is characterized in his fallen state by understanding, feeling, will, and conscience. But his understanding is darkened, his emotions are perverted, his will is enslaved, and his conscience distorted. He is 'mind', but it is carnal, and enmity against God. And it is the dignity belonging to man as in the image of God that aggravates this depravity. When we think of man as metaphysically and inalienably in the image of God, we can never conceive of what he metaphysically is, apart from the moral and religious relations that pertain to him by reason of what he intrinsically is.

Up to this point the accent has fallen upon man on the psychical aspect of his being. The question arises: Is it only in respect of his being spirit that man is made in the image of God? It would be easy to say so. God has no body. But it is man in his unity and integrity who is made in the image of God (Gen. 1:26, 27; 2:7; 9:6). Man is body, and it is not possible to exclude man in this identity from the scope of that which defines his identity, the image of God. Sin and holiness are predicated of the body. This does not mean that God has a body. There is a radical difference between God and man even in respect of the spirit. The greater difference in respect of body is but an extension of this differentiation. Man's body and its functions are subject to moral judgment by way of approbation or censure. And only by virtue of responsibility could this be so. But the main consideration is that of man in his integrity is God's image predicated.

Another phase of the question must not be discounted. In Ephesians 4:24 and Colossians 3:10 the image of God is defined in terms of knowledge, righteousness, and holiness of the truth. It is the new man who is in view in both passages, the person created anew in Christ Jesus. They do not, expressly at least, refer to Adam as created, and by no means do they refer to man unregenerate. The only question is: Do they refer by implication to Adam in his original integrity?

There can be no question but Adam was created upright. He was 'very good' (Gen. 1:31) and, therefore, very good in terms of his being and functions. He could not be upright and good in terms of what he essentially was unless he had knowledge, righteousness, and holiness; and if God's image is defined in these terms, the inference would appear to be necessary that Adam was created in the image of God in respect of these qualities. Furthermore, as Calvin argues, that which holds the first place in the renovation of man must have held the first place in the first creation.[1] Finally, it is difficult to exclude from the passages concerned (Eph. 4:24; Col. 3:10) an allusion to Genesis 1:26; 5:1. If this position is maintained, then we should have to construe the image of God, as predicated of man, as having a twofold aspect, one as intrinsic and unloseable and the other as forfeited in the fall. This is the classic Reformed position as markedly distinct from the Lutheran. The distinction between the two aspects could be made in various ways as, for example, moral agency and moral excellence, generic and specific, metaphysical and ethical.

It should be understood, however, that the doctrine of man's original integrity, that he was created with positively holy and upright character, that this character was not a superadded gift nor a later self-developed acquisition but a concreated endowment[2], is not indispensably based on the premise that knowledge, righteousness, and holiness are included in the image and likeness of Genesis 1:26. Undoubtedly the doctrine would derive added support from such a premise. But this premise is not indispensable to the doctrine of original integrity as defined above.

It will have to be granted that the thesis of a twofold aspect derived from or based upon these passages (Eph. 4:24, Col. 3:10) is not as

---

[1] *Inst.* I, xv, 3 and 4; cf. Laidlaw: *The Bible Doctrine of Man*, pp. 106, 135.

[2] cf. Thornwell: *Collected Writings*, I, pp. 238ff.

conclusive as it might appear to be. Re-creation is undoubtedly after God's image in the respects specified. But that this is intended in Genesis 1:26; 5:1 is not necessarily the case. In the context of Genesis 1:26 it is the nature and dignity of man in contradistinction from all other animate creatures (vss. 24, 25) that are being emphasized. It is man's specific character that is thrown into prominence, and it may well be that it is this identity that is intended, and not the moral and religious excellence with which man was also endowed. Genesis 5:1 is dealing with the history of mankind fallen. But there is no intimation that so radical a change had taken place in the context of the image of God as would be the case if knowledge, righteousness and holiness were ingredients of what was comprised in the image and likeness of Genesis 1:26 and the likeness of Genesis 5:1. The upshot of these considerations would, therefore, appear to be that as far as man in the image of God is concerned, after the pattern of Genesis 1:26; 5:1; 9:6; 1 Corinthians 11:7; James 3:9 (cf. also Genesis 5:3), no more may be in view than that which belongs to man as man, and may not comprise the moral excellence referred to in Ephesians 4:24 and Colossians 3:10.

Dominion over the Creatures. Some Reformed theologians regard this dominion as an element in the divine image. It would appear preferable, however, to regard dominion as a function or office based upon the specific character defined as the image of God. The latter fits him for the dominion to be exercised. Man is made in God's image. He is, therefore, constituted God's viceregent. It belongs to God's being to be sovereign over all creation. It belongs to man's being to execute delegated dominion.

Psalm 8 is the echo of Genesis 1:26, 27. It is not the insignificance of man that is its theme, but the amazing dignity bestowed upon him. 'For thou hast made him a little lower than the angels, and hast crowned him with glory and honour' (vs. 5). This is confirmed by the application in Hebrews 2:5-9.

VARIOUS VIEWS OF MAN IN THE IMAGE OF GOD

1. *Roman Catholic*
(i) *Status Naturae Purae.* Man was created of soul and body, distinct and diverse elements, the soul with the higher exercises of reason, conscience,

and will, the body with corporeal impulses and desires.[1] This is man's primitive condition, in which he is endowed simply with *dona naturalia*, and is designated the state of *in puris naturalibus*; man possessed of all the attributes necessary to his nature as man, but destitute of the graces and accomplishments that adorn human nature.

In this natural state there was no sin. According to certain theologians this natural state involved creation in the divine image.[2] This applied to the higher portion of man's nature.

(ii) *Pugna Concupiscentiae*. The state of pure nature, though not one of sin, was a state, nevertheless, in which there was a *tendency* on the part of the corporeal impulses and desires to assert themselves and to break through the limits of reason.[3] In Moehler's words, 'A struggle would by degrees have naturally arisen between the sensual and spiritual nature of man'.[4] While the term 'tendency' expresses the case in some theology, in some of the ablest and most representative theologians it is construed as a conflict.[5] Thomas Aquinas calls it *pugna concupiscentiae*, but in no way derogatory to human nature; it does not involve blame or penalty because the defect was not caused by the will of man.[6] But in any case, whether construed as tendency or conflict (*pugna*), it provides the reason for superadded gifts.

(iii) *Dona Superaddita*. In some Roman Catholic theology this is spoken of in the singular as the gift of *justitia originalis*, by which the sensuous and supersensuous components of human nature were kept in undisturbed harmony, the lower to the higher, the corporeal in subjection to the dictates of reason. It also brought man into the closest communion with God and exalted man above human nature and made him participate in the nature of God.[7]

---

[1] cf. Brunini: *Whereon to Stand*, pp. 41ff.

[2] cf. *Catechism of the Council of Trent*, Tr. by Donovan, Part I, *Art.* I, p. 30; Moehler: *Symbolism*, E.T., p. 30.

[3] cf. *Catechism*, as cited, pp. 126f., 311f., 358.

[4] *op. cit.*, p. 27.

[5] cf. Bellarmine: *Disputationes*, Tome IV, p. 10, Col. 2 quoted in Hodge: *Syst. Theol.*, II, p. 104.

[6] cf. Pohle-Preuss: *Dogmatic Theology*, III, pp. 194f.; ed. G. D. Smith: *The Teaching of the Catholic Church*, I, p. 328.

[7] cf. Moehler: *op. cit.*, pp. 25–30.

But much of Rome's theology divides the gifts into preternatural and supernatural. The preternatural are integrity and immortality, and the supernatural is sanctity. Integrity consisted in the harmony established between the components of man's being, whereby man was freed from the *pugna concupiscentiae* and the lower impulses made subject to the dictates of reason. Immortality was the gift of freedom from the necessity of dying. Immortality is not natural, 'death being a necessary resultant of the synthesis of body and soul'.[1] The supernatural gift of sanctity is the sanctifying grace whereby man was made a partaker of the divine nature, elevated to a higher order of existence, endowed with what is above the essence of any created nature, adopted into the position occupied by the only-begotten Son, and given the capacity for the beatific vision.[2] The distinction is sometimes drawn in terms of *supernaturale relativum* and *supernaturale absolutum*.

(iv) *Imago Dei*. Some theologians have distinguished between image and likeness and regarded the former as *de natura* and the latter as *de gratia*. But others do not make this distinction and regard both as *de gratia*, allowing that in some sense man was by nature in the divine image.[3] But in view of 2 Peter 1:4; 1 John 3:2 *et al.* the image and likeness are more properly regarded as supernatural.[4]

On the question of the time of endowment with preternatural, and particularly with supernatural grace, there has been dispute. The Scotists maintained that an interval elapsed between creation *in puris naturalibus* and elevation to grace.[5] Thomas Aquinas contended for contemporaneity. This appears to be the prevailing view. The Council of Trent was non-committal and avoided *creatus in justitia*. Instead it adopted the term *'constitutus'*—*'in justitia constitutus'*.

(v) *Lapsus Adae*. In the fall there was the loss of the superadded gifts, and the consequence is reversion to the state of pure nature. Bellarmine is

[1] Pohle-Preuss: *op. cit.*, III, p. 195.

[2] cf. M. J. Scheeben: *The Mysteries of Christianity*, pp. 214ff.; *Synopsis Theologiae Dogmaticae*, Tom. II, pp. 529ff.; *ed.* Smith: *op. cit.*, I, pp. 320ff.

[3] caliquo modo Dei imaginem in anima nostra gerimus'—*Synopsis Theologiae Dogmaticae*, II, p. 535.

[4] *Synopsis*, II, pp. 535f.; Pohle-Preuss: *op. cit.* III, pp. 179–218; *ed.* Smith: *op. cit.*, I, pp. 520ff.

[5] *e.g.* Lombard and Bonaventura.

explicit to this effect. 'Quare non magis differt status hominis post lapsum Adae a statu eiusdem in puris naturalibus, quam differt spoliatus a nudo, neque deterior est humana natura, si culpam originalem detrahas, neque magis ignorantia, et infirmitate laborat, quam esset et laboraret in puris naturalibus condita. Proinde corruptio naturae, non ex alicuius doni carentia, neque ex alicuius malae qualitatis accessu, sed ex sola doni supernaturalis ob Adae peccatum amissione profluxit. Quae sententia communio Doctorum Scholasticum veterum, et recentiorum.'[1]

Criticism. (i) Rome entertains a degrading view of man's metaphysical being. There is a native incompatibility and strife between the component elements, body and soul, flesh and spirit; in Bellarmine's terms a *morbus* or *languor* that needed a remedy; in Aquinas' terms the *pugna* which required supernatural grace to prevent sinful concupiscence which otherwise would result. On the most restrained position, conflict between the objects of sense and those of reason necessarily arises. This conception runs wholly athwart the biblical representation that there is no intrinsic incompatibility in the being of man, that the being of man, as made, was very good in terms of its own purpose, character, and functions.

(ii) The Scripture affords no support to a construction of man's origin in terms of a twofold action, one of creation and the other of superadded grace. The only action is that of making or creating (both terms are used) man in the image and likeness of God, and not the remotest suggestion of a superadded action to meet a defect in man's nature. There is in Scripture no making of *man* apart from his identity as made in God's image. And if we predicate a defect inevitably leading to sin, then we impinge upon the goodness of God's handiwork.

(iii) Rome entertains an inadequate view of the gravity of the fall and of

[1] *Disputationes*, Tom. 4, p. 11, col. 2. 'Hence the condition of man since the Fall of Adam is only different from his condition in the state of pure nature like this: the former has been bereft of his clothes, whereas the latter has not yet put them on. Human nature is no worse (leaving original sin out of the question) and is no more afflicted with ignorance and weakness, than if it were in a state of pure nature. So then, the corruption of man's nature does not flow from the lack of some gift, nor from the advent of some evil property, but solely from the loss of the supernatural gift on account of Adam's sin. This is the universal view of the subject held by the old Schoolmen and by more recent writers.'

its implications in human depravity. It regards the issue of the fall as consisting in relapse into *status naturae purae*. But, according to Rome's own premises, this was not a state of sin, only one of a tendency to sin. The fall, therefore, produced only forfeiture of superadded grace, and not corruption of nature; relapse into *pugna concupiscentiae* but not the concupiscence that is sinful. How contrary to the biblical view of the origin of sin (cf. James 1:13, 14)!

(iv) Rome's position is, in effect, to regard sin as proceeding from the corporeal, the assertion of the lower impulses beyond the limits of reason and integrity (*justitia*). But it is wholly unscriptural to regard sin as originating from the sensuous, or from conflict between the sensuous and supersensuous. It was an appeal to what was intensely 'spiritual': 'Ye shall be as God, knowing good and evil'; 'A tree to be desired to make one wise'. These are the pivots. Sin had its origin and seat in the spirit of man. It began with the acceptance by Eve of an allegation that was an attack upon God's veracity. This is the iniquity of both temptation and fall. So, totally alien to Genesis 3, is an account of the fall that construes it as an assertion of lower, corporeal impulses above the dictates of reason. In Rome's position there is a dualism that is gnostic and Manichean in its affinities and presuppositions.

2. *Lutheran*

The evangelical Lutheran view is that the image of God in which man was created consisted in knowledge, righteousness, and holiness and, therefore, in what was lost in the fall. It is admitted that man, as fallen, retains vestiges of the divine image but these vestiges are construed in terms of knowledge and virtue, the knowledge the natural man possesses and the natural virtue he may exhibit.

Evaluation (i) Scripture predicates the divine image of man in his fallen state. Any deviation from Scripture is fraught with danger.

(ii) The view that the divine image defines the specific nature of man is correlative with a proper assessment of human depravity. Lutheran theology is defective in its doctrine of man's depravity. It regards man as capable of non-resistance to the gospel. It may be that the position respecting the divine image is bound up with the failure properly to assess the depravity with which man is afflicted. It may seem paradoxical, but the higher our view of man's nature, the more aggravated becomes the depravity that characterizes man as fallen.

3. *Barthian*

Barth's view is that the natural man is not in the image of God. God does not have contact with the natural man. This is related to his view of revelation as an ever-recurrent act to this man, and to no other, in a concrete confrontation and crisis. This revelation carries with it the impartation of the divine image. The revelatory Word of God has no permanent existence in Scripture. The Bible is the medium of, or witness to revelation, but is not a deposit of revelation. Revelation has not become inscripturated and thus has not taken on abiding form or content. Two consequences follow. First, there is no revelation on God's part that is constantly addressed to men; second, there is no capacity in man that makes him addressable in terms of God's Word.

Criticism. According to Scripture, revelation has become inscripturated; it is the voice of God to every one to whom it comes. It is the Word of God written, and addressed to men indiscriminately. It is addressed to the natural man and makes an impact upon him. This impact is the precondition of saving faith. For faith is of hearing and must never be abstracted from the effect which the Word of God makes upon a person before he becomes a believer. Effective address, and the corresponding impact, can be called the point of contact for the saving address of the Word and believing response. In other words, there must be some conviction created by the Word of God, and some cognition of the import of the gospel in order to make the act of faith meaningful and purposeful. This antecedent conviction and cognition are the vestibule of faith. It is Scripture as the speech of God, and the doctrine of man in the image of God, that makes intelligible this antecedent state of conviction and cognition, and makes possible the point of contact. All of this Barth cannot hold on his own premises and, as a matter of fact, vigorously denies. It is impossible for him to give a biblical version of the origin of faith, or of the data to which Scripture bears witness in connection with the gospel (cf. Acts 8:13, 16–23; 24:25; Rom. 7:7–13; 2 Pet. 2:20–22; also seed sown on rocky and thorny soil). For Barth, faith must be as unrelated an occurrence as is the act of revelation itself, on his construction.

5

The Adamic Administration

MAN was created in the image of God, a self-conscious, free, responsible, religious agent. Such identity implies an inherent, native, inalienable obligation to love and serve God with all the heart, soul, strength, and mind. This God could not but demand and man could not but owe. No created rational being can ever be relieved of this obligation. All that man is and does has reference to the will of God.

But man was also created good, good in respect of that which he specifically is. He was made upright and holy and therefore constituted for the demand, endowed with the character enabling him to fulfil all the demands devolving upon him by reason of God's propriety in him and sovereignty over him.

As long as man fulfilled these demands his integrity would have been maintained. He would have continued righteous and holy. In this righteousness he would be justified, that is, approved and accepted by God, and he would have life. Righteousness, justification, life is an invariable combination in the government and judgment of God. There would be a relation that we may call perfect legal reciprocity. As this would be the minimum, so it would be the maximum in terms of the relation constituted by creation in the image of God.

This relation falls short in two respects of what may readily be conceived of as higher. (1) It is a contingent situation, one of righteousness but mutably so, and likewise of justification and life. There is always the possibility of lapse on man's part and, with the lapse, loss of integrity, justification, life, the exchange of these for unrighteousness, condemnation, death. (2) There is the absence of full-orbed communion with God in the assurance of permanent possession and increasing knowledge.

In addition to the account given of man's creation and of the creation ordinances, we find a special series of provisions dispensed to our first parents. In other words, there are data which cannot be construed in terms simply of creation in the divine image and the demands of awards belonging to that relationship.

THE DATA

God gave to Adam a specific command or, more accurately, a specific prohibition. The term prohibition is significant. It is negative and, as such, differs from all the other ordinances. It is in character and intent not in the same category and stands off in this distinctness (Gen. 2:17). It applied to Adam and Eve alone and had relevance to the particular conditions of Eden. We are constrained to ask: Why or for what purpose?

To disobedience was attached the threat of death (Gen. 2:17). Failure to comply with the other ordinances would have been disobedience and disobedience would carry the consequences of penal judgment. But only in connection with the tree of the knowledge of good and evil was this eventuality enunciated. Again we ask: Why?

There was also in Eden the tree of life (Gen. 3:22, 24). As the other tree represented the knowledge of good and evil, this tree must have been symbolic of life, and we may infer that in some way it would have been the seal of everlasting life (Gen. 3:22—'take also of the tree of life, and eat, and live for ever'; also Gen. 3:24 in that Adam having forfeited life was prevented from access to it—'to keep the way of the tree of life'). There must have been in the institution some provision for eternal life. And it is natural, if not necessary, to infer that it is the opposite of what actually transpired that would have secured this life, that to obedience was appended the promise of life, after the analogy of Genesis 2:17 in respect of disobedience. Although from Genesis 3:22 we infer that Adam had not partaken of the tree of life, and although it was not forbidden as was the tree of the knowledge of good and evil (cf. Gen. 2:16), yet, apparently, by the arrangements of providence or of revelation, it was recognized as reserved for the issue of probationary obedience. This would explain Genesis 3:22, 24 (cf. Rev. 2:7; 22:2, 14, especially the expression, 'right to the tree of life').

We know that Adam acted in a public capacity. Not only his destiny but that of the whole race was bound up with his conduct for good or for evil (Rom. 5:12-19; 1 Cor. 15:22, 45, 46).

The race has been confirmed in sin, condemnation, and death by Adam's trespass. Surely this principle of confirmation would have been applied with similar consistency in the direction of life in the event of obedience on Adam's part.

Analogy is drawn between Adam and Christ. They stand in unique relations to mankind. There is none before Adam—he is the first man. There is none between—Christ is the second man. There is none after Christ—he is the last Adam (1 Cor. 15:44-49). Here we have an embracive construction of human relationships. We know also that in Christ there is representative relationship and that obedience successfully completed has its issue in righteousness, justification, life for all he represents (1 Cor. 15:22). So a period of obedience successfully completed by Adam would have secured eternal life for all represented by him.

The Adamic administration is, therefore, construed as an administration in which God, by a special act of providence, established for man the provision whereby he might pass from the status of contingency to one of confirmed and indefectible holiness and blessedness, that is, from *posse peccare* and *posse non peccare* to *non posse peccare*. The way instituted was that of 'an intensified and concentrated probation', the alternative issues being dependent upon the issues of obedience or disobedience (cf. G. Vos: *Biblical Theology*, 22f).

This administration has often been denoted 'The Covenant of Works'. There are two observations. (1) The term is not felicitous, for the reason that the elements of grace entering into the administration are not properly provided for by the term 'works'. (2) It is not designated a covenant in Scripture. Hosea 6:7 may be interpreted otherwise and does not provide the basis for such a construction of the Adamic economy. Besides, Scripture always uses the term covenant, when applied to God's administration to men, in reference to a provision that is redemptive or closely related to redemptive design. Covenant in Scripture denotes the oath-bound confirmation of promise and involves a security which the Adamic economy did not bestow.

Whether or not the administration is designated covenant, the uniqueness and singularity must be recognized. It should never be confused with what Scripture calls the old covenant or first covenant (cf. Jer. 31:31–34; 2 Cor. 3:14; Heb. 8:7, 13). The first or old covenant is the Sinaitic. And not only must this confusion in denotation be avoided, but also any attempt to interpret the Mosaic covenant in terms of the Adamic institution. The latter could apply only to the state of innocence, and to Adam alone as representative head. The view that in the Mosaic covenant there was a repetition of the so-called covenant of works, current among covenant theologians, is a grave misconception and involves an erroneous construction of the Mosaic covenant, as well as fails to assess the uniqueness of the Adamic administration. The Mosaic covenant was distinctly redemptive in character and was continuous with and extensive of the Abrahamic covenants. The Adamic had no redemptive provision, nor did its promissory element have any relevance within a context that made redemption necessary.

THE NATURE OF THE ADMINISTRATION

The administration was sovereignly dispensed by God. It was not a contract or compact. Sovereign disposition is its patent characteristic.

That Adam was constituted head of the human race and acted accordingly, we necessarily infer from the following considerations:

1. All that befell Adam as a consequence of his disobedience has as much reference to posterity as to Adam. Death is the lot of mankind, not through a repetition of the temptation and fall of Eden, but by solidarity with Adam. The earth is cursed for all, even though they do not individually pass through the crisis of Adam's fall and the direct pronouncement of God's judgment. The same is true of the judgment upon Eve.

2. The solidarity is clearly implied in Romans 5:12–19; 1 Corinthians 15:22.

3. The plan of redemption is erected on the principle of representative identification, and the parallel by which righteousness, justification, and life come to lost men is that exemplified in sin, condemnation, death through Adam.

4. The principle of representation underlies all the basic institutions of God in the world—the family, the church, and the state. In other words, solidarity and corporate relationship is a feature of God's government. We should expect the prototype to reside in racial solidarity. At least, racial solidarity is congruous with what we find on a less inclusive scale in the other institutions of God's appointment.

We need not suppose that Adam knew of this headship nor of the consequences issuing for posterity. All we know is that God constituted Adam the head. We do not know how much Adam knew of this relationship.

THE CONDITION

The condition was obedience. Obedience was focused in compliance with the prohibition respecting the tree of the knowledge of good and evil. The effect, however, was not to confine the demand for obedience to this prohibition. It was not the only command given to Adam, but it served to exemplify in an acute and condensed way the obedience owing to God, obedience unreserved and unswerving in all the extent of divine obligation. The ambit of obligation was not contracted, but the intensity required was thereby illustrated.

In order to appreciate the significance of the tree as the test of obedience we must observe the twofold circumstance under which the obedience was to be rendered, probation and temptation.

1. *Probation.* It was symbolized by the tree of the knowledge of good and evil. The question we may ask is: What is denoted by the knowledge of good and evil? There are four possibilities.

(i) The good and evil would refer respectively to the issue of a successful or unsuccessful probation, the knowledge of good in the former event and of evil in the latter. But there are two objections.

(a) The phrase scarcely allows for this view. It is the knowledge of good *and* evil, not good *or* evil. Good and evil are correlatives and not alternatives.

(b) In the sequel of an unsuccessful probation it is said that 'man is become as one of us to know good and evil' (Gen. 3:22), not simply evil, as the interpretation in question would require.

(ii) The tree derived its name from the foreordained result. This view has the advantage of relating the designation to an event; it eliminates the question: How the knowledge of evil on the alternative of a successful probation?

It is difficult to rule out the relevance to the alternative of a successful probation since there are elements in the situation that do have reference to this alternative. Besides, since evil was present in the universe, it would seem necessary for Adam's enlarged knowledge to include this phase of God's all-embracive providence. Eve, at least, encountered this evil in the state of integrity. So, to some extent, it came within her acquaintance, and the knowledge derived from this encounter would have been hers even if she had resisted the temptation.

(iii) The tree had reference exclusively to the knowledge to be attained through successful probation. This would require us to regard Genesis 3:22a as irony, not as a statement of fact, an interpretation scarcely tenable, since verse 22a is given as the reason for verses 22b, 23. Irony would not provide the ground for the liability and the expulsion of these two verses.

(iv) We seem, therefore, to be shut up to the fourth view that the knowledge of good and evil describes the issue of either alternative of the probation.

In the event of a successful probation the experience of the crisis of temptation, and the experience of assured and indefectible goodness, would have imparted a renewed and greatly increased knowledge of the contrast between good and evil, and a renewed appreciation of the good as the opposite of evil. Furthermore, as suggested above, Adam, if elevated to a higher state of knowledge, would be given enlarged knowledge, not only of God but also of created reality and of God's providential order. The latter would include the system of evil of which Satan was the prince. Empirically, knowledge is knowledge of good and evil as co-related and contrasted realities.

In the event of unsuccessful probation, the event that actually occurred, the experience of all the evils that befell our first parents gave them a vivid sense of the bitterness of sin and its consequences in contrast with the good of their former condition. They knew the good of integrity; they came to know the evil of apostasy.

We must not suppose that the knowledge would have the same

content in either case. How diverse the states of consciousness! By the fall there invaded man's consciousness elements that would never have crossed the threshold, the sense of guilt, of fear, of shame. There entered a new dispositional complex of desires, impulses, affections, motives, and purposes. We may never conceive of knowledge as a state of mind apart from the total condition of heart and will.

Yet in both cases the description applies, the knowledge of good and evil. This advises us that, in the usage of Scripture, two diverse states of mind, totally diverse in complexion, may be denoted by the same term. It also reminds us that of man as fallen is predicated the knowledge of good and evil, though we cannot ascribe to the knowledge predicated the qualities that belong to man's knowledge when renewed and illumined by the Holy Spirit in the operations of saving grace.

Probation in the nature of the case must be limited in duration. A destiny contingent upon an event can never become settled until the event has occurred. We see this exemplified in Adam, the elect angels, and Christ himself. How significant is Christ's word from the cross, 'It is finished' (cf. also John 17:4)!

2. *Temptation.* This was symbolized by the serpent (cf. John 8:44; Matt. 13:38, 39; Rom. 16:20; 2 Cor. 11:3; 1 John 3:8; Rev. 12:9). The sense in which temptation is used in this instance is that of solicitation to sin and the placing of an inducement to sin in the way of another. It is temptation in this sense that is denied of God (James 1:13). He did not solicit sin in Adam and Eve; he did the opposite. He warned them against it and placed the inducement in the opposite direction. God did try our first parents. He was the agent of the probation. The serpent was the agent in the temptation. It is of God to try and prove with a view to moral and religious strength, confirmation, and increased blessing (cf. Gen. 22:1, 12, 16–18). It is satanic to seduce and it is designed for weakening and degradation.

In the temptation our first parents were accosted by the serpent as the instrument of Satan and were subjected to doubting, unbelieving, and apostatizing suggestions and allegations. These suggestions did not originate in the mind of Eve. They were injected. It was not sin for Eve to have been confronted with these suggestions and solicitations, and it was in the circumstance of this temptation that our first parents were called upon to fulfil the condition of the administration. The temptation was of divine appointment, though Satan, not God, was the agent.

It was in the double circumstance of probation and temptation that our first parents were called upon to obey. The probation was epitomized in the prohibition, the temptation was directed to the contravention of the prohibition. Thus the stringency of the condition was pointed up in the tension between the demand for obedience to the divine prohibition and the pressures of temptation in the tempter's allegations. Our first parents had the ability to resist the temptation and to obey the prohibition. But they did not will to obey[1] and so they fell.

PROMISE

That there was a promise, though not expressly enunciated, we infer from the following data:

1. The tree of life represented everlasting life (Gen. 3:22). But it could not have this application unless there had been some provision connected with Eden which contemplated such life. Adam's expulsion signified forfeiture of that which the tree of life symbolized and was complementary to the fulfilment of the threat of Genesis 2:17 and the pronouncement of 3:19. It must have represented the opposite of death, as its designation also clearly indicates. Furthermore, the references to the tree of life (Rev. 22:2, 14) hark back to Genesis 3:22, 24 and they are fraught with this meaning.

2. The analogy of Romans 5:12–19 would require that confirmation in righteousness would carry the same of life.

3. In view of the foregoing, and the usage of Scripture in general that a negative in command implies the positive, we should infer the promise of life from the threat of death (Gen. 2:17).

It may be that Genesis 3:22 implies a disposition on Adam's part to grasp at the life he knew he had forfeited, and thus sacrilegiously to partake of the tree. If so, then Adam must have known of its significance and therefore of the promise involved. But we cannot be sure of this. Genesis 3:22 may imply no more than the liability on Adam's part to

[1] cf. Calvin: *Inst.*, I, xv, 8.

partake of the tree which now, by reason of his sin, could not have for him any benefit, but rather the opposite, and would entail further judgment. It would have been sacrilege for him to partake, and mercy as well as judgment is evident in expulsion from access to it.

Difficulty resides in the words 'eat and live for ever' (Gen. 3:22). How could this be when Adam had forfeited the life signified, and of which the tree would have been the sign and seal? It is possible that the words do not refer to what would have been the actual sequel, but to Adam's intent in eating, namely, that he should live for ever and thus attempt to defeat the judgment of God. In that event we would have to suppose knowledge on Adam's part of the purpose of the tree. However, this construction is harsh. 'Live for ever', in the syntax, points rather to a result. On this assumption what is the import? A dogmatic answer is not warranted. But a possible solution can be proposed.

We found that the knowledge of good and evil described the result on either alternative of the probation. This is striking because in Scripture knowledge is equated with life. Yet the double reference is required. A radical difference is necessary between the two states in the respective cases, as observed already. In one case it is knowledge in a state of death, in the other it is knowledge in a state of indefectible blessedness and life. By analogy, may we not regard the tree of life as having likewise a twofold reference, the sign and seal of life on the highest level of realization on the one hand, and also of that life in death and misery to which Adam by sin degraded himself on the other? In this condition and state the tree would still have its sealing significance, but in the opposite direction, confirmation in the life of sin and death. In Adam's expulsion we should find, therefore, a signal manifestation of preventive grace, not only the grace of preventing an aggravation of Adam's sin, as noted already, but of preventing *confirmation* in sin, misery, and death, of preventing a sin that would have sealed his doom. God shielded Adam from the sin that would have put him outside the sphere of redemption.

In connection with the promise of life it does not appear justifiable to appeal, as frequently has been done, to the principle enunciated in certain texts (cf. Lev. 18:5; Rom. 10:5; Gal. 3:12), 'This do and thou shalt live'. The principle asserted in these texts is the principle of equity, that righteousness is always followed by the corresponding award. From the promise of the Adamic administration we must dissociate all notions of meritorious reward. The promise of confirmed integrity and blessedness was one annexed to an obedience that Adam owed and, therefore, was a promise of grace. All that Adam could have claimed on the basis of equity was justification and life as long as he perfectly obeyed, but not confirmation so as to insure indefectibility. Adam could claim the fulfilment of the promise if he stood the probation, but only on the basis of God's faithfulness, not on the basis of justice.[1] God is debtor to his own faithfulness. But justice requires no more than the approbation and life correspondent with the righteousness of perfect conformity with the will of God.

THREATENING

The threat was death (Gen. 2:17; 3:17–19). Death has a threefold aspect, spiritual (moral and religious), judicial, and psycho-physical. In Genesis 2:17, as interpreted by the pronouncement of Genesis 3:17–19, the emphasis falls upon psycho-physical death (cf. Rom. 5:12–19). It may well be that this is the only aspect expressly intended. But in the broader context of Scripture we shall have to take account of the other aspects. For example, when Paul describes the condition of the unregenerate as being 'dead in trespasses and sins' (Eph. 2:1), we cannot exclude this death from the death threatened in the original reference to death. Again, judicial death, as will be noted, consists in separation from God and the infliction of the curse. But sin is said expressly to be the cause of both separation and curse (Isa. 59:2; Gal. 3:10). This separation is symbolized in expulsion from Eden, for it meant expulsion from that which betokened the favour of God.

Spiritually our first parents became dead in the day they sinned. Their sin constituted this death; they estranged themselves from God and their mind became enmity against God. *Judicially* they also died the day they sinned; they became subject to the curse. *Psycho-physical* death can be said to have befallen them the day they sinned, in that mortality became their lot. They became mortal even though the actual dissolu-

---

[1] cf. Shedd: *Dogmatics*, II, p. 153; Witsius: *Economy of the Covenants*, I, pp. 61, 91.

tion did not take place. This death consists in the separation of the integral elements of their being, and exemplifies the principle of death, namely, separation. Since it is this aspect of death that is in the foreground in Genesis 2:17 and 3:17-19, and properly so, because of the prominence given to what is phenomenal in the administration as a whole, we are advised of the significance of this aspect in the judgment upon sin. It is not a mere incident. It consists in the disintegration of man's person, and demonstrates as such the gravity and total abnormality of sin and of its consequence. The body returns to dust and sees corruption, and the spirit, though it continues to be active, is no longer existent or active in its normal and natural relationship. Death is not merely a physical event; it is separation of body and spirit; and disembodied existence for man is punitive and expresses God's condemnation.

Spiritual death describes man's moral and religious condition; judicial death describes his status in reference to God; psycho-physical death describes the disruption of his very being.

THE RELEVANCE OF THE ADAMIC ADMINISTRATION

We may subsume the necessary observations under two captions, negative and positive:

Negative

1. The special prohibition of Eden does not apply to us now. It was restricted to the conditions and circumstances of Eden and has no relevance outside the same. The whole-souled obedience it was intended to exemplify is our obligation, but not this way of discharging it.

2. As individuals we do not undergo probation in terms of the Adamic administration. It is totally wrong to say we are all Adam, and sin as he did. His sin was unique, in that it was from integrity he fell. We do not individually fall from integrity. Hence to construe the probations that we undergo as individuals, or even in our corporate responsibilities, in terms of the Adamic probation, fails to take account of the unique character of Adam's situation and relationships.

3. We cannot attain to life in terms of the Adamic institution. This possibility was once for all forfeited for Adam and posterity by the fall

of our first parents. And the Adamic institution had no redemptive provisions.

Positive

1. We all stood the probation in Adam as our representative head, and failed in Adam. His sin was our sin, his fall our fall, by reason of solidarity with him. Likewise the fulfilment of the threat draws posterity within its scope. All who die, die in Adam, and in Adam all died (cf. Rom. 5:12; 1 Cor. 15:22). The threat exercises its sanction with unrelenting severity, unless totally different provisions of redemptive grace intervene.

2. Christ's vicarious sin-bearing on behalf of the new humanity included the Adamic sin as well as all other sins. This aspect should not be overlooked.

3. The obedience Christ rendered fulfilled the obedience in which Adam failed. It would not be correct to say, however, that Christ's obedience was the same in content or demand. Christ was called on to obey in radically different conditions, and required to fulfil radically different demands. Christ was sin-bearer and the climactic demand was to die. This was not true of Adam. Christ came to redeem, not so Adam. So Christ rendered the whole-souled totality obedience in which Adam failed, but under totally different conditions and with incomparably greater demands.

We are liable to regard the Adamic administration as abstract, unrelated to our situation and practical interest, and so far removed from us that it has little or no relevance. If we are inclined to think so, it is because we do not have a biblically conditioned way of thinking. The Adamic institution is intensely relevant if our thought is regulated by the biblical revelation.

We are sinners and we come into the world as such. This situation demands explanation. It cannot stand as an empirical fact. It requires the question: Why or how? It is the Adamic administration with all its implications for racial solidarity that alone provides the answer. This is the biblical answer to the universality of sin and death.

We need salvation. How does salvation come to bear upon our need? Racial solidarity in Adam is the pattern according to which salvation is wrought and applied. By Adam sin-condemnation-death, by Christ righteousness-justification-life. A way of thinking that makes us aloof to solidarity with Adam makes us *inhabile* to the solidarity by which salvation comes. Thus the relevance of the Adamic administration to what is most basic, on the one hand, and most necessary, on the other, in our human situation.

6

Free Agency

In dealing with this topic it is helpful to begin with human action and to proceed from action to that which determines action. By this progression we may arrive at a more satisfactory analysis of what is involved in free agency or, as it has sometimes been denoted, natural liberty (cf. *Westminster Confession of Faith*, IX, i). In the matter of terminology it is necessary at the outset to distinguish between 'free agency' and 'free will'. No necessary objection can be made to the latter term. A term denotes the concept understood by it, and a proper connotation can be given to the term 'free will'. But frequently this designation has been used to express that concept of the will whereby the 'will' of man is regarded as autonomous and undetermined, and capable of volition good or bad, apart from any previous conditioning by our moral and religious character.

1. *The Reality of Human Action.* The thought hereby expressed is that man is endowed with power to perform certain actions within the realm of his created and dependent existence. In other words, man's agency is not illusory; within the all-embracive providence of God he is possessed of agency which is exercised in action.

2. *The Responsibility of Human Action.* Man's acts are worthy of blame or approval. Moral law, law of obligation, applies to him. His acts are within the sphere of ought and ought not. This obtains because he is made in the image of God and his actions must be in conformity with the likeness that defines his identity. God's likeness is the pattern in accord with which man's action is to be performed. The law that prescribes action or forbids it is the transcript of God's perfection, the

perfection of God coming to expression for the regulation of conduct consonant with it.

3. *The Freedom of Human Action.* The responsibility referred to above rests upon the fact that the action is the result of volition. Man wills or chooses to act. If he does not will to act, or if the act is contrary to his will, then the event occurring through his instrumentality is not in reality his action. He is the victim of some other power or agent over which he is not able to exercise control, and so he is not responsible for the event. We sometimes use the expression, 'I did it against my will'. This is not correct. We may do things reluctantly, do things we detest. But if we do them, it is because we *will* to do them. We will to do the distasteful rather than not to do it. Something may *be* done against our will and, strictly speaking, we are not the agents. But when we *do* something, it is always because we willed the same.

We are responsible for our acts because they are the result of our volition, and volition is the choice thus to act.

4. *The Determinant of Volition.* It is a platitude to say that we will because we have the power to will. But the power of volition does not explain why we exercise this power in a certain way. Two men have the power to earn a livelihood. One does it by honourable labour, the other resorts to theft. What explains the difference? It is not the power of volition, for both are endowed with this quality. It is apparent that we must go beyond the power of volition and the mere exercise of this power in actual volition. This that lies back of the power and its exercise is the character. And because there is a radical difference of character volition is exercised in totally different ways. The character is the *habitus* of the person, the whole complex of desires, of motives, propensions, principles. This may conveniently be called the dispositional complex, and the complex comprises all that goes to make up the distinguishing moral and religious bent, aim, purpose, and propension. Scripture calls this the heart. 'Out of the heart are the issues of life' (Prov. 4:23). Our Lord is express. 'Out of the abundance of the heart the mouth speaks. The good man out of the good treasure sends forth good things, and the evil man out of the evil treasure sends forth evil things' (Matt. 12:34, 35). 'For from within, out of the heart of man, proceed evil thoughts, fornications, thefts, murders, adulteries' *etc.*

(Mark 7:21, 22). The Scripture throughout is replete with this emphasis upon the heart as the fountain of both good and evil. Volition then is determined by the inward disposition. Dr. Shedd calls the one, immanent volition, and the other, executive volition. But whatever terms are used, the upshot is that much more belongs to a man than his metaphysical constitution and the series of volitions registered, and this is the determinant of the moral and religious character of his actions and course of life.

5. *The Self-determination of Volition and Action.* If volition is determined by the dispositional complex, in what does freedom consist? We are not free because the will or power of volition is in a state of indifference or indeterminancy. It is not an autonomous power or agent that can register any series of volitions by virtue of its unconditioned prerogative. Volition is causally determined by what the person most characteristically is. The liberty or freedom consists in the fact that the series of volitions is determined by the self; in the sense relevant to our topic, volition is self-determined. Action is self-action, volition is self-volition, determined by what the person is, and not by any compulsion or coercion extraneous to the person. 'God hath endued the will of man with that natural liberty, that it is neither forced, nor, by any absolute necessity of nature, determined to good, or evil.'[1] James 1:13, 14 enunciates this description of the process of human action. 'Every man is tempted when he is drawn away by his own lust and enticed.' This principle applies to all human situations in good and evil. It holds true in the fall and in regeneration. In the fall man's disposition changed and this resulted in the overt act of transgression. In regeneration a new disposition is given and new volitions are the result. In no case is the volition contrary to the immanent disposition of heart and mind. Nothing can make a man will against immanent disposition of heart and mind. Such a supposition would amount to a violation of the *nature* with which we are endowed.

This is not to deny the influences brought to bear upon man for good or for evil, influences of suasion to good or of temptation to evil. The consideration is simply that the person must come to acquiesce in that

---

[1] *Confession of Faith*, IX, i.

which the solicitation involves. The disposition of the person is affected, not by compulsion, but by adoption or acceptance.

Freedom is thus defined negatively and affirmatively, as the absence of compulsion and *self*-determination respectively. A man is responsible for his acts because they are due to *his* volitions. He is responsible for his volitions because they are self-propelled, exercised without compulsion and expressive of what he is in the innermost bent, bias, and disposition of heart and mind. Understood thus, freedom is rational spontaneity.

6. *The Inclusiveness of Freedom.* This freedom is not restricted to the sphere of volition and action. It applies to the heart, the dispositional complex. The heart of man is his own. Man is depraved, but this depravity is his and he is responsible for it. In the fall the disposition of man became unholy. Though great mystery surrounds this change, yet the unholy disposition was his, and for all its movements he was responsible for this reason. In regeneration God gives a new heart. But once given, it belongs to the person regenerated and, though efficaciously imparted, it is not a disposition compulsively imposed so that the new disposition does not violate that which is most characteristically his. In other words, whatever the immanent disposition is, it is his with consent, and not by compulsion contrary to his will.

7. *The Power of Contrary Choice is not of the Essence of Free Agency.* In dealing with this proposition it is necessary to distinguish between *contrary* choice and *alternative* choice. *Contrary* choice is the ability to choose between alternatives that are morally antithetical, between good and bad regarded not relatively but absolutely in terms of God's judgment. *Alternative* choice, on the other hand, is the choice between alternatives that are ethically of the same character, alternatives that are both good or both bad. The proposition applies only to contrary choice. We may examine the proposition and define it both negatively and positively.

(i) *Negatively.* It does not mean that there are no situations in which man had the power of contrary choice. Adam in his state of integrity had the power of contrary choice. To deny this would mean that sin was a necessity of his nature. Adam sinned. But he was able not to sin because he was created upright and holy.

63

Regenerate man has the power of contrary choice, the ability to good in virtue of the holiness implanted in regeneration, and the ability to sin because of indwelling sin. Romans 7:25 is explicit to this effect.

(ii) The proposition does not mean that fallen, unregenerate man is destitute of the power of alternative choice. He is under an unholy necessity of sinning. He is totally depraved and cannot choose what is good and well-pleasing to God (Rom. 8:7; Eph. 2:1). But within the realm of bondage to sin there are numberless alternatives from which he is able to choose. Likewise regenerate man, although he cannot will certain things because of his confirmed state of holiness (cf. 1 John 3:9), yet there are many situations in which he has alternative choice in the categories of both good and evil.

(iii) The proposition is not dealing with the determinism arising from foreordination. It is true that all our choices and acts are foreordained, and only foreordained acts come to pass. But this is not the factor or consideration contemplated in the proposition. To suppose that it is, confuses two things that must be kept distinct. If this were the consideration, then the power of both alternative and contrary choice would be eliminated from the realm of human agency and possibility. The power of contrary choice would not be predicable of Adam in the state of integrity, a position that must be maintained without any equivocation. The distinction to be borne in mind is that foreordination, though all-inclusive, does not operate so as to deprive man of his agency, nor of the voluntary decision by reason of which he is responsible for his actions. Similarly foreordination does not rule out the power of contrary choice in those cases where this obtained or obtains. Just as foreordination does not conflict with or rule out human responsibility, so it does not conflict with or rule out the power of alternative choice, nor does it conflict with or rule out the power of contrary choice where this power is necessarily posited.

(ii) *Positively*. The proposition is concerned *solely* with the truth that, in a state of confirmed holiness or unholiness, the absence of the power to choose the morally opposite does not interfere with free agency in the sense defined in the foregoing analysis. In the state of sin we are unable to love God and choose what is well-pleasing to him. This inability does not deprive us of free agency. In fact it is only in virtue of free agency that the indictment of bondage to sin could apply. Likewise, in the regenerate state, and particularly in the glorified state, the holy necessity of doing good and the impossibility of the opposite, does not interfere with free agency. Again, it is the fact of free agency that makes the characterization possible and relevant.

The proposition has respect to moral and religious condition exclusively, and to the necessities belonging to a condition of confirmed goodness or badness, not to the necessity arising from God's foreordination. Every proposition has its own universe of reference and is applicable only within that universe. The anthropological importance of the proposition appears particularly in three connections:

i) The prelapsarian power of contrary choice was not a necessary condition of Adam's free agency. If Adam had been confirmed in his integrity he would still be a free agent. The power of contrary choice was for purposes of probation.

ii) Total inability for good in the state of sin does not rule out free agency. Inability for good is one thing; responsible agency is another.

iii) In grace relatively, and in glory completely, confirmation in holiness does not make us automatons. It is in such confirmation that free agency achieves its highest expression and realization.

The essence of free agency is that we act without compulsion from without, according to our nature or character. Free agency thus construed applies to all conditions of men and angels.

8. *Free Agency is Consistent with Certainty.* The principle here asserted is that an act may be certain as to its futurition, but free as to the mode of its occurrence. The proposition goes athwart every position which supposes that uncertainty and contingency are necessary to freedom, that certainty of occurrence is incompatible with the nature of a free act. This position is analogous to that which would deny foreordination in favour of human responsibility. The answer is that, although we are not able so to analyse the relations of God's foreordination and human agency that we can discover and perceive the perfect *concursus* that obtains, yet we must maintain both without any infringement upon the province, reality, and integrity of each. The foreknowledge of God presupposes certainty of occurrence; his foreordination renders all occurrence certain; by his providence what is

foreordained is unalterably put into effect. Only within the realm of all-inclusive providence is our free agency a fact, and only thus is it maintained. In God we live and move and have our being. Providence in fulfilment of foreordained purpose is not only compatible with the freedom indispensable to our being; it is indispensable to the existence of our freedom and never functions so as to interfere with it.

7

The Fall of Man

THE FACT OF THE FALL

Man was created upright and therefore with the character that constituted him for, and endowed him with the ability to perform, righteousness. Such a position is demanded by the fact that he was very good and was created in the divine image. If he was very good he was such in terms of the categories that define his nature as man, and if he bore the divine image he must have borne it in the fullest terms of the Scripture definition (Eph. 4:24; Col. 3:10). At the suggestion of Satan man disobeyed and fell into sin and under its guilt. The fact that it was at the suggestion of Satan that man fell advises us, or at least reminds us, of two important facts.

1. Sin was present in the universe prior to the fall of man. Already there was a kingdom of sin and of evil. Of that kingdom Satan was the head, a spirit of obviously exceptional ingenuity, skill and power. This pushes back the origin of sin and evil beyond the sphere of human life and experience. And it pushes back the problem of the origin of sin also. The mystery associated with the origin of sin goes back to, and enshrouds, the fall of Satan and of the angels who kept not their first estate.

This consideration, however, provides us with no relief from the problem of the origin of sin in our first parents, or of the problem connected with sin as such. Neither does it provide us with any extenuation of the guilt of Adam's sin. It neither solves the problem nor does it alleviate the wrong.

2. It serves to remind us of the reality and activity of Satan and of the demonic order. Back of all that is visible and tangible in the sin of this world there are unseen spiritual powers. Satan is the god of this

world, the prince of the power of the air, the spirit that now works in the sons of disobedience. The arch-foe of the kingdom of God is not the visible powers arrayed against it; for behind these visible agents and manifestations of evil is the ingenuity, craft, malicious design, instigation and relentless activity of the devil and his ministers. It was this of which Paul was fully aware when he said, 'We wrestle not against flesh and blood, but against the principalities, against the powers, against the world rulers of this darkness, against the spiritualities of wickedness in the heavenlies' (Eph. 6:12). Because we have given way to the impact of naturalistic presuppositions, and to the anti-supernaturalistic and anti-praeternaturalistic bias, we are far too liable in these days to discount this truth of Christian revelation. We are liable to discard it in our construction and interpretation of the forces of iniquity. To the extent that we do so, our thinking is not Christian.

In this connection it is most significant that the work of Christ, which is so central in our Christian faith, is essentially a work of destruction that terminates upon the power and work of Satan. This is not a peripheral or incidental feature of redemption. It is an integral aspect of its accomplishment. Our Lord himself, as he was approaching Calvary, said, 'Now is the judgment of this world; now shall the prince of this world be cast out' (John 12:31). These words appear in a context that is pregnant with allusions to the necessity and results of the cross. We find the same emphasis in John's first Epistle: 'For this purpose the Son of God was manifested, that he might destroy the works of the devil' (1 John 3:8). And in Hebrews 2:14, 15: 'that through death he might destroy him that had the power of death, that is the devil, and deliver them who through fear of death were all their lifetime subject to bondage.' The relevance of Colossians 2:15 to this same triumph has been called in question.[1] But Meyer presents an able argument in support of the interpretation that the verse refers to the destruction of Satanic powers in the cross—'He spoiled principalities and powers, and made a show of them openly, triumphing over them in it'.[2]

Satan tempted man to sin; this temptation was the *occasion* of man's fall. It was not, however, the *cause*. No external power or influence can

[1] See Alford *in loco*, and compare Colossians 1:16; 2:10.
[2] see Meyer *in loco*.

cause a rational being to sin. The sin of Adam was a movement of defection and apostasy and transgression in Adam's heart and mind and will, and for that movement he was responsible and he alone was the agent and subject. The temptation of Satan did not constitute the sin of Adam. It was the voluntary acquiescence in that suggestion, the embrace or sympathetic entertainment of it. For that acquiescence man was solely and wholly responsible. Satan was responsible for the malicious and seductive intent of the temptation, and for its character as seduction. Satan incurred guilt thereby. But for the fall of Adam, Adam alone was responsible. Satan incurred guilt in connection with the sin, but it was not Satan who ate of the tree.

God gave to man the power of contrary choice. Man of his own will, by no external compulsion or determination, used that power in the commission of sin. There was no necessity arising from his physical condition, nor from his moral nature, nor from the nature of his environment, why he should sin. It was a free movement within man's spirit. To use Laidlaw's words, 'It arose with an external suggestion, and upon an external occasion, but it was an inward crisis.'[1]

The outward act of transgression, like all overt acts, was determined by inclination, propension, character. Since the character that produced the act cannot be different as to its moral character from the act itself, we must conclude that the inclination, disposition or character of Adam changed from holiness to unholiness. It was that change of moral character that alone can explain the overt act of sin. The inward change was signalized or manifested by the overt act of disobedience.

This analysis can be shown on exegetical and psychological grounds. The overt act must be traced to its source in the movement of defection in man's heart and mind. And that movement of defection consisted in doubt of the divine goodness, wisdom and love, disbelief of the divine Word, coveting of the divine prerogatives. This movement of doubt, unbelief and lust issued in direct disobedience to the divine command. 'The woman saw . . . that the tree was to be desired to make one wise, and she took.'

In Shedd's words, 'Eve looked upon the tree of knowledge not only with *innocent* but with *sinful* desire. She not only had the natural created

[1] *The Biblical Doctrine of Man*, John Laidlaw, Edinburgh 1879, p. 142.

desire for it as producing nourishing food, and as a beautiful object to the eye, but she came to have, besides this, the unnatural and *self-originated* desire for it as yielding a kind of *knowledge* which God forbade man to have. She "lusted" after that "knowledge of good and evil" which eating of the fruit would impart. . . . This lusting of Eve for a knowledge that God had *prohibited* was her apostasy.'[1]

James Fisher's Catechism speaks as follows:

'Question: Were not our first parents guilty of sin before their eating the forbidden fruit?

Answer: Yes, they were guilty in hearkening to the devil and believing him, before they did actually eat thereof.

Question: Why then is their eating of it called their first sin?

Answer: Because it was the first sin finished (James 1:15).'

In reference to 1 Timothy 2:14, Shedd says 'According to St. Paul, Adam was seduced by his affection for Eve, rather than deceived by the lie of Satan. He fell with his eyes wide open to the fact that if he ate he would die' (*ibid*. p. 176).

The fall, then, was complete moral revolt against the sovereignty, supremacy, authority and will of God. In the command given to Adam there was epitomized the sovereignty, authority, wisdom, justice, goodness, and truth of God. Disobedience to it was an assault upon the divine Majesty, repudiation of his sovereignty and authority, doubt of his goodness, dispute with his wisdom, contradiction of his veracity. Sin is transgression of law ($\dot{\alpha}\nu o\mu\dot{\iota}\alpha$), and law is the expression of all that God is in the moral sphere in relation to man, as absolute and sovereign Creator and Ruler and righteous Judge. Sin is all along the line of divine perfection a contradiction of each.

In ethics the ultimate question is, What has God commanded?, not, What is the most expedient?, nor, What, according to the nature of things, is the good or the best? And the ultimate test of our loyalty is preparedness to obey simply and solely because God has commanded. When man fails here it intimates the bankruptcy of moral character.

THE IMMEDIATE EFFECTS OF THE FALL

1. *Internal Revolution*. This refers to man's subjective condition. The

[1] *Dogmatic Theology*, Vol. II, 174, 175.

pivot on which this internal revolution turned was his changed attitude to God. 'And the eyes of them both were opened, and they knew that they were naked.' 'And the man and his wife hid themselves from the presence of the Lord God amongst the trees of the garden.' 'I heard thy voice in the garden and I was afraid, because I was naked, and I hid myself.' All of this betrays the fact that there was a radical change in man's mental attitude. Man was made for the presence and fellowship of God and, as created, would have found his supreme delight in the presence of God. He now flies from the face of God. A new complex of disposition, feeling, and emotion took possession of his heart and mind. He experienced shame and fear, indicating to us the operation of a guilty conscience and the attempt to get away from the light. 'God is light'. 'He that doeth evil hateth the light, neither cometh to the light, lest his deeds should be reproved' (John 3:20).

2. *Revolution in God's Relation to Man.* God changed his relation to man. God is unchangeable in being, nature, character, intradivine relations, and in his relations to men. This change is not mutability but a necessary expression of his own immutable perfection. It evinces the inevitable reaction to that which is contrary to his immutable character.

We must note that the rupture between God and man was not one-sided, though the reason for the rupture was the fault of man. This rupture appears in the manifest difference of tone after Genesis 3:9. Previously there were on all sides the tokens of favour, peace, and harmony. Not only is the note of reproof and displeasure absent, but also of discord. Now an aspect of the divine character appears that is entirely new in divine–human relations, and that previously was not even suggested. It is that of anger, reproof, retribution, curse, and condemnation. 'Unto the woman he said, I will greatly multiply thy pain and thy conception. In pain thou shalt bring forth children, and thy desire shall be to thy husband, and he shall rule over thee' (Gen. 3:16). To the man he said, 'Cursed is the ground for thy sake . . . In the sweat of thy face shalt thou eat bread till thou return to the ground . . . Dust thou art and to dust thou shalt return' (Gen. 3:17f.). 'Therefore the Lord God sent him forth from the garden of Eden to till the ground from whence he was taken. So he drove out the man . . .' (Gen. 3:23f.). These are the arrows of the Almighty. They are the echoes of displeasure and condemnation.

Sin causes disruption and makes a difference not only in our mental attitude, and in our relations to God, but also in God's relation to us. It separates us from the favour of God and separates between us and our God.

3. *Cosmic Revolution.* Sin is an event in the spiritual realm of man's mind. Sin originates in the spirit and resides in the spirit. It is not a disturbance in the physical world, not maladjustment to physical conditions. It is a movement in the realm of spirit. But it drastically affects the physical and non-spiritual. Its relationships are cosmic. 'Cursed is the ground for thy sake; thorns also and thistles shall it bring forth to thee' (Gen. 3:17). 'The creation was made subject to vanity'. 'The whole creation groans and travails in pain' (Rom. 8:20, 22). Not until the reconciliation accomplished by Christ shall have achieved its final purpose will the creation be delivered from the bondage of corruption into the liberty of the glory of the children of God.

4. *Revolution in the Human Family.* It had its effect not only upon Adam but upon the race. It has affected mankind organically and there is corporate corruption. The immediate sequel in the unfolding history of Adam's family is the catalogue of sins—envy, malice, hatred, homicide, polygamy, violence. 'I have slain a man for wounding me and a young man for bruising me. If Cain shall be avenged sevenfold, truly Lamech seventy and sevenfold.' 'The wickedness of man was great in the earth.' 'The earth was filled with violence.' 'All flesh had corrupted its way upon the earth.'

5. *Disintegration in Man's own Constitution.* Death. How eloquently this is advertised in Genesis 5! Notwithstanding the longevity of man, he cannot escape the fulfilment of the divine threat, and must prove that the wages of sin is death.

INSOLUBLE PROBLEMS CONNECTED WITH THE FALL

1. *The Ontological Problem.* The question here is that of the divine causality in connection with sin. There are two positions that must be maintained in order to conserve the balance of truth and the proportion of emphasis.

(i) There is divine *predetermination* or *foreordination* in connection with sin. The fall was foreordained by God and its certainty was therefore guaranteed. And as divine foreordination ensured the certainty of occurrence, so it was accomplished in the realm of his all-controlling providence. The first sin, like all other sins, was committed within the realm of God's all-sustaining, directing and governing power. Outside the sphere of his foreordination and providence the fall could not have occurred. The arch-crime of history—the crucifixion of our Lord—was perpetrated in accordance with the determinate counsel and foreknowledge of God (Acts 2:23). So, too, was the fall.

(ii) God is not the author of sin. For sin as sinfulness, man alone was responsible, and he alone is the agent of execution. He alone did it. God did not do it. God did not work in the heart and mind of man so as to constrain or induce apostasy. He did not cause to be the act of eating the forbidden fruit. Adam and Eve ate the fruit; they were the agents of the sinful act and of the movement of defection and apostasy of heart and of mind that lay back of and came to expression in the overt act of transgression. *The responsibility for the act as sin and as guilt rested with Adam.*

It was God alone who foreordained the act; it was in God's providence, and in his alone, that it was accomplished. For the inclusion of it in his decree and within the sphere of his providence God was truly responsible, if we may use that expression. It was his sovereign prerogative and his alone to foreordain what comes to pass. But within the sphere of divine decree and providence man's agency and responsibility were real facts. They were not suspended nor even curtailed by the foreordination and providence of God. And with man's agency rested the responsibility for sin, and therefore the guilt or blameworthiness of it. With him rested the wrong and therefore with him the sin. *The foreordination determined the act; it was accomplished in God's providence; but neither of these acted so as to deprive man of his freedom, responsibility and agency.*[1]

Now here is the problem. How can it be that, from the aspect of the divine plan, there is immutable predetermination and accomplishment, and yet from the aspect of man's agency no coercion or compulsion, no

[1] cf. *Westminster Confession of Faith*, III, i; V, iv; Calvin: *Inst.*, I, xviii, 1, 2.

curtailment of his freedom and responsibility, and no alleviation of his guilt? It is a mystery beyond our comprehension. We cannot so diagnose or analyse the interrelations of these correlative facts that we shall be able to see the perfectly harmonious co-working of these two distinct agencies or factors. There is convergence of both in the one act of the fall. But how they converge, how there can be the combination of divine and human agency in the same event and yet no interference with or curtailment of either, is a matter beyond our understanding. This is what we mean when we say that we are faced with an insoluble problem.

To point up the problem perhaps even more acutely, we must say that something occurs by the decretive will of God which is in direct contradiction to his revealed will. God decretively wills what he preceptively forbids, decretively ordains what is contrary to his preceptive ordinance. Personify the decree and it would say: This will certainly come to pass. Personify the precept and it would say: This thou shalt not bring to pass.

We must, of course, remember that this problem emerges not only in connection with the fall, but in connection with all sin, and the problem is not basically different in connection with all free and responsible acts. The problem, however, becomes particularly patent in connection with the fall, because here we have the origin of sin, the beginning of that which is the contradiction of God's perfection.

2. *The Dispensational Problem.* The question here is: Why did God decree sin? Of course, the ultimate end of all that God decrees, great and small, good and evil, is the manifestation of his glory (cf. Eph. 1:11; Rom. 11:33–36; Prov. 16:4). But why God chose this particular way of showing forth the glory of his perfections is hid in the counsels of his own good pleasure and will. It is not ours to scan the reasons of his unrevealed counsel. It is ours to bow in humble adoration and say, 'Shall not the judge of all the earth do right?' And if we are disposed to say, 'Why hast thou made me thus?', we should remind ourselves of the inspired reply, 'Who art thou, O man, that repliest against God? Shall the thing formed say unto him that formed it, why hast thou made me thus?'. We cannot know the Almighty unto perfection. 'It is high as heaven, what canst thou do?, deeper than hell, what canst thou know?

The measure thereof is longer than the earth and broader than the sea'
(Job 11:8, 9). We see the outskirts of his ways, but how little a portion
do we know of him! (Job 26:14). 'Touching the Almighty, we cannot
find him out' (Job 37:23). 'Clouds and darkness are round about him
but justice and judgment are the habitation of his throne' (Ps. 97:2).
How much must this be true when we are dealing with the reason
of his ultimate counsel!

3. *The Psychogenetic Problem.* How could a being perfectly holy and
upright become sinful? How could sin originate in a holy soul and find
lodgment and entertainment there? We cannot tell. It constitutes an
insoluble psychological and moral problem. Every reason was against
the commission of sin. It was in the deepest sense an irrationality. As
James Fisher says, 'This sin was aggravated in being committed when
man had full light in his understanding, a clear copy of the law in his
heart; when he had no vicious bias in his will, but enjoying perfect
liberty; and when he had a sufficient stock of grace in his hand, whereby
to withstand the tempting enemy; in being committed after God had
made a covenant of life with him, and given him express warning of the
danger of eating the forbidden fruit' (*ibid*. Q.19).[1]

Though these problems emerge in connection with the origin of sin,
we are not to think that it is only in connection with the biblical doctrine
that difficulties arise. It is true that we can eliminate these specific problems if we deny the Christian positions on which they rest. But it by
no means follows that we eliminate difficulty. And it certainly does not
follow that we can offer a more satisfactory interpretation and solution
of the facts. Furthermore, if we try to eliminate these problems, or tone
down their acuteness on a less consistent Christian basis, we land ourselves ultimately in greater difficulty, because we shall find ourselves
struggling with the inconsistency of the attenuated residuary of
Christian truth which we try to retain.

The doctrine as presented, though it involves incomprehensible
mystery, is nevertheless the only doctrine that preserves the two polar
truths of theism on the one hand, and human responsibility on the
other, the absolute sovereignty of God and human guilt. Without either
there is no sin in the proper sense of the term. Without the holy

[1] See Shedd: *ibid.*, vol. II, p. 165.

sovereignty of God there can be no responsibility for man. And without the real guilt of man, guilt arising from his total responsibility for sin, there can be no holy sovereignty for God. For then we should be unable to justify the evils with which man is inflicted.

Dualistic philosophy posits the eternity of something else than God and denies the sole eternity and absoluteness of God. It sets up an eternal antithesis.

Theistic evolution makes God responsible for sin by making it a necessity of man's nature.

The biblical doctrine leaves us with mysteries beyond our comprehension, but these are, as Laidlaw says, 'solvents, not sources of difficulty. Into the problem of evil, Scripture introduces elements of explanation. It accounts for man's present moral and physical condition, for the broad phenomena of life and death in a way that is thinkable and intelligible'.[1]

The humble Christian is content to contain these unresolved problems. They do not disturb his peace of mind because, in the last analysis, the ground of all peace of mind is the conviction of the sovereignty, justice, goodness of God. What he cannot resolve he believes God does. It is the apex of Christian piety to trust in God, just as it is also the foundation, to say, 'I do not know, but I do know that God does'. Christian piety leaves unresolved problems in the hand of God, remembering that, if we knew all, then we would be as God, and worship and adoration would be at an end. Clouds and darkness are round about him but justice and judgment are the habitation of his throne.

[1] *op.cit.*, p. 139.

8

The Nature of Sin

1. *Sin is a real evil*. Real in opposition to all theories which regard sin as illusion, and in opposition to all theories that conceive of sin as negation, privation or limitation. Sin is a positive something (*prava dispositio* not *otiosa*) not simply the absence of something. And evil in opposition to all views which make sin necessary to the promotion of good. Pantheism makes sin a necessary step in the self-realization of God, the antagonism view makes it the condition of virtue. We hold that God has decreed sin and embraced it in his plan for wise and holy ends, but not because it is necessary for himself nor for the existence of good.

2. *Sin is a specific evil*. Disease, calamity, death are evils, but sin belongs to a different category. These are the consequences of sin but sin has features that these other evils do not have.

3. *It is moral evil*.

(i) It is wrong. As such its specific character is disclosed. This is the first feature by which it is distinguished. Sin belongs to the sphere of moral relations. It is recognized as something that ought not to be. It is a coming short of moral imperative. It is not something simply unwise, or inexpedient, or hurtful, or painful, or calamitous, or unfortunate. It is a violation of the category of *ought*; it is wrong; it ought not to be.

(ii) Violation of law. Sin has relation to law and is violation of it. The word 'ought' can have no meaning apart from a rule or standard of right, that is apart from law. Morality cannot be reduced to lower terms than obedience to law, or sin to lower terms than violation of unconditional obligations. The ethical standard is not our highest good or best interests, nor the greatest good of the greatest number, but the categorical imperative that is the imperative of simple command, the imperative not of prudential or utilitarian considerations but of the law that binds the conscience. Sin then is moral evil because it is a contravention of that which by its own right, apart from any extraneous considerations, binds and demands.

(iii) Violation of God's Law. The law that sin violates is the law of God. The categorical imperative binds, demands and commands because it proceeds from the authority of God, and the authority of God inheres in his being and nature as God. The law of God is simply the expression or transcript of his moral perfection for the regulation of thought and life consonant with his perfection. It is not the law of cosmos, nor the law of reason; it is the law that expresses the nature and will of the supreme personality who has authority over us and propriety in us, to whom we owe complete submission and absolute devotion. We are bound to love the Lord our God with all our heart and soul and strength and mind, and such love is the fulfilling of the law. Herein appears the perverseness of the idea that the moral law may be abrogated and is superseded by love. Law for us is the correlate of the nature of God, in us and to us the correlate of the divine perfection. Love is the fulfilling of the law. But love is not an autonomous, self-instructing and self-directing principle. Love does not excogitate the norms by which it is regulated. Love fulfils the law but love itself is not the law. Sin is therefore the violation of the law which love fulfils. Abrogate law and we abrogate sin, and we make love an emotion abstracted from all activity and meaning. Sin is ἀνομία and because so it is *culpa*, blame and blameworthy.

(iv) The Pervasiveness of God's Law. The law of God extends to all relations of life. This is so because we are never removed from the obligation to love and serve God. We are never amoral. We owe devotion to God in every phase and department of life. It is this principle of all-inclusive obligation to God, and of the all-pervasive relevance of the law of God, that gives sanctity to all of our obligations and relations. Because of the ordinances which God has established in this world we have obligations to other creatures. We owe subjection to them under certain conditions. But these obligations are not obligations unless they are first of all embraced in a higher divine obligation. All subordinate obligation is derived: we owe subjection to our fellow men, and to the ordinances and laws imposed by them, only insofar as these ordinances originate in divine institution and authority. For when any institution of human character or composition trespasses or exceeds the limits of God-given authority, then we are not under obligation to obey. (The violation of a law humanly imposed, and not the legitimate exercise of God-given authority, does not involve sin.) Nothing is sin except that which involves the violation of a divine obligation. There is only one Lawgiver. If the ordinances of men require us to violate the law of God, then we must obey God rather than men, and must violate the human ordinance. If human ordinances do not require us to sin but are in excess of divinely authorized prerogative, then compliance is to be determined by expediency in relation to all the circumstances of the situation. But violation, when required by higher considerations, is not sin. If the ordinances are a legitimate exercise of the God-given authority, then disobedience is violation of God's law and not merely of man's (cf. fifth commandment). Such disobedience is sin because the ultimate sanction on which such a law is based is the authority of God. This is clearly the force of Romans 13:1–7. 'Let every soul be subject to the higher powers, for there is no power but of God: the powers that be are ordained of God. Therefore he that resisteth the power resisteth the ordinance of God, and they that resist shall receive to themselves damnation . . . Wherefore ye must needs be subject, not only for the wrath but also for conscience sake.' 'For conscience sake'. Surely God alone is Lord of the conscience. Yes! But in the ordinance referred to there is divine law.

It is violation of divine law that is sin. Standards by which sin is to be judged are not therefore variable. Circumstances and conditions have to be taken into account as constituting the concrete situations in which we find ourselves and in relation to which the law is to be applied. And circumstances and conditions will aggravate or alleviate the heinousness of our sin and the degree of our guilt. But the law by which sin is to be judged is not variable. He that knew not his Lord's will and did things worthy of stripes will be beaten with few stripes. But he is still beaten with stripes and is not regarded as innocent. They who sin without law will perish without law, but they will perish because they sin.

(v) Sin involves both pollution and guilt (*macula et poena*).

(a) *Pollution*. This refers to the depravity of disposition and character. Man is totally unholy. All his functions and exercises are unholy because they lack conformity to the will of God; they come short of the perfection which his holiness demands. Man's understanding is darkened, his will enslaved, his conscience perverted, his affections depraved, his heart corrupted, his mind enmity against God. 'Mansit igitur intellectus sed obtenebratus; mansit voluntas, sed depravata; mansit appetitus inferior, sed totaliter vitiatus' ('Man's understanding still remains, but in a darkened condition; his will-power remains, but only in a depraved state; his lower affections remain, but they are wholly corrupt'[1]). Man stands in contradiction to the holiness of God, and he stands thus in every aspect and in every relationship.

(b) *Guilt*. Guilt is twofold: demerit and the judgment of demerit, ill desert and the infliction of the desert owing. In Latin it may be expressed as *dignitas judicii aut poenae* and *poena aut judicium demeriti* ('the deserving of judgment or punishment', and, 'the punishment or judgment of demerit'), or, the distinction between *demeritum* and the *judicium demeriti* ('demerit', or 'ill-desert', and 'the judgment of demerit'). The former is called *reatus potentialis* ('potential guilt') and the latter *reatus actualis* ('actual guilt') by Reformed theologians. It is obvious that *reatus actualis* (actual guilt) may be suspended, as in forbearance, or completely annulled, as in remission. But this is not so with *reatus potentialis* (potential guilt). For, wherever there is sin there is the unworthiness and demerit which it entails, whether the penalty of that demerit is inflicted or not.

Sometimes the distinction has been drawn between *reatus culpae* and *reatus poenae* ('the guilt of sin', and 'liability to punishment'). The classic Reformed theologians of the seventeenth century rejected this distinction as improper and as a distinction without a difference.[2] Van Mastricht says: 'Est ergo reatus medium quid, inter culpam et poenam: ex culpa enim *oritur*, et ad poenam *ducit*, adeo ut *unus* sit reatus culpae et

[1] Wallebius: *Compendium C.T.*, Lib I, Cap. x, para. x.
[2] Cf. Amesius: *Medulla*, XII, 3; Leydecker: *Medulla*, IX, XV; Van Mastricht: *Theoretica—Practica Theologia*, Lib IV, Cap. 11, par. viii; Turretine: *Institutio*, Locus IX, Quaestio 111, Sect. vi.

poenae, qui inter istos terminos quasi *medius* incidit, et ab utroque ex aequo denominatur.'[1] ('So *reatus* is a sort of middle term standing midway between *culpa*, sin, and *poena*, punishment. It springs from *culpa* and leads to *poena*. In effect, *reatus culpae*, the guilt of sin, and *reatus poenae*, liability to punishment, are one and the same. The term *reatus* falls in between these two other terms and may be equally well described by either term.') We often use the word 'guilty' in the sense of perpetrating wrong. When we say a person is guilty we mean that he has perpetrated the wrong with which he has been charged. And thus we also use the word 'guilt' in the sense of wrong committed. When a person acknowledges guilt we mean he acknowledges his wrong, in a word, his sin. So guilt, in common parlance is sometimes the synonym of transgression, but as the translation of the Latin word *reatus* it has reference rather to the obligation to justice or penalty (*obligatio ad poenam*) in which sense the word 'guilt' is sometimes used, and in which sense it is used in this connection to denote the consequences of sin and not the sin itself.

These aspects of sin with which we have been dealing need to be guarded and emphasized. We may find a great deal of emphasis upon the undesirability of sin, the unfortunateness, the odiousness, ugliness, disgustingness, even filthiness of sin, without any truly Christian assessment of sin as lawlessness, pollution and guilt. The Christian estimate of sin is that it is wrong, that it ought not to be. It is not only undesirable; it is damnable in the strongest sense of the word. It is this concept of wrong that gathers up into itself all that has been said regarding sin as violation of the law of God. It is contradiction of God's perfection and cannot but meet with his disapproval and wrath. (And not only is it wrong, but it also makes us subject to the execution of God's wrath.) Since it is the contradiction of God's perfection, he must react with holy indignation and displeasure, and inflict that indignation upon the ungodly. Here we come face to face with a divine 'cannot' that bespeaks not divine weakness but everlasting strength, not reproach but inestimable glory. He cannot deny himself. To be complacent towards that which is the contradiction of his own holiness would be a denial of himself. So that wrath against sin is the correlate of his holiness. And

[1] *op. cit.*

this is just saying that the justice of God demands that sin receive its retribution. The question is not at all: How can God, being what he is, send men to hell? The question is: How can God, being what he is, save them from hell? This is the import of *reatus*.

9

Inability

ORIGINAL sin deals with our depravity. Inability deals with the fact that our own depravity is humanly irremediable. Man is totally unable to change his character or act in a way that is different from it.

DEFINITION
Negatively, it is not:
1. Metaphysical; it is not due to the loss or absence of any component element of our own being, nor to any incompatibility between the component elements in our being, nor to any limitation belonging to our being as creatures.
2. It did not belong to man originally. We must distinguish between what man is unable to be, become, or do because of his finitude, and the moral inability arising from sin. In his original state man had plenary ability to fulfil all of God's demands. To maintain otherwise would mean that sin was a necessity of the condition in which he was created. For all failure to meet the full demands of God is sin.
3. Inability does not mean the loss of natural liberty. This refers to free agency, namely, that man exercises volition according to his character. Inability presupposes liberty.
4. Inability does not deny the possibility of *justitia civilis*, that is natural and social virtue.
Positively, inability means that in sin man is not only indisposed and made opposite to all good but that he is totally unable to be otherwise. It is inability to discern, love, or choose the things that are well pleasing to God. He cannot know them because they are spiritually discerned; he

cannot love them because his mind is enmity against God; he cannot choose them because those in the flesh cannot please God. It is the *ou dunatai* (cannot) of the natural man.

BIBLICAL BASIS OF THE DOCTRINE

1. The Scripture, of course, requires us to do what we do not have the moral ability to perform. God's command can never be reduced to the level of our sinful impotence. For the command must reflect the holiness of God and the demand of that holiness upon us. The minimum and maximum coincide, namely, that we should love the Lord our God with all our heart, our soul, our strength, our mind and our neighbour as ourselves. Yet the Scriptures do not attribute to us the ability to fulfil that demand; they do not predicate of man the ability to change his character nor the ability to act otherwise.

2. On the contrary the Scripture asserts unmistakably man's total inability to transform character. Jeremiah 13:23 states the principle when it says, 'Can the Ethiopian change his skin or the leopard his spots? Then may ye also do good that are accustomed to do evil.'

But the truth of inability is expressly asserted:

(i)   Matt. 7:17–18
      Matt. 12:33–35
      Luke 6:43–45

'Generation of vipers, how can ye being evil speak good things? For out of the abundance of the heart the mouth speaks. The good man out of the good treasure brings forth good things, and the evil man out of the evil treasure brings forth evil things.' Note the occurrence of *agathos* (good) three times in the first clause of Matthew 12:35 and *ponēros* (evil) three times in the second. But in Matt. 7:18 our Lord goes further and says, 'A good tree cannot bring forth evil fruit, neither can a corrupt tree bring forth good fruit' (*ou dunatai*).

(ii) John 6:44, 45, 65.

In John 6:37 Jesus says, 'Everything (*pan ho*) that the Father gives to me shall come to me, and him that cometh unto me I will in no wise cast out.' Jesus is here speaking of the coming to him which consists in faith and which has its issue in the salvation that reaches its apex in the resurrection at the last day. The former is shown by vs. 40 and the latter by vss. 39, 40. It is therefore of the faith in Jesus unto salvation that he speaks in vss. 44, 45, 65.

Now, obviously, as men are confronted with the gospel the most elementary demand, the demand that is the only avenue to the fulfilment of all other demands, is to believe in Christ. But of that Jesus says man is incapable. It is a psychological, moral, and spiritual impossibility apart from an efficacious drawing which is of the nature of a gift from the Father. It is therefore of that faith in Christ that Jesus says 'No one can come unto me except the Father who sent me draw him' (*oudeis dunatai elthein pros me*), and 'On this account I said to you that no one can come unto me except it were given to him of my Father' (*oudeis dunatai . . . ean mē ē dedomenon autō ek tou Patros*).

Nothing therefore can be plainer than this, that the act of true and simple faith in Christ is impossible apart from the drawing and gracious gift of the Father.

(iii) Romans 6:6, 16, 20. The sinner is in bondage to sin.

Romans 7:1. 'Or are ye ignorant, brethren, for I speak to them that know the law, that the law hath dominion over a man for so long a time as he liveth?' When we take this along with the argument that follows it means that until delivered from the law by the body of Christ the sinful passions which are through the law work in our members and bring us into bondage to sin. This simply means that we are bondservants to sin until delivered by redemptive grace.

(iv) Romans 8:7, 8. This text not only asserts that the carnal mind is enmity against God but also that the carnal mind cannot be subject to the law of God (*oude gar dunatai*). Those who are in the flesh cannot please God (*Theō aresai ou dunantai*), cf. Heb. 11:6.

(v) 1 Corinthians 2:14. 'The natural man receiveth not the things of the Spirit of God; neither can he know them because they are spiritually discerned' (*kai ou dunatai gnōnai, hoti pneumatikōs anakrinetai*).

John 3:3, 5. Except a man be born again he cannot see or enter into the kingdom of God.

All of which is to the effect of demonstrating that man in his natural state is psychologically, morally, and spiritually incapable of the understanding, affection and will which will enable him to be subject to the law of God, respond to the gospel of his grace, appreciate the things of

85

the Spirit of God, or do the things well-pleasing to him. Neither under-standing, nor affection, nor will is capable of rendering that response which is appropriate to and required by the relation of God's will in law and gospel.

OBJECTIONS

1. How can the doctrine of inability be reconciled with the commands of God? Does not a command presuppose a modicum of ability? When God created man perfect in holiness, ability did limit obligation. But since man has fallen ability does not limit obligation. The obligation remains unchanged but the ability does not. God deals with man accord-ing to the measure of responsibility and obligation, not according to the measure of ability.

(i) The commands of God must be the transcript of his own perfection. He cannot lower his demands to the level of our sinful inability for that would be to reduce them to vanishing point. It would be the contra-diction of the divine nature and of the relation that man sustains to him as dependent rational creature. The minimum of divine claim is just the maximum, that we should love the Lord our God with all our heart and soul and strength and mind, and, in view of sin and the gospel, repent and believe as the only way to the attainment of that standard.

(ii) If obligation presupposes ability, then we shall have to go the whole way and predicate total ability of man, that is, to adopt the Pelagian position. For obligation is total and cannot be reduced to any lower terms. To what purpose would be a modicum of ability, a token ability?

The law of God, furthermore, in addition to being the inescapable claim of the divine perfection, serves many useful purposes. It restrains sin and convicts of it. 'I was alive without the law once' etc. 'I had not known lust except the law had said, Thou shalt not covet.'

2. It is objected that this doctrine is inconsistent with the use of means. Means are ordained by God in every sphere of human activity and it is just as absurd to argue that our inability makes the use of means futile and meaningless here as it would be in any other sphere where the effect is not produced solely by the means humanly used. Dr. Hodge says, 'In every department of human activity the result depends on the co-operation of causes over which man has no control.'

(i) God ordains means and commands us to use them. They are the channels of divine grace.

(ii) Ordinarily the result is not attained except in the use of the means.

(iii) The promise of God is given to those who use the means. To exclude the use of means would be as sensible as to deny the relevance to us of the commands of God, for the use of means is part of the divine institution that bears upon us.

The neglect of the means therefore is an offence against the wisdom and counsel of God, and therefore sinful and dishonouring. To justify the neglect of means on the basis of human inability is to justify one sin on the basis of another; it is to exculpate sin on the basis of sin. Our inability is our responsibility and our sin.

3. It is urged that it encourages delay and is a counsel of despair for the lost. There is no gainsaying the fact that the doctrine of total inability has been perverted to this end by the indolent and careless, and has been the occasion for temptation to despair in the case of the truly anxious. But perversion does not refute the truth of the doctrine perverted. It is ours to protect the wayward against perversion, but it is not ours to suppress the truth because it has been perverted. And we must not keep back truth or suppress it because the defiled and unbelieving turn it into lasciviousness.

But that the doctrine of total depravity and inability is in reality a counsel of despair is grossly untrue. It is rather the very truth that lays the basis for the glory of the gospel of grace and for the exercise of that faith that is unto life eternal. Nothing is more soul-destructive than self-righteousness. And it is self-righteousness that is fostered by the doctrine that man is naturally able to do what is good and well-pleasing to God. To encourage any such conviction is to plunge men into self-deception and delusion and such is indeed the counsel of despair.

What is faith? It is trust in God's grace and in that alone. It is alleged that this is a counsel of despair and that the gospel offer, the appeal for faith, and the assertion of human responsibility in reference to the offer and demand of the gospel are not compatible with the presupposition of total depravity and inability. It is true enough that there are many who cannot preach what they conceive to be the gospel on the basis of this doctrine. What are we to say?

(i) Is this doctrine the doctrine of Scripture? If it is, then the doctrine of the gospel must be compatible with it.

(ii) Is this the doctrine of the only revelation God has given to us? We shall have to revise our conception of the gospel, in order that the gospel we conceive of and preach will be one that can presuppose total inability. The gospel is one of grace and therefore rests upon despair of human resources and potency.

(iii) The only gospel there is is a gospel which rests upon the assumption of total inability. It is this truth that lays the basis for the glory of the gospel of grace. Nothing is more inimical to the interests of the gospel than the assumption that there is some point at which the sovereign grace of God is dispensable, that there is some power in man operative unto salvation that is not the fruit of God's own saving grace. It is the doctrine of man's utter sinfulness and inability that leads men to cease to trust in themselves and shuts them up to reliance upon God's grace. The doctrine of ability makes men self-sufficient and that is the contradiction of the gospel and makes them immune to its appeal.

Furthermore, experience will show that there is no conviction more basic as the preparation for the reception of the gospel than that of complete impotence. Conviction in us must correspond with reality, with truth. Are we to say that conviction that falls short of the truth promotes the interests of salvation? The gospel dovetails our helplessness and when convinced of the same it is into the conviction that the overtures of grace come with *power*. It is not the conviction of helplessness that keeps men away from Christ; it is the opposite.

This doctrine does not hinder evangelism. One of the greatest hindrances to the spread of the gospel is the lack of it. It is only on the presupposition of total depravity and complete human impotence that the full glory and power of the gospel can be declared. Then shall the lame man leap as a hart and the tongue of the dumb sing. In the wilderness shall waters break out and streams in the desert. The blind will receive their sight, the deaf hear, the dead be raised up and the poor have the gospel preached to them.

GENERAL CONCLUSIONS ON THE DOCTRINE OF SIN

We have found that sin involves both guilt and pollution. It is this doctrine of sin that supplies the basis for the doctrine of salvation on both its objective and subjective sides. Guilt involves our liability to the divine wrath and curse. It is with that that salvation on its forensic and objective side deals. Pollution deals with the defilement of sin and is formulated under total depravity and inability. This is the presupposition of salvation on its subjective, internal and ethical side. As the guilt of sin serves as the basis for the great doctrines of atonement and justification, so the doctrine of original sin and inability serves as the basis for regeneration and sanctification. If we eviscerate guilt, we eviscerate Christianity in its objective accomplishment; if we deny original sin we eviscerate Christianity in its subjective application and fruition.

II

10

Common Grace[1]

THE subject of common grace is not only of particular but also of very urgent interest to the person who accepts the witness of Scripture regarding the total depravity of human nature by reason of sin. For if we appreciate the implications of total depravity, then we are faced with a series of very insistent questions. How is it that men who still lie under the wrath and curse of God and are heirs of hell enjoy so many good gifts at the hand of God? How is it that men who are not savingly renewed by the Spirit of God nevertheless exhibit so many qualities, gifts and accomplishments that promote the preservation, temporal happiness, cultural progress, social and economic improvement of themselves and of others? How is it that races and peoples that have been apparently untouched by the redemptive and regenerative influences of the gospel contribute so much to what we call human civilization? To put the question most comprehensively: how is it that this sin-cursed world enjoys so much favour and kindness at the hand of its holy and ever-blessed Creator?

Elementary acquaintance with the history and literature of this world will convince us that even the heathen have their noble examples of what, to human norms of judgment at least, may be called courage, heroism, honesty, justice, fidelity, and even mercy. Common grace concerns itself with the reason and meaning of this 'rich stream of natural life' which existed before Christianity made its appearance and even now continues to flow 'underneath and side by side with the Christian religion'.[2]

[1] Reprinted from *The Westminster Theological Journal*, Vol. V. i, 1942.
[2] Herman Bavinck, 'Calvin and Common Grace': *The Princeton Theological Review*, Vol. VII, 1909, p. 437.

In this field of inquiry no name deserves more credit than that of the renowned reformer, John Calvin.[1] No one was more deeply persuaded of the complete depravation of human nature by sin and of the consequent inability of unaided human nature to bring forth anything good, and so he explained the existence of good outside the sphere of God's special and saving grace by the presence of a grace that is common to all, yet enjoyed by some in special degree. 'The most certain and easy solution of this question, however, is, that those virtues are not the common properties of nature, but the peculiar graces of God, which he dispenses in great variety, and in a certain degree to men that are otherwise profane.'[2] The elect alone are sanctified by the Spirit; they alone are healed of sin; they alone are created anew. But all creatures by the energy of the same Spirit are replenished, actuated and quickened 'according to the property of each species which he has given it by the law of creation.'[3]

On this question Calvin not only opened a new vista but also a new era in theological formulation. Having thus stated the question and indicated the line along which the greatest of the Reformers answered it, we may now proceed to attempt an elucidation and exposition of our topic.

DEFINITION OF COMMON GRACE

Dr. Charles Hodge in his *Systematic Theology* defines common grace as 'that influence of the Spirit, which in a greater or less measure, is granted to all who hear the truth.'[4] This definition given at the outset of his treatment is reiterated and unfolded in his ensuing discussion. 'The Bible therefore teaches that the Holy Spirit as the Spirit of truth, of holiness, and of life in all its forms, is present with every human mind, enforcing truth, restraining from evil, exciting to good, and imparting wisdom

[1] Dr. Herman Kuiper has made us his debtor for his comprehensive and careful work, *Calvin on Common Grace*, Oosterbaan & Le Cointre, Goes, Netherlands and Smitter Book Company, Grand Rapids, Michigan, 1928. He has furnished us with a complete survey of Calvin's teaching on this subject as set forth in the *Institutes* and in his commentaries.
[2] *Inst.* II, iii, 4.
[3] *Inst.* II, ii, 16.
[4] Charles Hodge, *Systematic Theology*, Vol. II, p. 654.

or strength, when, where, and in what measure seemeth to Him good. In this sphere also He divides "to every man severally as He will." (I Cor. 12:11) This is what in theology is called common grace.'[1] 'As God is everywhere present in the material world, guiding its operations according to the laws of nature; so He is everywhere present with the minds of men, as the Spirit of truth and goodness, operating on them according to the laws of their free moral agency, inclining them to good and restraining them from evil.'[2] 'The evidence therefore from Scripture, and from experience, is clear that the Holy Spirit is present with every human mind, and enforces, with more or less power, whatever of moral or religious truth the mind may have before it.'[3] To this presence and influence of the Spirit then, according to Dr. Hodge, we are indebted for all the order, decorum, refinement and virtue, as well as the regard for religion and its ordinances, which exist in the world.[4] To it we owe 'the skill of artisans, the courage and strength of heroes, the wisdom of statesmen'.[5]

It is obvious that this series of definitions evinces a rather restricted view of the nature and scope of what is called common grace. The word 'grace' in the definition is limited to 'the influence of the Spirit of God on the minds of men',[6] and so in accord with that limited concept of the word 'grace' the following restrictions are made in the definition of the nature and scope of common grace. (1) Common grace is restricted to the human sphere. (2) It is restricted to the rational, moral and religious spheres. (3) It is restricted to those operations of the Spirit, on the minds, consciences and hearts of men, that are mediated through the truth.

To the same effect is the definition given by Dr. A. A. Hodge. ' "Common grace" is the restraining and persuading influences of the Holy Spirit acting only through the truth revealed in the gospel, or through the natural light of reason and of conscience, heightening the

[1] *Idem*, p. 667.
[2] *Idem*, p. 668.
[3] *Idem*, p. 670.
[4] Cf. *idem*, pp. 671, 674.
[5] *Idem*, p. 666.
[6] *Idem*, p. 655.

natural moral effect of such truth upon the understanding, conscience, and heart. It involves no change of heart, but simply an enhancement of the natural powers of the truth, a restraint of the evil passions, and an increase of the natural emotions in view of sin, duty, and self-interest.'[1]

There can be no question but these definitions given by Charles and A. A. Hodge embrace what is perhaps the most important phase of common grace, and very often in common usage it is this phase of God's favour we have in mind when we use the term 'common grace'. But this rather restricted definition does not embrace other important aspects of the divine favour which should naturally and logically be included in the definition. It will provide us with a broader basis for discussion of the topic and will be found to be more in accord with the witness of the Scripture on this subject to regard the word 'grace' in the title as referring to any gift or favour bestowed upon, and enjoyed by, creatures, rather than, in the more limited sense accepted by Dr. Hodge, as 'the influence of the Spirit of God on the minds of men'. If this broader definition of the word 'grace' is adopted, it will include the influence of the Spirit of God on the minds of men, but it will also include gifts bestowed upon other creatures as well as upon men and it will also include the grace bestowed upon men that cannot conveniently be defined as an influence of the Spirit upon their minds.

The word 'common' in the title of the topic is not used in the sense that each particular favour is given to all without discrimination or distinction but rather in the sense that favours of varying kinds and degrees are bestowed upon this sin-cursed world, favours real in their character as expressions of the divine goodness but which are not in themselves and of themselves saving in their nature and effect. So the term 'common grace' should rather be defined as *every favour of whatever kind or degree, falling short of salvation, which this undeserving and sin-cursed world enjoys at the hand of God.*

This is a comprehensive definition and it is apparent that the favours bestowed and enjoyed fall into different categories. The best classification with which the present writer has become acquainted is that offered by Dr. Herman Kuiper in the work aforementioned. In classifying the various manifestations of grace recognized by Calvin he gives three

[1] A. A. Hodge, *Outlines of Theology*, Chapter XXVIII, Section 13.

groups. The first category is that of the 'grace which is common to all the creatures who make up this sin-cursed world . . . a grace which touches creatures as creatures'.[1] This Dr. Kuiper calls *universal common grace*. There is, secondly, the grace recognized by Calvin as 'common to all human beings in distinction from the rest of God's creatures . . . a grace which pertains to men as men'.[2] This Dr. Kuiper calls *general common grace*. Thirdly, there is the grace common not to all creatures and not to all men but to all 'who live in the covenant sphere . . . to all elect and non-elect covenant members'.[3] This Dr. Kuiper calls *covenant common grace*. There is, of course, within each classification the general and the particular. For the gifts bestowed upon each group of creatures are not indiscriminately dispensed. In each group there are differing degrees of the favour bestowed. This classification is inclusive and it also provides us with necessary and convenient distinctions. In the order stated we find the circle becomes more limited, but just as the limitation proceeds so does the nature of the grace bestowed become higher in the scale of value.[4]

THE NATURE OF COMMON GRACE

1. *Restraint*. It is natural that writers on this subject should place in the forefront of their discussion the notion of restraint. It is perhaps the most striking and readily granted feature of the non-saving grace that God dispenses to this undeserving and sin-cursed world. God restrains sin and its consequences.

---

[1] *op. cit.*, p. 179.

[2] *Ibid.*

[3] *Ibid.*

[4] It is scarcely necessary to mention the fact that the sphere of common grace is posterior to the fall of man. There was grace manifested prior to the fall and this grace may be spoken of as common. But in theological terminology the term 'common grace' must be restricted to the post-lapsarian and pre-consummation period. It is the fact of the fall that introduces the need for this kind of grace. The word 'common' is synonymous with non-saving, and so the whole construction and formulation of the doctrine of 'common grace' is in contrast with, and in relation to, saving or redemptive grace. But saving grace did not begin to operate until there was the need for it, namely, the fall. The grace that was in operation prior to the fall was not 'saving' grace, and neither was it, in the sense of the doctrine we are now discussing, 'common' grace.

It is not, of course, to be supposed that the restraint God places upon sin and its effects is complete, nor is it uniform. Complete restraint would imply eradication, for even though restraint in itself does not mean eradication, yet a restraint that would be complete would involve the removal of the exercise of sinful affection and impulse and removal of the very primary consequences of sin. Neither does the notion of restraint suppose that such restraint is always present. Paul tells us that because men did not like to retain God in their knowledge God gave them over to a reprobate mind and gave them up to uncleanness so that they were filled with the fruits of unrighteousness.[1] But what the notion of restraint does involve is that in the forbearance and goodness of God he does place restraint upon the expressions and consequences of human depravity and of unholy passion.

There are three respects in which the notion of restraint may be applied.

(i) *Restraint upon Sin.* God places restraint upon the workings of human depravity and thus prevents the unholy affections and principles of men from manifesting all the potentialities inherent in them. He prevents depravity from bursting forth in all its vehemence and violence. In the words of Jonathan Edwards, 'There are in the souls of wicked men those hellish principles reigning, that would presently kindle and flame out into hell-fire, if it were not for God's restraints. There is laid in the very nature of carnal men, a foundation for the torments of hell: there are those corrupt principles, in reigning power in them, and in full possession of them, that are the beginnings of hell-fire. These principles are active and powerful, exceeding violent in their nature, and if it were not for the restraining hand of God upon them, they would soon break out, they would flame out after the same manner as the same corruptions, the same enmity does in the hearts of damned souls, and would beget the same torments in them as they do in them. The souls of the wicked are in Scripture compared to the troubled sea, Isaiah 57: 20. For the present, God restrains their wickedness by his mighty power, as he does the raging waves of the troubled sea, saying, "Hitherto shalt thou

---

[1] Cf. Romans 1:18–32. Even in such cases it is probably necessary to posit a certain kind of restraint. Otherwise the persons concerned would have been consigned immediately to eternal perdition and thus have been separated from all the tokens of God's favour.

come, and no further;" but if God should withdraw that restraining power, it would soon carry all before it. Sin is the ruin and misery of the soul; it is destructive in its nature; and if God should leave it without restraint, there would need nothing else to make the soul perfectly miserable. The corruption of the heart of man is a thing that is immoderate and boundless in its fury; and while wicked men live here, it is like fire pent up by God's restraints, whereas if it were let loose, it would set on fire the course of nature; and as the heart is now a sink of sin, so, if sin was not restrained, it would immediately turn the soul into a fiery oven, or a furnace of fire and brimstone.'[1]

This restraint upon the tendency inherent in sin appears very early in the history of fallen humanity. It is, no doubt, exceedingly difficult to know the exact meaning and intent of Genesis 3:22, 23. 'Behold, the man is become as one of us, to know good and evil: and now, lest he put forth his hand, and take also of the tree of life, and eat, and live for ever: therefore the Lord God sent him forth from the garden of Eden, to till the ground from whence he was taken.' But it seems rather certain that the eating of the tree of life after man had completely forfeited every right to that of which it was the sign and seal would have been an act of gross presumption, sacrilege and rebellion. It is surely an act of gracious restraint on the part of God that he thrust him out from the garden so as to prevent the commission of so heinous and desperate a sin. This consideration is not offset by the other fact that the expulsion from the garden was an act of divine judgment for the first sin. A divine act may have diverse grounds according to the aspect from which it is viewed.

Again, perhaps more conclusive and significant is the case of Cain. Profane and godless as he was, a halo of sanctity was placed around his life to protect him from the violence that sinful passion would tend to execute upon him. 'And the Lord set a mark upon Cain, lest any finding him should kill him' (Gen. 4:15). Provision was made by God to restrain and prevent in others the murderous impulse that was so signally characteristic of Cain himself.

In the case of Abimelech we have a direct statement to the effect that

[1] Jonathan Edwards, *Works*, Vol. IV, p. 315, New York, 1881. Cf. John Calvin, *Inst.* II, iii, 3.

God kept him from sin. 'Yea, I know that thou didst this in the integrity of thy heart; for I also withheld thee from sinning against me: therefore suffered I thee not to touch her' (Gen. 20:6). We do not have reason to suppose that Abimelech truly feared God, and so we have an example of an unbeliever restrained by divine intervention from the commission of sin. This fact is not in the least disproven by the objection that it was for Abraham's sake that this restraint was exercised. Whatever may have been the reason or reasons, it is still a fact that God prevented the sin of which Abimelech would otherwise have been guilty.

In the case of Sennacherib his rage against the Lord was curbed and the evil purpose of his mind frustrated. 'But I know thy abode, and thy going out, and thy coming in, and thy rage against me. Because thy rage against me and thy tumult is come into my ears, therefore I will put my hook in thy nose, and my bridle in thy lips, and I will turn thee back by the way by which thou camest' (2 Kings 19:27, 28).

(ii) *Restraint upon the Divine Wrath.* There is restraint upon the divine vengeance, suspension of the full measure of the divine wrath due to sin. It should not be forgotten that all the evil that exists in the world is ultimately traceable to the divine displeasure. Even the evil that is present in the physical realm is the result of the divine curse, and the curse is but the expression of his wrath. But there is also the direct infliction of divine displeasure, an infliction that is the necessary reaction of God's holiness to sin and guilt. It is the restraint upon this manifestation of God's wrath that we have in mind when we speak of restraint placed upon the execution of the divine wrath. Were it not for this restraint the wicked would be immediately consigned to everlasting perdition. The facts demonstrate that this world's history is a dispensation of the divine forbearance and longsuffering. Restraint is therefore not only restraint upon the unholy passion of man's heart but also restraint upon the holy wrath of God.

One of the most forcible examples we have of this is in the period prior to the flood. 'My Spirit shall not always strive with man, for that he also is flesh: yet his days shall be an hundred and twenty years' (Gen. 6:3). Whether the word should be translated 'strive' or 'rule', this text implies that God did bear with men in his forbearance and longsuffering. Notwithstanding much provocation, the pent-up forces of God's indignation were to be restrained for one hundred and twenty years. And though the main point of this text is that there is a limit to the divine longsuffering, nevertheless the longsuffering does operate. We have allusion to this on the part of Peter and confirmation is given to the correctness of this interpretation. Peter refers to the period before the flood as the time 'when the longsuffering of God was waiting in the days of Noah' (1 Pet. 3:20).

When Paul, referring to past generations of the history of the world, says that the times of ignorance God overlooked (Acts 17:30), he is not referring to any indifference or connivance on the part of God his first chapter of the epistle to the Romans disproves any such interpretation—but among other things he is making reference to the fact that God refrained from executing the full measure of his judgment. It is true that God did not manifest his grace as *now* when he commands that men should all everywhere repent, but in the word we have translated 'overlooked' there is also implied the 'passing by' of forbearance.

Romans 2:4 and 2 Peter 3:9[1] may have believers particularly in mind, but, even so, the longsuffering mentioned in both passages involves the suspension of judgment over periods of time, and such suspension of judgment draws even the wicked and reprobate within its scope.

(iii) *Restraint upon Evil*. Sin introduces disintegration and disorganization in every realm. While it is true that only in the sphere of rationality does sin have meaning—it originates in mind, it develops in mind, it resides in mind—yet sin works out disastrous effects outside the sphere of the rational and moral as well as within it. God places restraint upon these effects, he prevents the full development of this disintegration. He brings to bear upon this world in all its spheres correcting and preserving influences so that the ravages of sin might not be allowed to work out the full measure of their destructive power.

The curse pronounced upon Adam as distinct from that pronounced upon the serpent and upon Eve had particular reference to this effect of

---

[1] 'Or despisest thou the riches of his goodness and forbearance and longsuffering; not knowing that the goodness of God leadeth thee to repentance' (Rom. 2:4). 'The Lord is not slack concerning his promise, as some men count slackness; but is longsuffering to usward, not willing that any should perish, but that all should come to repentance' (2 Pet. 3:9).

sin. 'Cursed is the ground for thy sake' (Gen. 3:17). But the ground, though not yielding henceforth its strength and although its strength was to be sapped by thorns and thistles, was yet to bring forth enough for the sustenance of life.

The ferocity of the animals that leads them to destroy human life we must regard as unnatural and as a consequence of the disruption and discord that sin brought in its train. If from no other consideration, we may infer this from the sanction by which the life of man is protected against this form of predatory ferocity, 'And surely your blood of your lives will I require; at the hand of every beast will I require it' (Gen. 9:5). But that this destructive impulse in the animal kingdom is restrained is intimated in Genesis 9:2. 'And the fear of you and the dread of you shall be upon every beast of the earth, and upon every fowl of the air, upon all that moveth upon the earth, and upon all the fishes of the sea.' However we may explain the origin of this fear, it cannot be doubted that it holds in check a destructive tendency that is part of the curse of sin upon the animal order.

We thus see that restraint upon sin and its consequences is one of the most outstanding features of God's government of this world—the history of this present world exists within an administration that is one of restraint and forbearance.

2. *Bestowal of Good and Excitation to Good.* This caption means that common grace is more than negative and preventative; it is also positive, in the bestowal and production of good. God not only restrains the destructive effects of sin in nature but he also causes nature to teem with the gifts of his goodness. He not only restrains evil in men but he also endows men with gifts, talents, and aptitudes; he stimulates them with interest and purpose to the practice of virtues, the pursuance of worthy tasks, and the cultivation of arts and sciences that occupy the time, activity and energy of men and that make for the benefit and civilization of the human race. He ordains institutions for the protection and promotion of right, the preservation of liberty, the advance of knowledge and the improvement of physical and moral conditions. We may regard these interests, pursuits and institutions as exercising both an expulsive and impulsive influence. Occupying the energy, activity and time of men they prevent the indulgence of less noble and ignoble

pursuits and they exercise an ameliorating, moralizing, stabilizing and civilizing influence upon the social organism.

The Biblical evidence to be adduced in support of the immediately foregoing propositions will have to be classified:

(i) *Creation is the recipient of divine bounty.* That the animate and inanimate creation, groaning and travailing in pain and made subject to vanity though it be, yet receives the showers of divine blessing, is the theme of some of the stateliest lyrics we have in the Scripture. 'By terrible things in righteousness wilt thou answer us, O God of our salvation; who art the confidence of all the ends of the earth, and of them that are afar off upon the sea: Which by his strength setteth fast the mountains; being girded with power: Which stilleth the noise of the seas, the noise of their waves, and the tumult of the people. They also that dwell in the uttermost parts are afraid at thy tokens: thou makest the outgoings of the morning and evening to rejoice. Thou visitest the earth, and waterest it: thou greatly enrichest it with the river of God, which is full of water: thou preparest them corn, when thou hast so provided for it. Thou waterest the ridges thereof abundantly: thou settlest the furrows thereof: thou makest it soft with showers: thou blessest the springing thereof. Thou crownest the year with thy goodness; and thy paths drop fatness. They drop upon the pastures of the wilderness: and the little hills rejoice on every side. The pastures are clothed with flocks; the valleys also are covered over with corn; they shout for joy, they also sing' (Psalm 65:5–13). The majestic music is carried perhaps to even loftier strains in Psalm 104. 'He watereth the hills from his chambers: the earth is satisfied with the fruit of thy works. He causeth the grass to grow for the cattle, and herb for the service of man: that he may bring forth food out of the earth; And wine that maketh glad the heart of man, and oil to make his face to shine, and bread which strengtheneth man's heart. The trees of the Lord are full of sap; the cedars of Lebanon, which he hath planted; Where the birds make their nests: as for the stork, the fir trees are her house. The high hills are a refuge for the wild goats; and the rocks for the conies. He appointed the moon for seasons: the sun knoweth his going down. Thou makest darkness, and it is night: wherein all the beasts of the forest do creep forth. The young lions roar after their prey, and seek their meat from God. The sun ariseth, they gather themselves together, and lay them down in their dens. Man goeth forth unto his work and to his labour until the evening' (vss. 13–23). It is this review of the riches of God's goodness in the work of his hand and of the wisdom of the provision and arrangements for each of his creatures that causes the psalmist to exclaim, 'O Lord, how manifold are thy works! in wisdom hast thou made them all: the earth is full of thy riches' (vs. 24). The truth of all this as bearing upon our topic is very directly summed up in the words of another psalm, 'The Lord is good to all: and his tender mercies are over all his works. . . . The eyes of all wait upon thee; and thou givest them their meat in due season. Thou openest thine hand, and satisfiest the desire of every living thing' (Psalm 145:9, 15, 16).

Lest we should entertain any doubt as to the character of this teeming bounty as one of grace and lovingkindness we need but be reminded of that psalm which, in the extolling of the praises of creation and redemption, ever reiterates the refrain, 'For his mercy endureth for ever'. At its conclusion we read, 'Who giveth good to all flesh: for his mercy endureth for ever' (Ps. 136:25).

(ii) *Unregenerate men are recipients of divine favour and goodness.* The witness of Scripture to this fact is copious and direct. Attention will be focused on a few of the most notable examples.

In Genesis 39:5 we are told that 'the Lord blessed the Egyptian's house for Joseph's sake'. Truly it was for Joseph's sake and for Joseph as the instrument through whom the chosen people were to be preserved and God's redemptive purpose with respect to the world fulfilled. But, just as we have found already in the case of Abimelech, the reason for the blessing bestowed does not destroy the reality of the blessing itself.

Perhaps the most significant part of Scripture bearing upon this phase of our subject is the witness of Paul and Barnabas at Lystra in Iconium. 'Who in the generations gone by suffered all the nations to walk in their own ways. Nevertheless he left not himself without witness, doing good, and giving rains to you from heaven and fruitful seasons, filling your hearts with food and gladness' (Acts 14:16, 17). The 'generations gone by' of this passage are the same as 'the times of ignorance' mentioned by Paul in his speech on Mars' hill (Acts 17:30). Paul and Barnabas in this case are referring to the past of those who had served dumb idols. They expressly state that although God allowed them to walk in their own idolatrous ways yet God did not leave them without a witness to himself. The particular witness mentioned here is that he did good and gave them rains from heaven and fruitful seasons, filling their hearts with food and gladness. This is the most direct and indisputable assertion that men, left to their own ungodly ways, are nevertheless the subjects of divine benefaction. God showed them favour and did them good, and the satisfaction and enjoyment derived from the product of rains and fruitful seasons are not to be condemned but rather regarded as the witness, or at least as the proper effect of the witness, God was bearing to his own goodness. And it would be wanton violence that would attempt to sever this 'doing good' from a disposition of goodness in the heart and mind of God. Paul says that the 'doing good' and 'giving rain from heaven and fruitful seasons' constituted the witness God gave of himself. In other words, the goodness bestowed is surely goodness expressed.

The testimony of our Lord himself, as recorded in Matthew 5:44, 45; Luke 6:35, 36, establishes the same truth as that discussed in the foregoing passage. 'But I say to you, love your enemies and pray for those who persecute you; that ye may be sons of your Father who is in heaven, for he maketh his sun to rise on the evil and the good, and sendeth rain on the just and the unjust.' 'But love your enemies, and do them good, and lend, never despairing; and your reward shall be great, and ye shall be sons of the Most High: for he is kind toward the unthankful and evil. Be ye merciful, even as your Father is merciful.' Here the disciples are called upon to emulate in their own sphere and relations the character of God, their Father, in his own sphere and relations. God is kind and merciful to the unthankful and to the evil; he makes his sun to rise upon evil and good, and sends rain upon just and unjust. Both on the ground of express statement and on the ground of what is obviously implied in the phrases, 'sons of your Father' and 'sons of the Most High', there can be no escape from the conclusion that goodness and beneficence, kindness and mercy are here attributed to God in his relations even to the ungodly. And this simply means that the ungodly are the recipients of blessings that flow from the love, goodness, kindness and mercy of God. Again it would be desperate exegetical violence that would attempt to separate the good gifts bestowed from the disposition of kindness and mercy in the mind of God.

Finally, we may appeal to Luke 16:25, 'Son, remember that thou in thy lifetime receivedst thy good things, and likewise Lazarus evil things: but now here he is comforted, and thou art tormented'. The rich man was reprobate; but the gifts enjoyed during this life are nevertheless called 'good things'.

It is without question true that good gifts abused will mean greater condemnation for the finally impenitent. 'To whom much is given, of the same shall much be required' (Luke 12:48). But this consideration, awfully true though it be, does not make void the fact that they are good gifts and expressions of the lovingkindness of God. In fact, it is just because they are good gifts and manifestations of the kindness and mercy of God that the abuse of them brings greater condemnation and demonstrates the greater inexcusability of impenitence. Ultimate condemnation, so far from making void the reality of the grace bestowed in time, rather in this case rests upon the reality of the grace bestowed and enjoyed. It will be more tolerable for Sodom and Gomorrha in the day of judgment than for Capernaum. But the reason is that Capernaum was privileged to witness the mighty works of Christ as supreme exhibitions of the love, goodness and power of God.

The decree of reprobation is of course undeniable. But denial of the reality of temporal goodness and kindness, goodness and kindness as expressions of the mind and will of God, is to put the decree of reprobation so much out of focus that it eclipses the straightforward testimony of Scripture to other truths.

(iii) *Good is attributed to unregenerate men.*[1] We have no reason to

---

[1] In connection with this proposition we have to recognize what may be called the paradox of common grace. This paradox appears in the teaching of Scripture itself as well as in the discussions of the greatest exponents of the doctrine. The paradox consists in making apparently contradictory statements. On the one hand, there is the undeniable witness of Scripture to the fact that by nature 'there is none righteous, no, not one: there is none that understandeth, there is none that seeketh after God. They are all gone out of the way, they are together become unprofitable; there is none that doeth good, no, not one' (Rom. 3:10-12). The mind of those unrenewed by the Spirit is enmity against God and is not only not subject to the law of God but also cannot be. They that are in the flesh cannot please God (Rom. 8:7, 8). Yet on the other hand, as is

suppose that Jehu truly feared and served the Lord God of Israel. We are told that 'from the sins of Jeroboam the son of Nebat, who made Israel to sin, Jehu departed not from after them, to wit, the golden calves that were in Bethel, and that were in Dan' (2 Kings 10:29). Yet we are told that the Lord said to Jehu, 'Because thou hast *done well in executing that which is right in mine eyes*, and hast done unto the house of Ahab according to all that was in my heart, thy children to the fourth generation shall sit on the throne of Israel' (2 Kings 10:30). Jehu did what was right in God's eyes in executing vengeance upon the house of Ahab. He did what was good, and for this good temporal reward was administered to him and to his house.

Because of his defection after the death of Jehoiada there is good reason to doubt that Jehoash truly feared God.[1] Yet we are told that he 'did that which was right in the sight of the Lord all his days wherein Jehoiada the priest instructed him' (2 Kings 12:2).

In the context of passages already discussed Jesus says to his disciples, 'For if ye love them that love you, what reward have ye? do not even the publicans the same?' (Matt. 5:46), 'For if ye do good to them who

---

shown in the text of this article, good is attributed to unregenerate men. The paradox is real but it does not involve a real contradiction. The good attributed to unregenerate men is after all only relative good. It is not good in the sense of meeting in motivation, principle and aim the requirements of God's law and the demands of his holiness. The fundamental character of the unregenerate man, however much relative good he may perform, is still unholy, just as the fundamental character of the regenerate man, however imperfect he may be, is nevertheless that of holiness.

The Westminster Confession of Faith expresses the distinction when it says, 'Works done by unregenerate men, although, for the matter of them, they may be things which God commands, and of good use both to themselves and others; yet, because they proceed not from an heart purified by faith; nor are done in a right manner, according to the word; nor to a right end, the glory of God; they are therefore sinful, and cannot please God, or make a man meet to receive grace from God. And yet their neglect of them is more sinful, and displeasing unto God' (Chapter XVI, Section vii). The ploughing of the wicked is sin, but it is more sinful for the wicked not to plough.

The seeming contradiction is unavoidable if we are to declare the whole counsel of God. It is for this reason that seeming contradiction appears in all the great expositions of the doctrine. The paradox does not deny the doctrine of total depravity on the one hand nor the doctrine of common grace on the other.

[1] See 2 Chron. 24:17–27.

do good to you, what thanks have ye? Sinners also do the same' (Luke 6:33). Here love, at least of some sort, love as bestowed upon fellow-men, is attributed to publicans, and sinners are said to reciprocate in doing good to one another. It is indeed true that the form in which the exhortation to the disciples is cast implies a low standard of motivation among the publicans and sinners of whom Jesus speaks, and upon the disciples he enjoins the disinterested love worthy of children of the Most High. But even recognizing this to the fullest extent the fact still remains that sinners do become the beneficiaries of a love and a good that sinners bestow upon them. This must be recognized and appreciated for what it is.

The statements of the apostle in Romans 2:14, 15 have been the occasion of much discussion anent the subject of common grace. Admittedly the text offers difficulties in the matter of exact interpretation. And such difficulties it is not the purpose of this article to solve. So far as the thesis of the present subdivision of the subject is concerned, it is not dependent upon Romans 2:14, 15 for its establishment. But this text does add to the evidence in support of the thesis and it presents certain propositions wholly pertinent to that thesis.

Paul is, no doubt, speaking in this text of those who are outside the pale of special revelation. They do not have the law written upon tables of stone. But while ignorant of this special revelation they are not without the work of the law. In other words, they are not entirely removed from the operation of the law. The law has another way of making its demand and influence felt, and the law makes its impact upon these Gentiles *in that way*. Hence they are affected by it.

The following propositions may readily be elicited from the text: (1) The Gentiles are the subjects of the work of the law. (2) They are the subjects of this work because it is written in their hearts. The work of the law is engraven upon that which is constitutive and determinative of their personal life. (3) As a result they do by nature the things of the law. In other words, they evince, to some degree at least, a certain conformity to the law. Their conduct is characterized to some extent by the things required by the law. (4) Their consciences bear joint witness. This is just saying, in effect, that the work of the law is not something that escapes consciousness. The work of the law rather pushes itself into their consciousness and registers itself there in the attestations of conscience. That the work of the law is not mechanical but drawing within its embrace the conscious functions of personality is further confirmed by the presence of self-accusing and self-excusing reasonings or judgments.

All of this has important bearing upon that phase of the subject we are now discussing, to wit, that relative good is attributed to unregenerate men. Romans 2:14, 15 lays the basis for such predication. The norm of moral good is the law of which Paul is speaking. It is only in relation to that norm that any predication of moral good can be made. The text we are now discussing establishes the fact that that precise norm is operative in men to the end of producing conduct that in the sense and to the extent intended by the apostle may be said to be conformable to it. The divinely established norms of conduct have relevance to, and even effect upon, those who are outside the pale not only of redemptive grace but also of that special revelation that is the medium of its application in the hearts and lives of men.[1]

(iv) *Unregenerate men receive operations and influences of the Spirit in connection with the administration of the gospel, influences that result in experience of the power and glory of the gospel, yet influences which do not issue in genuine and lasting conversion and are finally withdrawn.*

There are a few passages in the New Testament which so plainly attest the reality of such influence and resultant experience that no detailed exegesis is necessary.

We have spoken of this experience on the part of unregenerate men as that of the power and glory of the gospel. In the parable of the sower those who are compared to the rocky ground are those who hear the word and immediately with joy receive it. This implies some experience of its beauty and power. Yet they have no root and endure but for a while. When tribulation and persecution arise they just as immediately stumble and bring forth no fruit to perfection. The passages in Hebrews 6:4–8; 10:26–29 refer to experience that apparently surpasses that spoken of in the parable of the sower. At least, the portraiture is very much more

---

[1] If the truth here clearly taught by Paul is true in the case of those who are outside the pale of special revelation, how much more must this be true of those who have not only the work of the law written in their hearts but also the added reinforcement of the work of the law as revealed in the Scriptures.

elaborate in its details and the issue much more tragic in its consequences. The persons concerned are described as 'those who were once
enlightened and tasted of the heavenly gift, and were made partakers
of the Holy Spirit, and tasted the good word of God and the powers of
the age to come' (Heb. 6:4, 5), as those who had received the knowledge
of the truth and had been sanctified by the blood of the covenant (Heb.
10:26, 29). We shudder at the terms in which the experience delineated
is defined.[1] Yet we cannot avoid its import, nor can we evade the
acceptance of the inspired testimony that from such enlightenment,
from such participation of the Holy Spirit and from such experience of
the good word of God and the powers of the age to come men may fall
away, crucify to themselves the Son of God afresh, put him to an open
shame, tread the Son of God under foot, count the sanctifying blood
of the covenant an unholy thing and do despite to the Spirit of grace.
Here is apostasy from which there is no repentance and for which there
is nought but 'a fearful looking for of judgment and fiery indignation
which shall devour the adversaries.'

It is here that we find non-saving grace at its very apex. We cannot
conceive of anything, that falls short of salvation, more exalted in its
character. And we must not make void the reality of the blessing enjoyed
and of the grace bestowed out of consideration for the awful doom resultant upon renunciation and apostasy. As was pointed out already in
other respects, it is precisely the grace bestowed in all its rich connotation

---

[1] The remarks of Dr. Charles Hodge on this subject are pertinent. 'No strictness of
inward scrutiny, no microscopic examination or delicacy of analysis, can enable an
observer, and rarely the man himself, to distinguish these religious exercises from those
of the truly regenerated. The words by which they are described both in the Scriptures
and in ordinary Christian discourse, are the same. Unrenewed men in the Bible are said
to repent, to believe, to be partakers of the Holy Ghost, and so taste the good Word of
God, and the powers of the world to come. Human language is not adequate to express
all the soul's experiences. The same word must always represent in one case, or in one
man's experience, what it does not in the experience of another. That there is a specific
difference between the exercises due to common grace, and those experienced by the
true children of God, is certain. But that difference does not reveal itself to the consciousness, or at least, certainly not to the eye of an observer. "By their fruits ye shall
know them." This is the test given by our Lord. It is only when these experiences issue in
a holy life, that their distinctive character is known' (*Systematic Theology*, Vol. II, p. 673).

as manifestation of the lovingkindness and goodness of God that gives ground for, and meaning to, the direful judgment that despite and rejection entail.

The teaching of such passages is corroborated by others that are to the same or similar effect. Peter in his second epistle devotes a considerable part to similar instruction and warning, and concludes with what is clearly reminiscent of the teaching of the epistle to the Hebrews. 'For if after they have escaped the pollutions of the world through the knowledge of the Lord and Saviour Jesus Christ, they are again entangled therein, and overcome, the latter end is worse with them than the beginning. For it had been better for them not to have known the way of righteousness, than, after they have known it, to turn from the holy commandment delivered unto them. But it is happened unto them according to the true proverb, The dog is turned to his own vomit again; and the sow that was washed to her wallowing in the mire' (2 Pet. 2:20–22). And Paul in his first chapter of the epistle to the Romans portrays for us the process of inexcusable abandonment of knowledge and of worship by which the heathen nations had lapsed into idolatry and superstition. But the knowledge they had relinquished is plainly represented as good, as that which should have been jealously cherished and as that for which they should have been thankful.

(v) *The institution of civil government is for the purpose of restraining evil and promoting good in the whole body politic.*

Civil magistrates are sent by God 'for the punishment of evil-doers, and for the praise of them that do well' (1 Pet. 2:14). Notwithstanding all the miscarriage of justice and all the faults that have characterized civil government in the course of history, the purpose of this divine institution has not completely failed. The Roman state in the days of the apostles was characterized by gross corruptions that defeated the very end for which government was instituted. Yet it was of such government that Paul could say, 'For rulers are not a terror to good works, but to the evil. Wilt thou then not be afraid of the power? do that which is good, and thou shalt have praise of the same: for he is the minister of God to thee for good' (Rom. 13:3, 4). While particular governments do themselves often perpetrate the grossest injustices, yet the testimony of Scripture and of experience is that apart from the restraints imposed and the order promoted by civil government the condition of this world would be one of moral and economic barbarism.

Civil government as such is not a redemptive ordinance. But it provides, and is intended to provide, that outward peace and order within which the ordinances of redemption may work to the accomplishment of God's saving purposes. It is on this basis and to the end of fostering in believers the recognition and appreciation of it that Paul says to Timothy, 'I exhort therefore, first of all, that supplications, prayers, intercessions, thanksgivings, be made for all men; for kings, and all that are in authority, that we may lead a quiet and peaceable life in all godliness and honesty' (1 Tim. 2:1, 2).

The tranquillity and order established and preserved by the ordinances of government are benefits enjoyed by all. This blessing arising from divine institution we must regard therefore as a common blessing and therefore as one of the institutions of common grace.

The evidence drawn from Scripture, then, compels the conclusion that the world as a whole, though subject to the curse incident to sin, receives the showers of manifold blessing, that men who still lie under the divine condemnation of sin, including even those who will finally suffer the full weight of that condemnation in perdition, are the recipients in this life of multiple favours that proceed from God's lovingkindness, that of unregenerate men is predicated moral good that externally or formally is that required by the law of God, that unregenerate men who come into contact with the revelation of God's grace in the gospel may even taste the good word of God and the powers of the age to come, and that in the institutions of civil righteousness and order we have a divine provision that ensures even for the ungodly restraint upon their evil works and outward tranquillity and peace. So that viewing God's government of this world, even from the aspect of his common or non-saving grace, we may say, the earth is full of the glory of the Lord and all peoples see his glory.

THE PURPOSE OF COMMON GRACE
Though it is true that the glory of God is the ultimate end of common grace, as it is of every other phase of God's providence, yet we have to inquire as to the more proximate and specific ends promoted by com-

mon grace in subordination to the final end, which is also the final end of all things, namely, the manifestation of the perfections that constitute the divine glory. The specific ends cannot be reduced to the simplicity of a single purpose. There is, however, at least one proximate purpose that is immediately apparent and has already been shown in some of the texts discussed. It is that common grace serves the purpose of special or saving grace, and saving grace has as its specific end the glorification of the whole body of God's elect, which in turn has its ultimate end in the glory of God's name.

The redemptive purpose of God lies at the centre of this world's history. While it is not the only purpose being fulfilled in history and while it is not the one purpose to which all others may be subordinated, yet it is surely the central stream of history. It is however in the wider context of history that the redemptive purpose of God is realized. This wider context we have already found to be a dispensation of divine forbearance and goodness. In other words, it is that sphere of life or broad stream of history provided by common grace that provides the sphere of operation for God's special purpose of redemption and salvation. This simply means that this world upheld and preserved by God's grace is the sphere and platform upon which supervene the operations of special grace and in which special grace works to the accomplishment of his saving purpose and the perfection of the whole body of the elect. Common grace then receives at least one explanation from the fact of special grace, and special grace has its precondition and sphere of operation in common grace. Without common grace special grace would not be possible because special grace would have no material out of which to erect its structure. It is common grace that provides not only the sphere in which, but also the material out of which, the building fitly framed together may grow up into a holy temple in the Lord. It is the human race preserved by God, endowed with various gifts by God, in a world upheld and enriched by God, subsisting through the means of various pursuits and fields of labour, that provides the subjects for redemptive and regenerative grace. God could raise up children to Abraham out of the stones. As a matter of fact he does not follow this method but rather perfects his body the church out of those redeemed *from among men*.

If we view God's redemptive purpose from the viewpoint of the church we find that the latter does not exist in abstraction from the context of the wider history of this world. The church is not of the world but it is in the world. The church, whether we regard it from the standpoint of the individuals that compose it or from the standpoint of its collective organism, exists in relation to what is not the church. The members of the church do business with unbelievers, they often derive their sustenance from pursuits and employments that are conducted by unbelievers. Even the most segregated communities of believers who attempt to separate themselves from the life of the world are unable to isolate themselves from dependence upon the relationships and institutions of common grace. Their existence and even the segregation in which they live are guarded by the state. The food they eat, the clothing they put on, the material out of which their houses are constructed, are derived from the earth blessed with rain, sunshine, verdure, and flocks that benefit the ungodly as well as themselves. It is divine wisdom that speaks of the tares and the wheat, 'Let both grow together until the harvest'. And it is by divine inspiration Paul wrote to the Corinthians, 'I wrote unto you in an epistle not to keep company with fornicators: yet not altogether with the fornicators of this world, or with the covetous, or extortioners, or with idolaters; for then *must ye needs go out of the world*' (1 Cor. 5:9, 10).

Even when we deal with the individual who is to become a subject of saving grace, we must not think of his regeneration as effecting a complete rupture with all that he was and was made to be prior to his regeneration. A radical moral and spiritual change there must indeed be. He is translated from the kingdom of darkness into the kingdom of light. And that change affects all of life and every relationship. All that he was undergoes transformation by the regenerative influences of God's Spirit. But all that he was is not nullified and discarded. His personality is not changed, and the various endowments and qualities, gifts and possessions, with which he had previously been blessed of God are not destroyed. In other words, though spiritually he become as a little child, yet he does not have to become psychologically an infant all over again. He enters the kingdom of God and exercises his membership and place in it as the person formed and moulded as to his distinct individuality by the antecedents and processes that fall outside the sphere of saving grace. We need but remind ourselves of Paul as the student who sat at the feet of Gamaliel or of Moses learned in all the wisdom of the Egyptians. Long lines of preparation in the realm of common grace, designed in the plan of God's all-comprehending providence, have fitted the most blessed of God's servants for the particular rôle they were to play in the kingdom of God.

Furthermore, when we come to the point of actual conversion, the faith and repentance involved in conversion do not receive their genesis apart from the knowledge of the truth of the gospel. There must be conveyed to the mind of the man who believes and repents to the saving of his soul the truth-content of law and gospel, law as convicting him of sin and gospel as conveying the information which becomes the material of faith. To some extent at least there must be the cognition and apprehension of the import of law and gospel prior to the exercise of saving faith and repentance. 'Faith cometh by hearing, and hearing by the word of God' (Rom. 10:17). But this apprehension of the truth of the gospel that is prior to faith and repentance, and therefore prior to the regeneration of which faith and repentance are the immediate effects in our consciousness, cannot strictly belong to the saving operations of the Spirit. They are preparatory to these saving operations and in the gracious design of God place the person concerned in the psychological condition that is the prerequisite of the intelligent exercise of faith and repentance. In other words, they place in his mind the apperceptive content that makes the gospel meaningful to his consciousness. But since they are not the saving acts of faith and repentance they must belong to a different category from that of saving grace and therefore to the category of non-saving or common grace.

We may thus say that in the operations of common grace we have what we may call the vestibule of faith. We have as it were the point of contact, the *Anknüpfungspunkt*, at which and upon which the Holy Spirit enters with the special and saving operations of his grace. Faith does not take its genesis in a vacuum. It has its antecedents and presuppositions both logically and chronologically in the operations of common grace.[1]

[1] In this connection it must not be forgotten that the truth-content of the gospel that is

Both in the individual sphere and in the sphere of organic and historic movement, the onward course of Christianity can never be dissociated from the preparations by which it is preceded and from the conditions by which it is surrounded, preparations and conditions that belong not only to the general field of divine providence but also to the particular sphere of beneficent and gracious administration on God's part, yet gracious administration that is obviously not in itself saving, and therefore administration that belongs to the sphere of common grace.

To conclude this part of the discussion, common grace provides the sphere of operation of special grace and special grace therefore provides a rationale of common grace. It does not follow that the achievement of God's redemptive purpose is the sole rationale or sole end of common grace. While it is assuredly true that the elect people of God, the righteous, are the salt of the earth, and while it is probably necessary to apply on the wide scale of the world's history the principle expressed by the prophet that 'except the Lord of hosts had left unto us a very small remnant, we should have been as Sodom, we should have been like unto Gomorrah' (Isa. 1:9), and while it is true that it is for the sake of the wheat that the tares are allowed to grow until the harvest, it still does not necessarily follow that the whole purpose of common grace is to serve the interests of special grace. Special grace is a precondition of the operation of common grace and yet the purposes served by common grace may go beyond the interests that are peculiar to special grace. This follows from the simple distinction that one fact may be the condition of the existence of another fact and yet not be the sole end of the existence of that other fact.

What the other ends promoted by common grace may be it might be precarious to conclude. Of one thing we are sure that the glory of

---

brought to the attention of unregenerate men through the various means of propagation and proclamation is not itself the product of common grace. It is the product of special revelation in deed and word. All that has been said above is simply that the operations in the individual and subjective sphere whereby that truth-content has become the property of consciousness, prior to the acts of regeneration and faith, are operations that are not in themselves saving and therefore belong to the category of common grace.

God is displayed in all his works and the glory of his wisdom, goodness, longsuffering, kindness and mercy is made known in the operations of his common grace. In subservience to that ultimate end it may well be that a group of proximate reasons is comprised within that goal of glorifying him, of whom and through whom and to whom are all things.

THE PRACTICAL LESSONS

As special grace supervenes upon the platform of life provided by common grace we must not suppose that it negatives everything it finds in that sphere. It is indeed true that we must jealously guard the distinction between the grace that is common and the grace that is saving. To change the terms, we must not obliterate the distinction between nature and grace. Saving grace differs in its nature, it differs in its purpose and it differs in its effect. But we must beware of a false dualism whereby we incline to regard special grace as nullifying or annihilating the good things it finds in that sphere upon which it falls. Common grace is after all God's grace. It is a gift of God and 'every good gift and every perfect gift is from above, and cometh down from the Father of lights, with whom is no variableness, neither shadow of turning' (Jas. 1:17). Special grace does not annihilate but rather brings its redemptive, regenerative and sanctifying influence to bear upon every natural or common gift; it transforms all activities and departments of life; it brings every good gift into the service of the kingdom of God. Christianity is not flight from nature; it is the renewal and sanctification of nature. It is not flight from the world; it is the evangelization of the world.

The practical effect of this principle is very great. It means a profound respect for, and appreciation of, every good and noble thing, and it is this philosophy and ethic that has made Christianity in its true expression a force in every department of legitimate human interest and vocation. Christianity when true to its spirit has not been ascetic or monastic. Rather has it evaluated everything that is good and right as possessing the dignity of divine ordinance. It has recognized the measureless variety of God's gifts in nature, not only for the subsistence of man and beast but also for their pleasure and delight. It has appreciated the endless variety of human aptitude, skill, art, and vocation. It has not spurned the most humble and menial tasks. It has embraced the divine command, 'Whatsoever thy hand findeth to do, do it with thy might' (Eccl. 9:10). It has placed around all the halo and dignity of divine vocation. It has sought to bring all of life into the service of the King of kings. It has striven to give expression to the Christian faith in politics, economics, industry, education, art, science and philosophy, for its controlling conception has been the absolute sovereignty of God in all of life. While it has recognized itself as constituted in those who are pilgrims and strangers in the earth, looking for a city which hath foundations whose builder and maker is God, it has sought to give full-orbed expression to the truth of God in all the paths of their pilgrimage. It has not been isolationist with respect to the life that now is while waiting for the new heavens and the new earth wherein dwelleth righteousness. Its anthem has been 'The earth is the Lord's, and the fulness thereof; the world, and they that dwell therein' (Ps. 24:1), 'O Lord, how manifold are thy works! in wisdom hast thou made them all: the earth is full of thy riches' (Ps. 104:24). And its practical outlook has been, 'For every creature of God is good, and nothing to be refused, if it be received with thanksgiving: for it is sanctified by the word of God and prayer' (1 Tim. 4:4, 5).

It is true that Christianity in its truest expression has been awfully severe and it has realised the cost of holiness, 'If thine eye offend thee, pluck it out, and cast it from thee: it is better for thee to enter into life with one eye, rather than having two eyes to be cast into hell fire' (Matt. 18:9). Christianity *must* know severity, for it is a warfare not against flesh and blood but against principalities and powers, against the rulers of the darkness of this world, against spiritual wickedness in high places. Its war is with sin in all its agents and manifestations. But it is just for the reason that its war is with sin and the agents of sin that Christianity has been severely jealous not to dissipate its forces and miss its holy crusade by making war on the good gifts and blessings, ordinances and institutions, of God. Sin does not reside in the creatures and institutions of God but rather in the hearts of men and demons. And so Christianity has sought to encompass all of God's grace and bring every thought into captivity to the obedience of Christ. In that warfare it is upheld by the conviction that the prince of this world, though active, has been cast out, that the Captain of salvation spoiled principalities and powers and made a show of them openly, triumphing over them in his death, and that 'He shall not fail nor be discouraged, till he hath set judgment in the earth: and the isles shall wait for his law' (Isa. 42:4). 'All thy works shall praise thee, O Lord; and thy saints shall bless thee. They shall speak of the glory of thy kingdom, and talk of thy power; To make known to the sons of men his mighty acts, and the glorious majesty of his kingdom. Thy kingdom is an everlasting kingdom, and thy dominion endureth throughout all generations' (Ps. 145:10–13).

III

11

The Plan of Salvation

IN a systematic treatment of Christian doctrine the plan of salvation is the first topic that calls for treatment. The reason for this is twofold. First, salvation is of the Lord and the plan is therefore God's plan. Second, if it is God's plan it is eternally designed, and the design is prior to all phases of execution, and all the aspects of execution and realization are fulfilled in accordance with the heavenly design (cf. Eph. 1:11).

If God has provided for the salvation of men, it must be salvation that takes effect in the sphere of human existence, that is, in the temporal, historical realm. Salvation as accomplished in time comprises a great many elements, factors, and aspects. There is this diversity for two reasons.

1. Salvation takes account of our manifold needs in sin, misery, and death. If any one facet of our need or liability were overlooked, then salvation would not be complete.

2. The salvation God has provided is not a minimal salvation from sin and its evil consequences. It is maximal salvation, expressing and correspondent with the depth of the riches of God's goodness, wisdom, power, grace, and love. It is salvation *to*, as well as salvation *from*; salvation to a destiny the highest conceivable, not merely by angels and men but also by God himself. Thus it is salvation manifold.

If so, then the eternal counsel must have designed this manifold diversity, and it is necessary for us to take account of the diverse elements as they are comprised not only in actual execution but also in the counsel that lies back of the historical realization.

Furthermore, the diverse elements of salvation as executed are related to one another in orderly fashion. They are not haphazard, unrelated occurrences. And it is necessary for us to seek to understand what these relations are. And if there are these necessary relationships in salvation wrought, there must likewise be necessary relationships in the elements as designed in the eternal counsel. This is to say that there must be in the eternal plan or design as archetype, what corresponds to that which is fulfilled in execution.

The distinct elements comprised in the design or plan have often been spoken of as the distinct decrees. If this term is adopted, then the expression 'the order of the divine decrees' means the same as the order that the various elements of salvation sustain to one another in the eternal counsel of God. This is why the treatment of the plan of salvation is often conducted in terms of the order of the divine decrees.

If we focus attention upon the central fact of the salvation process, we can see not only the propriety but the necessity of what belongs to our topic. God the Father sent his Son into the world to redeem men. This central fact in accomplishment must have been central in the design. God decreed to send his Son into the world in the fullness of time. We are required to make the following analysis:

1. God set his love upon men.
2. In consequence he decreed their salvation.
3. In order to achieve this end, he decreed to send his Son to secure their salvation.

In this very brief outline we have a plan of salvation. We have an order of divine decrees. In other words, the central fact stands in necessary relations to other elements of the divine counsel and must be construed in these relationships; it cannot stand alone.

Historically speaking, the distinguishing features of the various theologies appear in their respective constructions of the plan of salvation. The sacerdotalist conception is governed by the thesis that the church is the depository of salvation and the sacraments the media of conveyance. Among evangelicals there are the Lutherans, the Arminians, and Reformed. The Lutherans and Arminians orient their construction of the plan of salvation to the contention that what God does looking to salvation, he does on behalf of all equally, and the diversity of the issues depends upon the differences of response on the part of men. The

Reformed, on the other hand, maintain that *God* makes men to differ, and that the diversity of the issues finds its explanation ultimately in God's sovereign election of some to salvation. The differences among the Reformed arise in connection with the place accorded to the decree of election in the order of the divine decrees. Much debate has been devoted to the difference between Supralapsarians and Infralapsarians, But into this question we cannot now enter.

In connection with our topic these are the crucial questions and it is well to focus discussion on them. My thesis may be stated in three propositions.

1. God's electing purpose is the fountain from which salvation in all its phases and elements emanates; the whole process of salvation is consequent upon, subordinate to, and is the unfolding of God's electing love and predestination.

2. God's electing love is sovereign; it consists in the sovereign counsel of his own will and is not determined by any foresight on his part of autonomous activity or absence of activity on the part of men.

3. The process of salvation moves from electing grace as fountain, to its goal in the praise of the glory of God's grace in the glorification of those who are the objects of electing love and the participants of redeeming grace.

It will not be possible to adduce all the evidence derived from Scripture in support of this thesis, or of the propositions in which the thesis has been propounded. But a few passages will demonstrate the lines along which the biblical teaching proceeds. To begin we shall consider:

EPHESIANS 1:3–14
I shall deal with this passage under three main captions.

1. *Spiritual Blessing*. There are two observations in particular respecting this subject.

(i) *The Denotation*. It is 'spiritual blessing in the heavenlies'. This is not to be construed as referring merely or even primarily to blessing to be enjoyed in heaven in the life to come. Paul is speaking of blessing in possession now. The Father 'has blessed' believers with this spiritual blessing. Colossians 3:3 is an index to the force of 'the heavenlies in

Christ': 'For ye died, and your life is hid with Christ in God'. The blessing is thus characterized because it proceeds from Christ who is now in
the heavenlies, and the life of the believer is hid with Christ in God.
Christ is the one in whom all the fulness dwells, and believers are complete in him, and only in virtue of what he is. Furthermore, it would be
exegetically impossible to exclude from the scope of the spiritual blessing
the blessings specified in the immediately succeeding context—adoption
(vs. 5), redemption and the forgiveness of sins (vs. 7), the knowledge of
the mystery of God's will (vs. 9), the inheritance (vs. 11), and the seal of
the Holy Spirit as the earnest of this inheritance (vss. 13, 14).

(ii) *The Pattern*. All spiritual blessing bestowed is after the pattern of
election in Christ (vs. 4). Just as those concerned were chosen in Christ,
so they were blessed. This pattern is pretemporal and eternal; it was
election before the foundation of the world. Hence the election is
logically and causally prior to all blessing bestowed. In other words, that
in accordance with which all spiritual blessing is bestowed and is in the
possession of the believer, is something that antedates all history,
namely election. This order cannot be reversed. Anything that falls into
the category of spiritual blessing cannot be regarded as in any way
conditioning election. For election provides the pattern of all that is
embraced in spiritual blessing.

2. *Election and Predestination*. It is highly probable that verses 4 and 5
are exegetical of each other, that they are two ways of expressing the
richness of the grace involved in this counsel of God's will before the
foundation of the world, and that election to be holy (vs. 4) is parallel to
predestination to adoption. If 'in love' is to be taken with verse 5, rather
than with verse 4, then election is explicated in terms of predestinating
love. But be this as it may, the following observations are inescapable.

(i) Those concerned were elected to be holy and predestinated to
adoption. Holiness flows from election and therefore all that is com-
prehended in holiness, and is necessarily associated with it, is the fruit
of election. Here again is an order of causation or, if you will, of
conditioning, that cannot be reversed.

(ii) The Conditioning Determinant. Here our interest is the expressions,
'being predestinated . . . according to the good pleasure of his will' (vs. 5),
'the mystery of his will, according to his good pleasure which he

purposed in him' (vs. 9), 'having been predestinated according to the purpose of him who works all things according to the counsel of his will' (vs. 11). The central issue of the plan of salvation can be staked on these expressions. They deal with the determining factor in predestination, and of what in verse 9 is called the mystery of his will. This latter expression is surely the will unto salvation revealed in the gospel with which the whole passage is concerned. As respects both—predestination and the mystery of his will—it is to trifle with the plain import of the terms, and with the repeated emphasis, to impose upon the terms any determining factor arising from the will of man. If we say or suppose that the differentiation which predestination involves proceeds from or is determined by some sovereign decision on the part of men themselves, then we contradict what the apostle by eloquent reiteration was jealous to affirm. If he meant to say anything in these expressions in verses 5, 9, and 11, it is that God's predestination, and his will to salvation, proceeds from the pure sovereignty and absolute determination of his counsel. It is the unconditioned and unconditional election of God's grace. In like manner, if we assess the word 'grace' and observe that 'the praise of the glory of his grace' is the goal to which the good pleasure of his will in predestination is directed (vss. 6, 12), we are provided with confirmation that grace is the determining factor in all that belongs to the mystery of God's will. It is scarcely necessary to show that the determinate purpose, in accord with which predestination took place, is the eternal purpose. That election is eternal is expressly stated in verse 4. The parallelism of verses 4 and 5 would require the inference that predestination is likewise eternal, and therefore also the good pleasure of his will in accord with which God did predestinate. Hence the purpose and the counsel of his will, in accord with which God does all things, must be the eternal purpose and counsel of his will.

3. *Union with Christ.* Pervasive in the passage is the formula 'in Christ' or its equivalent. It is 'in Christ' that we are blessed with all spiritual blessing (vs. 3). It is 'in the beloved' that we were abundantly favoured with grace (vs. 6). It is 'in him' that we have the redemption (vs. 7). 'In Christ' all things will be summed up (vs. 10). 'In him' we have obtained the inheritance (vs. 11). 'In him' we are sealed with the Holy Spirit (vs. 13). The blessings mentioned, at least most of them, are

blessings bestowed, and therefore in actual possession. We ask the question: What is the origin of this relationship? The answer is given in verse 4—'chosen in Christ before the foundation of the world'. It did not therefore begin in time in the bestowment of the blessing in actual possession. Hence all phases of union with Christ, and all blessing accruing from union with him, proceed from the union constituted before the foundation of the world in election. The spiritual blessing is 'in Christ' (vs. 3). But, as noted earlier, the spiritual blessing, as bestowed and possessed, finds its antecedent and pattern in election in Christ before the foundation of the world. If $\grave{\epsilon}\nu$ $\alpha\grave{v}\tau\hat{\omega}$ in verse 9 refers to Christ, then the good pleasure of his will (vss. 5, 9, and 11) is also in Christ, and so the determinate purpose that conditions predestination is likewise conceived of (cf. 2 Tim. 1:9) as determined in Christ. So again we are advised that the determinate purpose is in Christ, and so the unison is traced back to God's eternal counsel.

ROMANS 8:28–30; 2 TIMOTHY 1:9

In Ephesians 1:3–14 we found that the purpose in accord with which predestination was determined is sovereign and eternal, that is, it proceeds from God's own unconditioned and unconditional will in the counsel of eternity. We also found that the same sovereignty must be applied to the election in Christ which is expressly stated to have been before the foundation of the world. This analogy will have to be applied to the 'purpose' of Romans 8:28—'called according to purpose'. 2 Timothy 1:9 expressly enunciates both features of the 'purpose' in accord with which we are both saved and called. The pure sovereignty is expressed negatively and positively—'not according to our works but according to his own purpose and grace'. The negative speaks indeed of *works* or *deeds* but, when taken in conjunction with the positive emphasis, the effect must be to set in sharp contrast any determining factor emanating from us, with the determinate will of God. And two features of the affirmative part of the text thrust into prominence the God-conditioned nature of the purpose—it is his *own* purpose and it is *grace*. The word 'own' ($i\delta\acute{\iota}\alpha\nu$) harks back to the negative that precedes, and certifies that the purpose is not in any respect ours, nor does it derive any determination from us, but is severely and only his own. The co-ordination of purpose and grace accentuates the sovereignty of the counsel specified. It may be that the words 'and grace' should be taken as a characterizing addition to the effect of saying 'gracious purpose'. In that event the word 'grace' would reinforce the free sovereignty implicit in 'his own purpose'. But if taken more independently, the co-ordination of purpose and grace serves to remind us that the determinate purpose is one associated with grace, and therefore is of grace. That the purpose and grace are eternal is expressly stated—'given in Christ Jesus before times eternal'.

In this passage also we have the same truth respecting union with Christ, and the assurance that the calling with a holy calling is after the pattern of a union with Christ existing from eternity. For the purpose and grace were given in Christ Jesus before times eternal.

Romans 8:28–30 merits further examination. That it is in important respects parallel to Ephesians 1:4, 5 needs no argument. 'Whom he did foreknow he also did predestinate' is a succinct enunciation of the more expanded statement in Ephesians 1:4,5. Exegetical considerations demand that 'foreknow' be understood in terms of electing love and the thought is therefore identical with Ephesians 1:4a. And if 'in love' is construed with Ephesians 1:5, 'in love having predestinated' is, in turn, the most condensed way of expressing the thought of Romans 8:29. When 'foreknow' is understood in terms of electing love, and the parallel to Ephesians 1:4a recognized, then the foreknowledge and predestination of Romans 8:29 must be conceived of as eternal. This could be demonstrated from its own terms, but the parallel in Ephesians 1:4, 5 puts this beyond dispute. Furthermore, the 'purpose' of Romans 8:28 must be the eternal purpose, as noted earlier, and the purpose is obviously explicated as consisting in foreknowledge and predestination in verse 29. For our present interest, therefore, Romans 8:28–30 shows that the fountain of the whole process of salvation is God's electing love, and that calling, justification, and glorification, with all other aspects of the salvation process bound up with them, are conditioned by, and are the fruit of foreknowledge and predestination as the elements of God's eternal and sovereign purpose of grace.

This will suffice to establish the three propositions of the thesis stated at the outset. This is the crucial question of the plan of salvation. God's electing love is the fountain from which salvation in all its elements emanates. This love is sovereign, and as it is sovereignty predestinating in its origin, so it is sovereignty secure in its outcome, to the praise of the glory of God's grace.

There is, however, another angle from which the plan of salvation must be viewed. To say the least, there is another aspect of God's counsel of salvation that must be appended to the discussion of the plan of salvation, apart from which our construction of the plan of salvation fails to take account of what is necessarily germane. If we are alert to the demands of exegesis we will have detected this requirement. Much has been said of the electing love of God as the fountain, and as that which conditions salvation in all its phases. But it is God the Father who is the subject. This is apparent in the passages on which we have focused attention. God the Father is the subject in Ephesians 1:4, 5, as is shown by verse 3: 'Blessed be the God and Father of our Lord Jesus Christ'. It is apparent also in Romans 8:29, for the subject is the person of whom it can be said that he 'predestinated to be conformed to the image of his Son.' The Father alone sustains such a relationship to the Son and therefore it is the Father in his distinguishing identity who foreknew and predestinated as well as called, justified, and glorified. Much else could be adduced from Scripture to the same effect. In a word, therefore, our concept of the plan of salvation is bereft of what is most precious, if it fails to take account of the trinitarian economy in terms of which it is both devised and executed.

This aspect of truth has not been neglected in Reformed theology. It has been constructed and developed in covenantal terms and has been called the covenant of redemption as distinct from the covenant of grace, the eternal covenant as distinct from its temporal administration, the covenant of peace, and the *pactum salutis*. It is not necessary to make much of an issue respecting terminology. But it may not be remiss to observe that the term 'covenant' in Scripture refers to temporal administration, and it is not strictly proper to use a biblical term to designate something to which it is not applied in the Scripture itself. For this reason it is not well, and is liable to be confusing, to speak of this economy in terms of covenant. I prefer some such designation as the inter-trinitarian economy of salvation. This title is inclusive enough to comprise all aspects of the economy, eternal and temporal, pre-temporal design and fulfilment in time and in the ages to come. Whatever term is adopted, the truth concerned is all-important. For it is not only proper, it is mandatory that in the plan of salvation as eternally designed and as executed in time, we discover the grandeur of the arrangements of divine wisdom and love on the part of the distinct persons of the Godhead, and recognize the distinguishing prerogatives and functions of each person and the distinct relations we come to sustain to each person as we become the partakers of God's grace. After all, our study of the plan of salvation will not produce abiding fruit unless the plan captivates our devotion to the triune God in the particularity of the grace which each person bestows in the economy of redemption, and in the particularity of relationship constituted by the amazing grace of Father, Son, and Holy Spirit. The fellowship of the living God is the fellowship of the Father, and of the Son, and of the Holy Spirit.

12

The Person of Christ

THE particular aspect of the doctrine of the person of Christ with which we are now concerned belongs to the locus of soteriology and presupposes all that falls within the locus of theology proper, namely, the immanent and eternal relations of the Son to the other persons of the Godhead, the Son's essential Deity, and his activities as eternal Son in the economics of creation and providence. We now deal with that phase of the doctrine of Christ's person which is directly related to the economy of salvation and, therefore, with his becoming man for our salvation. The first subdivision of this doctrine is the incarnation.

THE INCARNATION

1. *The Fact.* It is on the premises of his eternal identity as God, his eternal subsistence as the only-begotten Son, his creative activity at the beginning, and his continued activity in sustaining all created reality, that we can conceive the fact and meaning of the incarnation. The doctrine of the incarnation is vitiated if it is conceived of as the beginning to be of the person of Christ. The incarnation means that he who never began to be in his specific identity as Son of God, *began* to be what he eternally was not. We must appreciate the historic factuality and temporal occurrence of the incarnation and the sustained contrasts involved. The infinite became the finite, the eternal and supratemporal entered time and became subject to its conditions, the immutable became the mutable, the invisible became the visible, the Creator became the created, the sustainer of all became dependent, the Almighty infirm. All is summed up in the proposition, God became man. The

title 'God' comprehends all the attributes that belong to God and the designation 'man' all the attributes that are essentially human.

The thought of incarnation is stupendous, for it means the conjunction in one person of all that belongs to Godhead and all that belongs to manhood. It would have been humiliation for the Son of God to have become man under the most ideal conditions, humiliation because of the discrepancy between God and his creation, between the majesty of the Creator on the one hand, and the humble status of the most dignified creature on the other. But it was not such an incarnation that took place. The Son of God was sent and came into this world of sin, of misery, and of death. These describe the situation into which he came. Paul draws our attention to this by the use of a formula that is on the verge of peril—'in the likeness of sinful flesh' (Rom. 8:3). He could have used other expressions—'made of the seed of David according to the flesh' (Rom. 1:3), 'made of a woman' (Gal. 4:4), 'made in the likeness of men' (Phil. 2:7), 'manifested in flesh' (1 Tim. 3:16). But, instead, in this case he uses a formula that staggers us by its uniqueness. When he uses the term 'likeness' he does not mean to suggest any unreality to the flesh of Christ (cf. Rom. 1:3). He employs the word to obviate any thought of sinfulness. For he could not have said that the Son was sent in sinful flesh. Why then the use of the expression 'sinful flesh'? The highest purpose is served by its use. Thereby is enunciated the great truth that the Son of God was sent in that very nature which in every other instance is sinful. The Son came by a mode that was supernatural, by a mode consonant with his supernatural person, and by a mode that guaranteed his sinlessness. But he came in a way that preserved fully his organic and genetic connection with us men who are all sinful flesh. He was made of the seed of David, of a seed that was sinful, and of a woman who was herself sinful and afflicted with the depravity incident to fallen humanity. He came into the closest relation to sinful humanity that it was possible for him to come without thereby becoming himself sinful. This is the incarnation that actually occurred.

Furthermore, having come as sin-bearer to redeem from sin, he bore in his flesh the marks which the vicarious endurance of sin impressed upon him. Unparalleled agony, reproach, shame, and curse were his. 'His visage was so marred more than any man, and his form more than the sons of men' (Is. 52:14). Sentimental art has distorted our Lord's human appearance. We have no data for an authentic portrait, but we can be sure that his appearance would not correspond with the creations that have not taken account of the realities of our Lord's mission and commission.

2. *The Mode.* The mode is often designated as the virgin birth. This is not improper. When we speak of the virgin birth we may not suppose, however, that the event of emerging from the virgin's womb was supernatural, or that the process of foetal and embryonic development in the virgin's womb was abnormal. It was when Mary's full time came that she brought forth her son (cf. Luke 2:5-7). The supernatural is to be found in three considerations:

(i) *Supernatural Begetting.* Jesus was not conceived in the womb by the conjunction of male and female, by spermal communication from the man to the woman. He was begotten by the Holy Spirit, and the miraculous consisted in this supernatural begetting. It is the absence of human begetting that made the birth a virgin birth. In this connection it is not proper, strictly speaking, to say that Jesus was conceived by the Holy Spirit. Mary did conceive by the power of the Holy Spirit. But Mary conceived and to say simply, 'conceived by the Holy Ghost', obscures the all-important truth that the function of Mary was to conceive and in this respect to participate in the event of Jesus' incarnation. The relevant texts bear this out emphatically (Matt. 1:20—τὸ γὰρ ἐν αὐτῇ γεννηθὲν ἐκ Πνεύματός ἐστιν Ἁγίου.; Luke 1:35—διὸ καὶ τὸ γεννώμενον ἅγιον κληθήσεται Υἱὸς Θεοῦ). Mary is expressly stated to have conceived (Luke 1:31—καὶ ἰδοὺ συλλήμψῃ ἐν γαστρὶ καὶ τέξῃ υἱόν). What is said of Elizabeth in reference to John (Luke 1:24, 26) is here said of Mary. The Holy Spirit begat, Mary conceived (cf. also Luke 2:21).

(ii) *Supernatural Person.* It was not a mere baby that was supernaturally begotten. It was the eternal Son of God in respect of his human nature. *He* was begotten of the Spirit and conceived by the virgin in human nature. The most stupendous fact of all is that this was the begetting, conception, embryonic development, and birth of a supernatural person. Because of this there was no point at which the supernatural was not present. The incarnation was supernatural through and through, because at no point was the supernatural identity of the person suspended. It is forgetfulness of this fact that opens the door for the entertainment of any doubt respecting the virgin birth and its antecedent of supernatural begetting. Supernatural generation is thoroughly in accord with the incarnation as properly defined. Natural generation, on the other hand, would be incongruous. 'It cannot be denied that the supernatural birth of Jesus enters constitutively into the substance of that system which is taught in the New Testament as Christianity—that it is the expression of its supernaturalism, the safeguard of its doctrine of incarnation, the condition of its doctrine of redemption.'[1]

This emphasis on the supernatural as always present by reason of the person, in no way excludes the natural processes operative in foetal and embryonic development and in emergence from the womb. In other miracles natural factors are not entirely eliminated (e.g. water into wine). There is a convergence of the natural and supernatural and, in this instance, the diverse interests of the incarnation are conserved and promoted by the combination. As, in the earthly life of our Lord, various needs were met by the provisions of general providence (hunger, thirst, weariness), so in the formation of his human nature in the womb. Just as the natural in the life of our Lord in no way interfered with his supernatural identity, so in the formation that took place in Mary's womb. (iii) *Supernatural Preservation*. This refers to preservation from defilement from the womb. This may reside entirely in the supernatural begetting, for it may be that depravity is conveyed in natural generation. In any case, natural generation would have entailed depravity (John 3:6). Yet it may not be correct to find the whole explanation of Jesus' sinlessness in the absence of natural begetting. So it may well be that preservation from the taint of sin (cf. Psalm 51:5) required another, supernatural factor, namely, the preservation from conception to birth of the infant Jesus from the contamination that would otherwise have proceeded from his human mother.

3. *The Nature.* The proposition 'God became man' could convey the thought of kenosis, subtraction, or divestiture; that the Son of God ceased to be what he was and exchanged divine identity for human; that

[1] 'The Supernatural Birth of Jesus' in *Christology and Criticism*, B. B. Warfield, 1929, p. 457.

divine attributes, prerogatives, and activities were surrendered, or at least suspended, in order that the human might be real and active. The various statements of Scripture are eloquent to the exclusion of such a conception.

In John 1:14 there is no hint that the Word in becoming flesh ceased to be that which he is defined to be as the eternally subsistent one, eternally co-ordinate with God, and eternally identified with God in John 1:1. And lest we should interpret the incarnation in terms of transmutation or divestiture, John hastens to inform us that, in beholding the incarnate Word, they beheld his glory as the glory of the only-begotten from the Father (John 1:14). And then he proceeds to identify the only-begotten in his unabridged character as 'God only-begotten who is in the bosom of the Father' (v. 18). Most significant is the fact that in this very identity he is represented as giving the revelation. In this respect the variant υἱός makes no difference in the context of the theology of John's Gospel (cf. John 5:17ff; 10:33ff). So the only construction that satisfies the terms of John's prologue is that the incarnation means addition and conjunction, not subtraction. Other statements of Scripture are to the same effect (cf. Phil. 2:6, 7; Col. 2:9; Heb. 1:1–3).

The incarnation, therefore, means that the Son of God took human nature in its integrity into his person with the result that he is both divine and human, without any impairment of the fulness of either the divine or the human. He is God-man.[1]

THE HYPOSTATIC UNION

This caption concerns the doctrine of the two natures in the one person. In the formulation of Chalcedon: 'one and the same Son, our Lord Jesus Christ, the same perfect in Godhead and also perfect in manhood, truly God and truly man . . . consubstantial with the Father according to the Godhead, and consubstantial with us according to the manhood . . . to be acknowledged in two natures, inconfusedly, unchangeably, indivisibly, inseparably; the distinction of natures not being taken away by the union, but rather the property of each nature being preserved, and concurring in one person and one subsistence, not parted or divided into two persons (εἰς ἕν πρόσωπον καὶ μίαν ὑπόστασιν),

[1] cf. Shedd: *Dogmatic Theology*, II, p. 267.

but one and the same Son, and only-begotten, God the Word, the Lord Jesus Christ.' This is admirably summed up in the Westminster Confession: 'Two whole, perfect, and distinct natures, the Godhead and the manhood, were inseparably joined together in one person, without conversion, composition, or confusion' (VIII, ii). The divine is not changed into the human, nor accommodated to the human, nor is the human transmuted into the divine—no conversion! The divine and human do not coalesce so as to form a third—no composition! Neither are the natures mixed—no confusion! The case is that of duality, with each nature possessing and exercising its own attributes without interference, curtailment, or modification, duality in every respect in which the created is the antithesis of the uncreated. What the person is in virtue of the one nature is in sharp contrast with what he is in virtue of the other. This contrast applies to the spheres of consciousness, intelligence, and will.

It was the person of the Son, and he alone, who took human nature to himself into union with his divine nature in the one divine person.

On this construction the catholic doctrine has been to the effect that the human nature was not itself hypostatic, that is, personal. There was only one person and this person was divine. This has been known as the Chalcedonian tenet of the *anhypostasia* of the human nature. A great deal of discussion has turned on this question in more recent times and there has been the tendency to speak of Jesus as a human person and to reject the Chalcedonian formula on this particular (εἰς ἕν πρόσωπον καὶ μίαν ὑπόστασιν). This tendency is not one to be lightly dismissed. In Scripture our Lord is referred to as a man or the man (ἀνήρ) in several instances (Luke 24:19; John 1:30; Acts 2:22; 17:31), and as the man (ἄνθρωπος) Christ Jesus (1 Tim. 2:5). We necessarily raise the question: Does the *anhypostasia* do justice to this emphasis? Is not all that belongs to human personality necessarily involved in such designations? Two remarks are in order:

First, it may not be possible for us to give adequate expression in our formulae, and particularly in the formulae of Chalcedon, to all that is involved in our Lord's humanness. This is to say, we may not be able to devise a precise formula that will guard the unity of his person, on the one hand, and the integrity of his humanity, on the other.

Second, it may be that the term 'person' can be given a connotation in our modern context, and applied to Christ's human nature, without thereby impinging upon the *oneness* of his divine-human person. In other words, the term 'nature' may be too abstract to express all that belongs to his humanness and the term 'person' is necessary to express the manhood that is truly and properly his.

At the same time there appears to be a great truth in the Chalcedonian insistence on one person. We do not find our Lord speaking or acting in terms of merely human personality. In the various situations reported to us in the Gospel record, it is a striking fact that he identifies himself as one who sustains to the Father his unique relationship as the only-begotten Son, as the one whose self-identity, whose self, is conceived of in such terms. It is indeed true that he speaks and acts as one who is human and intensely aware of his human identity. He shows the limitations inseparable from this identity, and also the limitations prescribed by the task given him to fulfil in human nature. But it is highly significant that in situations where his human identity, and the limitations incident to this identity and to his commission, are most in evidence, there appears the profound consciousness of his filial relationship and of his divine self-identity (cf. Matt. 24:36; 26:39, 42, 53; John 12:27. Cf. also John 5:26, 27; 17:1; Rom. 1:3; Heb. 5:7–9; 1 John 1:7). In such contexts the experiences that were his, in virtue of being human, are conspicuously in the forefront in all the intensity of their meaning. But just then the consciousness of his intradivine Sonship is in the foreground as defining the person that he is. And the inference would seem to be that our Lord's *self*-identity and *self*-consciousness can never be thought of in terms of human nature alone. Personality cannot be predicated of him except as it draws within its scope his specifically divine identity. There are two centres of consciousness but not of self-consciousness.

In this same connection it is worthy of special attention to observe how, in connection with the sacrifice of Christ which he offered in human nature, it is always he who is represented as offering himself, and in the contexts he is identified and defined in terms of what he is as divine (John 10:17, 18; 17:4; Rom. 8:32–34; Phil. 2:6–8; Heb. 1:3).

The Son of God did not become personal by incarnation. He became incarnate but there was no suspension of his divine self-identity. In these terms his self must always be defined. Jesus was God-man, not, strictly speaking, God and man.

CONSEQUENCES OF THE HYPOSTATIC UNION

1. *Theanthropic Constitution.* From the time of conception in the womb of the virgin, and for ever, the second person of the Godhead is God-man. This identity did not suffer dissolution even in death. The death meant separation of the elements of his human nature. But he, as the Son of God, was still united to the two separated elements of his human nature. He, as respects his body, was laid in the tomb and, as respects his disembodied spirit, he went to the Father. He was buried. He was raised from the dead. He was indissolubly united to the disunited elements of his human nature. When he was raised from the dead, human nature in its restored integrity belonged to his person, and it was in that restored integrity that he manifested himself repeatedly to his disciples and to various other persons, including more than five hundred at one time. It was in this human nature that he ascended to heaven and sat down at the right hand of God. It is as God-man he is exalted and given all authority in heaven and in earth. It is in human nature that he will return, and as God-man he will judge the world. The elect will be conformed to his image, and it is as the firstborn among many brethren that he will fulfil the Father's predestinating design (Rom. 8:29; cf. Phil. 3:21). The thought of ceasing to be the God-man is, therefore, alien to all that the Scripture reveals respecting his own glory and the glory of those for whose sake he became man.

2. *Economic Subordination.* By the incarnation and by taking the form of a servant, the Son came to sustain new relations to the Father and the Holy Spirit. He became subject to the Father and dependent upon the operations of the Holy Spirit. He came down from heaven, not to do his own will, but the will of the Father who sent him (cf. John 6:38). As the Father had life in himself, so gave he to the Son to have life in himself (cf. John 5:26). It is in this light that we are to interpret Jesus' statement, 'The Father is greater than I' (John 14:28). It is our Lord's servanthood that advertises this subordination more than any other office. As servant he was obedient unto death (cf. Phil. 2:7, 8).

Manifold were the activities of the Holy Spirit. By the Spirit he was begotten in Mary's womb. With the Spirit he was endued at the baptism in Jordan. By the Spirit he was driven into the wilderness to be tempted of the devil. In the power of the Spirit he returned to Galilee. By the Spirit he cast out demons. In the Holy Spirit he rejoiced and gave thanks (cf. Luke 10:21). Through the eternal Spirit he offered himself and fulfilled the climactic demand of his commission (cf. Heb. 9:12). According to the Spirit he was constituted the Son of God with power in the resurrection (cf. Rom. 1:4). By virtue of this, Christ is 'life-giving Spirit' (1 Cor. 15:45), and Paul can say, 'the Lord is the Spirit' (2 Cor. 3:17). He is given the Spirit without measure (cf. John 3:34).

3. *Mediatorial Investiture.* The authority with which he is invested as a result of his obedience unto death must be distinguished from the authority and government that he possesses and exercises intrinsically as God the Son. The latter is intrinsic to his deity (cf. Matt. 28:18; John 3:35; Acts 2:36; Eph. 1:20–23; Phil. 2:9–11; 1 Pet. 3:22). This authority and sovereignty is universal and all-inclusive. How it is related to the sovereignty that is intrinsic we cannot tell. Here is another aspect of the duality that exists all along the line in the mystery of the incarnation. The duality in this instance consists in the coexistence of the exercise of prerogatives belonging to him in virtue of his Godhood and of prerogatives which were bestowed upon him as Mediator and Lord. Mystery enshrouds this duality for us, but we may not deny the coexistence or the distinctions involved.

4. *Communio Idiomatum.* Whatever can be predicated of either nature can be predicated of the person. This is not properly stated as *communicatio idiomatum*. It is not a communication or transfer of the attributes of the one nature to the other. The Lutheran doctrine is that there is an impartation of divine properties to the human nature.[1]

The Reformed view is rather that what is true of either nature is true of the person, and the person may be *designated* in terms of one nature when what is predicated is true only in virtue of the other.
(i) The Person is the subject when what is predicated of him is true only in virtue of all that belongs to his Person as divine and human—Redeemer, Lord, Prophet, Priest, King.

[1] cf. H. Schmid: *Doctrinal Theology of the Evangelical Lutheran Church*, pp. 322–344, a περιχώρησις of the human by the divine. See also 'Formula of Concord', Art. IV.

(ii) The Person is the subject when what is predicated of him is true only in virtue of his divine nature—'Before Abraham was I am'; 'the glory which I had with thee before the world was'; 'Thou, Lord, in the beginning hast laid the foundation of the earth'. He may be designated, however, in terms of what he is as human (cf. Rom. 9:5—'Christ according to the flesh').

(iii) The Person is the subject when what is predicated is true only in virtue of his human nature—'I thirst'; 'Jesus wept'; 'they crucified the Lord of glory'; 'mother of my Lord'; ignorance of the day and hour of the advent. He may be designated in terms of deity when what is predicated is true only in virtue of human nature (Heb. 1:3).

13

The Atonement

THE atonement is a term appropriated by theology to designate the work of Christ, which in the express terms of Scripture is explicated as obedience, sacrifice, propitiation, reconciliation, and redemption. It needs no argument to demonstrate that these are the categories under which we must construe that which Christ wrought once for all in order to secure our salvation. These terms lie on the face of the biblical teaching and, though the interpretations placed upon them are various, no student of Scripture would deny that the atonement must be construed in these categories if it is to bear even the semblance of the biblical teaching. There is at least one other conception that has played an important rôle in the definition of the atonement, that is not expressly denoted by a biblical term. It is the satisfaction of justice. It is, however, a biblical conception, and we must not abandon it, even though the terminology is not overtly biblical. In Isaiah 53:10 we read of the Servant that his soul will make a trespass-offering, that is to say, he will offer himself as a trespass-offering.

There were four main types of blood-offering under the Old Testament. They each had their own distinctive features and significance. The trespass-offering was one of them, and it is apparent that the purpose of the trespass-offering was that of compensation or satisfaction. This is the governing idea, and, since Christ's offering is interpreted in terms of this offering, it must be construed in the light of this governing idea, namely, satisfaction for wrongs committed. In Romans 3:25, 26 we read that God set forth Christ a propitiation, to demonstrate his righteousness, 'that he might be just and the justifier of him who is of the faith of Jesus.' This states that which is satisfied or provided for in the propitiation, namely, the justice of God. So we have a biblical basis for the concept.

As indicated, the atonement refers to the work of Christ wrought once for all and therefore finished. The work of Christ includes more than that which is finished and completed. It includes the continued ministry of Christ in his exalted glory, a ministry discharged in all three offices as prophet, priest, and king. And when we are thinking of the *work* of Christ, we impoverish our faith and dishonour Christ whenever we think of it simply in terms of what is past and complete. But it is equally important to maintain the once-for-all character of the atonement. It is incomprehensible how, even within Protestant circles, there could be propounded the idea that atonement is eternal in the heart of God, not to speak of the Roman Catholic dogma of the sacrifice of the mass. The Epistle to the Hebrews is intensely concerned with the continued heavenly ministry of Christ, but in no other book in the New Testament is there more repeated emphasis upon the once-for-all character of his sacrifice. 'Now once, in the consummation of the ages, hath he been manifested for the putting away of sin through the sacrifice of himself' (Heb. 9:26). 'Christ was once offered to bear the sins of many' (Heb. 9:28). 'He needs not daily to offer up sacrifices . . . for this he did once for all when he offered up himself' (Heb. 7:27); cf. also Hebrews 9:12; 10:10; also Romans 6:10; 1 Peter 3:18. Our Lord himself testifies to a finished work of his (John 17:4; 19:30).

The atonement as a completed work of Christ must always be viewed in the light of the inter-trinitarian economy of salvation. We cannot over-emphasize the importance of this orientation. For only thus can the atonement be placed in its proper context, its relationships properly constructed, the distinctive functions of the three persons of the Godhead understood and appreciated, the nature and design of the atonement rightly interpreted, and the continued heavenly ministry of Christ, on the basis of the atonement, duly prized. Respects in which this becomes manifest can readily be furnished.

THE LOVE OF GOD

Much confusion, misunderstanding, and misrepresentation have arisen from failure to accord to the love of God the prominence that belongs to it as the source from which the atonement springs. This should not have been the case. The accent of Scripture is apparent and pervasive. The simple fact is too patent to be overlooked. But the analysis of both fact and implications has too frequently been neglected, and the faith of believers has thereby suffered, and attacks upon integral elements of the faith have frequently been advanced.

The love of God that is the source of the atonement is the love of God the Father specifically. This is obvious in the most relevant texts (John 3:16; Rom. 5:8; 1 John 4:9, 10). But too frequently this specificity escapes our attention, and here the particularity and its significance for the doctrine of salvation, are obscured if not distorted, with the result that our thought and faith come to be concentrated on the love of Christ, to the eclipse of the Father's love. There are several ways in which even Reformed believers have failed to do honour to the love and grace of God the Father, and this aspect of the Father's love is basic to the correction of this default of faith and devotion. Let us prize the love of the Redeemer himself. Let us know and reproduce that of which the apostle speaks (2 Cor. 5:14, 15; Gal. 2:19, 20). But this love of Christ is not in its biblical perspective unless we perceive that it is love constrained by and exercised in fulfilment of the Father's will, and the Father's will as the purpose flowing from his invincible love. We must be captivated by the Father's love. For this is love, not that we loved God, but that the Father loved us and sent his Son a propitiation for our sins (cf. 1 John 4:10).

When we acquire this perspective and enter thus into the holy of holies of the Father's love, our view of the source of the atonement is set within the plan and inter-trinitarian economy of salvation. As we found, the plan originates in the election of love in Christ before the foundation of the world, and the plan must be conceived of in terms of an inter-trinitarian economy because there are the distinguishing prerogatives, actions, and functions of the three persons. Foremost in this economy is the electing love of the Father. So the love of the Father as the source of the atonement is the love from which the whole plan of salvation takes its origin.

PROVISION OF THE FATHER'S LOVE

The next observation relevant to the orientation provided by the inter-trinitarian economy is that the atonement is the provision of the Father's love. This fact is the corrective of much confusion, and also of allegations that undermine some of the cardinal features of the atonement itself. We may think, first of all, of that objection frequently urged against the doctrine of propitiation as placating or propitiating the wrath of God, specifically the wrath of God the Father. It is alleged that this doctrine involves a mythical conception of God, that it introduces a dualism incompatible with the unity of God, because it represents the Father as actuated by unrelenting and vindictive disfavour, but the Son by mercy and love, and that the Son wins over the Father to grace by placating his wrath.

In dealing with this objection it is not necessary now to establish the doctrine of propitiation. It would be beyond the scope of our present task. Suffice it to be reminded that the essence of the judgment of God against sin is his wrath, his holy recoil against what is the contradiction of himself (cf. Rom. 1:18). If Christ vicariously bore God's judgment upon sin, and to deny this is to make nonsense of his suffering unto death and particularly of the abandonment on Calvary, then to eliminate from this judgment that which belongs to its essence is to undermine the idea of vicarious sin-bearing and its consequences. So the doctrine of propitiation is not to be denied or its sharpness in any way toned down. How then are we to deal with the objections?

It must be admitted that, if we were to think of the Father as actuated simply by wrath and the judgment that it involves, and conceive of him as won over to clemency by Christ, then we should certainly be guilty of what has been alleged. We should be denying all that is involved in our present topic, that the atonement is the provision of the Father's love. Calvary and its curse are the supreme expression of the Father's love. Any tendency in the interest of more dramatic homiletics to obscure this truth must be resisted and condemned. It assails the Father's honour and impugns his love. How then is the objection to be answered?

The answer resides in the simple truth that love and wrath are not contradictory. They can coexist in their greatest intensity in the same person at the same time. Wrath is not to be equated with hate. Failure to recognize this simple truth in the relations of men to one another, and in God's relations to men, is the capital error of those who make the objection concerned. It is an incomprehensible error. Because of the compatibility of love and wrath as coexisting, the wrath-bearing of the Son of God, pre-eminently upon the accursed tree, the vicarious infliction of the wrath of God against those whom the Father invincibly loved, is not only comprehensible, but belongs to the essence of the doctrine that Christ bore our sins in his own body upon the tree as the the supreme manifestation of the Father's love. God's glory is not only love. It is also holiness. And because he is holiness, his holy jealousy burns against sin, and therefore against sinners. For only as characterizing sinners does sin exist. The propitiation which God made his own Son is the provision of the Father's love, to the end that holiness may be vindicated and its demands satisfied. Thus, and only thus, could the purpose and urge of his love be realized in a way compatible with, and to the glory of the manifold perfections of his character. Paul sets forth this doctrine when he writes: God set forth Christ 'a propitiation . . . that he might be just and the justifier of him who is of the faith of Jesus' (Rom. 3:25, 26).

But not only is the compatibility of love and wrath the vindication of the doctrine of propitiation, it is also the key to the understanding of wrath inflicted upon Christ himself as the one upon whom the good pleasure of the Father rested, and the one whom the Father loved with unique and immutable love. The difficulty for many, some kindly disposed to the doctrine of propitiation and some hostile, is: How could Jesus be uniquely and immutably loved of the Father, and at the same time be the object of his wrath? The answer resides in the same principle, that love and wrath are not contradictory, that love in its intensest exercise can coexist with the exercise and infliction of wrath.

In the case of Christ's vicarious undertaking, however, we must go further. It is only because of the unique relation that the Father sustained to his own Son, and the unique love of the Father to the Son arising from this relation and inseparable from it, that the Son incarnate could be the object of such wrath. The wrath vicariously borne was unique, it was incomparable and without parallel. We have the index to this in Psalm 22 and 69, in the record of Gethsemane's agony, and in the dereliction of Calvary. Who could be equal to such an ordeal? None but the Son of God in his unchanged identity as the Son, and in the embrace of that love of which Jesus spoke when he said, 'The Father loveth the Son', a love also presupposed in the cry of dereliction, 'My God, why hast thou forsaken me?'.

But we have to take another step. Jesus spoke of the love of the Father constrained by the faithful discharge of the commission given him (John 10:17, 18). We cannot dissociate the death of Christ from its propitiatory implications. And so we must say that this love of the Father was at no point more intensely in exercise than when the Son was actively drinking the cup of unrelieved damnation, than when he was enduring as substitute the full toll of the Father's wrath. All of this is implicit in the saying of Romans 8:32, that the Father did not spare his own Son. And what perverse myopia afflicts the minds of men when they try to rob the unspeakable spectacles of Gethsemane and Calvary of that which is the only explanation! As we rob this unexampled ordeal of its meaning, we deprive ourselves of what brings us to the summit of amazement. What love for men that the Father should execute upon his own Son the full toll of holy wrath, so that we should never taste it! This was John's amazement when he wrote: 'This is love, not that we loved God, but that he loved us, and sent his Son the propitiation for our sins' (1 John 4:10).

Here is the economy of salvation. When the Father chose the elect *in Christ* before the foundation of the world, to nothing less than this appointment was the Son assigned. In the fulness of time God the Father sent the Son, and the appointment is declared in the witness of the Father on the occasion of Jesus' baptism: 'This is my beloved Son in whom I am well pleased' (Matt. 3:17), that is, 'in whom my good pleasure has come to rest' for the discharge of messianic commission. In all stages of fulfilment there was no suspension of the Sonship, nor of the love expressed in the term 'beloved'.

INTER-TRINITARIAN CO-OPERATION

As we think of the categories in terms of which the atonement is to be interpreted, it is to be borne in mind that only of Christ can the atoning accomplishment be predicated. He alone was obedient unto death, the death of the cross. He alone offered himself to God as a sacrifice to expiate guilt. He alone made propitiation so that he is the propitiation for our sins. We were reconciled to God by Jesus' blood. He redeemed us to God by his blood. It was he who made a trespass-offering and satisfied justice. The atonement is focused in the death of Christ, and this points up the exclusiveness. For only the Son of God died and bore our sins in his own body upon the tree. The atonement must more broadly be subsumed under the mediatorial work of Christ, and more specifically under the priestly office. But there is one Mediator, and Christ alone was called a High Priest after the order of Melchizedek.

But neither the Father nor the Holy Spirit were spectators in the great drama of redemption accomplished. It is surely to the Holy Spirit that the Epistle to the Hebrews refers when it says of Christ that 'through the eternal Spirit he offered himself without spot to God' (Heb. 9:14). And when we remember that the Holy Spirit rested upon the Saviour and was given to him without measure, it is impossible to think of the equipment with which Christ was furnished in learning obedience, apart from the constant enduement and operation of the Holy Spirit. It is, however, more frequently on the activity of God the Father that the Scripture reflects.

This is strikingly brought to our attention in the Old Testament passage which perhaps more than any other portrays for us the vicarious work of Christ (Isa. 52:13–53:12). It is in the capacity of Servant that the sin-bearer is presented, and it is as the Lord's Servant he performs the expiatory work. He is the Father's Servant. But when he is thus introduced we read: 'Behold my servant, whom I uphold' (Isa. 42:1; cf. vs. 6). And then we read: 'The Lord hath laid on him the iniquity of us all' (Isa. 53:6); 'Yet it pleased the Lord to bruise him: he hath put him to grief' (Isa. 53:10). Here is activity on the part of the Father most directly related to what is pivotal in the atoning work. In the New Testament no passage along this line is more arresting than that of Paul: 'Him who knew no sin he made sin for us, that we might become the righteousness of God in him' (2 Cor. 5:21).

Most significant of all in this connection are those passages in which the Father is stated to be the subject and agent of the atoning action. I am thinking particularly of 2 Corinthians 5:18, 19 and Colossians 1:19, 20. The initiative is with the Father, and the reconciling action is the Father's —'all things are of God who reconciled us to himself' (2 Cor. 5:18);

'God was in Christ reconciling the world to himself' (2 Cor. 5:19). In these contexts, in which the Father's initiative and action are emphasized, there is no suppression or eclipse of the action and mediacy of Christ. It is through Christ that the Father reconciles all things to himself. It was in Christ he was reconciling the world. It was through the death of his Son we were reconciled to God. It is in the body of his flesh through death. And it is through Christ that we receive the reconciliation. In Christ and through Christ the Father acts in his own reconciling accomplishment. The reason for this mediacy consists in what the reconciliation demands, the exigency for which the Father by his action alone could not provide. The exigency was death, obedience unto death, the shedding of blood. In the economy of salvation only God's Son had blood to shed and life to lay down in death. It should not surprise us, therefore, that Christ is also said to be the agent in the reconciling action (Eph. 2:16; Col. 1:22; cf. also Rom. 5:10).

We naturally raise the question: If only what Christ could perform in the body of his flesh through death could avail for reconciliation, why is there frequent reflection on the agency of the Father? We may suspect that there is much behind this question that surpasses analysis and understanding on our part. Yet since the revelatory data invite us to examination, and demand the appreciation of faith, there are some appropriate observations.

1. We are not only directed to the Father's love as the source of the atonement, and not only to the inflictions on the Father's part involved in Christ's sin-bearing, but also to agency in the atoning action constrained by the dictates of invincible love and made necessary by the inflictions of sin and its penalty. The love of the Father constraining the giving of the Son and the inflictions laid upon him would be sufficient to certify that the Father was no spectator in the humiliations to which Christ subjected himself, but when the Father is said to be actually reconciling the world to himself, any suggestion of spectatorship is severely excluded, and the Father is to be regarded as intimately related to that by which his alienation had been removed and his favour bestowed.

2. The Father's action in the reconciliation prevents any construction of the atonement in which Christ is set forth as the representative of love,

mercy, and compassion, and the Father, by way of contrast, as the representative of holiness, justice, and truth. The atonement we must ever maintain is the supreme manifestation and vindication of love and justice, mercy and truth, compassion and equity. But there may be no disjunction by which the claims of love and mercy are associated with Christ and the claims of justice with the Father. Reconciliation as action fulfils the claims of supreme love and of inflexible justice. But God the Father in the reconciliation is active in providing for the removal of his own holy alienation, so that the urge of invincible love may come to effect in his reconciled favour and peace. And thereby God the Father is recommending his own love toward us.

3. As observed already, we may not predicate of the Father the actions of Christ by which the reconciliation was accomplished. The Father did not humble himself and become obedient unto death. The humiliations were not those of the Father. The specific and exclusive work of Christ must be guarded and appreciated. But what needs emphasis now is what is entailed in Christ's mediation and agency. We must not so concentrate our thought on what Christ did that we overlook what is implicit in the *mediacy* that was his. It was God the Father who was reconciling *through* Christ, *in* Christ, *through* the death of his Son. The economy of salvation required the distribution of function. But the distribution by which the Son alone bore sin, wrath, curse, and alienation was that of the Father's commission and appointment. 'God commends his own love toward us in that while we were yet sinners Christ died for us' (Rom. 5:8).

We are but touching the fringes of the mystery of God's will and we should be aware that thought and word fail. Here we have unsearchable wisdom, facets of revelation that pertain to ways past finding out. But it is only as our feeble minds become engaged with this mystery and we seek to explore its depths that we catch glimpses of its marvel and we exclaim: 'O the depth of the riches both of the wisdom and knowledge of God!' (Rom. 11:33).

14

The Obedience of Christ

THE obedience of Christ is one of the categories in terms of which the Scripture defines the atoning work of Christ. It does not define the specific character of the other categories. But it does point to the capacity in which Christ discharged all phases of his atoning work.

In delineating the Saviour's expiatory accomplishment, no one passage in Scripture is more instructive than Isaiah 52:13–53:12. It is in the capacity of Servant that the personage is introduced (cf. Isa. 42:1; 49:6) and it is in this capacity he executes his expiatory work (cf. Isa. 52:13; 53:11). The title 'Servant' applies to him because he was the Lord's Servant, not the Servant of men (cf. Isa. 42:1; 52:13; 53:11). He was the Father's Servant. This office implies commission by the Father, subjection to, and fulfilment of, the Father's will. All of this involves obedience. So already we are advised that no category could more significantly express the execution of his vicarious work than obedience. The language of prophecy is again confirmatory: 'I delight to do thy will, O my God: yea, thy law is within my heart' (Psalm 40:8; cf. Heb. 10:5–10).

Early in our Lord's ministry we have his own witness to this effect. At the baptism in Jordan, in answer to John's demurral, Jesus replied: 'Suffer it to be so now: for thus it becometh us to fulfil all righteousness' (Matt. 3:15). This shows that the fulfilment of righteousness in all its detail and extent was the demand of Jesus' commission. His baptism by John pointed to his identification with the people he came to save, and should be associated with his later reference to the cross: 'I have a baptism to be baptised with' (Luke 12:50). There are also the more explicit utterances at various stages of his ministry. 'My meat is to do the will of him that sent me' (John 4:34). 'I came down from heaven, not to do mine own will, but the will of him that sent me' (John 6:38). 'Therefore doth my Father love me, because I lay down my life that I might take it again . . . This commandment have I received of my Father' (John 10:17, 18). Thus the pivotal events of redemptive accomplishment—death and resurrection—he fulfilled in pursuance of the Father's commandment in the exercise of messianic authority.

The apostolic teaching in a similar way accords centrality to Christ's obedience (Rom. 5:19; Phil. 2:7, 8; Heb. 5:8, 9; 10:9, 10).

The evidence indicates that our thought of the atonement is not biblically oriented unless it is governed by this concept of obedience. It is not remiss to be reminded in this connection of the perceptiveness of the father of Reformed theology, John Calvin: 'Now someone asks, How has Christ abolished sin, banished the separation between us and God, and acquired righteousness to render God favourable and kindly toward us? To this we can in general reply that he has achieved this for us by the whole course of his obedience.'[1] And we scarcely need to be reminded of the prominence given in later Reformed theology to the active and passive obedience of Christ in the formulation of the doctrine of the atonement.

In attempting to expound this category of obedience, we may do so under four divisions.

THE INWARDNESS

There is the danger that we view the obedience mechanically or quantitatively, as if it consisted merely in the sum-total of formal acts of obedience. But an act externally conformed to God's requirements may not be one of obedience. To be an act of obedience, the whole dispositional complex of motive, direction, and purpose must be in conformity to the divine will. It was not otherwise in the case of our Lord. It was in human nature that Christ rendered the obedience required by his commission and office, and so the psychology of human action was applicable to him in all the intensity of the demands arising from his unique and incomparable undertaking as the Lord's Servant. We shall presently

---

[1] *Inst.* II, xvi, 5; E.T., Philadelphia, 1960, I, p. 507; cf. also II, xii, 3.

see the relevance of this in the interpretation of at least one of the most striking New Testament passages. And in the witness of Scripture it is to this psychology our attention is drawn. 'I delight to do thy will, O my God.' 'My meat is to do the will of him that sent me.'

THE PROGRESSIVENESS

It is in this respect that much of orthodox thinking has failed, and that for the reason that the implications of our Lord's human identity have been so often overlooked, and in some instances even resisted, lest, as is erroneously thought, prejudice would thereby be offered to his deity. Our Lord was truly human. The moment we think of human nature we must posit growth, development, progression. And so of Jesus we read that 'he increased in wisdom and stature and in favour with God and man' (Luke 2:52). If he increased in wisdom he must have increased in knowledge, and this increase in knowledge must have applied pre-eminently to his understanding of the Father's will and of the purpose for which he came into the world. But parallel to this there was increase in wisdom and therefore in the proper application of knowledge to the diverse situations as they emerged. This implies increase in obedience as the demands devolving upon him became more and more exacting, until they reached their climax in the death upon the accursed tree. Besides, Jesus increased in the favour of God. This could only be because the increasing demands of the Father's will were fully discharged, and elicited corresponding degrees of complacency on the Father's part. Furthermore, we are told that Jesus 'learned obedience from the things he suffered' (Heb. 5:8). Learning clearly implies process and progression.

This progression does not involve disobedience at any time. As in the case of knowledge, increase did not mean error or fallibility at any point; all that is meant is expansion. So in respect of obedience. In all circumstances, at every stage of his humiliation, he was obedient to the full extent of divine demand. But the demands became more extensive and exacting as he went on to the climactic demand, and as the implications of his commission became more fully known. And these expanding demands required increasing resources of obedient disposition, resolution, and volition. He learned obedience from the things he suffered.

THE CLIMACTIC DEMAND

The death upon the cross was the supreme act of obedience. The stress that falls upon the giving of his life in the teaching of Jesus himself (cf. Matt. 20:28; Mark 10:45; Luke 24:26, 46; John 3:14; 6:33, 51, 53–56; 10:11, 17, 18; 12:24, 32), and upon the death of Christ in apostolic teaching, clearly points to the cross as the pivotal event in the accomplishment of redemption, and the climax, though not the terminus, of obedience (cf. Phil. 2:7, 8). We are too ready to overlook the stupendous character of death as undertaken and undergone by our Lord. Death is abnormal, the wages of sin, and the contradiction of what Jesus was as holy, harmless, undefiled, and separate from sinners. In and of itself death cannot be contemplated except with horror, dread, and recoil. It is God's judgment upon sin, the expression of his holy wrath and vengeance. When thus considered, death takes on in Jesus' case unique and incomparable meaning. It is bereft of nothing that belongs to it as God's judgment upon sin. But in our Lord's case it was not an event that overtook him. Strictly speaking, it was not an infliction. It was an undertaking, a commitment assumed, an act to be effected by himself, the exodus that he was to *accomplish* at Jerusalem (cf. Luke 9:31). In the event he poured out his soul unto death, he laid down his life, he dismissed his spirit, he rent asunder the bond uniting the constituents of his human nature. He wrought what was in reality the contradiction of what he was as spotlessly human.

It is not merely the event of death that has to be taken into account; it was the accursed death of the cross, and this is the index to the implications of shame and reproach.

We may focus attention upon our Lord's prayers in Gethsemane and by this means gain some insight into these implications and into their bearing upon his obedience. When Jesus prayed: 'O my Father, if it is possible, let this cup pass from me: nevertheless not as I will but as thou wilt' (Matt. 26:39), we must not suppose that he did not desire that the cup should pass from him. This would negate the reality that formed the background of the prayer and the sincerity that must be predicated of the Saviour. So we must ask: How could such a desire be entertained? He knew he was to die. To the necessity he gave repeated expression on earlier occasions. The only explanation is that at this time there was an unprecedented enlargement of knowledge in reference to what was entailed in his sufferings, particularly his suffering unto death upon the accursed tree. Mark tells us that 'he began to be amazed' (14:33). The inference is inevitable. There now invaded his consciousness such increased understanding and experience of the involvements of his commitment, that amazement filled his soul. Our Lord was now looking into the abyss already beginning to inundate his soul, the abyss that he was to swallow up in himself. The recoil of his whole soul was inevitable. If he had not recoiled from the incomparable ordeal, it would be unnatural in the deepest sense. We must reckon with the enormity of his agony and the reality of his human nature. Here was the unrelieved, unmitigated judgment of God against sin. It filled him with horror and dread. The recoil evidenced in the prayer is the proof of the ordeal and of the necessary sensibilities and sensitivities of his human nature.

The accent upon the necessity and reality of recoil, and of the prayer reflecting it, throws into relief the intensity of his obedience. The reservation in the first prayer, 'Nevertheless, not as I will, but as thou wilt', evinces complete resignation to the Father's will. At the next stage there would appear to be increased recognition of the inevitable and correspondingly greater resignation: 'O my Father, if this cup may not pass from me except I drink it, thy will be done' (Matt. 26:42). But at the final stage we have the triumphant protestation to Peter: 'Thrust thy sword into its sheath: the cup which my Father hath given me, shall I not drink it?' (John 18:11). We cannot but observe the contrast and therefore the development of our Lord's thought and resolution. How eloquently this exemplifies and corroborates the statement: 'He learned obedience from the things he suffered'. And it is the intensity of holy revulsion that accentuates his unflinching commitment to the Father's will.

The figure Jesus used bespeaks voluntary action on his part. The Father, indeed, gave the cup; gave it, as it were, into our Lord's hand. But he must drink it. He must drink it to its dregs. Any attempt to deny or tone down the reality of his recoil and revulsion betrays our failure to appreciate the bitterness of the cup and the intensity of his commitment to the Father's will. It was the cup of damnation voluntarily taken, vicariously borne, and finished in his agony.

THE DYNAMIC

We must ask the question: Whence the disposition, resolution, and volition constituting him equal to every demand and particularly that of his climactic undertaking? We may not entertain any mechanical notion of Christ's obedience. As observed earlier, it was in human nature he obeyed, and the psychology of human nature was fully operative in the rendering of this obedience. So the psychology of human nature is fully enlisted, enlisted on the highest level, in the fulfilment of a commission that has no parallel. It is to this psychology that two passages in particular bear witness. They are Hebrews 2:10 and 5:8, 9. 'It became him, on account of whom are all things and through whom are all things, in bringing many sons unto glory, to make the captain of their salvation perfect through sufferings.' 'Though he was Son, he learned the obedience from the things he suffered. And being made perfect, he became for all those that obey him the author of eternal salvation.' The 'being made perfect' has obvious reference to his being constituted to perfection as the captain and author of salvation, and can never be conceived of except in this office and relationship. But what is of special relevance to our present interest is that he was made perfect through sufferings, and learned the obedience from the things he suffered. His obedience was forged in the furnace of trial, temptation, and suffering. By these ordeals throughout the whole course of humiliation, his heart, mind, and will were framed, so that in each situation as it emerged in the unfolding of the Father's design he was able to meet all the demands, and at the climactic point of his commission, freely and fully to drink the cup of damnation and pour out his soul in death.

In conclusion it should be noted how these two passages relate the obedience of Christ to salvation in its inclusive and ultimate reference. In his identity as captain of salvation, Jesus is viewed as conducting the sons of God to the full possession of that designed for them, the sons brought to glory. As the author of salvation, it is *eternal* salvation he procures and bestows. The *obedience* is that by which he is furnished so as to fulfil these rôles, to conduct to salvation and to bestow it. In other words, the obedience is the accomplishment that procures salvation and ensures its bestowal. No consideration could more definitely institute the place that obedience occupies in the securing and imparting of salvation in its all-embracing connotation. In other passages the obedience of Christ is set forth as the basis or medium of more specific elements in salvation. In Paul's statement 'By the obedience of the one shall many be constituted righteous' (Rom. 5:19), the obedience of Christ is brought into relation to justification as its basis or ground. In Hebrews 10:10 the obedience is viewed as that by which we are sanctified, and this sanctifying is probably conceived rather as the purification from sin derived from Christ's expiatory offering. But in Hebrews 2:10 and 5:8, 9, it is salvation inclusively considered that is derived from the obedience of Christ. So we must say that the obedience of Christ is that which procured salvation in broadest compass. Salvation must never be conceived of in design, accomplishment, or actual possession, apart from Christ as the Saviour. And salvation is secured by the obedience of Christ, because it was by obedience that Jesus as God-man was constituted the all-sufficient and perfect Saviour.

IV

15

The Call

When we use this term 'the call', it is not immediately apparent what the precise reference is. The call of God has several applications. It is used of the vocation which in the providence of God we are called to fulfil (1 Cor. 7:20, 24). It is also used of call to special office in the church of God (Rom. 1:1; 1 Cor. 1:1). In reference to the gospel the appeal to sinners, without distinction, to repentance and faith, is designated the call of God (Prov. 8:4; Matt. 22:14). But it is striking that in the New Testament, with scarcely an exception, the terms when used of the call to salvation, are applied to the call that is effectual, conjoined with predestination, on the one hand, and union with Christ, justification, and glorification, on the other. Such passages as Romans 8:28–30; 1 Corinthians 1:9; Galatians 1:15, clearly indicate what the denotation and connotation are. This preponderant usage shows that when we use the term without further qualification we should think of the effectual call. If we are governed by the pattern of New Testament usage, it is not necessary to specify by the introduction of the word 'effectual'. What is denoted by this word is implied in the simple designation 'the call'. The call is within the compass of the application of redemption.

THE PRIORITY

Although no fundamental issue of theology, or specifically of soteriology, would be at stake if regeneration were given the priority in the application of redemption, yet the evidence shows that the call occupies this position. If we fail to accord to it the place which the exegetical considerations demand, we miss a great deal of the emphasis of Scripture and we are also liable to overlook what belongs to its specific and distinguishing character. The key passage evincing its priority is Romans 8:29, 30. There are so many indications of order in this passage that we are compelled to regard the apostle as enunciating the order: calling, justification, glorification, in verse 30, and also establishing calling as the act of grace directly joined to predestination, and as that which in the realm of application brings the latter to expression. Other passages, particularly those in the Pauline epistles, create the strongest presumption in favour of the conclusion which Romans 8:29, 30 would require (cf. 1 Cor. 1:9; Gal. 1:15; 2 Tim. 1:9; 1 Pet. 2:9; 5:10; 2 Pet. 1:10).

THE AUTHOR

God is the author. 'God is faithful by whom ye were called into the fellowship of his Son Jesus Christ our Lord' (1 Cor. 1:9). 'Be thou partaker of the afflictions of the gospel according to the power of God, who saved us and called us with a holy calling' (2 Tim. 1:8, 9; cf. also Gal. 1:15; 1 Thess. 5:23, 24; 2 Thess. 2:13, 14; 1 Pet. 5:10). This sustained emphasis should advise us that the call is an act of God's grace comparable in this respect to regeneration, justification, and adoption. It is an act of God, and of God alone, and does not derive its definition from any activity on our part, such as faith or repentance or conversion. Calling is not to be defined in terms of the responses which the called yield to this act of God's grace. As we examine the passages, this fact is forcibly thrust upon our attention and the lesson is apparent. The application of redemption begins with an act of God's grace that derives nothing of its character from any activity of ours. The pure sovereignty of God's grace is not suspended at the inception of the applicatory process.

God the Father is specifically the author. The evidence in support of this is copious (Rom. 8:30; 1 Cor. 1:9; Gal. 1:15; Eph. 1:17, 18). This aspect of biblical teaching is too frequently unobserved, and it is strange that students of Scripture should overlook it and neglect it. But how significant it is that God the Father is the agent in the inception of application! He is active in constituting the bond that unites to what he designed in his eternal counsel and accomplished through the redemptive work of his Son. It is God the Father who justifies and adopts. He also sanctifies. But we neglect something precious when we forget that it is God the Father who initiates salvation in actual possession by the call of his sovereign grace. To use the terms used by our Lord, he donates men to his own Son in the effectual operations of his grace (John 6:37).

THE CHARACTER

1. *An Act*. All the revelatory data would indicate that the call is an act and not a process. Those called are called to be saints (Rom. 1:7; 1 Cor. 1:2), and saintship in New Testament usage designates a status constituted. The call ushers into the fellowship of Christ (1 Cor. 1:9), a relationship once for all established. It is a call out of darkness into God's marvellous light (1 Pet. 2:9), into his own kingdom and glory (1 Thess. 2:12).

2. *Effective Summons*. When we consider the destination to which the call is directed—the fellowship of Christ, the kingdom of God, God's marvellous light, saintship, God's glory and virtue—the thought is that of being ushered into the blessings concerned. There is determinate action, and the call is invested with the efficacy that delivers to the destination intended. The call is God's action and it cannot be frustrated.

3. *Immutability*. Romans 8:28–30 puts this feature beyond dispute. The call is according to God's purpose; it finds its place in the centre of the chain which has its source in foreknowledge and its final issue in glorification. The prominence given to God's faithfulness in connection with the call, a faithfulness ensuring confirmation and preservation unto the end, is the guarantee that the calling of God is unrepented of on God's part. When Paul says 'God is faithful by whom ye were called into the fellowship of his Son' (1 Cor. 1:9), it is for the purpose of certifying that he will 'confirm you unto the end blameless in the day of our Lord Jesus Christ' (1 Cor. 1:8). And when he says, 'Faithful is he who calls you who also will do it' (1 Thess. 5:24), it is to assure those called that they will be sanctified wholly, their spirit, soul, and body being kept entire, and that they will be blameless at the coming of our Lord Jesus Christ (1 Thess. 5:23).

4. *High, holy, heavenly* (Phil. 3:14; 2 Tim. 1:9; Heb. 3:1), in its origin, intrinsic character, and destiny.

THE PATTERN

There are two considerations of particular importance.

1. *Eternal purpose.* That we are called according to purpose, and purpose defined in terms of foreknowledge and predestination is explicit in Romans 8:28, 29. And that the purpose is eternal is stated in 2 Timothy 1:9: 'according to his own purpose and grace, given to us in Christ Jesus before times eternal'. Thus the foreordination belonging to predestination to be conformed to the image of the Son is that in accordance with which the call takes place. The effect of all this is that as the determinate purpose cannot be annulled, so the call cannot fail of realization, nor can its grace be reversed. All the predestinated will be called, and the called will attain to the predestinated goal.

2. It is in Christ that the purpose was conceived. It is into union with Christ that the call ushers the partakers of it. But there is the union with Christ in accord with which the call takes place, and therefore precedent. Here is illustrated again the denotative co-extensiveness of design and realization. It is not only that the purpose was in Christ Jesus but the grace which the purpose embraced was given *us* in Christ Jesus before times eternal. So the *in Christ Jesus* has reference to the called before they existed and before they became the called. The distinction between the fellowship with Christ constituted by the call, and the precedent union with Christ, must be maintained. But the latter is the pattern and measure of the former. The eternal purpose must never be conceived of apart from Christ, and the call itself must never be thought of apart from the fellowship with Christ into which it ushers. The purpose is the purpose of the Father, the call is the Father's act. But neither the purpose nor the call is apart from Christ, and we have another example of inter-trinitarian conjunction. Significantly enough, it appears at the inception of the application of redemption.

TERMINUS AD QUEM

The fellowship of Christ (1 Cor. 1:9), the fellowship of the saints (Col. 3:15), the peace of God and good will to all men (1 Cor. 7:15; Gal. 1:15–16; 1 Pet. 3:9), holiness (1 Thess. 4:7; 5:23, 24), light (1 Pet. 2:9), liberty (Gal. 5:13), hope (Eph. 1:18; 4:4), patient endurance of persecution (1 Pet. 2:20, 21), God's kingdom of glory (1 Thess. 2:12), eternal life and glory (2 Thess. 2:14; 1 Tim. 6:12; 1 Pet. 5:10; Heb. 9:15; Rev. 19:9).

THE OBLIGATIONS

Since it is a high calling (Phil. 3:14), a heavenly calling (Heb. 3:1), and a holy calling (2 Tim. 1:9), the obligations correspond with the dignity involved in these characterizations. We are to walk worthily of it and of God who called.

Peter's exhortation (2 Pet. 1:10) is particularly noteworthy. He focuses attention upon the fount of salvation and upon the inception of its actual realization, the actions which are specifically those of the Father.

DEFINITION

Calling is the efficacious summons on the part of God the Father, in accordance with and in pursuance of his eternal purpose in Christ Jesus, addressed to sinners dead in trespasses and sins, a call that ushers them into fellowship with Christ and into the possession of the salvation of which he is the embodiment; a call immutable in its character by reason of the purpose from which its proceeds and the bond it effects.

These features, derived from the biblical data, show plainly that the theological formulation of this doctrine has not been successful in placing in the forefront the distinctive features of this act of God's grace. The definition of the Shorter Catechism illustrates this defect. It speaks of effectual calling as a work when, in terms of the usage of the Catechism, it should be designated an act no less than justification and adoption. Then the Catechism construes calling as specifically the action of the Holy Spirit, when the Scripture refers it specifically to God the Father. In accord with the terms 'work of God's Spirit' the Catechism defines the action in terms of subjective effects wrought in us by the Spirit and of response on our part in the embrace of Christ by faith. But the accent that falls upon God as the author should advise us that we may not define the act in terms of our response, nor in terms of the subjectively operative factors necessary to constrain that response. In this respect calling is to be co-ordinated with justification and adoption.

Neither of these takes place apart from faith. Yet neither is to be defined in terms of faith, nor in terms of the convicting, enlightening, and renewing operations of the Spirit necessary to faith. The same is true of calling.

The fact that calling is an act of God, and of God alone, should impress upon us the divine monergism in the initiation of salvation in actual possession. We become partakers of redemption by an act of God that instates us in the realm of salvation, and all the corresponding changes in us and in our attitudes and reactions are the result of the saving forces at work within the realm into which, by God's sovereign and efficacious act, we have been ushered. The call, as that by which the predestinating purpose begins to take effect, is in this respect of divine monergism after the pattern of predestination itself. It is of God and of God alone.

The fact that calling is the act of God the Father apprizes us that God the Father is the specific agent in the initiatory act of application, and when this is not perceived or sufficiently appreciated, we rob our faith of an all-important element in the economy of salvation. We think of the Father's love in election, of his love in sparing not his own Son, in making him sin for us. We are overwhelmed with adoring amazement. But let us not overlook the Father's love in the initial act of salvation possessed. It is he who constitutes the bond with the Saviour and therefore puts us in possession of all that the Saviour is. It is of the Father that Christ is made unto us wisdom, righteousness, sanctification, and redemption.

16

Regeneration[1]

W E are dealing with the application of redemption, with the question how men actually become partakers of the blessings of the eternal covenant ratified and sealed by the redemptive work of Christ. This application is initiated by an effectual call on the part of God. He summons men into union and fellowship with his Son so that, united to him in whom all spiritual blessings are treasured, they come to possess Christ and all that belongs to him in his capacity as Saviour and Redeemer.

We must bear in mind, however, that this call with which the *ordo salutis* begins involves not only an operation on the part of God but response on the part of those called. The very term *call* implies this. It is a call and is therefore addressed to our consciousness. It consequently involves the engagement and response of our consciousness.[2] It is not the efficacious grace, nor the Holy Spirit as the agent of that grace, that answers the call and appropriates the blessings entailed. It is the person called, enabled thus to act in virtue of efficacious grace. And our question in the topic 'regeneration' is: how does the Holy Spirit operate in man in order to produce this effect? What is wrought in man by the Spirit's agency so that the appropriate response to the call may be elicited?

First of all, it is necessary to demonstrate the need of antecedent efficacious grace and thus lay the basis for an understanding of the subject

[1] See: B. B. Warfield: 'The Biblical Notion of Renewal' in *Biblical Doctrines*, New York 1929, pp. 439ff. *Princeton Theological Review*, Vol. IX, pp. 242ff. *Biblical and Theological Studies*, Philadelphia 1952, pp. 351ff.
[2] For Professor Murray's later view that 'Calling is not to be defined in terms of the responses which the called yield to this act of God's grace', see p. 162.

we have now in hand, namely, 'regeneration'. In order to do this it is necessary to set forth the facts of *complete* and *universal* sinfulness:

1. *The Totality of Pollution* Man is totally corrupt; sin has taken possession of his whole being. The inmost springs of desire, disposition and motive are corrupted or depraved: the source of intellectual, emotional and volitional activity is enmity against God. Man is under the dominion of sin. 'Of whom a man is overcome, of the same is he brought in bondage' (2 Peter 2:19). The imagination of the thoughts of man's heart is only evil continually (cf. Gen. 6:5). 'The heart is deceitful above all things and desperately wicked' (Jer. 17:9). The imagination of the thought of man's heart is evil from his youth and we go astray from the womb speaking lies. We drink down iniquity like water. Out of the heart proceed evil thoughts, fornications, thefts, murders, adulteries, covetings, wickednesses, deceit, lasciviousness, an evil eye, railing, pride, foolishness; all these things come from within and defile us. The carnal mind is enmity against God. It is not subject to the law of God and cannot be.

Can a fountain send forth both sweet water and bitter? Can a corrupt tree bring forth good fruit? Who can bring a clean thing out of an unclean? How can we, being evil, speak good things? An evil man out of the evil treasure of his heart brings forth that which is evil.

This pollution has permeated every part of our being and there is no part, or member, or function immune to the taint of corruption. If some part were clean, there might be hope that through nurture, education and development, under the proper conditions, it might work restoration and recuperation in the surrounding mass of corruption. It might recapture the whole personality. But there is no such survival or area of immunity. There is no pure area, no part in alliance with God, no germ of holiness and truth (see Rom. 3:10–18). To them that are defiled and unbelieving is nothing pure but even their minds and consciences are defiled. The desires, impulses, principles and functions have all together become filthy. Education, development, evolution are out of the question for there is nothing pure to develop.

From the aspect of self-help and from the aspect of the resources of human nature, our case is hopeless. No combination of available or conceivable resources under heaven can cure a sin-diseased and sindistempered soul or heart. No invention or convention can eradicate the sinfulness of human nature. We are dead in trespasses and sins.

By death we do not mean the cessation of activity; trespasses and sins are states or conditions in which we are active. This death simply means that being alienated from God we totally cease to be active in ways that are well-pleasing to him and are active in ways displeasing to him and opposite to his will. The carnal mind is not dormant; it is enmity against God. There is no neutrality. With characteristic incisiveness and exclusiveness Jesus stated: 'He that is not with me is against me'. They that are in the flesh cannot please God.

2. *The Universality of Sinfulness* Sin is not only complete intensively; it is universal extensively. There are no exceptions. For all have sinned and come short of the glory of God. 'There is none righteous, no, not one: there is none that understandeth, there is none that seeketh after God. They are all gone out of the way, they are together become unprofitable; there is none that doeth good, no, not one' (Rom. 3:10–12).

If this is man's condition in sin, then there can be no pleasure in the will of God. Enmity against God must express itself in opposition to every manifestation of his holy will. How then can we expect that man will answer with delight the call to enter into God's kingdom of glory and virtue? How can a man dead in trespasses and sins, and at enmity with God, answer a call to the fellowship of the Father and the Son? How can a mind darkened and depraved have any understanding or appreciation of the treasures of divine grace? How can his will incline to the overtures of God's grace in the gospel? The overtures of grace are summed up in the call to acceptance of him who is the image of the invisible God, the brightness of his glory and the express image of his substance, the one in whom are hid all the treasures of wisdom and knowledge. If the carnal mind is enmity against God surely this enmity will come to its most violent and virulent expression at the point where the revelation of the divine glory reaches its zenith, and this is the point at which we have the supreme exhibition of the wisdom, and power, justice and holiness, love and mercy of God. How can a child of darkness come to walk in the light as God is in the light, and become an heir of the inheritance of the saints in light?

All along the line of the obligations, overtures and privileges of the divine call, there is an utter incongruity between the condition of the called and the calling. The response to the call is a whole-souled movement of loving subjection and trust in God. It is a totality act of man's soul, as Brunner says. It is a turning to God with the whole heart and soul and strength and mind. Now, whence the inclination and the desire, the motive and the will? How can there be a totality act of loving trust when the attitude of man is total distrust?

The answer to these questions is impossibility, moral and spiritual. None other than our Lord expresses and confirms this impossibility when he says, 'No man can come unto me, except the Father who hath sent me draw him' (John 6:44). 'No man can come unto me, except it were given unto him of my Father' (John 6:65). And Paul does the same when he says, 'They that are in the flesh cannot please God' (Romans 8:8); also 'The natural man receiveth not the things of the Spirit of God: for they are foolishness unto him: neither can he know them, because they are spiritually discerned' (1 Cor. 2:14).

But the question must have an answer in another direction, since the call is effectual and does meet with the appropriate response. The only possible answer is that there must be a change that man himself cannot initiate, a change that cannot take its origin from resources resident in human nature, a change radical and all-pervasive. The only outlet is that man's subjective disposition and *habitus* be renewed, that an all-pervasive moral transformation, changing the whole man in heart, disposition, inclination, desire, motive, interest, ambition and purpose, be effected.

The glory of the gospel in this connection is that the divine remedy for the contradiction descends to the lowest depths of man's need, and meets all the exigencies of man's moral and spiritual conditions. What is impossible with man is possible with God, for he calls the things that be not as though they were. We have to reckon with the revelation and exercise of God's recreative power and grace. In promise and fulfilment the message of the gospel is, 'A new heart also will I give you, and a new spirit will I put within you: and I will take away the stony heart out of your flesh, and I will give you an heart of flesh' (Ezek. 36:26; cf. Ezek. 11:19). 'If any man be in Christ, he is a new creature. Old things are passed away: behold, all things are become new' (2 Cor. 5:17).

There is a change that God effects in man, radical and reconstructive in its nature, called new birth, new creation, regeneration, renewal—a change that cannot be accounted for by anything that is in lower terms than the interposition of the almighty power of God. No combination, permutation or accumulation of earth-born forces can explain it or effect it. In the words of Stephen Charnock, 'It is not an excitation or awakening of some gracious principle which lay hid before in nature under the oppression of ill habits, as corn lay hid under the chaff but was corn still; not a beating up something that lay skulking in nature, not an awakening as of a man from sleep; but a resurrection as of a man from death; a new creation, as of a man from nothing. It is not a stirring up old principles and new kindling of them.'[1]

It is the Holy Spirit working directly, efficaciously and irresistibly upon man's heart and mind, making the man over again, and creating him anew after the image of Christ in holiness and righteousness of the truth. A revolution, a reconstruction takes place at the centre of man's moral and spiritual being: sin and pollution are dethroned in the citadel of man's being, and righteousness takes its place. 'Regeneration', says Charnock again, 'is a mighty and powerful change wrought in the soul by the efficacious working of the Holy Spirit, wherein a vital principle, a new habit, the law of God, and a divine nature, are put into and framed in the heart, enabling it to act holily and pleasingly to God, and to grow up therein to eternal glory . . . There is a change, a creation, that which was not is brought into a state of being.'[2] In the language of Jonathan Edwards, 'There is a new foundation laid in the nature of the soul for a new kind of exercise.'

This deep-seated transformation must express itself in all the relations of life. The governing disposition, the character, the mind and will are renewed and so the person is now able to respond to the call of the gospel and enter into the privileges and blessings of the divine vocation. He is enabled to embrace Jesus Christ as freely offered in the gospel and to enter into his kingdom and fellowship. Formerly he was at enmity with God but now he comes to find in him his supreme delight. Formerly dead in sins, he is now alive to righteousness. Formerly sitting in dark-

[1] *Complete Works of Stephen Charnock* (Nichol, Edinburgh) 1865. Vol. III, p. 92.
[2] *Idem.* Vol. III, pp. 87–88.

ness and in the shadow of death, now he comes to walk in the light as God is in the light.[1]

This change, as it is viewed in all its implications and consequences, is, of course, a complex event embracing a variety of factors and aspects. But the aspect in which we are now particularly interested is the inceptual act of God as it terminates on man's heart and mind, namely, that underneath all those acts of ours like faith, repentance, conversion, there is the mysterious, supernatural, efficacious activity of the Holy Spirit which precedes in the order of causation every activity of ours. This initial step is that in which God is active, as he is in the resurrection from death to life. It is the act of communicating or imparting life to the dead, it is the act by which God generates new life. It is true that once life is imparted it immediately becomes active. But the communication is one thing, the exercising of it another. To be born is one thing; to be active as a newborn child is another.

In Systematic Theology it is necessary to distinguish the various elements and factors in this total change and to define the relation between the agency of the Holy Spirit and the activities on the part of the human agent. In later Reformed theology the term *regeneration* has been chosen to designate the initial act, that act in which God alone is active, while *conversion* is frequently used to designate the logically subsequent phase in which the person is active as a result of the grace which in regeneration has been imparted to him, and in connection with which the person's consciousness is engaged in the exercise of faith and repentance. Regeneration in this restricted sense is logically antecedent to any saving response in the consciousness or understanding of the subject. Regeneration is a change wrought by the Spirit in order that the person may savingly respond to the summons, or demand of the call, embodied in the gospel call. God's call is an efficacious summons and therefore carries with it, carries as it were in its bosom, the grace that ensures the requisite response on the part of the subject.

THE OLD TESTAMENT BIBLICAL EVIDENCE

As on many other topics, the greater part of the evidence is derived from the New Testament, but because of the unity of revelation and the unity

[1] *cf.* B. B. Warfield—*Biblical Doctrines*, p. 439.

of what we call both Testaments, what is patent in the New is latent in the Old. The need is one, the covenant of grace and the way of salvation is one, the faith that saves is one. As our Confession says, 'This covenant was differently administered in the time of the law, and in the time of the gospel: under the law it was administered by promises, prophecies, sacrifices, circumcision, the paschal lamb, and other types and ordinances delivered to the people of the Jews, all fore-signifying Christ to come, which were for that time sufficient and efficacious.

'Under the gospel, when Christ the substance was exhibited, the ordinances in which this covenant is dispensed are the preaching of the word, and the administration of the sacraments of Baptism and the Lord's Supper . . . There are not therefore two covenants of grace differing in substance, but one and the same under various dispensations.'[1]

There are therefore in our subject Old Testament adumbrations. We need simply to look at such passages as Deuteronomy 10:16 'Circumcise therefore the foreskin of your heart, and be no more stiffnecked'; 30:6: 'And the Lord thy God will circumcise thine heart, and the heart of thy seed, to love the Lord thy God with all thine heart, and with all thy soul, that thou mayest live.'

Jeremiah 31:33: 'But this shall be the covenant that I will make with the house of Israel; after those days, saith the Lord, I will put my law in their inward parts, and write it in their hearts; and will be their God and they shall be my people.' (cf. 32:39). 24:7: 'And I will give them an heart to know me, that I am the Lord.' The difference is not absolute but relative. It is the speciality of the measure of grace under the New Covenant that is stressed; it is not a denial of regenerating or forgiving grace existing in the Old.

Ezekiel 36:25-27: 'Then will I sprinkle clean water upon you, and ye shall be clean: from all your filthiness, and from all your idols, will I cleanse you. A new heart also will I give you, and a new spirit will I put within you, and I will take away the stony heart out of your flesh, and I will give you an heart of flesh. And I will put my spirit within you, and cause you to walk in my statutes, and ye shall keep my judgments and do them.' (cf. also 11:19).

As Dr. Warfield says, 'The recreative activity of the Spirit of God is

[1] *Westminster Confession*, Chapter VII, v and vi.

made the crowning Messianic blessing (Isa. 32:15, 34:16, 44:3, 59:21, Ezek. 11:19, 18:31, 36:27, 37:14, 39:29, Zech. 12:10); and this is as much as to say that the promised Messianic salvation included in it provision for the renewal of men's hearts as well as for the expiation of their guilt.'[1]

There can then be no doubt that the Old Testament in prophecy testifies to regeneration as one crowning blessing, if not *the* crowning blessing, of salvation on its subjective side as it was to be realized in the Messianic age.

We cannot mistake the fact that in the foreground of such passages there is both a collective and prospective reference. Yet we cannot restrict their application to the collective aspect. The realization of the blessing in its collective features will have, as its prius, individual application; the regeneration of Israel will proceed in proportion to the regeneration of the individuals who compose it. The writer to the Hebrews cannot by any means be said to restrict the great Jeremiah prophecy to a merely national blessing. And besides, when we think of passages like 'They shall teach no more every man his neighbour, and every man his brother, saying, Know the Lord: for they shall all know me, from the least of them unto the greatest' (Jer. 31:34), and 'all thy children shall be taught of the Lord; and great shall be the peace of thy children' (Isa. 54:13), the individual aspect becomes explicit. God assumes relations to the individual, and operates and dwells in him. 'I dwell in the high and the holy place, with him also that is of a contrite and humble spirit, to revive the spirit of the humble, and to revive the heart of the contrite ones' (Isa. 57:15). 'To this man will I look, even to him that is poor and of a contrite spirit, and trembleth at my word' (Isa. 66:2).

THE TEACHING OF JESUS IN JOHN 3:3–8

In the teaching of Jesus the most relevant and explicit episode is the encounter with Nicodemus. We are not to think that Jesus' discourse in the third chapter of John's Gospel is an excrescence on his teaching and not harmonious with his uniform emphasis. (It is not only in line with his teaching elsewhere; the fact is that the doctrine of the new birth occupies a place which, if it were not filled, would leave an obvious

[1] *Biblical Doctrines*, p. 445. *Biblical and Theological Studies* pp. 357–8.

hiatus.) It is the logical link between his teaching respecting man's depravity, on the one hand, and his teaching respecting the demands and requirements of the kingdom of God on the other. The Sermon on the Mount would be unintelligible without the presupposition of the new birth. 'For I say unto you, that except your righteousness shall exceed the righteousness of the scribes and Pharisees, ye shall in no wise enter into the kingdom of heaven' (Matt. 5:20).

Jesus has nothing good to say about the unregenerate heart. There is nothing from without a man that entering into him can defile him, but the things that come out of him, these are the things that defile him (cf. Mark 7:18–23). If the fountain of man's character is polluted thus, how can anything good come out of him? This is the very question our Lord asks: the answer is a decisive negative. 'How can ye, being evil, speak good things?' 'Either make the tree good, and his fruit good; or make the tree corrupt and his fruit corrupt . . . A good man out of the good treasure of the heart bringeth forth good things: and an evil man out of the evil treasure bringeth forth evil things' (Matt. 12:33–35).

The only answer to the situation of the corruption predicated of man in our Lord's teaching is divine monergism. And again that is precisely what our Lord's teaching provides. After the meeting with the rich young ruler, commendable in so many respects but wedded to his riches and not prepared to meet the cost of discipleship, Jesus turned to his disciples and said, 'Verily I say unto you, that a rich man shall hardly enter into the kingdom of heaven.' The disciples were amazed at the apparent impossibility of a camel going through the eye of a needle and they replied, 'Who then can be saved?' Jesus' reply is so significant: 'With men this is impossible; but with God all things are possible' (see Matt. 19:16–26).

Our Lord's discourse in John 6 is to the same effect. 'No man can come to me, except the Father which hath sent me draw him'. 'No man can come unto me, except it were given unto him of my Father'. A true apprehension and appropriation of Christ is the one thing indispensable to salvation. But that true assessment can only be as it is given of the Father. 'As the Father raiseth up the dead, and quickeneth them; even so the Son quickeneth whom he will' (John 5:21).

The discourse to Nicodemus is Jesus' commentary on his own teaching elsewhere both in John and the Synoptics. Here it is the radical nature of the change that is the most prominent feature. No external privilege, no hereditary quality, no birthright, no amount of good works, no self-discipline, no amount of adherence to rules, no degree of human effort, will make members of the kingdom of God. Membership is not an attainment, not a reward, not a prize. It is not what a person does that counts here. It is what occurs with reference to a person. It is not what a person effects but that of which a person is the recipient. There is no appreciation of, no entrance into, no life in, the kingdom of God except by a change as radical and momentous as birth. A person does not cause his birth to be; he is the subject of it. And this all ran completely counter to the most cherished notions of Pharisaical conceit. John 3 verses 3 and 5 are the declarations of what streaks through all of Jesus' teaching respecting the kingdom of God. 'Except ye be converted, and become as little children, ye shall not enter into the kingdom of heaven' (Matt. 18:3).

John 3:3 'Jesus answered and said unto him, Verily, verily, I say unto thee, Except one be born anew, he cannot see the kingdom of God.'

The word *anōthen* has been rendered both locally and temporally, 'from above' and 'anew'. Interpreters are divided. Meyer, for example, says that conformably to Johannine usage the only right rendering is the local, not only linguistically, but out of consideration to usage, for John apprehends regeneration, not according to the elements of repetition, a being born again, but a divine birth: cf. John 1:13; 1 John 2:29; 3:9; 4:7; 5:1, 4, 18. The idea of repetition, he says, is Pauline and Petrine and when *anōthen* is used temporally it does not mean *iterum* or *denuo* but *ex archēs*, 'from the beginning onwards' or 'throughout'. Bernard agrees with Meyer that in John the new birth is not conceived of after the manner of repetition but as birth into a higher sphere.

On the other hand Alford observes that in the Syriac, which goes back to the native soil of the language, the word used is one that means 'afresh' or 'anew' (cf. also Thayer: *Lexicon, in loco*, who disputes Meyer's insistence on the meaning 'from above'). It must also be noted that Nicodemus in his reply uses *deuteron* ('the second time', v.4). This latter fact need not be regarded as conclusive, because even if the word used by our Lord clearly meant 'from above' and was so understood by

Nicodemus, the latter might have used 'a second time' in his reply, because, not understanding the doctrine, he might have given expression to his bewilderment by focusing attention on the impossibility of a second birth, even though the word used by our Lord clearly indicated the supernatural character of the birth mentioned. Nicodemus might have been thinking of the mode whereas *anōthen* does not reflect on the mode but on the nature or character. The incomprehensibility of it might have been focused in his attention in the thought that it was a second birth. Or to put it otherwise, he might have been trying to justify his lack of understanding by concentrating on the thought of repetition. If we do not wish to think too prejudicially of Nicodemus we might say that he focused attention upon the thought of repetition as the consideration that was weighted with the greatest mystery for him. As if he should say, Yes, I can reckon with supernatural power but I cannot see how supernatural power can cause a man to be born anew again, how a man can enter again into his mother's womb and be born?

When we examine the usage of the New Testament we do find that the preponderant meaning is 'from above.' Cf. Matthew 27:51 ('from the top'); Mark 15:38 ('from the top'); John 3:31 ('he who comes from above is above all'); John 19:11 ('except it were given thee from above'); John 19:23 ('woven from the top throughout'); James 1:17 ('every perfect gift is from above'); James 3:15 ('this wisdom cometh not down from above'); James 3–17 ('but the wisdom from above is first pure').

The only instance in the New Testament where it has the meaning 'again' is Gal. 4:9 and there it appears in conjunction with *palin-hois palin anōthen douleusai thelete* ('whereunto ye desire again to be in bondage')

In Luke 1:3; Acts 26:5 it has the meaning 'from the beginning'. *anō* has always the meaning 'from above' or 'up'. It is used nine times in the New Testament.

These are all the instances of its occurrence in the New Testament.

This consideration of the preponderant usage of the New Testament, together with the fact that John emphasizes the new birth as birth 'from God' and 'from the Spirit', makes out a very strong case for the meaning 'from above'. But there still remains an element of uncertainty even though it be slight. No great question is at stake, however, for even though the meaning be 'again', the context makes it plain that it is also 'from above' because it is *gennēthē*. Should this be rendered 'be born' or 'be begotten'? Bernard and Westcott, for example, contend for the latter, and that the analogy is not the female function in the bearing of children but the male function, namely, that of begetting—the Spirit is conceived of as the *begetter* of life.

As we study the New Testament usage of *gennaō* we find both senses, 'to beget' and 'to bear'.

In the active voice *gennaō* means 'to beget' in the following: passive in Matthew 1:2–16a; Acts 7:8,29 and 'to bear' (give birth to) in Luke 1:13,57; 23:29; John 16:21. Galatians 4:23 is doubtful; most probably it means 'to give birth to' but it may mean 'to beget'.

In the non-metaphorical instances of the passive, the meaning 'to be born' preponderates. But there are two instances in which the meaning 'begotten' is the more natural, namely, Matthew 1:20; Luke 1:35.

In the metaphorical instances, with which we are now concerned, the meaning 'beget' appears in Acts 13:33; Hebrews 1:5; 5:5, and it is the more natural if not necessary meaning in 1 Corinthians 4:15; Philemon 10. In all the other instances of the figurative—John 1:13; 3:3, 5, 6, 8; 1 John 2:29; 3:9; 4:7; 5:1, 4, 18 (2 Tim. 2:23 is different)—the question is therefore open. In 1 John 3:9 the thought appears to be derived from the analogy of human begetting, cf. 1 John 5:1. If so, then this would be the preferable rendering throughout 1 John. We cannot rule out the rendering 'to be born'. But 'to be begotten' is distinctly possible.

There is one thing we must say in this connection, that in the matter of the 'new birth' we must discount the distinction between 'begetting' and 'being born'. There is no warrant for positing a distinction between the divine begetting and the divine birth. That would be a pure fancy without doctrinal or exegetical or biblico-theological warrant. To be 'begotten again' and to be 'born again' are synonymous terms.

The use of this word *gennēthē* is most significant in the understanding of the Biblical teaching. It is obviously based on the analogy of human generation. The following observations are obviously to the point therefore:

1. When a baby is born or begotten a new individual life begins to exist. It is not the continuation, development, extension or transmigra-

tion of some other individual personal life. Though generated from the parents it has its own individual personal identity distinct from the parents of which it is born—there is an absolutely new individual life. So in the spiritual realm we must apply this principle. Something new and radical occurs. It is not a continuation or development of the natural life of the person concerned. It informs us that no amount of education, manipulation or nurture of the powers resident in man's natural life can produce it. Life must begin anew. There must be a radical beginning, a start as new and momentous as when in the sphere of nature a man is born.

2. This new thing is life.

3. The person begotten or born is passive. It is not by volition or determination on our part that we are born naturally. We were not born because we decided to be born. We were simply born. So the new birth is an event of which man is wholly the subject and not the agent. We were not born again because we decided to be born. In the words of John 1:13, 'born not of blood, nor of the will of the flesh, nor of the will of man, but of God'.

This new birth is indispensable to 'seeing' and 'entering into' the kingdom of God. In view of the context we cannot regard *idein* ('see', v. 3) and *eiselthein* ('enter', v. 5) as separable events but there is no doubt a distinction in concept. 'To see' may express the idea of intelligent understanding, cognition, appreciation, not mere observation in the sense of being spectator; and 'entering into' means actual entrance into the kingdom as members in the realm of life and privilege.

Verse 5: 'Jesus answered, Verily, verily, I say unto thee, Except one be born of water and the Spirit (*gennēthē ex hudatos kai Pneumatos*), he cannot enter into the kingdom of God.'

Here Jesus more fully explains what he means by *gennēthē anōthen* ('born again').

The first question is: are we to distinguish these two genitives or regard them as expressing one idea (*hendiadys*)? The latter is the view of Calvin. 'Ergo *aqua* nihil aliud est quam interior Spiritus Sancti purgatio et vegetatio. Adde quod non est risolens copulam exegetice sumi, quum scilicet posterius membrum explicatis est prioris'.[1] It is, of course, true, as we shall see later, that there is the very close co-ordination of two facts or factors, perhaps better still phases, but our Lord apparently wanted to lay stress on some particular aspect or implication of this birth by the use of *hudor* and lest we should miss something of this distinction we should look for the more exact and distinctive meaning.

The second question is: what is the precise significance of *hudōr* (water)?

There are many who regard the *hudōr* as an express reference to baptism. There are three modifications of this view.

1. The crassly sacerdotal view, that baptism is the indispensable medium of regeneration, and works *ex opere operato*.

2. The view entertained, for example, by Meyer, that baptism is the *causa medians* and the Holy Spirit the *causa efficiens*. There is of course a sacerdotalist bias and tendency in this view, but it may be distinguished from it in that baptism is not regarded as working *ex opere operato*, and that there must be conjoined with baptism the spiritual grace of the Holy Spirit regarded from a rather distinctly evangelical standpoint. Baptism is the *loutron palingenesias* 'the washing of regeneration' (Titus 3:5), but only as the divinely appointed means whereby the Holy Spirit works efficiently and efficaciously. There is in this view a bias to sacerdotalism on the one hand and to evangelicalism on the other.

3. The view of a goodly number of evangelical interpreters, represented, for example, by Alford, that baptism is the outward sign of the spiritual grace brought by the Holy Spirit. Baptism is not the means of regeneration but the sign and confirmation of it. Alford thinks that the key to the interpretation of this verse is the distinction between John's baptism as that of water and Jesus' baptism as that by the Holy Spirit. What Jesus is saying to Nicodemus in effect is that there must be complete baptism, the baptism of the Spirit that Jesus himself dispenses.

A view along this line need not be regarded as inconsistent with the

[1] Com. *in loco*, 'By water, therefore, is meant nothing more than the inward purification and invigoration which is produced by the Holy Spirit. Besides it is not unusual to employ the word *and* instead of *that is*, when the latter clause is intended to explain the former.'

context nor with the analogy of Scripture. Possibly baptism may be meant, and related to regeneration in a fashion similar to that which baptism, in the words of Peter, sustains to the remission of sin. 'Repent, and be baptized every one of you in the name of Jesus Christ for the remission of sins' (Acts 2:38). Baptism may be regarded as the outward pledge of the reality of our internal regeneration as well as the token of our sincerity.

The objection to this view is that faith is presupposed in baptism and there would have to be dislocation somewhere.

If we regard *hudōr* as baptism then we shall have to give to baptism an efficiency coordinate with *Pneumatos* (Spirit). The third view above does not do justice to the expression. It should be borne in mind that there is a sense in which various baptisms represented what water means. The following considerations, however, have to be borne in mind:

(i) The text does not say 'baptism'; it says 'water'. We must not too readily assume that the allusion is to baptism. We must not take it for granted that Jesus means baptism unless there is some compelling reason for thinking that in using the word *water* he meant the water of baptism. But there are, on the contrary, good reasons for thinking that he did not refer to baptism but to something else.

(ii) Christian baptism was not yet instituted when Jesus spoke these words. Meyer says the reference is to Christian baptism, but the kingdom of God existed and men were entering into it before Christian baptism was instituted. This is relevant. For how could Jesus be speaking to Nicodemus respecting a rite that had not yet been instituted?

(iii) Christian baptism is the sign and seal of regeneration rather than the means of effecting it.

(iv) Though Christian baptism represents regeneration, yet it would appear that the central significance and characteristic idea of baptism is union with Christ. It is difficult to bring this conception into relevant relation to this particular conversation, whereas the interpretation about to be developed would be calculated to bring to the attention of Nicodemus a great truth most pertinent to his need, intelligible to his mind, and directly germane to the subject of regeneration.

What then was the religious use of water that would or should be familiar to Nicodemus? We should keep in view the situation in which

Jesus spoke these words. He was engaged in a dialogue with Nicodemus on a basic religious question. Jesus wanted to convey to Nicodemus an idea of religious import which would be directly relevant to the subject of interest, and intelligible to Nicodemus. Now what religious idea would we expect to be conveyed to the mind of Nicodemus by the use of the word *water*? Of course, the idea associated with the religious use of water in the Old Testament and in that religious tradition and practice which provided the very context of Nicodemus' life and profession! And that simply means the religious import of water in the Old Testament, in the rites of Judaism, and in contemporary practice. When we say this, there is one answer. The religious use of water, that is to say, the religiously symbolic meaning of water, pointed in one direction, and that direction is purification. All the relevant considerations would conspire to convey to Nicodemus that message. And that message would be focussed in his mind in one central thought, the indispensable necessity of purification for entrance into the kingdom of God.

(a) In the Old Testament water often signified washing and purifying from the pollution of sin (cf. Psalm 51:2, 3; Isa. 1:16; Jer. 33:8; Ezek. 36:25; Zech. 13:1). The mention of water in the context of the conversation would be calculated to convey the message of purification and cleansing. Perhaps also proselyte baptism.

(b) John's baptism had just stirred the whole of Judea. In this very chapter we have reference to it (v. 23). John's baptism was unto purification from sin; it was unto repentance and remission of sin. It was, of course, baptism with water.

(c) We are told that, though Jesus himself baptized not but his disciples, yet baptism with water did accompany the ministry of Jesus at this time (cf. John 3:22, 26; 4:2). This also had purificatory meaning.

All these facts of religious usage and ritual would have been familiar to Nicodemus and would conspire to bring to the thought of Nicodemus one lesson, namely, that of purification. All lines would converge to impress upon him the absolute need of cleansing.

We know also that it was the manner of Jesus' teaching in dealing with particular cases to lay his finger very directly upon the characteristic sin and aberration of those with whom he was dealing. The characteristic sin of the Pharisees was self-complacency and self-righteousness. What they needed most was conviction of sin and pollution and of their need of radical purification. The word 'water' would convey this lesson most effectively. For Nicodemus was a Pharisee. We are told that the Pharisees rejected the counsel of God against themselves, being not baptized of John (Luke 7:30).

Gennēthē ex hudatos ('born of water'), would therefore mean to Nicodemus that entrance into the kingdom of God could only be by what was utterly repellent to him as a Pharisee, namely, thorough spiritual purification from the pollution and defilement of sin.

Water would then appear to point to three thoughts directly germane to this topic:

It points to the fact of pollution.

It points to the need of having that pollution thoroughly purged away.

The new life requisite for entrance into the kingdom of God must emerge from thorough purification. Cleansing is, as it were, the womb from which it must issue.

We *may* call this the negative aspect of regeneration; we *must* call it the purificatory. We must not, however, regard it as separable from the more positive, indicated, as we shall see, by *Pneumatos*. The very construction precludes this, for the whole phrase is *ex hudatos kai Pneumatos* (of water, and of the Spirit). The purification itself is by the agency of the Spirit. It is birth of the Spirit that includes the cleansing from pollution and the impartation of life.

There is no room for question but that the *Pneumatos* is the Holy Spirit—v. 6 says *ek tou Pneumatos* (cf. also v. 8, and, John 2:29; 3:9; 4:7; 5:1, 4, 18; John 1:13). Any other view would wreck the force of what is expressly stated in these other passages, to wit, that it is 'of God'. It is birth, then, of a specifically divine and supernatural character.

Ek Pneumatos, The Holy Spirit is the source of this begetting or birth.

Gennēthēnai, Entrance into the kingdom of God is by a method that involves our passivity as much as does our birth in the realm of nature. We are wholly dependent upon the agency of the Holy Spirit. The Holy Spirit is the sole agent or author. Man is the subject of an action of which the Holy Spirit is the sole author. Not by synergism or co-operation do we enter into the kingdom of God. We are now informed that it is by the determination, decision, and operation of the Holy Spirit that we enter into this life and are born into the kingdom of God.

Four thoughts are to be distinctly stressed. It is the *Holy Spirit* who effects this change. He effects it because he is the *source* of it. He effects it by the mode of *generation*. Since he effects it by this mode he is the *sole author* or *active agent*.

John 3:5 sets forth the two aspects from which the new birth must be viewed—it purges away the defilement of our hearts and it recreates in newness of life. The two elements of this text—'born of water' and 'born of the Spirit'—correspond to the two elements of the Old Testament counterpart: 'Then will I sprinkle clean water upon you, and ye shall be clean: from all your filthiness, and from all your idols, will I cleanse you. A new heart also will I give you, and a new spirit will I put within you: and I will take away the stony heart out of your flesh, and I will give you an heart of flesh' (Ezek. 36:25, 26). This passage we may properly regard as the Old Testament parallel of John 3:5, and there is neither reason nor warrant for placing any other interpretation upon 'born of water' than that of Ezekiel 36:25: 'Then will I sprinkle clean water upon you, and ye shall be clean'. These elements, the purificatory and the renovatory, must not be regarded as separable events. They are simply the aspects which are constitutive of this total change by which the called of God are translated from death to life, and from the kingdom of Satan into God's kingdom, a change which provides for all the exigencies of our past condition and the demands of the new life in Christ, a change which removes the contradiction of sin and fits for the fellowship of God's Son. (Cf. also Psalm 51:2, 7, 10.)

Verse 6: 'That which is born of the flesh is flesh; and that which is born of the Spirit is spirit.'

Sarx (flesh) is sometimes used in the New Testament without ethical depreciation. If so used here, then *sarx* refers to human nature. What would be affirmed in that case is that human nature propagates human nature and does not produce anything that transcends the conditions under which human nature finds itself. Like propagates like. Since human nature is under the dominance of sin, human nature cannot overcome these sinful conditions and cannot propagate anything but human nature labouring under these conditions.

However, as in John 6:63; 8:15, the depreciatory quality so frequently characterizing *sarx* in the usage of the New Testament appears to be present in this case.[1] It is not impossible to think of *sarx* in the first instance as used without ethical import, and in the second as with it. For that with which it is contrasted here does bear ethical quality: 'that which is born of the Spirit is spirit'—that is, human nature under the dominance of the Holy Spirit. And when 'flesh' is used with ethical connotation it carries ethical depreciation and means human nature as dominated by sin; in a word, sinful human nature. 'Born of the flesh' would then mean, 'born of human nature under these sinful conditions'. The principle that like propagates like holds in the moral and spiritual sphere as well as in the psychico-physical. Sinful human nature cannot transcend the conditions. Human nature is in this respect wholly impotent and hopelessly sterile. That which is born of the flesh is flesh, namely, human nature under the direction and control of sin.

Two thoughts are then emphasized here: 1. It is by natural generation that human nature under the dominance of sin is propagated; 2. natural generation inescapably produces that kind of human nature, human nature bound to, and characterized by, sinful conditions.

Pneuma (spirit) is human nature under the dominance of the Holy Spirit. Human nature of this sort is generated by the Holy Spirit. There are, again, two thoughts stressed. (i) It is by generation from the Spirit that human nature under the control of the Holy Spirit is produced; (ii) such spiritual generation inevitably produces that kind of human nature, human nature bound to, and characterized by, the control and direction of the Holy Spirit. Such generation cannot fail in its beneficent result and cannot be frustrated by human perversity. The person who is born of the Spirit is *pneumatikos* and he is *anthrōpos pneumatikos* (a spiritual man).

To sum up, we find in this verse that the distinction drawn is qualitative, not quantitative. The leading thought is that there are two kinds of birth and that each birth completely conditions the character of its

[1] For fuller examination of the New Testament usage of 'flesh' see the author's *The Epistle to the Romans*, vol. I, 1959, pp. 244–45 and elsewhere.

product. The natural cannot produce anything but the natural, and by an invariable law does produce the natural. The supernatural alone produces the supernatural, and it infallibly secures the supernatural character of its issue. That which is born of the Spirit is spirit, and it is *only* that which is born of the Spirit that is spirit. It follows, of course, that there are two classes of person in view—this is a consequence flowing from that which is expressly stated in the text.

Scripture and Christian history are strewn with lessons illustrative and corroborative of this truth. Many regenerated persons show uncouthness, so much so that we marvel how God's children can be so uncomely and even repellent. But in the day of trial they stand the test. The work of regenerating grace cannot be repressed or overcome and it evidences itself with striking vigour and beauty. In the final outcome the work of grace is vindicated and demonstrated. 'That which is born of the Spirit is spirit', is the truth emblazoned on the final outcome of their career. On the other hand many others show a great deal of adornment and refinement, so that they pass for excellent specimens of grace and virtue. But in the day of trial their beauty is consumed like a moth and the unregenerate heart appears in all its ugliness, unsanctified perversity and enmity. 'That which is born of the flesh is flesh', is the truth emblazoned on the final outcome of their career. Nature can never be whipped up to generate the work and fruit of the Spirit—'that which is born of the flesh is flesh'.

Verse 8: 'The wind bloweth where it will, and thou hearest the voice thereof, but knowest not whence it cometh, and whither it goeth: so is every one that is born of the Spirit.'

Alford argues that since *pneuma* occurs some 370 times in the New Testament and only here has been translated by the word 'wind' that this is an irrefutable argument against the accuracy of that rendering. Hence he contends that the proper rendering is, 'The Spirit breathes where He wills'. Origen, Augustine and Bengel, for example, adopt this rendering, and Bernard argues that the context removes all ambiguity.

If this rendering is followed then the comparison instituted is that between the generic activity of the Holy Spirit and the specific. To put it otherwise, the general features of the Holy Spirit's operation, to wit, invisibility, irresistibility, and sovereignty, are brought to bear upon regeneration; they are eminently and characteristically present in regeneration. In the apodosis it is the *ho gegennēmenos* ('every one who is born') that bears the emphasis.

The interpretation is tenable and, if adopted, does not radically affect the teaching of the verse. The emphasis and import remain the same. There are, however, some considerations that are pertinent and perhaps turn the scales in favour of the ordinary rendering of the text.

1. It is not the most natural rendering. We do not find in the analogy of Scripture usage that the work of the Spirit is compared with the work of the Spirit. It is more natural to suppose that the work of the Spirit is compared with something else.

2. It is in accord with the analogy of our Lord's teaching to institute comparison between the phenomena of nature and the truths respecting the kingdom of God. It would be entirely in accord with our Lord's method to find a parable here by which he illustrates the great truth of which he is speaking. In view of this we should expect that since the one side of the comparison is the work of the Spirit (the apodosis), the other side, that with which the work of the Spirit is compared, is not the work of the Spirit but rather that which illustrates it. So it is in accord with analogy and is therefore wholly natural to regard the protasis as referring to the wind. Following this rendering and yet not forgetting that the other will yield substantially the same results, we find the following emphases:

(i) The invisibility and mysteriousness of the Spirit's operation in the new birth—'thou dost not know whence it comes and whither it goes' (cf. 'As thou knowest not the way of the wind, nor how the bones do grow in the womb of her that is with child, even so thou knowest not the works of God that maketh all'. Eccl. 11:5).

(ii) The irresistibility and efficaciousness of the new birth—'the wind blows' (there is personification of the wind in this case). We cannot resist the wind nor change its course.

(iii) The sovereignty of the Spirit's operation in the new birth— 'where it wills'. We cannot control the wind nor can we cause it to blow when or where or how we wish.

(iv) The necessary observable fruit—'thou hearest the sound thereof'. While the wind is invisible, irresistible and not subject in any way to our will, it does manifest its presence where it is: we hear its effects. So is it with the new birth. It manifests itself in the fruit of the Spirit—'that which is born of the Spirit is *spirit*'.

By a secret, incomprehensible operation when, where, and how the Spirit pleases, he begets, or gives birth to, men, and this is a birth that becomes manifest in the fruits that are appropriate to its nature and purpose.

General Conclusion. To sum up the teaching of our Lord in this passage, it is to the effect that understanding of, and entrance into the kingdom of God, the discernment of its meaning and the enjoyment of its privileges, rights and blessings, are conditioned upon a sovereign, mysterious, efficacious activity, of which the Holy Spirit is the specific agent and man the subject, an activity that consists in cleansing or purifying from the pollution of sin and the constituting of a new man, indwelt, controlled and directed by the Holy Spirit, a birth inscrutable as to its mode of operation, nevertheless manifest in the observable fruit of the Spirit consonant with and evidential of, membership in the kingdom of God.

THE TEACHING OF PAUL

In the teaching of Paul we believe we have this same doctrine. As B. B. Warfield says, 'It is doubtless the peculiarly immediate and radical nature of his operation at this initial point which gives to the product of his renewing activities its best right to be called a new creation (2 Cor. 5:17; Gal. 6:15), a quickening (John 5:21; Eph. 2:5), a making alive from the dead (Gal. 3:21)'.[1] We do find, however, in Paul that the new birth in the priority of its conception as a creative act of God, is indissolubly related to the broader notion of renewal, including at least the earlier and probably later stages of conscious experience on the part of the renewed person. We proceed now to formulate Paul's doctrine rather briefly, i.e. his doctrine of renewal with specific reference to regeneration. But in so doing we meet with great difficulty because of the intertwining of his teaching with respect to regeneration, in the precise

[1] *Biblical Doctrines*, p. 456; *Biblical and Theological Studies*, p. 369.

sense of the initial step of renewal, with the subsequent processes of renewal which involves the exercises of our conscious minds. This only serves, however, to corroborate our contention that regeneration in its restricted sense is inseparable from faith and repentance and the subsequent life of new obedience.

Summarizing Paul's teaching however we have:

1. *Terminus a quo*

It is death in trespasses and sins, wherein men once walked according to the course of this world, according to the prince of the power of the air. It was a life lived in the lusts of the flesh and of the mind when men were by nature the children of wrath even as others. The understanding was darkened, being alienated from the life of God through the ignorance that was in them, because of the blindness of their heart. The works of the flesh were manifest—adultery, fornication, uncleanness, lasciviousness, idolatry, witchcraft, hatred, variance, emulations, wrath, strife, seditions, heresies, envyings, murders, drunkenness, revellings, and such like. By virtue of these, and the estrangement of heart and mind whence they proceeded, men were excluded from the kingdom of God, for no whoremonger, nor unclean person, nor covetous man who is an idolater hath any inheritance in the kingdom of Christ and of God. Men were, therefore, far off and enemies in their minds by wicked works, without God and without hope in the world. In a word, the old man was corrupt according to the deceitful lusts (1 Cor. 6:9, 10; Gal. 5:19–21; Eph. 2:1–3, 11–13; 4:18, 22).

2. *The Source of regeneration*

The source is the grace, mercy and love of God. It does not take its starting point from anything in us. It indeed finds its necessity in our corruption but its source is entirely in the free self-determining love of God. 'Not by works of righteousness which we have done but according to his mercy he saved us by the washing of regeneration and the renewing of the Holy Spirit' (Titus 3:5; Eph. 2:4–10).

3. *The Agent*

God is the agent. 'We are his workmanship, created in Christ Jesus unto good works.' More particularly it is God in the person of the Holy Spirit. 'Such were some of you, but ye are washed, but ye are sanctified, but ye are justified in the name of the Lord Jesus and by the Spirit of our God.' The law of the Spirit of life in Christ Jesus it is that has made us free from the law of sin and death. The letter killeth but the Spirit giveth life. The Holy Spirit as the specific agent is the Spirit of God, the Spirit of Christ, the Spirit of him that raised up Jesus from the dead, the Spirit of life in Christ Jesus; all which designations are replete with meaning as to the nature of his operation and the renewing effects of it in the renewed person (cf. Eph. 2:10; 1 Cor. 6:11; Rom. 8:2; 2 Cor. 3:16, 18; 1 Cor. 15:45).

4. *The Mediator.*

Christ is the Mediator.

Ephesians 2:10, 'Created in Christ Jesus unto good works'.

2 Corinthians 5:17, 'If any man be in Christ he is a new creature (*ktisis*)'.

5. *The Nature of the Operation and Product.*

(a) A new creation (Eph. 2:10; 4:24; 2 Cor. 5:17; Gal. 6:15).

(b) A new life (Eph. 2:1–5).

(c) A new man (Eph. 4:24; Col. 3:10).

6. *The Internal Sphere of Operation.*

The spirit of the mind (Rom. 12:2; Eph. 4:23).

7. *The Pattern* after which this renewal is fashioned is God's image (*kata theon*) (Col. 3:10; Eph. 4:24; 2 Cor. 3:18).

8. *The Terminus ad quem.*

They are renewed unto knowledge (*eis epignōsin*) and good works (Col. 3:10; Eph. 2:10).

9. *The Practical Exhortation*

Be renewed in the spirit of your mind (Eph. 4:23). Put off the old man with his affections and lusts, and put on the new man (Eph. 4:22, 23). Put on the Lord Jesus Christ. If we live in the Spirit let us also walk in the Spirit. Put off anger, wrath, malice, blasphemy, filthy communication out of your mouth (Col. 3:8, 9).

The practical exhortation, so far from being superfluous, in view of the sovereign and efficacious working of God rather flows from it as the natural consequence. The sovereign working of God, instead of making our activity superfluous, or discouraging unceasing effort on our part, is the very urge to it and dynamic in it. The more convinced we are of our dependence upon God and of his efficacious working in us, the more diligent we are in the use of those means and the exercise of those graces of which he is the author.

The exhortation does not imply that the initiation is a mark or act of ours, nor that its continued progress has its secret in our diligence, nor that its perfection lies in our power and will. But that God is the initiator, and the indwelling and operation of his Spirit the condition of its progress to completion, does, paradoxically as it may appear, involve the constant urge 'to that diligent co-operation with God in the work of our salvation to which he calls us in all departments of life, and the classical expression of which in this particular department is found in the great exhortation of Philippians 2:12, 13 where we are encouraged to work out our own salvation thoroughly to the end with fear and trembling on the express ground that it is God who works in us both the willing and the doing for his good pleasure.'[1]

In a word the realization of our complete dependence upon God, both in that act in which there is no co-operation on our part, for it is a new creation from God, and in those processes in which we do co-operate, is the proper condition of, and urge to, and dynamic in, our diligent, fervent and persistent application to the duties and works of the Christian vocation; in a word in the putting off of the old man and in the putting on of the new.

THE TEACHING OF JOHN

John 1:12, 13

Sonship rests upon a right given by God. *Exousia* denotes and connotes rightful, legitimate authority.

Tekna theou ('children of God'). *Tekna* comes from *tektein* which means 'to beget'. *Teknon* probably implies therefore a real communication of life from God. The thought may be that of 'the first origin of the new life, and not of the introduction of the living being into a new region', as Westcott contends.

There are in any case three things in the text:

1. The persons concerned are designated as *tekna theou*.

2. They are described as those who believe and those born, not of

---

[1] *Biblical Doctrines* p. 451; *Biblical and Theological Studies*, p. 363.

blood, nor of the will of the flesh, nor of the will of man, but of God.'

3. The authority by which they became sons.

Hoi ouk ex haimatōn-hoi refers to *tekna* as its antecedent according to *constructio ad sensum.*

The plural might be taken with Augustine to mean the two sexes, or as some think as having reference to the multiplicity and variety of ancestors who contribute to our nature and position—the Jews prided themselves on the variety of the lines of ancestry they had—or it might be taken as referring to the multiplicity of the elements of which the blood as the basis and seat of life is constituted, as Godet and Meyer and probably Bernard, or as denoting the element out of which the material body is formed (Westcott); but diversity of interpretation does not and ought not to obscure the main thought, namely, that generation of this sort is not by natural physical procreation, descent or heredity. That which is born of the flesh is flesh. The sonship of which John speaks is not of human generation. 'The negative statement exhibits them as those in whose coming into existence human generation has no part whatever.'

To this negation are added two additional negations expressed by two disjunctive negatives *oude . . . oude.*

Oude ek thelēmatos sarkos ('not of the will of the flesh'). Not by physical instinct, not by sexual desire, not by impulses that spring from the operation of the flesh, not by human volition or purpose, whether with or without ethical depreciation.

Oude ek thelēmatos andros ('nor of the will of man'). *Anēr* is used of the male in distinction from the female. It is not even by the volition and purpose of man.

These negations are cumulative in their effect and there may be a gradation from the lowest form of natural, human potency to the highest as it respects human generation. The implication is that in the whole realm of nature there is no element, impulse, instinct, desire, volition or purpose, and no combination or collusion of these, that will meet the demands correlative with the bestowment of authority to become children of God, *tekna theou.* To whatever height the present form of transmission may rise, it cannot overleap the limit traced by the first creation, that of the physico-psychical life. The generation that is co-ordinate with reception of Christ and the bestowal of authority to become children of God, and which is to result in confiding and the abiding trust in his name, is a generation from God.

God is the agent and God alone is the agent. There is no determination that proceeds from man. If a human factor could be conceived of as the determining one, this would annul both the positive and negative sides of the sentence. God is the agent or begetter without co-operation or collusion on the side of man. Here it is not convergence of divine and human factors. John piles up negatives to exclude human determination. The notion of synergism would wreck the whole purpose of the negatives and of the antithesis.

1 John 2:29; 3:9; 4:7; 5:1, 4, 18.

In 1 John 2:29; 4:7; 5:1, 4, 18 all that can be demonstrated is invariable concomitance of the divine begetting and the other qualities or characteristics mentioned: in 2:29 the concomitance of the divine begetting and doing righteousness; in 4:7 of the divine begetting and loving; in 5:1 of the divine begetting and believing that Jesus is the Christ; in 5:18 of divine begetting and not sinning, of divine begetting and keeping, of divine begetting and immunity to the touch of the evil one. But in 3:9 the causal relation is expressly and incontestably stated, so that not only are we told that there is unfailing concomitance of the divine begetting and not doing sin, of the divine begetting and incapacity to sin, but also that the reason why the person concerned does not commit sin and cannot sin is that he is begotten of God. Not sinning, and inability to sin, find their logical and efficient cause in the divine begetting. This, in other words, is to assert the logical priority of regeneration. In this verse this is asserted twice in the two clauses introduced by *hoti-hoti sperma autou en autō menei* ('for his seed remaineth in him'), and *hoti ek tou theou gegennētai* "because he is born of God'). The fruits mentioned follow of necessity from the impartation and abiding presence of the divine seed (*sperma*), the former asserted in the second *hoti* clause and the latter in the first.

In 1 John 5:4, while the *hoti* clause, like 2:29; 4:7; 5:1, 18, asserts the concomitance of the divine begetting and overcoming the world, yet it does also state a logical relation between the fact that the commandments are not grievous, on the one hand, and the other two concomitant facts on the other, assigning the logical causation to the latter or at least to the overcoming of the world. The reason then why God's commandments are not burdensome or grievous is that the person concerned has overcome the world, and the overcoming of the world stands in the closest co-ordination with the divine begetting. But the fact that the divine commandments are not grievous is very intimately connected with the doing of righteousness, the loving of one's neighbour, and the not doing of sin, mentioned in 2:29; 4:7; and 5:18 respectively. We should therefore be justified in concluding that these virtues also find their logical cause in the same consideration for which God's commandments are not grievous, namely, that every one begotten of God overcomes the world. That is to say, that a certain causal relationship exists between the divine begetting and the doing of righteousness, loving and not doing sin. We are, at least, warranted in concluding that these virtues mentioned in 2:29; 4:7; 5:18 do not stand on their own feet, but find their explanation in some other fact, namely, overcoming the world, which in turn stands in the closest co-ordination with the divine begetting.

Since the logical relation is expressly stated in 3:9, we should conclude that the same logical relation holds in all the other cases. This should be obvious from a study of 5:18. Though the logical or causal relation is not stated there, yet the teaching is closely parallel if not identical with 3:9, and so the priority of regeneration must be implied though not overtly stated. From 3:9 and 5:18 we discover then a principle that must apply to all the other cases. Therefore the necessary inference is that doing righteousness, not sinning, inability to sin, loving God and our fellowmen, believing that Jesus is the Christ, overcoming the world and willing subjection to the divine commandments, keeping oneself, and immunity to the defiling touch of the evil one, are all the logical consequence of regeneration.

When this principle is established from 3:9, we can add confirmation from a study of some of the passages themselves. In 2:29 the thought is: that God is righteous; God is the begetter of the new life; like begets like; therefore every one begotten of God does righteousness. The order of causation is apparent. In 4:7 the thought is: God is love; therefore love is of God; like begets like; therefore everyone begotten of God loves, and everyone who does not love is not begotten of God. As B. B. Warfield says, the 'new life will necessarily bear the lineaments of his new parentage'.[1]

To state the whole matter in slightly different order and terminology, the teaching of these passages in 1 John is to the effect that faith that Jesus is the Christ, overcoming the world, immunity from the dominion of the devil, self-control, abstinence from sin, inability to sin, righteousness of behaviour, delight in the commandments of God, love to God and to our fellow men, all are the fruits, unfailing accompaniments and evidences of the divine begetting, and they are such because in this sphere the principle that like begets like holds true in the highest degree. We see that John here covers the whole range of those virtues which characterize the image of God in us, knowledge, righteousness and holiness. To take them in order, they proceed from faith (5:1) to love (4:7). To use an expression of Bengel, 'Faith leads the band, and love brings up the rear'. If we look at 2 Peter 1:5-9, we find great similarity to the catalogue of virtues provided by John in this epistle: 'to your faith virtue . . . and to brotherly kindness love.'

CONCLUSION ON THE BIBLICAL EVIDENCE

To conclude our examination of these passages in the Gospel and Epistles of John, the new birth, to use Dr. Warfield's words, is 'brought before us . . . in the purity of its conception; and we are made to perceive that at the root of the whole process of "renewal" there lies an immediate act of God the Holy Spirit upon the soul by virtue of which it is that the renewed man bears the great name of son of God. Begotten not of blood, nor of the will of the flesh, nor of the will of man, but of God (John 1:13), his new life will necessarily bear the lineaments of his new parentage (1 John 3:9,10; 5:4,18): kept by him who was in an even higher sense still begotten of God, he overcomes the world by faith, defies the evil one (who cannot touch him), and manifests in his righteousness and love the heritage which is his (1 John 2:29; 4:7: 5:1)'.[2]

In these passages we have without question the biblical warrant for

[1] *Biblical Doctrines* p. 956; *Biblical and Theological Studies* p. 368.
[2] *ibid.*

conceiving of regeneration, in the restricted sense, as the initial step in the process of subjective renewal in which God, by a creative act, works directly in the heart of man, recreating man after his image and bringing him from death to life by the impartation of what is generated after his own moral likeness.

If regeneration is an immediate act of creative power it cannot be said to be wrought through the instrumentality of the Word of God in the sense of the gospel. For when we use the term the Word of God in such a sense we mean the Word of God proclaimed to us, addressed to our consciousness, operative in our consciousness, and engaging our consciousness with the appropriate effects. In other words, we do not mean the word of divine fiat, for that we must posit as the action of regeneration.

Now if this is so, it is to be understood that regeneration is not mediated through the Word as that Word engages our consciousness in the understanding of our faith.

In view of this how are we to understand such passages as James 1:18; I Peter 1:23?

In James 1:18 the verb is *apokueō* which literally refers to emergence from the womb, the part the mother plays in the bearing of a child—*boulētheis apekuēsen hēmas logō alētheias* ('of his own will begat he us with the word of truth'). It is possible that this does not refer to the specific act of regeneration. But is is also possible that it does. If so, then the Word of truth of the gospel is represented as the medium and therefore as instrumental in our understanding and will. (It is very likely that it is God's regenerative act that is referred to). There is a distinct similarity between that denoted by the verb and the very idea of birth. Besides, the accompanying thoughts are entirely consonant with those emphasized elsewhere in connection with regeneration. It is 'from above' (*anōthen*) as in verse 17; it is of God's sovereign good pleasure (*boulētheis*) as in verse 18. That is to say, the emphasis upon the supernatural and the sovereign would make it wholly congruous with regeneration, as the act contemplated in *apekuēsen*.

In I Peter 1:23 there can be no doubt but regeneration is in view, and undoubtedly through the instrumentality of the proclaimed gospel word—*anagegennēmenoi . . . dia logou zōntos theou kai menontos* ('being

born again . . . by the word of God which liveth and abideth for ever'
cf. v. 25—*to de rhēma Kuriou . . . to rhēma to euangelisthen* 'But the
word of the Lord . . . the word which by the gospel is preached unto
you'). Regeneration is conceived of as taking place through the Word
of the gospel as that Word engages our consciousness in saving understanding and response.

What is to be our solution? It must be that regeneration is used in
two distinct senses in the New Testament:
(1) in the restricted sense of recreative action on the part of God in which
there is no intrusion in contribution of agency on our part; (2) in a
more inclusive sense, that is to say, a sense broad enough to include the
saving response and activity of our consciousness, a saving activity
which is always through the Word of the truth of the gospel. In this
sense it is virtually synonymous with the word *conversion*. It is in accord
with the Scripture to regard the word of the gospel as living and powerful (cf. John 6:63; Rom. 1:16; 1 Cor. 4:15; Heb. 4:12).

There is no good reason why we should not recognize the propriety
of this twofold use of the concept regeneration. Regeneration in its
restricted sense, the sense particularly apparent in John 1:13; John
3:3–8; 1 John 2:27; 3:9; 4:7; 5:1,4,18, must never be abstracted from
its context. The context of regeneration in the restricted sense is one
that has no meaning apart from the truth of the gospel addressed to and
engaging our consciousness. Regeneration takes place in connection
with the effectual call; it pushes itself into consciousness in the responses
of faith and repentance. It has no relevance except as it is concomitant
with these other aspects of the *ordo salutis*. It would be quite natural that
the terms should on occasion be used in a sense broad enough to include
the elements of this context. This only serves to confirm our earlier
contention that regeneration must not be separated from calling on the
one hand and faith and repentance on the other. The call that comes
through the Word—the effectual call—is logically prior even to regeneration, and the grace wrought by regeneration is but the grace in-
wardly wrought by the Spirit in order that the appropriate response to
the efficacious call may be elicited in us. Regenerative grace is carried
to us in the bosom of the effectual call, and since the latter is by the
Word we must never think of regeneration even in the restricted sense

as wrought outside of a context that has reality and meaning only as a result of the Word. God's efficacious call through the Word becomes vocal in our consciousness, and is responded to by our consciousness, because our hearts have been renewed, because the ears of our souls have been opened to receive the Word.

THE COROLLARIES OF THE CAUSAL PRIORITY OF REGENERATION
We must emphasize certain corollaries:

1. *Regeneration and Conversion*

The causal priority of regeneration to any saving activity on our part does not mean that the regenerate person may still live in sin and be unconverted. The passages in 1 John make this perfectly plain for not only does John emphasize in these passages the logical and causal priority of regeneration, but also, and perhaps even more overtly, the invariable concomitance of regeneration, on the one hand, and, on the other, the doing of righteousness (2:29), the loving of our fellow men and knowing God (4:7), the not sinning and inability to sin (3:9; 5:18), believing that Jesus is the Christ (5:1), willing subjection to the commandments of God, and overcoming the world (5:4). It is quite impossible to think of regeneration as existing in abstraction from this catalogue of virtues, and that is the equivalent of saying that these virtues must coexist with and accompany regeneration. That is to say, regeneration cannot be conceived of apart from the new life which it begets.

The regenerate person is the person called into the fellowship of God's kingdom of glory and virtue, and regeneration pushes itself into consciousness and expresses itself in the exercises of faith and repentance. It is true that, except a man be regenerated, he cannot enter into the kingdom of God, but it is also just as true that every person regenerated has entered into the kingdom of God—'that which is born of the Spirit is spirit'.

2. *Regeneration and Responsibility*

The causal priority of regeneration is no excuse for our unbelief and no alibi for sloth or indifference or despair. We may never plead our own depravity as any reason for not believing, nor our inability as any excuse for unbelief. To argue that we should not repent and believe until we are regenerated is to introduce confusion into the relations that regeneration sustains to our responsibility. We never know that we are regenerated until we repent and believe. The gospel of grace addresses itself to our responsibility in the demand for repentance and faith. Just as the unknown purposes of God are not the rule of our conduct nor the grounds upon which we act, so the inscrutable operations of God are not the rule or ground of our action, but his revealed will. The rule for us in every case is the revealed will presented to our consciousness, not his mysterious operations below the level of consciousness. Our belief, our knowledge that we have been regenerated is never the ground upon which we exercise faith in Christ, even though the fact of regeneration is always the source from which issues the exercise of faith and repentance.

3. *Regeneration and Free Agency*

The priority of regeneration does not violate our free agency. If we remember that man, though a free agent, is able to exercise that free agency only in the service and bondage of sin and is unable to release his free agency from that bondage, the interposition of supernatural grace simply ensures the release of his free agency to the end that it may exercise itself in the doing of that which is holy and good. God in his sovereign grace delivers man from his servitude in sin, so that he may be able freely to will that in which God's purpose and our blessedness consist. This is no violation of liberty but rather the emancipation of liberty, to the true exercise of it unto the glory of God.

4. *Regeneration in Infancy*

The priority of regeneration and the fact that it must not be separated from faith must be borne in mind even in the case of regenerate infants. In the nature of the case the infant is incapable of that conscious and intelligent activity in terms of which we must define faith and repentance. But where regeneration takes place in the case of an infant there is the immediate transition from the kingdom of darkness to the kingdom of God, and even though intelligent faith cannot be in exercise, nevertheless there is that which we may and must call the germ

of faith. It is impossible for us to determine the extent to which regeneration affects the rudimentary consciousness of the infant, but it
must affect that rudimentary consciousness just as radically as sin does.
If infants are depraved they may also be holy. The regenerate infant is in
this respect radically different from the unregenerated infant. The regenerate infant is not under the dominion of sin, is not a child of wrath,
but a child of God and a member of his kingdom. He grows up in the
nurture of the Lord in the highest sense of that term. It will take years,
of course, for the infant concerned to arrive at explicit consciousness of
the implications of that regeneration and of the salvation it involves.
But it is a fact that makes a radical difference in the developing or unfolding consciousness of the infant.

We must not, therefore, conceive of the regenerate infant as regenerated in infancy and then converted when he reaches years of
understanding and discretion. No, not at all! When the infant is regenerated, that infant is converted in the sense that there occurs in the
infant mind something which in the rudimentary sphere corresponds to
conversion, that is to say, the direction in which the heart and mind—
germinal and rudimentary though they be—are turned is towards God,
towards faith in him, love and obedience to him. As the infant grows up
under the sanctifying influences of the indwelling Holy Spirit, he re-
sponds in expanding experience and to increasing knowledge in a way
consistent with his membership of the kingdom of God; in a way consistent with the indwelling of the Spirit as the constantly directing and
controlling agency, he grows up to hate sin and love righteousness. If
in the case of unregenerate infants we can say, as we must, that they go
astray from the womb speaking lies, so of the regenerate infants we must
say that from the point of regeneration they in principle walk in the way
of holiness, speaking the truth. In a word, they are holy, just as others
are unholy.

Of course, oftentimes persons regenerated in infancy pass through
experiences when they grow up that closely resemble the experience of
conversion and they may themselves think that, prior to that event, they
were under the dominion of sin. But such experience is in these cases but
a crisis through which the regeneration that took place earlier comes to
explicit expression in their consciousness, and is focused in their in-

telligent experience. In many other cases, however, there has been no such critical or explosive experience at any particular time, and so many of the most intelligent Christians never remember a time when they can say that they were then without God and without hope in him. They were not only regenerated in infancy, but nurtured in the bosom of Christian instruction, so that simple faith in Jesus dates back as far as memory can penetrate.

17

Justification[1]

THE application of redemption begins with the sovereign efficacious summons on the part of God to partake of the covenant blessings. In order that this call may be answered, and the blessings of the high calling of God enjoyed, the inward supernatural regeneration and renewal of the Spirit is necessary. In it God begins to save from the subjective depravation of character. This change of heart mainfests itself in faith and repentance, which are the responses of our whole inner man to the revelation of the gospel, away from sin and towards God.

But, as James Buchanan says, guilt 'cannot be extinguished by repentance or even by regeneration; for while these may improve or renew our character, a divine sentence of condemnation can only be reversed by a divine act of remission'.[2] And sin, we must remind ourselves again, involves not only pollution but 'guilt'. It involves divine condemnation. The application of redemption, then, must embrace removal of guilt no less than the removal of defilement. It must involve a change in God's judicial relation to us as well as change in our attitude to God.

Justification is that aspect of the application of redemption whereby God delivers us from condemnation, and accepting us as righteous in his sight receives us into his favour and fellowship. It is the blessing of which

[1] *The Doctrine of Justification*, James Buchanan, Edinburgh 1867; *Justification as Revealed in Scripture*, James Bennett, London 1840; *The Doctrine of Justification by Faith*, John Owen, *Works* V. 1ff., Goold Edition, London 1851; *A Treatise of Justification*, George Downame, London 1633; *Faith and Justification*, G. C. Berkouwer, English translation Grand Rapids 1954; See also, *The Epistle to the Romans*, John Murray, volume I, Grand Rapids 1959, pp. 336–362.
[2] op. cit. p. 258.

Isaiah speaks 'And in that day thou shalt say, O Lord I will praise thee; for though thou wast angry with me thine anger is turned away and thou comfortedst me. Behold God is my salvation; I will trust, and not be afraid; for the Lord Jehovah is my strength and my song; he also is become my salvation' (Isa. 12:1–2).

Justification is not the eternal decree of God with respect to us, nor is it the finished work of Christ for us, when once-for-all he reconciled us to God by his death; nor is it the regenerative work of God in us, nor is it any activity on our part in response to and embrace of the gospel, but it is an act of God, accomplished in time wherein God passes judgment with respect to us as individuals.[1]

Justification would have been the basic religious question even if man had never sinned because it would be the question: how can man be just with God? How can a man be right with his Maker? But since man has sinned the question is: how can man *become* just with God? There is no more important or ultimate question than our individual relation to God. It is the basic religious question.

It may be safe to say that the greatest event for Christendom in the last 1500 years was the Protestant Reformation. What was the spark that lit the flame of evangelical passion? It was, by the grace of God, the discovery on the part of Luther, stricken with a sense of his estrangement from God and feeling in his inmost soul the stings of his wrath and the remorse of a terrified conscience, of the true and only way whereby a man can be just with God. To him the truth of justification by free grace through faith lifted him from the depths of the forebodings of hell to the ecstasy of peace with God and the hope of glory. If there is one thing the Church needs today it is the republication with faith and passion of the presuppositions of the doctrine of justification and the re-application of this, the article of a standing or falling Church. 'Being justified freely by his grace through the redemption that is in Christ Jesus: Whom God hath set forth to be a propitiation through faith in his blood, to declare his righteousness for the remission of sins that are past, through the forbearance of God; To declare, I say, at this time his righteousness: that he might be just, and the justifier of him which believeth in Jesus' (Romans 3:24–26).

[1] cf. Buchanan, op. cit. pp. 251–2.

As over against the flabby and unintelligent sentimentalism that has brought God down to the level of ourselves, approving our sin and condoning the faults of his erring children, we must assert the stern realism of the awfulness of human sin and guilt, and the power, liberty and joy of justification by faith alone.

We must regain and reassert high views of the majesty and righteousness of God and of the exceeding sinfulness of sin, so that coming into the joy of justification by faith we may know the peace that passeth knowledge and rejoice in the hope of the glory of God.

How can a man be just with God?

THE NATURE OF JUSTIFICATION
1. *The Meaning of the Term*
Justification is a judicial or forensic term and refers to a judgment conceived, recognized, and declared with respect to judicial status. It does not mean to make righteous or upright or holy in the subjectively factitive and operative sense but to pronounce or declare to be righteous. This is shown by the following considerations:
(i) It is used with reference to judgments where the factitive or operative concept cannot apply.
Deuteronomy 25:1—'They will justify the righteous'.
Proverbs 17:15   —'he that justifieth the wicked . . . even they both are an abomination to the Lord'.
Job 32:2   —'he justified himself rather than God'. (Elihu respecting Job)
Luke 7:29   —'they justified God'.
There are numerous other instances.
(ii) The antithetic expressions show this—it is contrasted with condemnation.
Deuteronomy 25:1; 1 Kings 8:32; Proverbs 17:15; Romans 5:16; 8:33, 34; Matthew 12:37.

Condemnation is not to make wicked and justification no more means to make righteous than condemn means to make wicked.
(iii) The correlative expressions are those which imply a process of judgment.
Psalm 143:2—'enter not into judgment with thy servant: for in thy

204

sight shall no man living be justified' (Qal imperfect may mean here 'be righteous' rather than 'be justified').

Romans 8:33—'Who shall lay anything to the charge of God's elect?'

Romans 3:19,20.

(iv) Synonymous expressions—to impute for righteousness or to impute righteousness.

Romans 4:4,5,6,9,11; 2 Corinthians 5:19,21; cf. Psalm 32:1; Romans 4:6.

Justification affects the judicial relation to law and justice. In our relation to God it must mean that we are reckoned in his judgment as free from guilt and sustaining an upright relation in terms of the criterion of his judgment, that is to say, we are reckoned as sustaining a relation which meets the requirements of law and justice, and pronounced to be such.

The forensic character of justification as to its precise nature is not affected by the ground upon which the judgment or sentence rests. Even when the character or conduct of the person is the *ground* of justification, justification is still forensic, because the justification in such a case is not the forming of the character or the framing of the conduct; but only the recognition and declaration of the status that belongs to that person in virtue of his character or conduct or both (e.g. Adam in innocence and Christ as holy and undefiled). In reality therefore it is inexcusably misleading to speak of the alternatives of moral and forensic justification. Justification is always forensic. The controversy regarding soteric justification should never have been stated in terms of the antithesis between moral and forensic justification. The real question in the controversy is whether the ground of justification is moral character infused, moral character developed, righteousness inherent and righteousness performed on the one hand, or righteousness imputed, on the other. If moral character developed were the ground, as the Pelagian avows, or holiness infused, as the Romanist contends, it should be recognized that, as regards nature, justification is forensic since it denotes simply and solely the judgment registered as a result of the character or holiness contemplated.

Unfortunately this has not been recognized and a great deal of the controversy in the history of debate has turned on the question as to whether justification is moral or forensic, operative or declarative. But there ought to have been unanimity in the question that, as respects nature, it is forensic, and exclusively so. If this had been recognized it would not by any means have removed the controversy nor would it have solved in any way the real question at issue. But it would have placed the controversy in its proper focus and form and would have made the issue, therefore, less confused and more sharply defined. For if all were agreed, as they ought to have been without compromising their respective positions, that justification is forensic, the debate would be concentrated just as vigorously as ever on the question: what is the ground of God's justification of sinners? Is it infused righteousness or is it imputed righteousness?

2. Soteric Justification

Justification means to declare to be righteous—it is a judgment based upon the recognition that a person stands in a right relation to law and justice. Or it is a pronouncement based upon the judgment that a person is free from guilt and stands approved in relation to the standard in law relevant to the case. Obviously both in ordinary usage and in the soteric application of the term, the existence of the state is presupposed in the declaration of the fact. The mere declaration does not constitute the state which is declared to be. Hence when the justification is warranted, there must be first of all the recognition that the relation exists antecedently. In a word, the declaration of the fact presupposes the existence of the fact.

(i) *Uniqueness.* When we come to the question of soteric justification, we are faced with what appears to be a dilemma. Sinners are under the sentence of divine condemnation. The only sentence that can properly belong to them as sinners is condemnation, and, of course, condemnation is the opposite of justification—the one cannot co-exist with the other. How can God justify the *ungodly*? How can he justify the *condemned*? God's judgment is always according to truth and therefore that which is declared to be a fact must be a fact. The question is: what is antecedent which guarantees that the declaration is a declaration according to truth?

It is here that we find the uniqueness and distinctiveness of soteric justification. We cannot expound the nature of soteric justification in terms simply *of what justification is in other instances of its use.* Other instances of its use determine for us that it is *forensic* and that it cannot change its basically forensic character when it is applied to soteric justification. But no other instance of its use and not all other instances of its use put together can provide us with the *distinctive* and *specific* character of this forensic act in God's part. What is this specific character? It is this, that God's justification of the ungodly *presupposes or comprises within itself*—that is to say the action of God denoted by justification of the ungodly—another action *besides that which is expressed by our English word 'declare righteous',* and another action besides that which is denoted by *tsadaq* and *dikaioō* in every other instance of its use. This action is one in which he *actually causes to be the relation which in justification is declared to be.* He effects a right relation as well as declares that relation to be. In other words, he *constitutes* that state which is declared to be. Hence the justifying act either includes or presupposes the constitutive act. This alone will make the declaration to be a declaration according to truth.

It is to be distinctly noted, however, that the constitutive act that must be posited in this case is the *constituting of a new judicial relation.* In other words, it must be a constitutive act *that will be consonant with the forensic character of justification,* a constitutive act that will supply a proper and adequate ground for the pronouncement which justification involves, namely, the pronouncement or declaration that the person concerned is reckoned in God's sight as free from guilt and sustains to law and justice a relation or status whereby he is accepted as righteous.

(ii) *Corroboration.* This unique feature of soteric justification is not only an inference required by the situation which soteric justification contemplates, not only an inference necessary to the concept of God's justification of the ungodly, but it is also expressly intimated in equivalent expressions.

(a) We have, first of all, Romans 5:19—'even so by the obedience of the one shall the many be constituted righteous'. This is an express statement to the effect that constituting righteous is involved in justification. Paul is dealing here exclusively with justification, not with regeneration or sanctification. The expression in verse 19 is parallel to the expression in the protasis, that by the disobedience of the one the many have been constituted sinners, and it is synonymous with the apodosis of verse 16, 'the free gift is of many offences unto justification' and the apodosis of verse 18, 'even so through one righteous act judgment came upon all men unto justification of life'. It is the analogy of sin—condemnation—death in the Adamic relation—and of righteousness, justification, life in the relation to Christ that Paul is instituting. Hence it is within the ambit of justification without any abatement of the forensic meaning or curtailment or interference that this expression has meaning. It is either a synonym for justification, or an essential element in the integral act of justification.

(b) Not only is there Romans 5:19, there is also 5:17 which refers to the receiving of the free gift of righteousness. It is not only through the one righteous act (Romans 5:18) but it is by the bestowal of the free gift of righteousness. That is to say justification has not only righteousness as its proper ground, it is not only that God has respect to righteousness, but it is also a bestowment of righteousness and, because so, there is the assurance of life. This leads us quite naturally to the next consideration, the concept of imputation.

(c) So we have, thirdly, the concept of the imputation of righteousness —*logizetai dikaiosunēn* or *eis dikaiosunēn*, in Romans 4:3, 5, 6, 9, 11, 22–24; Galatians 3:6; James 2:23 and the negative statements in Romans 4:8; 2 Corinthians 5:19 (cf. Romans 4:2; 1 Corinthians 4:4).

Now if there is an imputation of righteousness this is the clearest indication of that in which the constitutive act consists. That answers our question as to what the constitutive act is. If there is an imputation of righteousness, such righteousness meets the requirement of establishing a new relationship which not only warrants the declaration but elicits and demands it and ensures the acceptance of the person as righteous in God's sight.

(iii) *Comprised in the Justifying Act.* In connection with the question: Is this constitutive act comprised in the act which is called justification or is it simply the presupposition of it? There is good reason for suspecting that it is conceived of as actually involved in the act of justification as it applies to the justifying of the ungodly. There are the following considerations which would favour this conclusion.

(a) Presumptive argument. In some important instances of the use of the word *dikaioō* one may feel that the mere notion of 'declaring righteous' is scarcely adequate. We may properly feel that it is not rich enough to express the thought. In Luke 18:14, referring to the publican, Jesus says 'this one went down to his house justified' (*dedikaiōmenos*). Does it not mean that he went down to his house righteous, that is to say, righteous in the sense relevant to justification? If so, it means constituted righteous, in a righteous state established. Likewise in certain passages in Romans there is a paucity of conception which one feels if the bare notion of 'declaring righteous' is all that we have. In Romans 3:24, 'being justified freely by his grace through the redemption that is in Christ Jesus', we may properly sense a pregnancy of thought that can only be supplied by the idea of constituting righteous. Also in Romans 5:1, 'Therefore being justified by faith we have peace with God', the greater fulness supplied by the constitutive idea seems much more consonant with the thought. In a word, in all of these and such instances the thought is surely that of a relation established and the establishment of the relation is that which is expressed by the constitutive act.

(b) We should expect that the justification (*dikaiōma*) of Romans 5:16 and the justification of life of Romans 5:18 (*dikaiōsin zōēs*), and receiving the free gift of righteousness of Romans 5:17, and the constituting righteous of Romans 5:19, are all variations of expression to denote the same unified action which is called justification, and the specific ideas expressed by some of the expressions are simply ways of unfolding the differing facets of the action which is most frequently expressed as justification.

(c) It is quite likely that the very term 'justify' or 'justification' when denoting an action of God in reference to the ungodly is charged with this creative or constitutive ingredient after the analogy of Scripture teaching elsewhere that the word of God and the call of God call into existence—'he calls the things that be not as though they were'—and that God speaks and it is done. The pronouncement, the judgment is not simply one which recognizes existence but causes it to be. His declarative word carries with it the effectuation of that which is declared.

If we then find the specific idea of justification in the imputation of righteousness our inquiry is advanced as far as it can be so far as the topic of the nature of justification is concerned. It does not of itself settle the question what the righteousness attributed is. Conceivably it might be an inherent righteousness. In abstraction it might be this but when we proceed to the next topic, the ground of justification, we shall find that this cannot be.

THE GROUND OF JUSTIFICATION

In our study of the nature of justification we found that justification is forensic and respects a juridical judgment to the effect that the person justified is pronounced or declared to be free from guilt and liability in reference to law and justice and is regarded as standing in an un-impeachable relation to the law. When this is applied to soteric justification it means that God declares the ungodly to be free from condemnation and to be reckoned in his sight as standing in an upright relation to the demands of law and justice. Since God justifies those who are ungodly and therefore under the sentence of condemnation, the declarative act of God in justification presupposes a constitutive act on the part of God whereby he constitutes a new and upright relation to his law and to his righteousness. We found that the Scripture expressly indicates this constitutive act in such phrases as 'constitute righteous' (Romans 5:19) and 'impute righteousness' or 'impute for righteousness' (*passim* in Romans 4 etc.). So we might say that justification finds its specific character or at least finds its necessary presupposition in the imputation of righteousness (This is indeed required if the judgment of God is to be according to truth. If God declares that the demands of law and justice are reckoned by him as satisfied, this must involve righteousness as reckoned to the account of the justified). And the question is: What righteousness? A righteousness that will warrant such a judgment must be a perfect righteousness. Justification is an act, complete and irrevocable. It is not a progressive nor a comparative judgment, and so it must have respect to a righteousness that is undefiled and undefilable. So we ask; what is this righteousness?

1. *Not a righteousness generated or wrought in us*

(i) We must remember that an infused righteousness even though it were perfect and eliminated all future sin would not be adequate to what is included in justification. For such would not obliterate the sin and un-righteousness of the past. But justification includes the remission of all sin and judicial liability. There is no condemnation to them who are in Christ. Consequently the righteousness must be of the kind that will care for remission of the past as well as insurance for the future. Infused righteousness does not measure up to this need.

(ii) The righteousness infused in regeneration is never in this life perfect. Consequently the infused righteousness does not measure up to the standard required for a perfect justification. Only a perfect righteousness can supply the ground of a complete, perfect and irreversible justification.

(iii) We must bear in mind that justification secures eternal life (Romans 5:17,18,21). But even perfect inwrought righteousness cannot ground the reward of eternal life.

We must therefore look elsewhere for the righteousness that is to validate the justifying act.

2. *It is not of works*

It is not a righteousness wrought by us. It is not by our obedience to the law of God.

Romans 3:20, 'From the works of the law (*ex ergōn nomou*) no flesh will be justified'.

Romans 4:2, 'For if Abraham were justified by works he hath whereof to glory but not before God'.

Galatians 2:16, 'Knowing that a man is not justified by the works of the law' (*ex ergōn nomou*).

Galatians 3:11; 5:4, cf. Romans 10:3,4; Philippians 3:9; Titus 3:5.

Paul says in Romans 2:13 that the doers of the law will be justified, but he goes on to show that there are none such, for all have sinned and come short of the glory of God.

3. *We are justified by grace*

Romans 3:24–26; Romans 5:15–21; cf. Romans 4:16; Galatians 3:12.

'Therefore it is of faith that it might be according to grace'; 'But the law is not of faith but he who has done these things shall live in them'.

The fact that it is of grace means that this act finds its source and ex-planation in what God is; it is *not elicited by anything in us but proceeds from the free and unmerited favour of God.* Furthermore, if we bear in mind that the righteousness is not one *infused* nor one *outwrought,* then the grace involves a *donation* which is different in character from that of righteousness imparted or even of grace enabling us to the doing of righteousness. The only kind of gift that will fall into accord with these other considerations is one that consists in the righteousness of putative bestowment, in other words, a righteousness which is not constituted by or receives any ingredients from our own righteousness of character or performance.

These three foregoing considerations put the ground entirely outside of ourselves and our thought is therefore directed to something else.

4. *It is in Christ we are justified*

Isaiah 45:24,25; Acts 13:39; Romans 8:1; 1 Corinthians 6:11; Galatians 2:17; Ephesians 1:7. Therefore we are compelled to think that the ground resides in Christ himself and we are the beneficiaries of this judgment on God's part because of some virtue that belongs to Christ.

5. *It is through the redemptive work of Christ and particularly through his blood*

Romans 3:24,25; 5:9; 6:7; 8:33,34; 2 Corinthians 5:18–21. Hence the virtue belonging to Christ is specifically that which accrues from his redemptive accomplishment and it is to this that we are directed in our search for the righteousness demanded.

6. *It is the righteousness of God*

Romans 1:17; 3:21,22; 2 Corinthians 5:21 (*dikaiosunē theou*).
Romans 10:3 (*hē tou theou dikaiosunē, hē dikaiosunēn tou theou*).
Philippians 3:9 (*hē ek theou dikaiosunē*).

It should be noted that this righteousness is not our own, not of the law, but a righteousness revealed, a righteousness of the faith of Christ. This emphasis upon the righteousness of God can perhaps be most adequately and pointedly expressed by saying that it is a 'God-righteous-ness'. And to assess the force of this designation we may express it both negatively and positively.

(i) Negatively, it is contrasted not only with human unrighteousness but with human righteousness. It is not of human origin, not of human authorship, not of merely human quality. A human righteousness, however high in attainment, or however perfect it might be in character, could never measure up to the demands of the situation which God's justification of the ungodly contemplates. Herein lies the iniquity of every doctrine, Pelagian, Romish, Arminian, or Liberal, which conceives of human righteousness, whether it be that of character or performance, as constituting or contributing to the justifying righteousness. (ii) Positively, it is a God-righteousness, not simply because it is *provided* by God, nor simply because it is *approved by God*, nor simply because it is bestowed by God, but *chiefly* because it is a righteousness with divine quality or property. It is not, of course, the divine attribute of justice. But it is a righteousness with divine attributes. And, because so, it measures up to the demands of our sinful situation and to the requirements of a full, perfect, and irrevocable justification. And not only does it meet these demands and requirements, but since it is divine and therefore *perfectly correspondent with the inherent justice of God it always elicits the divine approbation* whenever it comes into operation. That is to say, not only does it warrant the justifying act but it demands the same. The justifying judgment must supervene upon it whenever it is bestowed. It is righteousness that is inviolable because it is divine.

7. It is the righteousness and obedience of Christ

Romans 5:17, 18, 19. It is this consideration that explains how, on the one hand, the righteousness that is operative unto justification and is mediated to us through faith can be the righteousness of God, and how, on the other hand, the righteousness of God can become ours by bestowment or imputation. It is the righteousness of God, characterized by divine quality or property because, though consisting of the obedience rendered in human nature, it is nevertheless the obedience of the Son of God manifest in the flesh and the quality is determined by his hypostatic identity as the God-man. It can become ours because it is only in his vicarious representative identity as our Redeemer and Saviour that this righteousness belongs to him; only in that capacity was there any necessity for it or any meaning to it.

In this connection it is important to appreciate the import of 2 Corinthians 5:21, that we become the righteousness of God in him—*hina hēmeis genōmetha dikaiosunē theou en autō*. The denotation of *en autō* is clearly specified by the preceding clause, 'him who did not know sin he made to be sin on our behalf'. This is, of course, Christ, mentioned as such in verse 20. It was on our behalf he was made sin. It was on our behalf he wrought righteousness. But the most significant thought of verse 21b is that we become this righteousness by union with him. We are made not only the beneficiaries of it; we are made the partakers of it and to such an extent that we are actually identified in terms of it. It is ours in the sense that our identity is defined in terms of it. Just as Christ became so identified with our sins that, though knowing no sin, he was made sin, so we being in ourselves utterly ungodly and therefore knowing no righteousness are so identified with Christ's righteousness that we are made the righteousness of God. In reality the concept is richer than that of imputation; it is not simply reckoned as ours, but it is reckoned to us and we are identified with it. Christ is ours, and therefore all that is his is ours in union with him and we cannot think of him in his vicarious capacity or of anything that is his in this capacity except in union and communion with his people. It is the truth of 2 Corinthians 5:21 that brings to fullest expression all that the apostle had said in Romans 5:17, 18, 19 in terms of justification as reception of the free gift of righteousness, as justification of life through the one righteousness of Christ, and so being constituted righteous through the obedience of the one. These are not legal fictions. They are the indispensable implicates of what union with Christ entails. For if we were not partakers of his righteousness and in that sense identified with it, the doctrine of union with Christ would be so attenuated and vitiated as to be bereft of meaning and efficacy, not to speak of comfort and assurance.

This doctrine is not only congruous with, but also confirmatory of, the forensic character of justification as an act. Soteric justification like all justification is forensic, but it implies or includes something that is never true in any non-soteric application of the term. When the righteousness contemplated in the constitutive act is not ingenerated righteousness but an objective righteousness, the obedience of Christ wrought for us, this righteousness verifies and brings into clear light the pervasively forensic nature of justification even in that unique and distinctive ingredient that is necessarily embraced in soteric justification. It verifies and vindicates the forensic character because it is putative in its nature, that is to say that the element peculiar to soteric justification, namely, the constitutive, is still strictly forensic in its nature. It is, in a word, the constituting of the judicial relation which is declared to be and it is such by the imputation to us of the righteousness and obedience of Christ.

THE INSTRUMENT OF JUSTIFICATION

Thus far in our analysis we have found that everything is objective to us. The constitutive and declarative acts are of God; the righteousness that provides the ground is the righteousness of God and the obedience of Christ. Does justification take place irrespective of any activity on our part? Is justification a judgment and donation given to sinners dead in sin upon which all saving activity on the part of the justified is consequent rather than precedent? The answer is that while God justifies the ungodly yet it is only those who believe in Jesus. We are justified by faith, *dia pisteōs*; *ek pisteōs*; *epi tē pistei*. But faith involves some saving response on the part of man and expresses some conscious activity on the part of the person concerned. This faith is not the response of the person to the justifying act, but is presupposed in the justifying act, and this faith is not the faith that we have been justified but is rather directed to the proper object in order that we may be justified. Justification is on the event of faith and not faith on the event of justification.

What then is the efficacy of faith in justification? In the Romish system faith as it precedes baptism is bare assent and is simply the occasional cause of first justification. Baptism is the instrumental cause of first justification. Faith simply leads the person to ask for baptism. Faith that issues from baptism is *fides formata*, faith informed with love, and is that subjective condition in virtue of which we do good works well-pleasing to God. These latter have *meritum condigni* and become the ground of second justification. *Fides formata* is the fountain of that which is the formal ground of justification. In either case faith is not the instrumental cause of justification. According to the Remonstrants, faith joined with evangelical obedience is the ground of justification. Though not perfect yet it is reckoned for righteousness by the grace of God.

According to the more classic protestant position faith is simply the instrument whereby justification is appropriated. The faith in view is not faith in justification but faith in Christ, the faith directed to him and commitment to him for salvation (cf. *Westminster Confession* XI, iv). The question may properly be asked: why is faith the instrument of justification? The emphasis placed on this truth in the Scripture from Genesis 15:6 to the most fully developed explication in the New Testament makes it not only appropriate but necessary to ask this question. There are several lines of thought which may be developed to demonstrate the congruity that there is between faith and the other elements comprised in the divine act of justification. Paul clearly expresses the congruity, indeed, the necessity, of justification by faith and justification by grace. 'It is by faith that it might be by grace . . . And if by grace then is it no more of works; otherwise grace is no more grace' (Romans 4:16; 11:6)—*dia touto ek pisteōs hina kata charin.* In a word it is not only consonant with grace; grace requires that it be by faith. We may proceed further. There is harmony between faith as the instrument, on the one hand, and the judicially constitutive and declarative nature of justification, and the righteousness of Christ as the ground of justification, on the other. Now why is there this congruity? It is not because faith is the gift of God. Sometimes that is given as the reason and Ephesians 2:8 is dragged in to do service for this truth. If the mere fact that faith is the gift of God were the explanation, then we could discover no reason why faith rather than repentance, or love, or hope, or patience is brought into this relation to justification. For all of these exercises of the regenerate person are due to the grace of God as much as is faith. In other words the fact that faith is the gift of God does not supply us with the differentia of faith and, therefore does not answer the question why it is by faith we are justified and not by repentance or love or hope. They are all the gift of God in the sense of being graciously wrought in us by the operation of the Holy Spirit. We shall have to look in some other direction then for the differentia of faith whereby its congruity with justification can be established. The differentiating quality of faith is that the nature and function of faith is to rest completely upon another. It is this resting, confiding, entrusting quality of faith that makes it appropriate to and indeed exhibitive of the nature of justification. It is consonant with its source as the free grace of God, with its nature as a forensic act, and with its ground as the righteousness of Christ. Faith terminates upon Christ and his righteousness and it makes mention of his righteousness and of his only. This is the Saviour's specific identity in the matter of justification—he is the Lord our righteousness. And in resting upon him alone for salvation it is faith that perfectly dovetails justification in him and in his righteousness. Other graces or fruits of the Spirit have their own specific functions in the application of redemption, but only faith has as its specific quality the receiving and resting of self-abandonment and totality of self-commitment.

This is both the stumbling-block and the irresistible appeal of the gospel. It is the stumbling-block to self-righteousness and self-righteousness is the arch-demon of antithesis to grace. It is the glory of the gospel for the contrite and brokenhearted—if we put any other exercise of the human spirit in the place of faith, then we cut the throat of the only confidence a sinner conscious of his lost and helpless condition can entertain. Justification by faith is the jubilee trumpet of the gospel because it proclaims the gospel to the poor and destitute whose only door of hope is to roll themselves in total helplessness upon the grace and power and righteousness of the Redeemer of the lost. In the words of one, 'cast out your anchor into the ocean of the Redeemer's merits'.

Faith is always joined with repentance, love, and hope. A faith severed from these is not the faith of the contrite and therefore it is not the faith that justifies. But it is faith alone that justifies because its specific quality is to find our all in Christ and his righteousness. This is clearly brought out by the fact that, in the Scriptures, justification is never said to be *dia pistin* (on account of faith).

APPENDICES

Justification and Remission of Sin

1. Admittedly remission of sin is an indispensable element in, or aspect of, justification. For if sin in its condemnation and curse remains, then condemnation continues and that is the opposite of justification.

2. Furthermore, the Scripture lays a great deal of emphasis upon remission of sin, and may on occasion imply by its use all that is embraced in justification.

3. Likewise in the conception of the believer himself forgiveness may loom so high in his perspective that the grace of justification is to a large extent construed in terms of remission. It is the burden of sin's guilt that occupies his consciousness, and remission of sin so fills him with gratitude that everything else comprised in justification suffers eclipse by way of comparison.

But it is prejudicial to the grace and nature of justification to construe it merely in terms of remission. This is so to such an extent that the bare notion of remission does not express, nor does it of itself imply, the concept of justification. The latter means not simply that the person is free from guilt but is accepted as righteous; he is declared to be just. In the judicially constitutive and in the declarative sense he is righteous in God's sight. In other words, it is the positive judgment on God's part that gives to justification its specific character. And remission is an implicate of justification precisely because justification has this positive character. In other words, it is inconceivable that justification should be registered without the remission of all sin. Justification is not simply an act of clemency. It is a judicial act in which all the claims of rectitude are declared to have been satisfied and vindicated.

Now the question arises: what is embraced in the remission which justification involves? It is true that forgiveness continues to be meted out to the justified person. Does this mean that justification is progressive? If it were, this would interfere with the definitive, complete, and irrevocable nature of justification and it would conflict with the express statement that there is no condemnation to them who are in Christ Jesus. We must therefore believe that there is a remission of all sin, past, present, and future in justification. If this is so, how are we to explain the need and fact of continued remission of sin? Perhaps the most satisfactory and proper way to express the distinction is that the judicial condemnation of all sin is removed in justification. Judicial wrath does not rest upon any justified person for sin that resides in him or which he continues to commit. This, however, does not make unreal the sin he commits nor does it eliminate the displeasure of God. All sin is the contradiction of God and so he must react against it with displeasure; he cannot be complacent to it. The relationship of God to the justified differs, however. And because of that new relationship, expressed particularly in that of Fatherhood, it is the fatherly displeasure that is evoked and it is the fatherly displeasure that is removed in the recurrent remission that is administered in response to repentance and confession. 'God doth continue to forgive the sins of those that are justified; and, although they can never fall from the state of justification, yet they may, by their sins, fall under God's fatherly displeasure, and not have the light of his countenance restored unto them, until they humble themselves, confess their sins, beg pardon, and renew their faith and repentance' (*Confession of Faith* XI, v).

Justification immediately and permanently changes the relation to God and to law and justice. It includes remission of the penalty of all sin, that is, it removes judicial, penal condemnation for past, present and future sins. God is no longer a condemning Judge but a loving Father. Nevertheless they by their sins fall under his fatherly displeasure and so they need daily forgiveness—the removal of this displeasure and restoration to the light of the divine countenance. Their sufferings therefore are not penal inflictions. They are either corrective to the end of their sanctification, or they may be grounded in the divine purpose to vindicate their godliness, or they may be dispensed in pursuance of the gospel so that they fill up that which is behind of the afflictions of Christ in their flesh for his body's sake, which is the church.

Justification and Good Works

It has been objected that the doctrine of justification by free grace through faith alone is inimical to the interests of ethical living and of good works, that it tends to the lascivious and licentious principle, 'let us do evil that good may come'. The apostle met this argument in his own day and Romans 6 is the answer—'How shall we that are dead to sin live any longer therein?' In connection with this objection and the misconception that underlies it we must observe the following:

1. The ultimate goal of the whole redemptive process both in its objective accomplishment and in its application is conformity to the image of

Christ. All the steps are subordinated to this purpose—they flow out of it and move to its realization. Christ gave himself a ransom that he might deliver his people from all iniquity. Justification is only one part or aspect of this redemptive process and must never be viewed in disjunction from its place in the context of all the other steps of the process and particularly the other aspects of the application of redemption. Any doctrine out of focus gives distortion to the whole system of truth and is therefore inimical to the ethical interests to be promoted by that system of truth. Redemption is unto holiness and justification as a part of the process of redemption cannot be to the opposite end.

2. Justification is the only basis upon which good works can be performed. For good works is the doing of that which is well-pleasing to God. There cannot be such well-doing if we are under God's wrath and curse. It is justification that removes alienation, wrath, and curse, and instates us in a relation of peace with God. Again, there can be no good works without confidence towards God which justifying grace imparts, and there can be no confidence except as we are brought near and have access into God's grace. It is then that we may serve God without fear in holiness and righteousness before him all our days (Luke 1:74, 75). Nothing makes God-service more impossible than guilt and in the sphere of experience nothing is more stultifying than the sense of guilt and alienation from God. 'I was alive without the law once: but when the commandment came, sin revived, and I died' (Rom. 7:9). When consciousness is awakened to the guilt and condemnation which sin entails, the invariable result is the death of which the apostle speaks. The only article of our faith that provides the remedy is justification by free grace through faith in Jesus' blood.

3. Justification is by faith and therefore can never be separated from it. What is this faith? It is trust in Christ for salvation from sin. It is to contradict the very nature of faith to regard it as anything else than a sin-hating, sin-condemning, and sin-renouncing principle. Since faith is a whole-souled movement of trust in Christ its very spring and motive is salvation from sin. How can it be an incentive to sin? This would be to attribute two mutually exclusive and antithetic qualities to the same thing.

As regeneration is the fountain of faith and faith is the logical precondition of justification, we can never think of justification apart from regeneration. And, again, the faith that justifies is faith conjoined with repentance.

4. Faith works itself out by love. The faith that does not work is not the faith that justifies: 'Shew me thy faith without thy works, and I will shew thee my faith by my works' (James 2:18).

5. While it makes void the gospel to introduce works in connection with justification, nevertheless works done in faith, from the motive of love to God, in obedience to the revealed will of God and to the end of his glory are intrinsically good and acceptable to God. As such they will be the criterion of reward in the life to come.[1] This is apparent from such passages as Matthew 10:41; 1 Corinthians 3:8-9, 11-15; 4:5; 2 Corinthians 5:10; 2 Timothy 4:7. We must maintain therefore, justification complete and irrevocable by grace through faith and apart from works, and at the same time, future reward according to works. In reference to these two doctrines it is important to observe the following:

(i) This future reward is not justification and contributes nothing to that which constitutes justification. (ii) This future reward is not salvation. Salvation is by grace and it is not as a reward for works that we are saved. (iii) The reward has reference to the station a person is to occupy in glory and does not have reference to the gift of glory itself. While the reward is of grace yet the standard or criterion of judgment by which the degree of reward is to be determined is good works. (iv) This reward is not administered because good works earn or merit reward, but because God is graciously pleased to reward them. That is to say it is a reward of grace. In the Romish scheme good works have real merit and constitute the ground of the title to everlasting life. The good works are rewarded because they are intrinsically good and well-pleasing to God. They are not rewarded because they earn reward but they are

---

[1] Cf. the remark made by Thomas Chalmers to James Buchanan, 'I would have every preacher insist strenuously on these two doctrines—a present Justification by grace, through faith alone—and a future Judgment according to works'. 'All faithful ministers have made use of both, that they might guard equally against the peril of self-righteous legalism on the one hand and of practical Antinomianism on the other'. *The Doctrine of Justification*. James Buchanan, Edinburgh 1867, pp. 238-9.

rewarded only as labour, work or service that is the fruit of God's grace, conformed to his will and therefore intrinsically good and well-pleasing to him. They could not even be rewarded of grace if they were principally and intrinsically evil.

18

Adoption[1]

ADOPTION is concerned with the Fatherhood of God in relation to the redeemed. But it is necessary to preface our discussion by distinguishing the several kinds of divine Fatherhood found in Scripture.

1. *Intertrinitarianism*

This is the exclusive property of the Father in relation to the Son in the mystery of the Trinity. It is immanent, eternal, and exclusive. No other person of the Trinity shares it and in reference to the Sonship involved no man or angel participates in it. This uniqueness is expressed in the *monogenēs* title as applied to Christ and in such expressions as the Father's own Son (Rom. 8:3, 32). This is the only Fatherhood that obtains in the *opera ad intra* and to think of it as belonging to the *opera ad extra* would deny its immanent and eternal character.

2. *Creative*

This is very seldom stated in terms of God's Fatherhood. But since it appears in such passages as Acts 17:28, 29; Hebrews 12:9; James 1:17, 18, we shall have to reckon with the fact that it is not improper to speak of God's creative relationship in terms of Fatherhood. Since all three persons of the Godhead were the agents of creation we cannot restrict this Fatherhood to the first person of the Trinity but we must think of the Godhead as sustaining this relation to angels and men.

1 T. J. Crawford: *The Fatherhood of God,* Edinburgh 1868; R. S. Candlish: *The Fatherhood of God,* Edinburgh 1865; R. A. Webb: *The Reformed Doctrine of Adoption,* Grand Rapids, r.i. 1947; J. Scott Lidgett: *The Fatherhood of God,* Edinburgh 1902; John Kennedy: *Man's Relation to God,* Edinburgh 1869.

Other texts, besides those cited, might appear to express this same truth. But some of these are clearly irrelevant and others cannot be shown to have the creative relation in mind.

In Matthew 5:45–48 God is not called the Father of all. He is called the Father of the disciples and it is true that he as their heavenly Father bestows his kindness upon just and unjust. But the text carefully refrains from stating or implying that it is because God is the Father of all that he sends rain and makes his sun to rise upon evil and good.

In 1 Corinthians 8:6—'but to us there is one God, the Father, of whom are all things, and we unto him'—there is no mention of a fatherly relation to all men. It is simply an identification of the first person of the Godhead by his distinguishing trinitarian name, and there is in the text indeed no necessary reflection upon his fatherly relation to men. In accord with Paul's usage it is the relation to the Son that is in view and, when he reflects on the fatherly relation to men, he calls him our Father.

Ephesians 3:15—'the Father, from whom the whole family in heaven and earth is named'—indicates that this cannot contemplate all mankind because it is restricted to the family of God.

Ephesians 4:6—'One God and Father of all, who is over all, and through all, and in all', must refer to the saints for of those specified as enjoying this relationship Paul proceeds to say, 'But to each one of us has been given grace according to the measure of the free gift of Christ'. Besides, in verse 4 the delimitation is clearly indicated—'One body and one Spirit even as ye were called in one hope of your calling'.

Malachi 2:10—'Have we not all one Father? hath not one God created us?'—might seem to refer to creation and therefore to universal fatherhood. But it is characteristic of the Old Testament to use the language of creation with reference to the work of redemption. Compare especially Isaiah 43:1, 7, 9 where *bara* and *yatsar* are used plainly in a restrictive and redemptive sense (cf. Isaiah 64:8, 9). Besides, the latter part of Malachi 2:10 refers to the covenant of the fathers and indicates that the theocratic relationship to Israel is in view in the earlier part of the verse.

It is noteworthy, therefore, how infrequently the creative relation is expressed in terms of fatherhood. Nowhere is God expressly called the Father of all men. Hence the concept of universal fatherhood, if used at all, must be employed with great caution and it is particularly necessary not to confuse this rare use of the term Father with the frequent use of the same term as it is applied to the redeemed.

In Luke 3:38 the word *huios* does not actually occur but it may be understood as carried over from verse 24 where the genealogy begins with *ōn huios, hōs enomizeto, Iōsēph, tou Elei tou Matthat*. This does not prove however that God may be regarded as the Father of all men in the sense in which he was the Father of Adam, for two reasons.

(i) The emphasis seems to be upon the fact that Adam owed his origin to God as no other man did. Adam was not generated by a human father.

(ii) Adam might have been a son of God by creation, but not in his fallen state. We might concede that Adam as created was a son of God without conceding that all men since the fall are sons of God. We must distinguish between Adam's sonship and the sonship of adoption. The latter entails a security that Adam did not possess.

3. *Theocratic Fatherhood*

This refers to God's adoption of Israel as his chosen people. It is the prototype of redemptive adoption as the Old Testament counterpart. Exodus 4:22, 23; Deuteronomy 14:1, 2; cf. 1:31; Deuteronomy 32:5, 6, 20; Isaiah 43:6; cf. Isaiah 1:2; Isaiah 63:16; Hosea 11:1; Malachi 1:6; Malachi 2:10; Romans 9:4.

This is not the exclusive property of the first person.

4. *Adoptive Fatherhood*

This must be distinguished from the fatherhood of the preceding caption, not because it is principially different but because it is the full-fledged sonship in distinction from the nonage sonship in the Old Testament period. The distinction is clearly drawn by Paul in Galatians 3:23–4:6. The difference is in line with the difference in general between the Old Testament and the New; the Old is preparatory, the New is consummatory. The Old is prepadeutic, the New is graduatory. The children of God in the Old Testament were as children under age. The grace of the New Testament appears in this that by redemption accomplished and by faith in him all without exception are introduced into the full blessing of sonship without the necessity of undergoing a period of tutelary preparation corresponding to the tutelary discipline of the Old Testament period. That is to say, New Testament believers from among Gentiles do not have to undergo in the realm of their individual development a preliminary period which corresponds to the Old Testament period in the broad sphere of progressive revelation and realization. There is no recapitulation in the individual sphere of what obtained in the realm of dispensational progression.

BIBLICAL TERMINOLOGY

The Greek term for adoption is *huiothesia*—Romans 8:15; 8:23; Galatians 4:5; Ephesians 1:5 (cf. Rom. 9:4). The most important passages in the New Testament bearing upon adoption are John 1:12, 13; Romans 8:14–17; Galatians 4:4–7; Ephesians 1:5; 1 John 3:1, 2, 10.

The words used in the New Testament to express the thought of sonship in relation to God are *huios, teknon, teknion*[1] and *paidion; pais*, though used on several occasions with reference to Christ and on two occasions with reference to David (Luke 1:69; Acts 4:25) is not used to express the relation with which we are now concerned.

Paidion is the regular word for child and is used of this relation in Hebrews 2:13, 14—cf. Isaiah 8:18—*teknion*—cf. John 13:33; 1 John 2:1, 12, 28; 3:7 (some mss. *paidia*), 18; 4:4; 5:21.

The standard terms are however *huios* and *teknon*. John uses *teknon* almost exclusively. Only in Revelation 21:7 does he use *huios*, in quoting 2 Samuel 7:14. Paul uses both *huios* and *teknon*. Romans 8:14–21 provides an interesting example of the facility with which Paul can pass from the one term to the other. *teknon* is derived from *tiktein* which means to bear or bring forth. *tekna* is the usual word for children in the New Testament and is used of both sexes, that is of son or daughter (cf. Luke 15:31; 16:25; Acts 7:5).

[1] It is questionable if *teknion* is used to express this relationship. Jesus uses it (John 13:33) and it may not here reflect upon the adoptive relationship but be a term of endearment. John has almost a monopoly since outside John it appears only in Galatians 4:19 where Paul addresses believers as *teknia mou* and the proper text is probably *tekna mou*. In John's usage it is a term of endearment as in John 13:33 (in addition to these occurrences all the instances are 1 John 2:1, 12, 28; 3:7, 18; 4:4; 5:21.) In this respect it is like *paidion* in John 21:5; 1 John 2:13, 18 and possibly 1 John 3:7 though the revised text reads *teknia*.

THE NATURE OF ADOPTION

Since *teknon* is derived from *tiktein* we might readily suppose that the word *tekna* would reflect upon divine parentage by generation. Much plausible support might appear to be derived from the fact that *tekna* is the common word for children in the New Testament and in reference to parents the birth from these parents is generally pre-supposed as that which constitutes the relation implied in the use of the term. Furthermore, in Johannine usage so much emphasis falls upon the fact that those who are begotten of God bear the lineaments of him who has begotten them that we might readily conclude that in the background of the term *teknon* is the assumption that they are children by divine begetting.

We must not, however, take for granted that the word *teknon*, because of its derivation or because of other assumptions which attach to its ordinary use, implies that we become children of God by regeneration or that it expressly reflects upon sonship as constituted by regeneration. Although it has been maintained in this connection that we become children of God both by deed of adoption and by participation of nature, it is not by any means so apparent that regeneration is to be co-ordinated with adoption as the way by which we become sons of God. We must appreciate the fact that the deed of adoption is clearly set forth in the New Testament, and it is apparent that adoption is quite distinct from regeneration. We may never think of sonship as being constituted apart from the act of adoption. If we should think of sonship as constituted by regeneration simply and solely then we should be doing serious prejudice to the necessity and the fact and the distinctive grace of adoption. And not only so. It is questionable if the generative act of God in regeneration is to be construed as an aspect of God's grace by which we are constituted sons of God. One other consideration may be mentioned in this connection. As will be noted later, it is to God the Father specifically and *par excellence* that the children of God sustain this relationship. It is God the Father who is our Father in heaven. We should expect then that it is by an action which is pre-eminently that of the Father that this relation is constituted. But regeneration is pre-eminently the act of the Holy Spirit. In any case, even if we allow that regeneration is to be co-ordinated with adoption as an ingredient in the total action by which we become sons of God, yet it is adoption that must be regarded as the distinctive and definitive act by which this relation is constituted. This is to say, that the privilege and status of sonship is not acquired simply by a subjectively operative action but by what must be called, by way of distinction, a judicial act that has its affinities with justification rather than with regeneration or sanctification. Calling, regeneration, pardon and justification are presupposed, and adoption supervenes upon the condition and status established by these other acts of God and initiates a status and introduces to a privilege which calling, regeneration and justification enlarged to the fullest extent do not themselves define or explicate. The case might be stated thus. Redemption contemplates and secures adoption as the apex of privilege. Calling ushers into the fellowship of God's Son. Regeneration effects that principial conformity to the image of God in righteousness and holiness. Justification accords acceptance with God as righteous and gives the title to the eternal life which the righteousness imputed demands. Sanctification prepares the people of God for the full and consummate enjoyment of the inheritance to which adoption entitles, the heirship of God. But it is in the act of adoption that God becomes to the redeemed a Father in the highest sense that divine Fatherhood can belong to creatures, or, rather, can be predicated of creatures.

We may not, however, rule out the significance of regeneration in connection with the sonship constituted by adoption. Regeneration it is that generates them anew after the image of God so that the adopted may be imbued with the disposition which is consonant with the responsibilities and privileges and prerogatives belonging to the status of adoption.

Now it is significant in this connection that not only do we have the explicit teaching of Paul to the effect that there is the adoptive act (Rom. 8:15; Gal. 4:5; Eph. 1:5), derived from the notion of a legal act whereby a person who is not a natural son is received into the rights and privileges of a son, but even in the teaching of John there is reflection upon the distinctive action by which we become sons of God. In John 1:12 he speaks of giving authority to become sons of God. Sonship, he indicates, is instituted by the bestowment of a right and this is to be distinguished from the regeneration spoken of in verse 13. When we apply John's own teaching elsewhere to this passage we are compelled to discover the following progression of logical and causal relationship—

regeneration (v. 13), the reception of Christ, the bestowment of authority, and becoming thereby children of God (v. 12). It is very likely that this same thought is alluded to in 1 John 3:1–3, 'Behold what manner of love the Father hath given to us that we should be called children of God, and we are'. Several things are to be noted. (1) It is the Father who is in view as the agent. (2) The Father bestows this privilege (*dedōken*—the same verb as in John 1:12). (3) The calling, whether it reflects on our being named children of God or contains a more efficient idea, that of being effectually called into being as sons of God, stresses the dignity of the status. (4) The emphasis upon the marvel of the Father's love points to the status contemplated as that which in the realm of possession is the apex and epitome of grace. (5) It is a present possession and not simply a future attainment. (6) The status insures that in the future we shall be conformed to his image and will enjoy the beatific vision.

In a word, the representation of Scripture is to the effect that by regeneration we become members of God's kingdom, by adoption we become members of God's family. And it may not be forgotten that on the only occasion in which this concept of the family of God is expressly mentioned in the New Testament, it is God the Father who is in view. 'For this cause', says Paul, 'I bow my knees unto the Father, of whom the whole family in heaven and upon earth is named' (Eph. 3:14, 15)[1].

THE SPIRIT OF ADOPTION

The grace of adoption embraces not only the bestowment of the status and privilege of sons but also the witness of the Spirit to the fact (Rom. 8:15, 16; Gal. 4:6). This includes, as we found already, two elements: (1) the creation and fostering within us of the filial affection and confidence which is the reflex in our consciousness of the status; (2) the conjoint witness of the Spirit to our spirits. The act of adoption is necessary to the possession of the prerogative of sons; the Spirit of adoption to the cultivation of these prerogatives and the fulfilment of the correlative obligations. It is the Spirit of adoption who produces the

[1] cf. James Buchanan, *The Doctrine of Justification*, pp. 262f. John Kennedy, op. cit., pp. 147f.

highest confidence that it is given to men to exercise in relation to God. The people of God thereby recognize not only Christ as their Redeemer and Saviour, high priest and advocate at God's right hand, not only the Holy Spirit as their sanctifier and advocate, not only the Father as the one who has called them into the fellowship of his Son but also as the one who has instated them in his family, and they enter into the holiest in the assurance that he, the God and Father of the Lord Jesus Christ, will own them and bless them as his *own* children. No approach to God partakes of comparable intimacy, confidence, and love with that of the simple, yet unspeakably eloquent, 'Abba, Father'. And they accept all the dispensations of his providence as those of the all-wise, all-holy, and all-loving Father in heaven. It is not without significance that the acme of privilege and the highest outreach of confidence toward God that flows from it should be directly attached to that which is pre-eminently and distinctively the action of the Father in the counsel of redemption, namely, election and predestination. 'In love having predestinated us unto adoption' (Eph. 1:5). Here we have the ultimate source and the highest privilege brought together. And in the consciousness of the sons of God it is inevitable that the assurance of the one should go hand in hand with the recognition of the other. The confidence implicit in the address 'Abba, Father' is one that draws to itself the assurance of predestinating love and these mutually support and encourage each other.

Finally, we may not overlook the example furnished in this matter of inter-trinitarian cooperation. It is the Father who sends the Spirit of adoption into the hearts of his children. It is to the end of ensuring the recognition and cultivation of the relation established by the Father and to the Father. And the activity of the Spirit is directed to the inducing of faith and love which have God the Father as their object in the particularity of his fatherly identity. It is the Father whom the Holy Spirit brings into the focus of the believer's faith, confidence, and love.

THE TITLE 'FATHER'

It has been assumed that it is God the Father who stands in this particular relationship to the sons of God. What is the evidence supporting this conclusion?

1. The title 'Father' is the distinguishing title of the first person of the

Godhead; it points to his incommunicable property. There is a certain presumption arising from this fact that the title as it applies to a divine relation to men would have in view that person who is distinctively the Father. In other words it would seem appropriate that the person who is Father should sustain to men the fatherly relation that is constituted through the mediation of the Son.

2. In John 20:17 Jesus said to Mary Magdalene, to tell the disciples 'I ascend unto my Father and your Father'. When he says 'my Father' he must mean the first person of the Trinity. In the usage of our Lord 'Father', 'the Father', 'my Father' always refers to the first person. And the same person must likewise be in view when he says 'your Father'. The coordination would require this inference. Besides, it is to 'the Father' he *ascended* and this is also said to be an ascension to the person who is identified as the disciples' Father. Here, therefore, without question 'the Father' is in view in the fatherly relation which God sustains to the disciples.

3. Jesus very frequently calls the first person 'my Father who is in heaven' in slightly variant forms:

ho patēr mou ho ouranios

ho patēr mou ho en tois ouranois

ho patēr mou ho en ouranois

ho patēr mou ho epouranios

He likewise speaks to the disciples of 'your Father who is in heaven' (Matt. 5:16, 45, 48; 6:1; 7:11; Mark 11:25, 26). The similarity of expression would naturally lead us to think that the same person is in view in both cases, even though Jesus never includes the disciples with himself and speaks of 'our Father who is in heaven'.

4. In the New Testament epistles the title 'the Father' is the personal name of the first person, as also quite frequently *ho theos*. The expression or its close parallel 'The God and Father of our Lord Jesus Christ' (Rom. 15:6; 2 Cor. 1:3; 11:31; Eph. 1:3; Col. 1:3; 1 Pet. 1:3) is unquestionably the first person. Likewise, 'God the Father' (Gal. 1:1; Eph. 6:23; Phil. 2:11; 1 Thess. 1:1; 2 Thess. 1:2; 1 Tim. 1:2; 2 Tim. 1:2; Tit. 1:4; Jas. 1:27(?); 1 Pet. 1:2; 2 Pet. 1:17; 2 John 3; Jude 1; Rev. 1:6). In nearly all these instances the Father is distinguished from the Son and in 1 Peter 1:2 from the Holy Spirit.

When we examine similar instances in the epistles where God is called the Father of believers we have close similarity of expression.

Romans 1:7: 'Grace to you and peace from God our Father and the Lord Jesus Christ' and the same in 1 Corinthians 1:3; 2 Corinthians 1:2; Galatians 1:3; Ephesians 1:2; Philippians 1:2; Philemon 3.

Galatians 1:4: 'According to the will of God and our Father'.

Philippians 4:20: 'But to God and our Father be the glory for ever and ever. Amen.'

Colossians 1:2: 'Grace to you and peace from God our Father.'

1 Thessalonians 1:3: 'before God and our Father'.

1 Thessalonians 3:11: 'But God himself and our Father and our Lord Jesus Christ'.

1 Thessalonians 3:13: 'before God and our Father at the coming of our Lord Jesus Christ'.

2 Thessalonians 1:1: 'to the church of the Thessalonians in God our Father and the Lord Jesus Christ.'

2 Thessalonians 2:16: 'But our Lord Jesus Christ himself and God our Father . . . comfort your hearts'.

But there is not only the similarity of expression between these instances and the others where God is called the Father of our Lord Jesus Christ but, even more significantly, when God is denominated 'our Father' the person contemplated is clearly distinguished from the Lord Jesus Christ in most of the instances quoted. And this conclusively shows that the person in view is God the Father as distinguished from the Son.

On these grounds we must infer that when God is contemplated in terms of adoption as 'our heavenly Father' it is the first person of the Trinity, the person who is specifically the Father, who is in view. This fact enhances the marvel of adoption. The Father is not only the God and Father of our Lord Jesus Christ but he is also the God and Father of those who believe in Jesus' name. The relation of God as Father to the Son must not be equated with the relation of God as Father to the adopted. Eternal generation must not be equated with adoption. Our Lord guarded this distinction most jealously in respect of relationship, address, and implication. He never included the disciples with himself or himself with the disciples in a common relationship designated 'our Father'. He never approached the Father in prayer with the disciples and said 'our Father'.

This is expressly marked in the word to Mary Magdalene. And the implications of the distinction are apparent in his word 'No one knoweth who the Father is but the Son' (Luke 10:22; cf. Matt.11:27). But while the distinction must be recognized and guarded we must not fail to appreciate that which is common, namely, that it is the same God and Father who sustains this relation to the only-begotten in the uniqueness of the sonship that is his and to the redeemed in the uniqueness of the sonship that belongs to them. This fact binds together the only-begotten and the sons by adoption in a bond of brotherhood. We could not dare to think of the relationship established in these terms unless we had the authority of Scripture. In Hebrews 2:11 (cf. Matt. 12:50; John 20:17; especially the latter when Jesus says 'Go to my brethren'.) we read, 'For both he that sanctifieth and they who are being sanctified are all of one: for which cause he is not ashamed to call them brethren', and then the writer appeals to Psalm 22:22; Isaiah 8:17, 18. The passage speaks of the sons to be brought to glory (v. 10—*pollous huious eis doxan agagonta*), of the children whom God had given (v. 13 *paidia*), and of the children (*paidia*) as partakers of blood and flesh (v. 14). We shall have to infer that the 'all of one' (*ex henos pantes*) refers to the fact that the Son (cf. 1:5), here designated the captain of salvation, and the sons to be brought to glory are of the Father and therefore together constituted a brotherhood by virtue of which the Son is not ashamed to call them brethren.

CONCLUSION

This doctrine of adoption is not only important in a positive way as setting forth the apex of redemptive grace and privilege, but it is also important negatively in that it corrects the widespread notion of the universal fatherhood of God and provides against its devastating implications. Though there is a sense in which the universal fatherhood may be maintained, yet to confuse this with adoptive fatherhood is to distort and even eviscerate one of the most precious and distinctive elements of the redemptive provision. For if we do not distinguish at this point it means one of two things; the denial of all that is specifically redemptive in our concept of the divine fatherhood, or the importation into the relation that all men sustain to God by creation all the privileges and prerogatives that adoption entails. On the former alternative God's fatherhood is emptied of all the rich content Scripture attaches to it. On the latter alternative we shall have to espouse universalism and the final restoration of all mankind.

It needs to be repeated that Scripture all but uniformly reserves the title Father as it respects men and the title son as it respects our relation to God for that relationship that is effected by the special act of God's grace that finds its place within the *ordo salutis*, namely, adoption. 'Adoption is an act of God's free grace, whereby we are received into the number, and have a right to all the privileges of the sons of God' (*Shorter Catechism*, Question 34).

19

Faith

THE discussion of the subject 'Faith' may be conveniently divided into three main subdivisions, Faith as a Psychological State, *Fides Generalis*, and *Fides Specialis*.

FAITH AS A PSYCHOLOGICAL STATE[1]

What we are concerned to discover in this part of the discussion is the meaning of 'faith' as a state of mind, and to distinguish it from other states of mind. That is to say, our concern is to arrive at a correct analysis and description of the state of mind we properly designate by the word 'faith' or 'belief'. In this part of the discussion we are not limiting ourselves to religious faith, or Christian faith, but rather considering faith in all the instances in which it may properly be used with reference to a certain state of mind. We cannot, of course, thereby determine the nature and grounds of Christian faith, whether it be *fides generalis* or *fides specialis*, because there are specific factors entering into Christian faith that do not enter into the more generic or common exercises of faith. But nevertheless we can in this way lay a groundwork for the proper understanding of the nature and grounds of Christian faith even though specific features enter into the latter which determine our concept and even analysis of its character.

When we use the word *faith* strictly and properly we mean that for certain reasons apprehended by us we are satisfied as to the reality,

[1] B. B. Warfield—'Faith in its Psychological Aspects', *Studies in Theology*, New York 1932 p. 313; also in, *Biblical and Theological Studies*, Philadelphia 1952, p. 375. Reprinted from *The Princeton Theological Review* ix, 1911, p. 537.

reliability or truth of a certain event, object or person. If faith has respect to an event we mean that we believe that the event has occurred. If faith has respect to an object we mean that we accept that object as trustworthy for the purpose we have in view. When it has respect to a person we mean that we credit him as trustworthy in respect of that character which is under consideration.

Not all alleged events and not all objects and persons evoke this mental state on our part. Why not? The reason is that the mind is not satisfied as to the truth of the report in the case of alleged event and not satisfied as to the reliability or trustworthiness of the object or person. If we press the question one step further and ask why not, the answer is that *to our apprehension* sufficient or adequate evidence has not been presented. Shall we not then say that faith is a state of mind determined by reasons apprehended by the understanding and evaluated by the judgment as sufficient? Whatever else it may be, it is nothing less than this.

There are, of course, two reservations that need to be made at this point:

First, this judgment on the part of the mind is not always the result of a conscious and deliberate process of reasoning and evaluation. Often the processes of reasoning are greatly speeded up, and they appear to us spontaneous and instantaneous and intuitive, so that we are unaware of the process by which we have arrived at a certain judgment. Sometimes our judgments are what we describe as intuitive. On other occasions the process of reasoning and evaluation has covered so long a period of time, and the evidence has been presented to our minds at such diverse times and in such diverse ways, that we are quite unable to analyse the process by which we have arrived at the state of mind which in a concrete instance we properly designate as faith. For example, our faith in certain persons—we are not able to remember the whole series and sum of impressions and experiences which have formed in our minds the trust we repose in them, or even for that matter the trust we refuse to repose in them.

Second, we are not forgetful that the mind makes many mistakes. It often judges evidence to be adequate that is not really such, and often judges evidence to be inadequate that really is adequate. The mind often believes when it should not and does not believe when it should believe.

But what we are insisting upon is that when faith is present it is because there has been a judgment of the mind that the evidence is sufficient, whether made consciously or unconsciously, hastily or slowly, whether it is justified or unjustified. Faith is a state of mind induced by what is considered to be evidence, presented to the understanding and evaluated by the judgment as sufficient.

We must add one other characteristic, and go one step further in our analysis of the phrase we have used, 'a state of mind induced by evidence'. Faith is *forced* consent. That is to say, when evidence is judged by the mind to be sufficient, the state of mind we call 'faith' is the inevitable precipitate. It is not something we can resist or in respect of which we may suspend judgment. In such a case faith is compelled, it is demanded, it is commanded. For whenever the reasons are apprehended or judged sufficient, will we, nill we, faith or belief is induced. Will to the contrary, desire to the contrary, overwhelming interest to the contrary, cannot make us believe the opposite of our judgment with respect to the evidence.

For example, in common parlance we say a man commands confidence. We do not trust a man simply because we have willed to, or even because we desire to. And we cannot distrust a man simply because we wish or will to do so. We trust a man because we have evidence that to us appears sufficient, evidence of trustworthiness. When to our apprehension a man presents evidence of trustworthiness we cannot but trust him, even though we hate his trustworthiness and would wish the opposite to be the case. His trustworthiness may be the ruin of what we think to be our interests, but we cannot but trust him (e.g. the criminal who wants to evade justice, arraigned before a judge whom he believes to be just and fair, may do everything in his power to do away with the judge. But why? Because he trusts him). We cannot but believe in his reliability and truthfulness.

To sum up, faith is trust. Trust presupposes an object. An object evokes trust when there is an antecedent judgment of the mind that the object is trustworthy. This judgment is formed by the evaluation of evidence as sufficient. It is a state of mind induced by considerations objective to ourselves though always apprehended by our minds. In Warfield's words, 'The conception embodied in the terms "belief", "faith", is not that of an arbitrary act of the subject, it is that of a mental state or act which is determined by sufficient reasons'. Faith is trust, and trust induced or compelled by evidence. It is forced consent.

In order to elucidate this view of faith, to vindicate its propriety, and to show its significance we must set it over against other views.

1. *Locke's Definition*

According to Locke's view faith is a persuasion of truth stronger than opinion but weaker than knowledge; it is assent of the mind to propositions that are probably, but not certainly, true. It must be conceded that there is a popular use of the word that accords with this definition. A popular use implies that we rise from opinion to belief, and from belief to knowledge, just in proportion to the degree of certainty attained. But this popular and loose use of the word 'belief' or 'believe' cannot fix for us the real meaning of 'faith' and provide us with its real differentia. There are exercises of faith into which the element of uncertainty does not enter. Our beliefs are among our firmest convictions. Evidence may be so overwhelming that unshakable conviction is the result, and so we cannot allow a loose popular use of the word to determine our definition of the psychological nature of the state of mind we call 'faith'.

2. *The Definition of Kant*

Opinion, he says, is a judgment resting on grounds that are both subjectively and objectively insufficient; belief is judgment resting on grounds that are subjectively sufficient but objectively insufficient; knowledge is a judgment resting on grounds that are both subjectively and objectively sufficient.

In criticism of this definition, may we not say that it is a psychological impossibility? Can there be subjective sufficiency except where there is a recognition of the sufficiency of the evidence? As Dr Warfield with able insight points out, the mind knows nothing of objectively and subjectively sufficient grounds in forming its convictions. All that the mind knows is the sufficiency or adequacy of the grounds on which its conviction rests. The moment the objective inadequacy is perceived, in that moment the subjective sufficiency ends; for objective sufficiency, if we may use the term, is nothing but the judgment of the mind with respect to the sufficiency of the evidence. 'To believe on the grounds of the inadequacy of which we are convinced is on the face of it an impossibility.... All it is conscious of is the adequacy or inadequacy of the grounds on which its convictions are based. If they appeal to it as adequate the mind is convinced; if they do not it remains unconvinced'.[1] Faith cannot be defined as anything less than conviction and is more than opinion or mere intuition.

3. *Those definitions that discover the distinguishing feature of faith in the element of desire or will.*
(i) 'Faith is determined by feeling, by our emotional attitude.'

It must be conceded that our feelings or emotional attitudes exercise a profound influence over our judgment. Feelings may stimulate or warp judgment, make us more sensitive to evidence, or unresponsive to evidence, alert to that which promotes our interest, indifferent to that which thwarts it. So it is perfectly true that our feelings may be the crucial factor in the explanation of a certain state of mind at a particular time. Strong feeling may induce us to imagine or create what we judge to be evidence. It may induce us to regard as evidence what is not evidence, regard as sufficient what is not sufficient, and vice versa. Feeling distorts our perception or it may clarify it.

Notwithstanding all these allowances, however, there are two observations:

(a) There are exercises of faith into which feeling does not enter to any appreciable extent, and sometimes our convictions are utterly repugnant to our feelings. We are compelled to believe what is directly counter to our most cherished feelings and desires.

(b) Even when feeling has warped our judgment or clarified it, it is not feeling that has induced faith, but judgment with respect to the evidence. Feeling influences the judgment but it is not feeling that makes the judgment.

(ii) Perhaps more widely current than the foregoing is the view that faith is determined by will. Faith is voluntary conviction in the sense

[1] B. B. Warfield, *Biblical and Theological Studies*, p. 381.

that our articles of faith are the result of a voluntary decision. In the thought-forms of William James we deliberately will to believe the validity of those religious emotions and feelings which work. As Warfield says in expounding this view, 'It is voluntary conviction, conviction determined not by the evidence of reality present to our minds but by our desire and will that it should be true—this desire or will expressing "some subjective interest or consideration of value".'[1] Knowledge rests on theoretical, conviction on practical grounds, not on evidence but on considerations of value. 'The pious man', says Strauss, 'receives religious truth because he feels its reality and because it satisfies his religious wants'. 'Failing knowledge we may take these things on faith because we perceive it would be well if they were true'.

There are certain admissions that have to be made:

(a) There is the closest interaction between our will and our judgment. Our willingness or unwillingness to accept evidence exercises a profound influence upon our judgment. Sometimes strong desire or will in a certain direction may lead us to evaluate as evidence what is not evidence, and to discount as evidence what really is evidence. But belief is not constrained by will but by judgment with respect to the adequacy of the evidence.

(b) We often act on the basis of what we would were true and we may think that this act is an exercise of faith. This, however, is a wrong choice of terms and rests upon faulty analysis. These are cases of supposition, hypothesis, conjecture, probability, venture.

(c) Considerations of value may be powerful arguments of reality, and workability of validity. Considerations of value may fill up the quota of evidence requisite to the exercise of faith and thus form an important part of the evidence.

But notwithstanding all these concessions we cannot grant that we ever believe simply because of advantages or values that accrue from believing. We believe not what we could wish were true but what we are convinced is true. And considerations of value never become the ground of faith until we have judged them to be evidence of the reality of what we believe to be valuable, and then they determine or induce faith only as they may be judged to constitute evidence of the reality of

[1] *Biblical and Theological Studies*, pp. 383–4.

that believed. We may be convinced that objects of such essential and all-important interest to us must be real, but what we do in such a case is to judge on the basis of such a consideration that the object is real. We believe, however, what we are convinced is real, and faith is not a projection of what we believe to be indispensable.

FIDES GENERALIS[1]

In our preceding discussion we found that faith is conviction induced by judgment of the mind with respect to the sufficiency of evidence. *Fides Generalis* is simply faith in the truth of the Christian religion. More specifically stated, it is the faith of the truth revealed in the holy Scripture. More pointedly it is the faith that holy Scripture is the Word of God; it is our full persuasion and assurance of the infallible truth and divine authority of Scripture as the Word of God.

If this persuasion is more than blind and unintelligent credulity, if it belongs to the category of faith, it must be indeed by an intelligent judgment of the mind on the basis of evidence competent to warrant such a judgment, that is, well-grounded and intelligent conviction. What is this evidence and where does it exist?

In this case it is useless or futile to try to ground this conviction upon rational argumentation based upon evidence extraneous to the sum total of the data with which the Christian revelation confronts us. It might seem that such argumentation is necessary in order to avoid the charge of arguing in a circle. But it will become apparent how impossible it is to produce by evidence extraneous to the Scripture the faith which has as its object the Scripture itself. The Reformers were aware of the fallacy attaching to argumentation on the basis of extrinsic evidence, and so they laid down the principle that Scripture is autopistic, that is, self-authenticating, and this means that the evidence validating the faith of Scripture as the Word of God is the Scripture itself. This is to say that it contains within itself the evidence of its divine origin, character, and authority.

1 *Bibliography*: John Calvin—*Institutes* I, vii; Caspar Wistar Hodge—'The Witness of the Holy Spirit to the Bible', *Princeton Theological Review*, VI, p. 41; B. B. Warfield—'The Knowledge of God', *Calvin and Calvinism*, New York, 1931, pp. 70–90; John de Witt—'The Testimony of the Holy Spirit to the Bible', *The Presbyterian and Reformed Review*, VI, p. 69; Bernard Ramm: *The Witness of the Spirit*.

It will readily be seen how necessary this principle is. If Scripture is the Word of God it must bear the marks of its divinity. This is parallel to the argument respecting God as Creator drawn from the visible creation. The invisible things of God—omnipotence, divinity, eternity—are clearly seen *(kathoratai)*, being understood *(noumena)* by the things that are made (Rom. 1:20). Just as the heavens declare the glory of God and bear witness to their Creator, so the Scripture as God's handiwork must bear the imprint of its divine authorship. In other words, only the evidence of God's hand could measure up to the requirements necessary to authenticate his handiwork. This is just saying that the evidence upon which faith in divinity rests must itself have the quality of divinity.

Of course we must allow that there could be evidence of divine character certifying to us the divinity of Scripture which would not itself be contained in Scripture. God could by continuous miracle or special revelation certify to us that Scripture is his Word, and such revelation would be sufficient to ground our faith in Scripture. But with respect to this supposition there are two things to be said: First, even such a supplementary revelation would not eliminate the fact or the necessity of the evidence inherent in Scripture itself. If otherwise certified to be his Word it would still be his Word and would bear the marks of divinity which would demand on our part the corresponding faith. And second, it is apparent that God does not supply us with that supplementary revelation and the reason is apparent. It is not necessary because Scripture contains within itself adequate evidence demanding faith and supplying all that is necessary to a well-grounded assurance of its divine origin, character, and authority. So it is the constraint placed upon the human mind by the perfections resident in Scripture that explains the full persuasion and assurance of its divine character. This is to say that the Word of God, addressed to us, must in the nature of the case be of such unique character, be invested with such authority, and be accompanied with such commanding power, that nothing else could be more convincing than this Word itself. In the realm of confrontation or encounter with God there could not be anything of higher evidential quality than God's Word to us. It is apparent, therefore, that if there is a Word of God at all, it must be self-evidencing, self-authenticating, autopistic.

We are now faced with the question: if Scripture is the Word of God and thus invested with the quality of divinity commanding faith, why is not faith the result in the case of every one to whom it is addressed? It is to be admitted, as we have found already, that faith is not induced by evidence itself; evidence does not create faith. Evidence must be evaluated by the judgment before faith is induced. There must be the corresponding mental response in the person who is confronted with the evidence. But in this case we have something so absolutely unique and transcendent that we should expect response to be always correspondent with the nature of the evidence. These considerations only accentuate the fact that nevertheless there is not always faith, and this but bears witness to the intensity of human blindness and depravity. 'The natural man receiveth not the things of the Spirit of God' (1 Cor. 2:14). It is here that the doctrine of the internal testimony of the Holy Spirit enters. And this doctrine is to the effect that, if faith in the Word of God is to be induced, there must be the interposition of another supernatural factor, a supernatural factor not for the purpose of supplying any deficiency that inheres in the Scripture as the Word of God, but a supernatural factor directed to our need. Its whole purpose is to remedy that which our depravity has rendered impossible, namely, the appropriate response to the Word of God. In this respect the internal testimony is co-ordinate and consonant with the Scripture itself. The Scripture is pre-eminently redemptive revelation; it is remedial of sin. The internal testimony is but another provision of God's redemptive, and therefore supernatural, grace, directed to the correction of that which sin has effected.

Our question now is therefore: what does the Scripture teach respecting this activity of supernatural grace which is directed to the end of inducing faith in men, the activity called the internal testimony of the Holy Spirit?

The Biblical Teaching

1. Matthew 11:25–27; Matthew 16:17; John 6:44, 45, 65; 1 Corinthians 12:3; 1 Corinthians 2:6–15; 2 Corinthians 4:3–6; Ephesians 1:17–18; Philippians 1:9–11; 1 John 2:20–27.

(i) *The Necessity*. God the Father sovereignly reveals the truth to some and refrains from revealing it to others. (Matt. 11:25–26). This sovereign revelation on the part of the Father is paralleled by a similar sovereignty on the part of the Son—'he to whomsoever the Son willeth to reveal him' (Matt. 11:27). It is not within the power of flesh and blood, not within the power of men, to discover or disclose the mysteries of God and particularly the mystery of the Father and the Son (Matt. 16:17). The wisdom and understanding of this world cannot unveil the hidden things of God or bring them within the compass of human knowledge and reception. It is the Spirit of God who reveals these things and imparts appreciation, discernment, judgment, and reception (1 Cor. 2:6–15). It is only in the Holy Spirit that one can say 'Jesus is Lord' (*kurios Iēsous*). We thus see that the three persons of the Godhead are active in this operation, though it is pre-eminently the agency of the Holy Spirit (1 Cor. 2:6–15; 12:3).

(ii) *The Nature*. This action or activity is called the drawing and instruction of the Father (John 6:44, 45). It is illumination of the heart (2 Cor. 4:3–6) *phōtismos*. It is the anointing of the Holy Spirit (1 John 2:20–27). It is the indwelling and energizing of the Spirit (1 Cor. 2:15)— *pneumatikos*.

(iii) *The Effect* in men is that they discern, know, judge, and receive the truth respecting these mysteries of God and his kingdom (Matt. 11:27; 1 Cor. 2:12–15); they receive them with joy (1 Thess. 1:6). They have certitude regarding the infallibility of the truth and are immovably established in that certitude. They are able to discern truth from error. They are not dependent upon human instruction; they are not dependent upon human testimony (1 John 2:20–27).

(iv) *The Focus*. This faith finds its centrum in the confession that Jesus is the Christ; the Son of the living God, Lord (Matt. 16:17; 1 Cor. 12:3; 2 Cor. 4:3–6).

2. 1 Corinthians 2:4, 5; 1 Thessalonians 1:5, 6; 1 Thessalonians 2:13.
In these passages the overt reference is to the character of the preaching of Paul and his colleagues as the ambassadors of Christ. It was not with the embellishments of rhetorical art nor with the persuasive words of human wisdom and eloquence that Paul delivered the gospel. It was in

demonstration of the Spirit and of power—that is, in the demonstration of the Spirit of God and the power of God. This undoubtedly refers to two interdependent and correlated considerations: First, the kind of influence by which the message which Paul preached was certified to be divine, and, second, that by which the message was borne home to the hearts and minds of its recipients, with such conviction and assurance as was appropriate to its divine character. It was that authentication and certification that elicited faith in the hearers at Corinth and Thessalonica. And it was upon that certification that Paul depended in his delivery of this divine message and it was for that reason that he did not resort to the arts of human wisdom and persuasion.

Paul calls this the demonstration of the Spirit and of power (1 Cor. 2:5), and the Holy Spirit and much assurance. We can call it the demonstration, power and assurance of the Holy Spirit. *Plērophoria* may refer to the persuasiveness of the Spirit's activity. In other instances, however, in which *plērophoria* occurs it refers to the full assurance entertained by us: the full assurance of understanding, Colossians 2:2; the full assurance of hope, Hebrews 6:11; the full assurance of faith, Hebrews 10:22.[1]

There can be no question but Paul is here speaking of a demonstration given by the Spirit of God which enabled Paul to preach the gospel with the fulness of confident assurance. But not only did this operation of the Spirit fill him with assurance in its delivery; it also filled the hearers with the same confident assurance. It was that demonstration, that power, which was the authentication and certification to the believers at Corinth and Thessalonica. It was this that enabled them to receive it 'not as the word of man but as it is in truth the Word of God' (1 Thess. 2:13). Furthermore we must recognize that it was an accompanying influence of the Holy Spirit. It is upon the word of the gospel that faith terminates; the demonstration of the Spirit is distinct from that which is believed. But it is by the demonstration that the Word is received as the Word of God. And it is this demonstration of the Spirit that constrains the acceptance in full and solid assurance of its divinity.

[1] See also Romans 15:29 in D*G for the other reading *plerōma: en* $\left\{ \begin{array}{l} plerōmati \\ plerōphoria \end{array} \right\}$ *eulogias Christou.*

Because it is so, the faith of these believers rested upon the divine certification of the power of God.

To sum up the conclusions derived from these passages, we can say that the reception of the Word of God in intelligent, discriminating, confident and abiding faith, is the effect of an activity of the Holy Spirit which is defined in terms of unction, demonstration, power, apart from which the Word itself is ineffectual in eliciting from us that response of faith and acceptance which its divine character demands.

The Nature of this Testimony

The question arises: what, more precisely, is the nature of this activity of the Holy Spirit? It has frequently been construed as consisting simply in the illumination which the Holy Spirit imparts, in regeneration on its noëtic side. If we were to use this expression, 'regeneration on its noëtic side', it is better to speak of it as regeneration in its noëtic expression.

Now it must be fully admitted that it cannot be less than illumination. The knowledge and discernment of which Paul speaks in 1 Corinthians 2:14, 15 implies the opening of our minds to discern the excellence and appreciate the truth of the things of the Spirit of God. It is regeneration in its noëtic expression because it is the affinity with the things of God implanted in regeneration coming to expression in our understanding in the response to the evidence Scripture contains of its divine character. But the question remains whether the notion of illumination is adequate as an interpretation of the biblical teaching. It is quite true that once we posit Scripture as containing within itself the evidence of its divinity, then all that we need to suppose is the illumination of our minds so that we may behold and properly evaluate that evidence. This is all we need to explain the result. If this is all that the internal testimony is, then in the strict sense it is not testimony. For, on this analysis, the testimony, strictly considered, resides exclusively in the Scripture itself, and there is nothing of the strict nature of testimony in the ever-present activity of the Spirit. The question must be pursued, however, whether something must be added to the concept of illumination in order to do justice to the language of Scripture.

When we examine 1 Corinthians 2:4, 5; 1 Thessalonians 1:5, 6, we must, first of all, remember that the demonstration and power of the

Holy Spirit is an accompanying operation of the Spirit; it is supplementary to the word of the gospel itself. But, secondly, and of more direct relevance to our question, it is spoken of as demonstration and power. The word 'demonstration' (*apodeixis*) has the notion of proof, or attestation, or confirmation, and it suggests, if it does not expressly indicate, the thought of testimony. It is, therefore, supplemental attestation. That it is not something inherent in the Word itself is shown by the fact that it always issues in the full assurance or conviction (*plērophoria*) of 1 Thessalonians 1:5; it has its result in the reception of the word 'not as the word of men but as it is in truth the word of God' (1 Thess. 2:13). There should be no question, therefore, that it is an additional attestation indispensable to the faith that rests not upon the wisdom of men but upon the power of God. Then again there is the accompanying and therefore supplemental power (*dunamis*). Since it is accompanying, and a power that constrains faith, it is distinct from the power inherent in the Word. It is the ever-recurrent power exercised by the Spirit in conjunction with the gospel.

The terms used point to the conclusion that this activity of the Spirit supplies confirmation, attestation, seal, by which the truth of the gospel is enforced and by which there is produced in us overwhelming conviction of its divinity. So the internal testimony is itself a positive testimony collateral and correlative with the evidence which the Scripture itself contains of its divine origin and authority. The internal testimony is both illuminative and testimonial, and the latter is necessary if we are to do justice to the biblical data. There is a compelling power which can be explained only in terms of the presence and authentication of God himself, and the effect is irresistible conviction.

The Internal Testimony and Revelation

Whether we view the internal testimony as merely illumination, or as illumination plus a positive supplementation construed as testimony in the stricter sense of the word, there is one principle which it is necessary to stress, namely, that the internal testimony does not convey to us new truth content. The whole truth content that comes within the scope of the internal testimony is contained in the Scripture. This testimony is directed to the end of constraining belief in the divine character and authority of the Word of God and upon that end alone. It gives no ground whatsoever for new revelations of the Spirit.

When Paul writes to the Thessalonians, 'Our gospel came not unto you in word only, but also in power and in the Holy Spirit and much assurance', he is surely making a distinction between the actual content of the gospel and the attendant power with which it was conveyed to them, and in virtue of which it was carried home with conviction to the hearts of the Thessalonians. Similarly in 1 Corinthians 2:4, 5 the content of Paul's word and preaching will surely have to be distinguished from the demonstration of the Spirit and of power by which Paul's message was effectual in the begetting of faith in the Corinthian believers. And we are likewise justified in recognizing a distinction between the truth which John says his readers already knew and the abiding anointing of the Holy Spirit.

Caveats:

1. The meaning of the internal testimony is not to be understood as though it was of the nature of a continuous revelation, calculated to supplement and perhaps supersede Scripture. This is an abuse to which it was subjected at the time of the Reformation and oftentimes since then. A correct understanding of the doctrine will exclude any such mis-application.

2. It in no way encourages false mysticism which derives from some mystical experience or from the inner light intimations of the will of God that are equal with, if of no higher authority than, the Scripture. False mysticism disparages the Word and displaces it from its place of final authority; it impinges upon the sufficiency and perfection of Scripture. The internal testimony of the Spirit has as its sole purpose the recognition of the divinity, authority and finality of Scripture. It is a witness to the truth of the Word. It is always by and with the Word in our hearts. There is no true and sound faith in Scripture apart from the inward testimony; there is no testimony of the Spirit apart from the Word.

3. A corollary is that the internal testimony is no part of the rule of faith. It is simply an activity of the Spirit extended upon and in our consciousness, so that we may be able to assent in confident faith to the

rule objectively given. There is no truth-content in the Spirit's operation, the truth-content is wholly in Scripture. He illumines our minds in truth objectively presented. 'The whole counsel of God concerning all things necessary for his own glory, man's salvation, faith and life, is either expressly set down in Scripture or by good and necessary consequence may be deduced from Scripture, unto which nothing at any time is to be added, whether by new revelations of the Spirit or traditions of men'.[1] When the Westminster Confession says, that 'the supreme Judge, by which all controversies of religion are to be determined and all decrees of councils, opinions of ancient writers, doctrines of men, and private spirits, are to be examined, and in whose sentence we are to rest can be no other but the Holy Spirit speaking in the Scripture' (I, x), it does not mean by the latter phrase the Internal Testimony, but the Scripture as the product of the Holy Spirit and through which he speaks. The expression 'the Holy Spirit speaking in the Scripture' is used in order to stress the fact that Scripture is not a dead word but the living voice of God the Holy Spirit, addressing itself to the various situations that arise for the individual and for the church. The expression itself should advise us that it is the Scripture that is intended and is not to be identified with the activity mentioned in section v, 'bearing witness by and with the Word in our hearts'. The one is 'in the Scripture', the other is 'in our hearts'. Besides, section vi points to Scripture as the whole counsel of God. The Holy Spirit speaking in the Scripture is to be sharply distinguished from the Spirit bearing witness by and with the Word in our hearts. The Holy Spirit speaks in Scripture because it is his word but he does not continue to write Scripture. His voice is in Scripture and to it nothing is to be added. If we once relinquish the principle of the finality of the objective rule then we have no norm by which we can distinguish the delusions of Satan from the light of God.

The Internal Testimony and the Authority of Scripture

The internal testimony does not make Scripture authoritative. It enables us to recognize the authority; it brings the Scripture home to us with authority. But it is not the authority-imparting factor. What makes Scripture authoritative is the divine authorship of Scripture, and it is of

[1] *Westminster Confession of Faith* I,vi.

divine authorship because it is inspired of the Spirit; it is God-breathed. If we fail to recognize this distinction between the operation of the Spirit by which it is authoritative and the operation of the Spirit by which that authority is borne home to our hearts with power and conviction, then we confuse inspiration and the internal testimony, and we deprive Scripture of its objective authority as God's Word. The Westminster Confession has been appealed to, and it has been interpreted as meaning, to use the words of Daniel Lamont, that 'Scripture is authoritative only as it is borne home to a man by the testimony of the Spirit.' In chapter I, section v, the Confession is not dealing with the ground of authority but with the way in which that authority is registered in our conviction. Section iv deals with the authority. And the Confession is drawn up in terms that obviate any possibility of confusion for any one who will pay attention to the development indicated by the order of the sections in Chapter I.

It is in this connection that we must deal with the Barthian theology. For Barth and his school, the Bible is not itself the Word of God in the sense of being revelation. The Bible simply witnesses to revelation and to the Word of God; it is the medium of revelation and it attests the Word of God. Revelation and the word of God to us is the ever-recurrent act of God in each existential situation when God speaks to this man and to no other in a concrete encounter. In the Bible we have merely human attempts to reproduce this Word of God that came to Isaiah, Jeremiah, Paul, and John. So in the Bible the human authors speak and this is not revelation. In revelation God speaks and God must act anew in revelatory word just as he did with Isaiah and others, and he does this through the medium of the witness which these past recipients of revelation bore to the revelation which they themselves received. The Bible becomes the Word of God only in these existential revelatory encounters. But there must be the ever-recurrent divine decision and act of grace. It is this action of God that is authoritative. Hence if we translate this act of God into the terms of the internal testimony, it is the latter and the latter only that is authoritative. Hence there need be no doubt that, for the dialectic theology, it is not Scripture as an existing entity or corpus that is authoritative, nor any quality inherent in it that makes Scripture authoritative, nor any past action of the Spirit by which it was produced, but only the intrusive act of God here and now.

Now it should be apparent how divergent this is from the witness of Scripture itself. In Scripture what we find repeatedly is that the inscripturated Word is appealed to as an end of all controversy. 'It is written' or 'Scripture says' are the formulae of our Lord and his apostles. It is the fact that it is *Scripture* that invests the Scripture with authority and not any concurrent witness of the Holy Spirit in and to our own hearts. It is the Word of God written and this is the only extant form of the Word of God. Inscripturation itself is the fact appealed to as that which imparts authority and finality.

There must be no suppression of the authority with which Jesus himself spoke, nor of the authority with which the apostles spoke and acted in terms of apostolic institution and commission. Both Jesus and the apostles recognized the authority and finality of the Scripture which was then in existence, and this is the attestation to us that when Jesus ascended and the apostles left this earthly scene, the form of authoritative word for the church would be inscripturated word. Since we have the witness of our Lord and of the apostles in inscripturated form, we must apply to that Scripture which incorporates their witness the same authority and finality as they accorded to the Scripture then extant. We are therefore shut up to Scripture as the only authoritative Word available to us and, following the witness of our Lord and the apostles, recognize its authority as derived from the fact that it is Scripture.

There is a plausible line of thought and argument characteristic of the dialectic theology in this connection and it may be proper to deal with it here. It is to the effect that Jesus himself is the Word of God. The word of God to us, and therefore always personal, because it is encounter with the Word incarnate. And thus the living Lord can never be identified with the written words of the Bible. The incarnate Logos can not be incarcerated in a static, impersonal corpus of written words. The incarnate Word and the words of Scripture must be distinguished. Jesus Christ is the focal point of the whole of Scripture, the soul of the Bible, and must be distinguished from the extant written message. Hence literal inspiration leads to bibliolatry and overlooks the fact that there is only one incarnation of the divine Word. Jesus Christ is the truth of God and so Scripture is never identical with the truth of God. To regard

Scripture as the truth is to incarnate the truth in a book and such a notion would interfere with the claims of the Logos as the only incarnation of the truth.

It is surely to be admitted that Jesus Christ is the focal point of Scripture. And the central purpose of Scripture is to bear witness to him and confront us with him as the incarnate Word, the image of God, the truth. It is only as we know him that we come to that knowledge of God which is eternal life. But how this fact interferes with or militates against the literal inspiration of Scripture is not apparent. And how literal inspiration leads to bibliolatry is not by any means obvious. The following considerations should make plain how monstrous is the travesty of sound reasoning when it is inferred from the fact that Christ is the focal point of Scripture that therefore literal inspiration is ruled out. What we shall seek to show is that literal inspiration is correlative with the central purpose of holy Scripture. There are two considerations:

1. Christ as the incarnate Word is never brought into contact with us apart from Scripture. Scripture itself is always the antecedent fact and we know nothing of him as the incarnate Word except as the Scripture confronts us with him. In reality the dialectic theology is compelled to recognize the antecedence of Scripture and our complete dependence upon it, and the use frequently made of Scripture could have no validity except on the assumption which the dialectic theologians are most jealous to controvert, namely, the indispensability of a written Word from which we derive truth-content respecting the incarnate Word.

2. The centrality of Christ as the Word incarnate can never be divorced from the manifestation of Christ in the days of his flesh and from the witness which he bore to himself and to the Father in that manifestation. This revelation of Jesus Christ can never be abstracted from the spoken word of Jesus. His spoken words were truly revelatory; they were the words of God. To think of the revelation of the incarnate Word apart from his spoken words is a pure abstraction that has no reality. Now these words he spoke were not deprived of their revelatory character by the fact that he was himself the incarnate Logos. In fact they were *necessarily* revelatory because he was God manifest in the flesh. Furthermore, the infallibility of the words he spoke would not in the least interfere with his centrality as the incarnate Logos. Indeed it is the fact

that he was the truth, God manifest in the flesh, that guaranteed the infallibility of his spoken Word. If his inerrant word was not incompatible with his centrality, but rather the means through which he confronted men in the days of his flesh with his own centrality as the incarnate Logos, then revelatory words or speech do not in the least interfere with revelation but are indispensable to it. But for us who do not have the Son of God manifest in the flesh and are not able to hear him speak, there must be some other way by which we are confronted with revelatory words. Otherwise we are completely shut off from contact with the incarnate Word, just as surely as those in the days of his flesh would have been shut off unless revelatory word were the medium of disclosure or revelation. Now if revelatory word, verbal communication, is thus indispensable to us, where are we to find it? Unless we find it in the inscripturated word, it is non-existent. And why should this mode or means of verbal communication interefere with the centrality of Christ any more than spoken words? Or why should the inscripturated word be less revelatory? What is there in the nature of inscripturation that makes that method of verbal communication less revelatory or authoritative? The witness of Scripture itself provides a decisive answer and it is 'Nothing'! Our Lord and the apostles appealed to Scripture as a finality. Their witness is to the effect that, as regards the mode of verbal communication, nothing could be more stable or authoritative than inscripturated word. This is an incontestable fact imprinted on virtually every page of the New Testament. Hence we have the guarantee of the finality and infallibility of that mode of verbal communication, of verbal revelation. Since, as we have found, verbal revelation is indispensable, then the inscripturated word is for us now the mode through which the word revelation comes to us, in distinction from the way in which it came to those who were the direct recipients of Jesus' spoken word, and in distinction from the ways in which word revelation came to those who were themselves the organs of revelation. And we must not forget that these other modes of word revelation were, in the case of Jesus and the apostles, collateral with the mode of inscripturated word which they also possessed in the Old Testament and which is confirmed to us as a mode of revelation by their own witness.

The whole bias of the dialectic theology, to deny the revelatory character of Scripture itself as the inscripturated Word of God, out of deference to the principle that revelation must be personal and engage us in personal encounter with God and particularly with the incarnate Word, fails to take account of the indispensable place which the word of utterance occupies, and must occupy, in the existential encounter with God and with his Christ. When the place of verbal communication, and infallible verbal revelation at that, as it obtained in the case of Christ's manifestation in the days of his flesh, is properly assessed, then the plausibility of the dialectic argument is shown to be a patent fallacy. The logic of its argument would lead to the conclusion that the words of Jesus were not themselves revelatory but only the witness to revelation.

FIDES SPECIALIS
Fides Generalis respects the belief that Scripture is the Word of God. This faith is inseparable from a state of salvation. Yet it is not faith in Scripture that saves but faith in Christ. It is with this specific exercise of faith that we now deal.[1] There are the following subdivisions:

1. *The Presupposition*
Saving faith is the faith that is elicited by, and is the response to, the overtures and claims of the gospel. The gospel is addressed to sinners, and has, therefore, no relevance apart from sin and condemnation. This is true in the realm of objective fact. But what is true objectively must also be reflected in subjective conviction. The gospel can have no appeal to any person unless there is to some extent a conviction of sin and need. This conviction is registered in varying degrees of intensity. In some it is articulate in a profound sense of condemnation, of the wrath of God, and of impending damnation. In others there may be little more than a sense of misery and need, a need, however, that is met by the overture of Christ in the gospel. Faith cannot have its origin in a vacuum; it always emerges in the context of knowledge and conviction. Faith is directed to Christ as Saviour, and he can have no intelligible

[1] This distinction between 'general' and 'special' faith is also to be found, among Reformed theologians, in Turretin. See the section on Vocation and Faith, question 11, par. 13–15, in his *Institutio Theologiae Elencticae,* Geneva 1688.

meaning in that identity except as there is the awareness of the need of salvation. Faith is meaningless when divorced from an antecedent conviction of sin and its desert. The more poignant is the conviction, the more intelligent and relevant is the commitment of faith.

2. *The Warrant*

By faith a person comes to rest upon Christ alone for salvation. The question now is: by what authority or warrant does a sinner come to Christ? What guarantee does a sinner have that Christ is able and willing to save? This is a question of paramount concern to a convicted sinner and it is also of the greatest importance for the proclamation of the gospel and for the faith that proclamation demands. Faith is not blind venture, nor conjecture, nor supposition, nor the plunge of desperation. It is confidence. And the question is both proper and indispensable: what grounds this confidence? There are four considerations:

(i) *Universal Invitation*. All without distinction are invited to Christ. It is striking that some of the most explicit instances are in the Old Testament (Isa. 45:22; Ezek. 33:11; cf. 18:23, 32). In Ezekiel 33:11 the appeal is significantly enforced by the terms—*negation*: 'I have no pleasure in the death of the wicked'; *affirmation*: 'but that the wicked turn from his way and live'; *asseveration*: 'As I live, saith the Lord God'; *exhortation*: 'turn ye, turn ye'; *protestation*: 'why will ye die?' In the New Testament we have similar invitations (Matt. 11:28; John 6:37; Rev. 22:17). It is with some reluctance that I use the term 'invitation'. It is scarcely adequate as a description of what is implied in the various expressions. They include invitation but there is more than mere invitation; there is the urgency of demand.

(ii) *Demand*. There are two senses in which demand is applicable, claim and command.

(a) Claim. The magnitude of the love, grace, and mercy revealed in the gospel, the glory of Christ's person and the perfection of his work both finished and continued, the sufficiency of Christ for all our needs, and the blessedness that accrues from believing response, all combine to make rejection an iniquity of incomparable gravity. Christ offers himself in the glory of his person, in the fulness of his grace, in the perfection of his finished work, and in the efficacy of his heavenly ministry. So the glory demands the response of total commitment to him.

(b) Command. In the gospel we have command in terms as imperative as are those of the law. In the gospel no less than in the law, God asserts his prerogative as Lord. 'This is the work of God, that ye believe in him whom he hath sent' (John 6:29; cf. 1 John 3:23). In his entreaties God covers the whole range of our highest interests—he entreats, exhorts, pleads. But he also enlists the demand of his own sovereignty in command. No text is more universal in its scope or more mandatory in its terms than Acts 17:30 (*pantes pantachou metanoein*). Here is universal overture in imperative terms.

(iii) *Promise*. The invitation and the demand are unconditional. But the promise is not. The promise respects bestowal and it is conditional on faith and is given to faith. Yet it is an unfailing promise to the effect that faith will always meet that to which it is directed (Matt. 11:28; John 3:16; 6:37; cf. 3:36). It is promise that the issue of faith can never be disappointment or disaster. To fulfilment is attached the faithfulness of him who is the truth.

(iv) *The All-sufficiency of the Saviour*. Christ's all-sufficiency resides in the fact that his identity is defined in terms of salvation, that is, in terms of that which meets our need in sin and condemnation (Matt. 1:21; 1 Tim. 1:15). The sufficiency is bound up with the work he came to accomplish and the ministry he still exercises at the right hand of God. The work accomplished and the ministry continued are intimately related and should never be dissociated. But we may focus attention upon the work accomplished as furnishing Christ an all-sufficient Saviour. The atonement, in other words, provides the basis for the free overture in the gospel. This might appear to require universal atonement. Correct analysis will show the opposite to be the case. It is only a definite atonement, an atonement that effectively redeems from sin in its guilt, power, and defilement, and thus secures salvation, that could ground the overture of a complete and perfect salvation. All that a universal atonement could provide would be the overture of a Saviour who died to make the salvation of men possible, or to make provision for the salvation of all. It is not such a Saviour who is presented in the gospel, and it is not such a salvation that is offered. Christ is presented as

Saviour and therefore as one who saves, as one who wrought salvation. What is offered to sinners is not the possibility of salvation, nor the opportunity of salvation, but salvation itself full and free. More properly stated, it is the Saviour who is offered and, still more properly, it is the Saviour who offers himself. It is effective atonement that constituted Christ the all-sufficient Saviour, in other words, made him perfect as the captain of salvation. So the doctrine of limited atonement, so far from being incompatible with the free and unrestricted offer, is in reality the only doctrine that provides the basis for the kind of overture we actually find, namely, salvation complete and perfect, and a Saviour who is himself the embodiment of the salvation professed.

Conclusion. The warrant of faith is, therefore, the full, free, and unrestricted overture of Christ in the gospel. This overture is not simply the warrant for believing in Christ for salvation. It places upon every one confronted with it the demand for repentance towards God and faith towards the Lord Jesus Christ, and it offers insult to the grace and faithfulness of God to require more as the warrant for faith. To interpose the necessity of additional information or of some precedent, saving experience to assure us of God's grace is to impugn the veracity of God's promises in the gospel. For a sinner to plead that it is presumptuous to believe in Christ for salvation until he receives some individual experiential assurance of Christ's willingness to receive him is to distrust the word of the Saviour in the free overtures of his grace. As respects warrant, all to whom the gospel comes are in the same position as to the opportunity, privilege, and responsibility.

The doctrine of election and the doctrine of limited atonement place no fence around the free offer. The free offer comes from the heart of God's sovereign will unto salvation, and it is definite atonement that grounds the kind of overture proclaimed in the gospel.

The Nature—its Constitutive Elements[1]

(i) *Notitia.* Faith respects an object and in this case Christ. But there can be no trust without knowledge of the person in whom trust is reposed. We do not trust any person unless we know something about him and,

[1] B. B. Warfield: 'The Bible Doctrine of Faith' in *Biblical Doctrines*, New York 1929, pp. 467ff.; *Biblical and Theological Studies* 1952, pp. 404ff.

more particularly, things pertaining to that in respect of which we have confidence. So it is with Christ. In this case, however, the knowledge must be proportionate to the issues of life and death, of this age and the age to come. Hence we must know that he is worthy of and equal to such confidence. Here lies the importance of doctrine respecting Christ. The doctrine defines Christ's identity, the identity in terms of which we entrust ourselves to him. Doctrine consists in propositions of truth.

Hence intelligible information must be communicated and there must be some intelligent cognition of the import of that information. Without this, Christ cannot be placed into our world of thought, he can have no meaning or relevance for us.

(ii) *Assensus*. This has two aspects: (a) Intellective and (b) Emotive.

(a) The information conveyed is recognized by us to be true (cf. Rom. 10:9, 10; 1 John 5:1); *pisteuō* with a simple dative or followed by *hoti* has this import.

(b) It is truth believed as applicable to ourselves, as supremely vital and important for us. Saving faith cannot be in exercise unless there is a recognition of correspondence between our needs and the provision of the gospel. Knowledge passes into conviction.

(iii) *Fiducia*. Saving faith is not simply assent to propositions of truth respecting Christ, and defining the person that he is, nor simply assent to a proposition respecting his sufficiency to meet and satisfy our deepest needs. Faith must rise to trust, and to trust that consists in entrustment to him. In faith there is the engagement of person to person in the inner movement of the whole man to receive and rest upon Christ alone for salvation. It means the abandonment of confidence in our own or any human resources in a totality act of self-commitment to Christ.[1] As *assensus* is cognition passed into conviction, so *fiducia* is conviction passed into confidence. Herein resides the unique and distinguishing character of this faith. It is abandonment to Christ against all issues, the deepest and most ultimate. *Pisteuein en* (with dative) implies steady confidence; *pisteuein epi or eis* (with dative) implies repose and reliance; *pisteuein epi or eis* (with accusative) bears the notion of 'movement towards'.[2]

[1] cf. *Biblical Doctrines*, p. 478.
[2] *op. cit.* p. 476; cf. also p. 505.

The Reformers laid much stress on faith as *fiducia,* in opposition to Rome which taught that faith was assent. The Romish doctrine is consonant with the place it accords the church as the depository and intermediary of salvation, and thus obscures the direct relationship of the person to Christ. On the other hand, the emphasis of the Reformation shows itself to be jealous for the evangelical principle, in teaching that faith brings the soul into direct contact with and reliance upon the Lord and Saviour.[1]

This fiducial character, consisting in entrustment to Christ for salvation, serves to correct misapprehensions. Faith is not belief that we have been saved, nor belief that Christ has saved us, nor even belief that Christ died for us. It is necessary to appreciate the point of distinction. Faith is in its essence commitment to Christ that we may be saved. The premise of that commitment is that we are unsaved and we believe on Christ in order that we may be saved. To require of sinners that they give assent to the propositions is to contradict truth and the consciousness of the sinner himself. The grandeur of *fiducia* is that it introduces no contradiction, and expresses that element that is exactly suited to the sinner's state and to the provision of the gospel. If we fail to assess this fiducial character we do prejudice to the doctrine of faith and to the free overture of Christ to which faith is the response (cf. John 3:16, 18, 36; Acts 16:31; 20:21). It is to lost sinners that Christ is offered, and the demand of that overture is simply and solely that we commit ourselves to him in order that we may be saved. In the gospel overture Christ is brought into the lap of lost sinners and placed there in all the glory of his person and the perfection of his ministry. Here is the grandeur of the ambassador's vocation. There should be no reserve or restraint. Christ cannot be brought too near to men in the free overtures of his grace.

It is necessary to guard against a wrong use of introspection. It is not by looking within, in the attempt to discover the movements of God's regenerative grace, that faith is evoked. It is preoccupation with the glories of the Saviour that constrains faith. We do not rest upon that which is done in us, far less upon that which is done by us. Faith does not feed upon the saving experiences that it evokes. It is well to ponder the

[1] B. B. Warfield: *Studies in Theology,* pp. 340 f.

fine words of B. B. Warfield: 'The *saving power* of faith resides thus not in itself, but in the Almighty Saviour on whom it rests. It is never on account of its formal nature as a psychic act that faith is conceived in Scripture to be saving. . . . It is not faith that saves, but faith in Jesus Christ. . . . It is not, strictly speaking, even faith in Christ that saves, but Christ that saves through faith . . . we could not more radically misconceive it (the biblical representation) than by transferring to faith even the smallest fraction of that saving energy which is attributed in the Scriptures solely to Christ Himself.'[1]

Conclusion

Though we must make these divisions in our analysis of the nature of faith, we do so only for the purposes of intelligible exposition. We are not to suppose that saving faith is a process of chronologically ordered steps answering to these logical divisions. Faith is a whole-souled movement of intelligent, consenting, and confiding self-commitment, and all these elements or ingredients coalesce to make faith what it is. Intellect, feeling and will converge upon Christ in those exercises which belong properly to these distinct though inseparable aspects of psychical activity. There is a consensus of all the functions of man's heart and mind. And not only so. There is an interpermeation of these various ingredients. Even in assent there is incipient trust. And in trust there is the full assent to the veracity of God's promise and to the word of Christ. But what we need to appreciate in connection with these elements is that faith, however simple it is as an act of trust, is a complex act and that diverse factors enter into its constitution. The trust of the infant may be said to be simple but, after all, it is complex, and we soon find that out if we try to substitute for the mother.

Again, we must make full allowance for the diversity of individual temperament and psychology. In some people the intellectual aspect may be more preponderant, in others feeling, in others will. And that feature is not annulled in the operations of grace. Hence in some the outstanding feature of their experience in the act of faith is the apprehension and discernment of the truth of the gospel. Perhaps the struggle

[1] 'Biblical Doctrine of Faith' in *Biblical Doctrines*, p. 504.

that preceded faith had to a large extent an intellectual complexion, and the change focused itself in their consciousness in the new light in the understanding. Another person may be more emotionally constituted and the new emotional experience may loom very high in his consciousness. What may be most in prominence is the attraction of the glory and beauty of the redeemer and falling in love with him. Another is more volitionally constituted, and perhaps what stands out most prominently in his experience is the critical decision. But making full allowance for the profuse diversity of human temperament and psychology and the variety of experience that arises from this diversity, what we must recognize in deference to the biblical teaching is that the whole person is active in faith, and that the specific character of faith as an act of self-commitment to Christ as Saviour demands that all these ingredients coalesce. They coalesce to make faith the proper exercise of intelligent, confident, loving trust.

APPENDICES
1. *Relation of Faith to Regeneration*

If faith is an act of whole-souled trust, we must be frank enough to acknowledge that the person dead in trespasses and sins, whose mind is enmity against God and whose characteristic attitude is one of hateful distrust, is incapable of exercising faith. The psychological, moral, and spiritual impossibility becomes more apparent when we consider that the manifestation of the glory of God is at no point more effulgent than in the person of Christ, and at no point is the enmity of the carnal mind more intense than at the point of the revelation of God in the face of Jesus Christ. It is to this impossibility that our Lord bears witness: 'No one can come unto me except the Father who hath sent me draw him' (*helkusē auton*); *helkuō* is a strong word, carrying the notion of effective impulsion (cf. John 12:32). There is an incongruity between the trust which the overture of Christ demands and the enmity which characterizes the person whom the overture confronts. The solution the Scripture offers to this contradiction is the grace of regeneration. It is, in the true sense, the gift of God, though not gift in the sense of adoption or justification, but in the sense of being graciously inwrought by the Holy Spirit, and the action of the Holy Spirit is that of regeneration. It is from the change effected in regeneration that the person is dispossessed of the enmity which makes faith impossible (he is born of water) and endowed with that new dispositional complex by which he is able to exercise the faith of self-commitment to Christ. We should readily see the relationship. Regeneration is not believing; it is the Holy Spirit who regenerates. Faith is not regeneration, for it is the person who believes. But it is by the washing and renewal of regeneration that the person is enabled to believe. Faith is of God, but faith itself is the whole-souled movement of the person in entrustment to Christ.

In this connection it is necessary to clear up a misconception that readily arises and which does prejudice to the teaching of Scripture that it is through faith that we are saved. Surely it needs no argument that we are saved through faith and that the unbeliever is still lost—the wrath of God abides on him who does not believe on the Son (John 3:36). 'By grace are ye saved through faith' (Eph. 2:8). But it may be objected that if regeneration precedes faith, then the person is saved before he believes and we have the anomaly of the person saved by regeneration while he is still an unbeliever. The answer to this objection is simply that there is no such state or condition of regeneration without faith always coincident; the priority of regeneration is logical and causal, not chronological. If we were to posit a case of regeneration without faith then we should have to say that the person merely regenerate is not saved. But there is no such case. We must appreciate the distinctive sanction of each activity in the manifold of actions belonging to the application of redemption. Regeneration is the act of God and of God alone, but it is directed to the renewal which produces faith as the specific instrument of salvation and justification. If a person were only regenerate he would not be saved, because the concept of salvation must be defined in broader terms than regeneration, and in the application of redemption there is no such disjunction of elements as would allow for regeneration without that broader context in which alone regeneration has meaning.

2. *Our Responsibility for Faith*

It is at the point of faith that our responsibility enters. It cannot be said to be our responsibility to regenerate ourselves, because regeneration is the kind of action that belongs to God alone—it is recreative. It is truly our responsibility to be what regeneration effects, namely, new creatures, trusting, loving, and obeying God with all our heart and soul and mind. And we are responsible for the depravity which makes regeneration necessary. But in terms of our present topic, it is in the demand for faith that our responsibility is engaged to the fullest extent. This is correlative with the truth expressed above, that faith is the activity of the person and of him alone. And every Godward response is, of course, our responsibility. This needs to be pressed home with the utmost emphasis.

If we approach the same question from another angle, the evidence constraining faith is wholly objective to ourselves. It is not our responsibility to create the evidence on which faith rests. But we are responsible for our judgment respecting the evidence and for the corresponding reaction.

20

The Assurance of Faith

THE MEANING AND NATURE OF ASSURANCE

When we speak of the assurance of faith we mean the assurance entertained by a believer that he is in a state of grace and salvation, the
knowledge that he has been saved, has passed from death unto life, has
become a possessor of eternal life and is an heir of glory. It is that to
which the Apostle John refers when he says, 'We know that we have
passed from death unto life, because we love the brethren' (1 John 3:14).
It is that which John has in mind as the knowledge coveted for believers
when he writes, 'These things have I written to you in order that ye may
know that ye have eternal life, to you who believe on the name of the
Son of God' (1 John 5:13; cf. 1 John 4:13). It is that to which the
apostle lays claim when he says, 'I am persuaded, that neither death, nor
life, nor angels, nor principalities, nor things present, nor things to
come, nor powers, nor height, nor depth, nor any other creature, shall
be able to separate us from the love of God, which is in Christ Jesus our
Lord' (Rom. 8:38, 39).

There is an obvious distinction between assurance or conviction and
the direct or primary act of faith. The primary and direct act of faith is
not the belief that we have been saved and are heirs of eternal glory, but
an act of entrustment to Christ, freely offered to us in the gospel, *in
order that we may be saved*. The primary act is trust in Christ for salvation,
the assurance of faith is the conviction that this salvation is ours. We
may distinguish these as the primary or direct act, and the secondary or
reflex act, of faith. But whatever we may call the respective acts the
distinction is too obvious to need any elaborate defence.

Since the assurance of faith is logically subsequent or reflex, this faith, in the nature of the case, cannot be of the essence of the primary act of faith. It is the very opposite that is of the essence of the direct and primary act of faith. For the latter proceeds not from the assurance that we are saved but from the conviction that we are lost.

The distinction between the primary and reflex acts of faith does not mean, however, that assurance of faith must always be separated chronologically from the primary act of faith. Far less does it mean that the assurance of faith is always attained by a process of syllogistic reasoning. This assurance may be instantly inwrought in the act of saving faith and thus be instantly registered in the consciousness of the believer.

The question that does arise quite properly is: granting that the assurance of faith is not of the essence of the primary act of faith, is it, nevertheless, an invariable accompaniment or consequence of saving faith? The answer must be in terms of a distinction between implicit and explicit assurance. The germ of assurance is surely implicit in the salvation which the believer comes to possess by faith, it is implicit in the change that has been wrought in his state and condition. However weak may be the faith of a true believer, however severe may be his temptations, however perturbed his heart may be respecting his own condition, he is never, as regards consciousness, in the condition that preceded the exercise of faith. The consciousness of the believer differs by a whole diameter from that of the unbeliever. At the lowest ebb of faith and hope and love his consciousness never drops to the level of the unbeliever at its highest pitch of confidence and assurance. In the words of the Westminster Confession: he is 'never utterly destitute of that seed of God, and life of faith, that love of Christ and the brethren, that sincerity of heart, and conscience of duty' (XVIII, iv). He has peace with God, and the peace of God keeps his heart and mind in Christ Jesus. But that the full consciousness of the implications of the change, the infallible assurance of being in a state of grace and salvation, is of the essence of a state of salvation is not apparent from Scripture. The exhortation to make our calling and election sure (2 Pet. 1:10), and John's care directed to the cultivation of this assurance (1 John 5:13), would be unnecessary if all Christians were fully persuaded of their own salvation. 'This infallible assurance doth not so belong to the essence of faith, but that a true believer may wait long, and conflict with many difficulties, before he be partaker of it' (XVIII, iii). See Psalm 51:8, 12, 14; 31:22; 77:1–10; Ephesians 4:30, 31; 1 John 5:13; cf. Matthew 26:69–72; Luke 22:31–34.

There are various considerations which account for this state of mind. In some cases it is due simply to immaturity in knowledge and grace and is often found in those who have passed from death unto life without any marked or explosive experience. The experience of some has been so gradual that they are not aware when the transition took place. Some have been regenerated in infancy or early youth, and although they have grown up in the nurture and admonition of the Lord they have not yet reflected consciously and intelligently on the question of their spiritual state. In other cases, however, the absence of full assurance is not due to any lack of reflection or development, but is due to inexcusable misconception and misapplication of the truths of the gospel and the nature of salvation, or to a weakness of faith springing from negligence in its cultivation and the fruits of the Spirit, disobedience to the commandments of God, backsliding, unwatchfulness, prayerlessness, excessive care for the things of this life, and worldliness. There are many sins which believers are prone to indulge and which, when indulged, weaken, cripple, bewilder, and cause to stumble, with the result that their Father's displeasure is manifest in the withdrawing of the light of his countenance, so that they are bereft of the joy of their salvation. Those who at one time enjoyed this assurance may lose it. In the words of the Confession: 'True believers may have the assurance of their salvation divers ways shaken, diminished, and intermitted; as, by negligence in preserving of it, by falling into some special sin which woundeth the conscience and grieveth the Spirit; by some sudden or vehement temptation; by God's withdrawing the light of his countenance, and suffering even such as fear him to walk in darkness and to have no light' (XVIII, iv).

This reservation, that an infallible assurance is not an invariable accompaniment of true faith, is not to be confused with any lack of certitude respecting the object of faith. Every believer is assured of God's reality and the truth of the gospel. These are the certainties which constitute the ground of faith itself, and it does not exist except as it entertains the assurance of these certitudes. Faith is not compatible with uncertainty as to its object, though it may consist with uncertainty as to the possession of the salvation which is the result of faith. Neither does it mean that there is any insecurity in the salvation of those who believe. The security does not rest upon the stability of the assurance the believer entertains of that security; the security resides in the faithfulness of the Saviour. Nor does the reservation give an encouragement to the believer to neglect the cultivation of this assurance. Neglect is dishonouring to God and impoverishing to the believer.

THE DUTY AND PRIVILEGE OF ASSURANCE

The Romish Church does not regard the full assurance of being in a state of grace and salvation as the safe and normal state of mind of the ordinary believer.[1] Rome believes that this assurance is attained by some exceptional and highly privileged persons. But ordinarily it is discouraged as ministering to pride and presumption, which are not compatible with the humility and contrition that Rome seeks to cultivate in its devotees.

The Arminian position is that, although the believer may be assured of a state of grace, yet this present state of grace is no guarantee of perseverance and so there can be no assurance of eternal salvation. The true believer may fall from grace and come short of glory.

In reality every brand of theology that is not grounded in the particularism which is exemplified in sovereign election and effective redemption is not hospitable to this doctrine of the assurance of faith. The pivot on which this assurance turns is the certainty that by the grace of God a believer is a child of God in accordance with the Father's eternal purpose, and is kept by the power of God unto the eschatological salvation in terms of the salvation secured and procured by the finished work of Christ. A few passages evince this most clearly. In 1 Peter 1:1–7 the assurance given is set within the points of the faith respecting the foreknowledge of God the Father and the inheritance incorruptible, undefiled, and that fadeth not away, reserved in heaven for them that believe. In Romans 8:28–39, the same foci are plainly evident—fore-

[1] See Sylvester J. Hunter: *Outlines of Dogmatic Theology*, III, pp. 47–51, 139–142, p. 599 and p. 639.

knowledge as the fount, glorification as the terminus. It is also significant that in 2 Peter 1:10 the apostle focuses attention upon election and calling. These are acts of God and of God alone, and what the believer is asked to ascertain is that of which God alone is the author—election as the ultimate fount, and calling as that with which salvation in actual possession begins. In a word, attention is focused upon the determinate actions of God. Hence it is no wonder that the doctrine of assurance should have found its true expression in that theology which is conditioned by the thought of the divine determinativeness of sovereign election, efficacious grace, definite atonement or effective redemption, the irreversibility of effectual calling, and the immutability of the gifts of grace. It is in connection with the emphasis upon such particularisms that the assurance appears in Scripture, and when these are denied we cannot expect the assurance to be in evidence; it is rather denied or discouraged.

The statement of the Westminster Confession is admirably framed to meet the fallacies of these opposing views. 'Although hypocrites and other unregenerate men may vainly deceive themselves with false hopes and carnal presumptions of being in the favour of God and estate of salvation; which hope of theirs shall perish; yet such as truly believe in the Lord Jesus, and love him in sincerity, endeavouring to walk in all good conscience before him, may in this life be certainly assured that they are in the state of grace, and may rejoice in the hope of the glory of God; which hope shall never make them ashamed.' (XVIII, i.)

That it is the duty of the believer to be certainly assured of being in a state of grace lies on the face of the New Testament. (See 2 Peter 1:4–11; 1 John 2:3; 3:14, 18, 19, 21, 24; 5:2, 5, 13; Romans 8:15, 16, 35–39; Heb. 6:11, 17–19; 2 Cor. 1:21, 22; 13:5; Eph. 1:13, 14; 4:30; 2 Tim. 1:12.)

The objection that the entertainment of this assurance develops presumption and highmindedness, carnal security and carelessness, self-sufficiency and pride, rests upon lamentable misunderstanding of the grace of God and of its effect in the life of the believer. No doubt this grace, like every other, is liable to perversion and abuse, and truly the perversion of the best is the worst. But to aver that it is to be discouraged and suppressed because of the perversions and abuses to which it has been subjected is to deny the sanctifying nature of God's grace. The true and necessary tendency of this grace when exercised is to promote humility, dependence, gratitude and holiness. Are we to say that the high and confident assurance of Paul in Romans 8:28–39 encouraged or developed in the apostle presumption and conceit, carnal security and sense of superiority? And these things were written for our admonition and learning. Paul is not speaking there of himself alone as if he were a highly privileged and exceptional case. He is rather identifying himself with believers, and as their advocate before the bench, pleading their defence in order to fortify them by providing them with the certitudes of God's grace against the accusations of the adversary. 'Who shall lay anything to the charge of God's elect?' is the challenge in connection with which he unfolds the case of the believer against all conceivable accusation.

The facts are that the more intelligent, the deeper and the more un-wavering the assurance of salvation is, the humbler, the more stable and the more circumspect will be the life, walk and conduct. Where close-ness of fellowship with God is maintained, where the highest privileges of redemption are appropriated, there holiness, love and obedience must reign. The nearer to God the greater will be the love of his perfection and the more vehement the fear of offending him. It was so with the apostle Peter when, after setting the points for the operation of this assurance, he says, 'Whom having not seen, ye love; in whom, though now ye see him not, yet believing, ye rejoice with joy unspeakable and full of glory.' (Cf. also the succeeding exhortations in 1 Peter 1.) It was so with Paul when, having defined the foci of the orbit within which this assurance must exercise itself, he says, 'Who shall separate us from the love of Christ?'.

Furthermore, its genius is not to despise those of weaker and more hesitating faith. It rather strengthens the weak hands and confirms the feeble knees. It says to them of a fearful heart, 'Be strong, fear not: behold, your God will come with vengeance, even God with a recom-pence; he will come and save you.' (Isa. 35:4.)

And again, this assurance does not raise the believer above conflict and encourage self-righteousness. It was the same Paul who wrote Romans 8 who also said in the same context, 'O wretched man that I am! who shall deliver me from the body of this death?' (Rom. 7:24), and again, 'I count not myself to have apprehended' (Phil. 3:13). The more confident and stable is the hope of eternal life, the more unrelenting and persevering becomes the battle with sin; 'every man that hath this hope in him purifieth himself, even as he is pure' (1 John 3:3). 'If we say that we have fellowship with him and walk in darkness, we lie and do not the truth' (1 John 1:6, 7).

THE GROUNDS OF ASSURANCE

When we speak of the grounds of assurance, we are thinking of the ways in which a believer comes to entertain this assurance, not of the grounds on which his salvation rests. The grounds of salvation are as secure for the person who does not have full assurance as for the person who has. What are the convictions which lead to this assurance and what are the evidences by which it is constrained?

1. An intelligent understanding of the nature of salvation. It is particularly relevant that the believer should appreciate the magnitude of the grace bestowed in salvation, that it is not salvation at all unless it is salvation in the highest reaches of privilege and blessing. Faith makes the believer an heir of God and a joint-heir with Christ. Too frequently believers entertain far too truncated a conception of salvation, as if, for example, it consisted merely in the forgiveness of sins and freedom from its penalty. Their conception is all too frequently a negative one. They thus fail to honour the grace of God and surreptitiously calculate on the basis of merit rather than on the basis of grace. It is right and necessary to consider our own unworthiness and ill-desert, but, when this sense of unworthiness leads us to think that it is presumption to lay hold upon the promises of God, then we have virtually denied the principle of grace.

2. The recognition of the immutability of the gifts and calling of God. The faith and love of the believer have their ebb and flow. They are subject to all sorts of fluctuation, but the security of the believer rests in the faithfulness of God and in the fact that the covenant of his peace will not be removed (Isa. 54:10). As indicated already it is upon the determinativeness and stability of God's gifts that our hearts must rest if we are not to be driven about by the fluctuating tempers or temperatures of

our own experience. From a different angle it may be much the same thing to say that it is in Christ Jesus that all the promises of God are yea and amen, and he is the same yesterday, today, and for ever. There is no fluctuation in his faithfulness and it is because of him that they are sure to us.

3. Obedience to the commandments of God. 'Hereby we do know that we know him, if we keep his commandments' (1 John 2:3). Disobedience and unfaithfulness, as we noted already, bring the divine displeasure and the withdrawal of the light of God's countenance; assurance is sure to suffer eclipse when we walk in the ways of disobedience. (But what is in view more particularly now is the way in which obedience to, and delight in, the commandments of God minister to our own assurance of the favour of God and the hope of eternal life.) This is not equivalent to resting upon works for salvation and it is not equivalent to self-complacency. Obedience simply constitutes the evidence that we love God and are members of his kingdom. In other words, the fruit of the Spirit is the evidence of that grace to which the promises are made, or of that grace within the orbit of which they are applicable. 'If our heart condemn us not, then have we confidence toward God' (1 John 3:21).

4. Self-examination (cf. 2 Pet. 1:10; 2 Cor. 13:5). One of the attitudes most detrimental to assurance is taking salvation for granted. Assurance is not to be confused with presumptuous self-confidence. There is much reason to fear that the Christian church has to a large extent neglected the duty of self-examination and that in consequence there is a form of godliness that denies its power. If we are to entertain this assurance it is because we face up honestly and frankly to the questions, Am I an heir of God? Do I bear the marks of the children of God? Do I have the title deeds to the resurrection of life and to the house not made with hands eternal in the heavens? We must not confuse morbid introspection with self-examination and we must not think that the latter ministers to a subjectivism that is morbid. There must be a subjectivism to selfexamination because we examine ourselves, and it is with the status and condition of our own persons that we are concerned in this exercise.

5. The inward witness of the Holy Spirit. Romans 8:15, 16; Galatians 4:6 (cf. 1 Cor. 2:12; 2 Cor. 1:21, 22; 2 Cor. 5:5; Eph. 1:13, 14). The

inward witness will have to be regarded as having two aspects or elements and it may be that the first aspect should not, strictly speaking, be included under this caption, but should rather be separately classified as the witness of the believer's own spirit as distinguished from the witness of the Holy Spirit. However, since they are so closely related we will deal with them under the same heading.

(i) The first aspect is that reflected on in Romans 8:15; Galatians 4:6. In the former believers are said to have received the Spirit of adoption by which they cry, 'Abba, Father'. I take it that in both instances in this verse *Pneuma* refers to the Holy Spirit and that the thought is that believers have not received the Holy Spirit as the Spirit of bondage but as the Spirit of adoption. But in any case they have received the Holy Spirit as the Spirit of adoption, and in him, or by him, there is generated within them that filial confidence which finds expression in the cry, 'Abba, Father'. They are conscious of that intimacy of relationship, so that they spontaneously give expression to it in the address and plea of God's fatherly relation to them. This is exemplified—and that is no doubt in the forefront of the apostle's thought in this passage—in the distresses which the believer is called upon to experience, by the simple cry 'Abba, Father'. This simple cry without any additional utterance is expressive of the confidence that he is able and ready to help us, that the relationship implicit in that utterance of itself is the guarantee of the Father's protecting and saving love. Implicit in the very address 'Father', as applied to God, is the witness that we are his adopted ones, and for that reason heirs to God and joint-heirs with Christ. It must be remembered that it is only by or in the Holy Spirit that believers are able to exercise the confidence which the utterance implies; and reflection upon the implications of this deep-seated spontaneous outburst, particularly in moments of distress, should provide to the believer evidence of his possession of the Spirit of adoption and therefore of the adoption itself. For, as Paul says in the parallel passage (Gal. 4:6), 'Because you are sons, God hath sent forth the Spirit of his Son into our hearts crying, Abba, Father'.

(ii) In Romans 8:16, Paul adds: 'The Spirit himself bears joint witness to our spirit that we are children of God.' Of course, the interpretation could be advanced that this is but another way of stating that which is adverted to in verse 15. But there are three considerations against this view: (a) The *sunmarturei* points to a joint testimony and therefore to something additional. (b) It is a witness *to* our spirit. If it were the same witness as that reflected on in v. 15, it would be difficult to see the point of v. 16. (c) A comparison of verses 15, 16 with verses 23, 26 would confirm this interpretation. For in the latter Paul speaks of the groanings of our own spirit and of the Holy Spirit, and the latter are distinct because he introduces the subject with the words *hōsautōs de kai* and again uses a composite verb with *sun*, namely, *sunantilambanetai*.

So apparently what Paul is saying in effect is that there is the witness borne through the Holy Spirit by our own spirits in the cry 'Abba, Father', and there is, in addition, the witness of the Holy Spirit to our spirits. In Meyer's terms, Paul distinguishes between the subjective self-consciousness, 'I am the child of God', and the accordant testimony of the Holy Spirit, 'Thou art the child of God'. So in verse 16 there is the witness which the Holy Spirit bears to the spirit of the believer. It must be construed therefore as something very direct. As in other phases of the operations of the Spirit there is inscrutability of mode. It is not something that can be subjected to any further analysis than a witness which is the seal of the Holy Spirit to the authentic character of the witness borne by our own spirits in the tenderness and confidence with which we approach to God and with which we lay hold upon all the provisions and resources of the Father's grace for the perfecting in us of the promises which reach their consummation in glorification with Christ.

In concluding, it may not be superfluous to mention that the Spirit's work in evoking filial affection and confidence, and in the direct witness to the sonship of believers, must never be divorced from the other activities of the Spirit in the sanctification of believers. The Spirit opens their understanding to understand the Scriptures. He unveils to them more and more of the glory of Christ. He sheds abroad in their hearts the love of God. He stirs up other holy affections and adorns them with the fruit of the Spirit. They thus increasingly approve the things that are excellent and prove what is the good and acceptable and perfect will of God. They grow in the grace and the knowledge of the Lord and Saviour Jesus Christ. They add to faith virtue, to virtue knowledge, to knowledge temperance, to temperance patience, to patience godliness, to godliness brotherly kindness, and to brotherly kindness charity. (2 Pet. 1:5ff.) Reflecting as in a mirror the glory of the Lord, they are transformed into the same image from glory to glory. This progressive conformity to the image of God's Son is authentic witness to the recognition that their alignments are not with the world that lies in the wicked one but with the kingdom which is righteousness, and peace, and joy in the Holy Spirit.

THE CULTIVATION OF ASSURANCE

Assurance is cultivated, not through special duties or counsels of perfection but through faithful and diligent use of the means of grace and devotion to the duties which devolve upon us in the family, the church, and the world. The means of grace are the Word, the sacraments, and prayer. This is not the privilege simply of exceptional sainthood but is the privilege of all who are the called of Jesus Christ. As the Westminster Confession says we may 'without extraordinary revelation, in the right use of the ordinary means, attain thereunto', and it 'is the duty of every one to give all diligence to make his calling and election sure' (XVIII, iii).

V

21

Definitive Sanctification[1]

WHEN we speak of sanctification we generally think of it as that process by which the believer is gradually transformed in heart, mind, will, and conduct, and conformed more and more to the will of God and to the image of Christ, until at death the disembodied spirit is made perfect in holiness, and at the resurrection his body likewise will be conformed to the likeness of the body of Christ's glory. It is biblical to apply the term 'sanctification' to this process of transformation and conformation. But it is a fact too frequently overlooked that in the New Testament the most characteristic terms that refer to sanctification are used, not of a process, but of a once-for-all definitive act.

We properly think of calling, regeneration, justification, and adoption as acts of God effected once for all, and not requiring or admitting of repetition. It is of their nature to be definitive. But a considerable part of New Testament teaching places sanctification in this category. When Paul, for example, addresses the believers at Corinth as the church of God 'sanctified in Christ Jesus, called to be saints' (1 Cor. 1:2), and later in the same Epistle reminds them that they were washed, sanctified, and justified (1 Cor. 6:11), it is apparent that he co-ordinated their sanctification with effectual calling, with their identity as saints, with regeneration, and with justification. Again, when in 2 Timothy 2:21 we read, 'If a man purge himself from these, he will be a vessel unto honour, sanctified, meet for the master's use, prepared unto every good work,' there need be no question but the term 'sanctified' is used in the same

[1] Published in *Calvin Theological Journal*, vol. 2, number 1, April 1967.

sense. And when Paul says that 'Christ loved the church and gave himself for it, that he might sanctify it, having cleansed it by the washing of water by the word' (Eph. 5:25f.), it is most likely that the sanctification referred to is explicated in terms of 'the washing of water by the word.' Although in Acts 20:32 and 26:18 'the sanctified' could have reference to the complete sanctification of the age to come, the usage in Paul's epistles would favour the signification whereby believers are viewed as the sanctified.

The substantive, 'sanctification', has a similar connotation. 'God hath not called us unto uncleanness, but in sanctification' (1 Thess. 4:7). 'God hath chosen you as first fruits unto salvation, in sanctification of the Spirit and belief of the truth, unto which he also called you through our gospel' (2 Thess. 2:13, 14).[1]

The terms for purification are used with the same import (Acts 15:9; Eph. 5:26; Tit. 2:14).

We are thus compelled to take account of the fact that the language of sanctification is used with reference to some decisive action that occurs at the inception of the Christian life, and one that characterizes the people of God in their identity as called effectually by God's grace. It would be, therefore, a deflection from biblical patterns of language and conception to think of sanctification exclusively in terms of a progressive work.

What is this sanctification? No passage in the New Testament is more instructive than Romans 6:1–7:6. The teaching here is oriented against the question with which Paul begins: 'Shall we continue in sin that grace may abound?', a question provoked by the exordium accorded to grace in the preceding context. 'Where sin abounded, grace superabounded, that as sin hath reigned in death, even so might grace reign through righteousness unto eternal life through Jesus Christ our Lord' (Rom. 5:20, 21). If the grace of God, and therefore his glory, are magnified the more according as grace overcomes sin, the inference would seem to be: let us continue to sin in order that God's grace may be the more extolled. It is this inference the apostle rejects with the most emphatic negative at his disposal, properly rendered in the corresponding Hebrew idiom, 'God forbid!' The perversity of the inference he lays

[1] cf. 1 Peter 1:2.

bare by asking another question: 'How shall we who are such as have died to sin live any longer therein?' (Rom. 6:2). The pivot of the refutation is: 'we died to sin.' What does Paul mean?

He is using the language of that phenomenon with which all are familiar, the event of death. When a person dies he is no longer active in the sphere or realm or relation in reference to which he has died. His connection with that realm has been dissolved; he has no further communications with those who still live in that realm, nor do they have with him. He is no longer *en rapport* with life here; it is no longer the sphere of life and activity for him. The Scripture brings this fact of experience to our attention. 'I saw the wicked in great power, and spreading himself like a green bay tree. Yet he passed away, and, lo, he was not; yea, I sought him, but he could not be found' (Ps. 37:35, 36). 'As for man, his days are as grass: as a flower of the field, so he flourisheth. For the wind passeth over it, and it is gone; and the place thereof shall know it no more' (Ps. 103:15, 16).

In accord with this analogy, the person who lives in sin, or to sin, lives and acts in the realm of sin—it is the sphere of his life and activity. And the person who died to sin no longer lives in that sphere. His tie with it has been broken, and he has been translated into another realm. In the most significant sense those who still live in the realm of sin can say: 'I sought him, but he could not be found.' This is the decisive cleavage that the apostle has in view; it is the foundation upon which rests his whole conception of a believer's life, and it is a cleavage, a breach, a translation as really and decisively true in the sphere of moral and religious relationship as in the ordinary experience of death. There is a once-for-all definitive and irreversible breach with the realm in which sin reigns in and unto death.

The antitheses which the apostle institutes in this passage serve to point up the decisive breach which this change involves. *Death in sin* means the service of sin as bondservants (vss. 6, 16, 17, 20); sin reigns in our mortal bodies (vs. 12); obedience is rendered to the lusts of sin (vs. 12); we present our members as instruments of unrighteousness to sin and as the bondservants to uncleanness and to iniquity unto iniquity (vss. 13, 19); we are free (footloose) in respect of righteousness (vs. 20); sin has dominion over us and we are under law (vs. 14). *Death to sin* means that the old man has been crucified and the body of sin destroyed —we no longer serve sin (vs. 6); we are justified from sin (vs. 7); we are alive to God and live to him (vss. 10, 11); sin no longer reigns in our mortal body and does not lord it over us (vss. 12, 14); we present ourselves to God and our members as instruments of righteousness to God, so that we are servants of righteousness unto holiness (vss. 13, 19); we are under the reign of grace (vs. 14); we render obedience from the heart to the pattern of Christian teaching (vs. 17); the fruit is unto holiness, and the end everlasting life (vs. 22). This sustained contrast witnesses to the decisive change. There is no possibility of toning down the antithesis; it appears all along the line of the varying aspects from which life and action are to be viewed. In respect of every criterion by which moral and spiritual life is to be assessed, there is absolute differentiation. This means that there is a decisive and definitive breach with the power and service of sin in the case of every one who has come under the control of the provisions of grace.

Although Paul is the chief exponent of this doctrine it is not to be forgotten that the same strand of thought appears also in one of Peter's epistles. Of Christ he writes: 'Who his own self bare our sins in his body upon the tree, in order that we, having died to sins, might live to righteousness' (1 Pet. 2:24).[1] And again Peter writes: 'Since, therefore, Christ hath suffered in the flesh, arm yourselves also with the same mind, because he who hath suffered in the flesh hath ceased from sin, to the end that no longer should he live the rest of his time in the flesh to the lusts of men but to the will of God' (1 Pet. 4:1, 2). I take it that, in the first passage quoted, the thought is after the same pattern that we find in Paul, that those for whom Christ died vicariously are reckoned also as having died in and with Christ, and, as Christ's death was death to sin once for all (cf. Rom. 6:10), so those dying with him die also to sin. And in the second passage the identification with Christ is indicated by the two clauses in identical terms, namely, 'suffered in the flesh', in the first instance applied to Christ and in the second to those being exhorted, with the implication that this suffering in the flesh has as its consequence cessation from sins. The interweaving of the indicative and

[1] ἀπογενόμενοι, though not used by Paul in this connection, and *hapax legomenon* in the New Testament, must be given the force of 'having died'.

the imperative is likewise reminiscent of what is so patent in Paul's Epistle to the Romans.

We may now turn to the apostle John. The incisiveness and decisiveness of John's first Epistle appear at no point more strikingly than where he, in terms peculiar to John himself, deals with the subject of our present interest. We think particularly of 1 John 3:6–9 in which the antithesis is more pronounced and might readily be interpreted as teaching sinless perfection. There are, however, several considerations which show that sinless perfection is not John's meaning:

1. If John's intent were to inculcate sinless perfection, then this passage would prove too much. In that event every regenerate person would be sinlessly perfect and only sinlessly perfect persons would be regenerate. The terms are that 'every one who is begotten of God does not do sin . . . and he cannot sin because he is begotten of God' (1 Jn. 3:9). On John's own teaching, sinless perfection is not the indispensable accompaniment of regeneration. In 1 John 2:1, John makes allowance for the incidence of sin in those whom he addresses as 'little children' and directs us to the provision for this eventuality: 'If any one sin, we have an advocate with the Father, Jesus Christ, the righteous.' Again, it is difficult, to say the least, to interpret the words, 'The blood of Jesus his Son cleanseth us from all sin' (1 Jn. 1:7), as not reflecting on the continuously cleansing efficacy of the blood of Christ. If there is provision for sin in the believer, then regeneration does not ensure sinless perfection.

2. John says expressly: 'If we say that we have no sin we deceive ourselves and the truth is not in us' (1 Jn. 1:8). If John in this case were thinking of past sin only, we should wonder why he uses the present tense. For, on the assumption of sinless perfection, there would be no present sin, and the use of the present tense would be misleading and constitute for his readers something of a contradiction to what on the premises would be one of the leading theses of the Epistle.

3. John insists that 'it hath not yet been manifested what we shall be' (1 Jn. 3:2). This is defined for us in the same verse as likeness to the Father, a conformity such as will be achieved when the children of God will see him as he is. Anything short of that conformity is not sinless perfection. But this is precisely the shortcoming John affirms—'It hath not yet been manifested.' This conformity is the hope entertained and,

because it is that hoped for, the outcome for the believer is self-purification after the pattern of the Father's purity. 'Every one who has this hope in him [i.e., the Father] purifieth himself even as he is pure' (1 Jn. 3:3). Self-purification implies impurity that needs to be cleansed.

4. John implies that sin may be committed by a believing brother: 'If any one see his brother sin a sin not unto death, he will ask, and he will give him life for those who sin not unto death' (1 Jn. 5:16). This is incontestably a reference to sin committed by a believer.

Sinless perfection cannot, for these reasons, be the import of 1 John 3:6–9; 5:18. What then does the decisive language of John mean? The usage of our Lord as reported by John in his Gospel provides us with an index to John's intent in the first Epistle.

In answer to the disciples' question concerning the man born blind: 'Who did sin, this man or his parents, that he was born blind?' Jesus said: 'Neither hath this man sinned, nor his parents, but that the works of God might be made manifest in him' (Jn. 9:2, 3). Jesus could not mean that the son and his parents were sinlessly perfect and had never sinned. The thought is simply that the blindness was not due to some specific sin for which the blindness had been inflicted as a punishment, the assumption underlying the disciples' question.

In the sequel to the foregoing incident Jesus said to certain of the Pharisees: 'If ye were blind, ye should not have sin; but now ye say we see; your sin remaineth' (Jn. 9:41). Again, sinless perfection cannot be in view in Jesus' statement, 'Ye should have no sin.' Jesus is thinking of the particular sin characteristic of the Pharisees, that of self-complacency and self-infatuation. From that sin they would be free if they were humble enough to acknowledge their blindness.

Finally, in John's Gospel, Jesus is reported to have said: 'If I had not come and spoken unto them, they had not had sin. But now they have no cloak for their sin' (Jn. 15:22). Obviously Jesus is speaking of the great sin of rejecting him and his Father (cf. Jn. 3:19).

Thus, in each instance, though the terms are absolute, some specific sin is in view, and the same principle must apply to the language of John with which we are concerned. Furthermore, in this Epistle, John himself gives us examples of the differentiation in terms of which we are to interpret his teaching. Whatever may be the sin unto death as distinguished from the sin not unto death (1 Jn 5:16, 17), there is undoubtedly radical differentiation in respect of character and consequence. It is the latter a believer is contemplated as committing, but not the former. Since, according to 3:6–9; 5:18, the regenerate do not commit sin, it is surely justifiable to conclude that the sin he does not commit is the sin unto death.

In 1 John 4:2, 3 the apostle propounds the test of Christian faith. It is the confession that Jesus Christ is come in the flesh. John's antithetic incisiveness appears here again. 'Every spirit that confesseth Jesus Christ come in the flesh is of God, and every spirit that confesseth not Jesus is not of God.' The force of verse 3 is that every one that does not confess Jesus in the identity defined in verse 2 does not confess Jesus at all. We must infer that the sin a regenerate person does not commit is the denial of Jesus as come in the flesh, or indeed the failure to confess Jesus Christ as come in the flesh. Speaking positively, everyone begotten of God believes and confesses that Jesus as come in the flesh is the Christ (cf. 1 Jn. 5:1). This is the faith that overcomes the world, and this victory is the mark of every regenerate person (cf. 1 Jn. 5:4). The upshot of these propositions is simply that the believer confesses Jesus as come in the flesh, believes that this Jesus is the Christ and that he is the Son of God, and cannot apostatize from this faith. The believer is the one who has secured the victory over the world, is immune to the dominion of the evil one, and is no longer characterized by that which is of the world, 'the lust of the flesh, and the lust of the eyes, and the pride of life' (1 Jn. 2:16). It is, therefore, in these terms that we are to interpret the sin that the person begotten of God does not commit and cannot commit.[1]

John's language and patterns of thought differ from those of Paul, but the doctrine is to the same effect, that for every believer in Jesus as the Christ and as the Son of God there is the decisive and irreversible

---

[1] The interpretation that the regenerate person does not habitually sin labours under two liabilities. (1) The term 'habitually' is not a sufficiently well-defined term. (2) This characterization leaves too much of a loophole for the incisiveness of John's teaching; it allows that the believer might commit certain sins, though not habitually. This would contradict the decisiveness of such a statement that the one begotten of God does not sin and cannot sin.

breach with the world and with its defilement and power. And on the positive side the characterization is no less significant of the radical differentiation from the realm of the wicked one. The person begotten of God does righteousness, loves and knows God, loves those who are begotten of God, and keeps the commandments of God (1 Jn. 2:3–6, 29; 4:7, 20, 21; 5:2, 3).

22

The Agency in Definitive Sanctification[1]

WHAT are the forces that explain this definitive breach with sin and commitment to holiness and righteousness? The answer is that the saving action of each person of the Godhead at the inception of the process of salvation ensures the decisive character of the change thereby effected.

The specific action of the Father is to call men effectually into the fellowship of his Son. In Jesus' own terms it is to donate men to his own Son in the efficacious operations of grace (cf. Jn. 6:37, 44, 65). The action bespeaks the radical character of the change. The specific action of the Holy Spirit is the washing of regeneration whereby men are instated in the kingdom of God as the kingdom of righteousness, power, life, and peace.[2] Again, the action, and that to which it is directed, indicate the momentous nature of the transformation. It is proper, however, to focus attention upon the action of Christ. This is so for two

---

[1] Published in *Calvin Theological Journal*, volume 2, number 1, April 1967.
[2] While regeneration is an all-important factor in definitive sanctification, it would not be proper to subsume the latter under the topic 'regeneration'. The reason is that what is most characteristic in definitive sanctification, namely, death to sin by union with Christ in his death and newness of life by union with him in his resurrection, cannot properly be referred to regeneration by the Spirit. There is multiformity to that which occurs at the inception of the Christian life, and each facet must be accorded its own particularity. Calling, for example, as the action of the Father, must not be defined in terms of what is specifically the action of the Holy Spirit, namely, regeneration. Definitive sanctification, likewise, must be allowed its own individuality. We impoverish our conception of definitive grace when we fail to appreciate the distinctiveness of each aspect, or indulge in over-simplification.

reasons. First, it is by virtue of what Christ has done that the action of both the Father and the Spirit take effect. Second, this aspect of biblical teaching has been more neglected. The bearing of Jesus' death and resurrection upon our justification has been in the forefront of Protestant teaching. But its bearing upon sanctification has not been sufficiently appreciated. It is here we find the basic consideration relevant to our present question.

In the teaching of Paul the pivots of the change in view are death to sin and newness of life. The starting point of Paul's argument in answer to the false inference that we may continue in sin that grace may abound is, as already observed, that the partakers of grace died to sin. His protestation, 'How shall we any longer live in it?' is immediately supported by appeal to the significance of baptism (cf. Rom. 6:3). It is baptism into Jesus' death that makes valid the pivotal proposition, 'we died to sin.' Then Paul proceeds to identify believers with Christ in his burial and resurrection (Rom. 6:3–5). This means, therefore, that not only did *Christ* die, not only was *he* buried, not only did *he* rise from the dead, but also all who sustain the relation to him that baptism signifies likewise died, were buried, and rose again to a new life patterned after his resurrection life. No fact is of more basic importance in connection with the death to sin and commitment to holiness than that of identification with Christ in his death and resurrection. And this relation of Jesus' death and resurrection to the believer is introduced at this point in the development of Paul's gospel, be it noted, not with reference to justification but in connection with deliverance from the power and defilement of sin. So it is the relation to sanctification that is in the focus of thought. What then is this relation?

It might be said that the relation is that which justification sustains to sanctification, that the death and resurrection of Christ are directly the ground of our justification, that justification is the foundation of sanctification in that it establishes the only proper relation on which a life of holiness can rest, and that the relation of the death and resurrection of Christ to *sanctification* is this indirect one through the medium of justification. Or it might be said that by his death and resurrection Christ has procured every saving gift. The death and resurrection are therefore the meritorious and procuring cause of sanctification as well as of justification, and in this respect are as directly related to sanctification as to justification. All of this is doctrinally true and does not violate the analogy of biblical teaching. But this analysis of the relation of the death and resurrection of Christ to sanctification does not do justice to Paul's teaching. He brings the death and resurrection of Christ into a much more direct relation to sanctification by way of efficiency and virtue than these foregoing proposals involve. The truth is that our death to sin and newness of life are effected in our identification with Christ in his death and resurrection, and no virtue accruing from the death and resurrection of Christ affects any phase of salvation more directly than the breach with sin and newness of life. And if we do not take account of this direct relationship we miss one of the cardinal features of New Testament teaching. It is not only in Romans 6 that this comes to expression. It is no less patent, for example, in Ephesians 2:1-6. It is the quickening from death in trespasses and sins that is in the forefront when the apostle says: 'But God being rich in mercy . . . hath made us alive together with Christ . . . and hath raised us up together.' And again in 2 Corinthians 5:14, 15 this thought is clearly in view—the death and resurrection of Christ ensure that those who are the beneficiaries live not to themselves but to him who died for them and rose again. In Colossians 2:20–3:4 the same doctrine is the basis of both rebuke and entreaty.

There are two questions, therefore, which require some discussion. First, what is this efficiency, in reference to sanctification, residing in the death and resurrection of Christ? and, second, when did believers die with Christ and rise again to newness of life?

In dealing with the first question it is well to turn to one of the most striking statements of Paul. It is Romans 6:7: 'For he who died is justified from sin.' It can be effectively argued that the uniform or, at least, all but uniform usage of Paul in reference to the term 'justify' must obtain in this instance and that the proposition must refer to justification and not to sanctification. It must be admitted that to suppose a meaning alien to the forensic import of 'justify' would be without warrant. But we have to recognize that it is characteristic of Paul to use the same term with different shades of meaning in the same context, and it is possible for him to use this term in its forensic signification without reference to what is specifically justification. The particular context must determine the precise application of a term, and in this case it must be observed that Paul is not treating of justification but dealing with what is properly in the sphere of sanctification, namely, deliverance from the enslaving power of sin. The proposition is adduced in support of the consideration that 'we no longer serve sin' (Rom. 6:6). 'Justified from sin' must be understood in a way that is appropriate to deliverance from the servitude of sin. If we paraphrase the thought it might be rendered, 'He who died is quit of sin.' And when we keep in view the forensic character of the term 'justify,' we readily detect what is forensic and at the same time consonant with the apostle's thesis, namely, the judgment executed upon sin in order that we may enjoy emancipation from its thraldom.

Admittedly it is difficult for us to grasp this juridical aspect of deliverance from the power of sin, and it is also difficult to make clear what is involved. But the difficulty arises perhaps from our failure to think through and appreciate this strand of New Testament teaching. In any case, we must look more carefully at the immediate context and the broader aspects of New Testament doctrine on this subject.

It should be noted that Paul in the context refers to the lordship of sin, of the law, and of death—of sin when he enjoins: 'Let not sin therefore reign in your mortal body' (Rom. 6:12), and when he asserts: 'Sin shall not lord it over you, for ye are not under law but under grace' (Rom. 6:14); of the law when he says: 'But now we have been discharged from the law, having died to that in which we were held, so that we might serve in newness of the Spirit and not in the oldness of the letter' (Rom. 7:6; cf. vss. 1, 4); of death when he reflects on the significance of Jesus' death and resurrection: 'Christ being raised from the dead dies no more: death no longer lords it over him' (Rom. 6:9). It is this notion of reigning power as applied to sin, the law, and death, that helps us to recognize not only the relevance but the necessity of the judgment executed if we are to be freed from their thraldom, judgment executed in Christ's death. The lordship wielded by sin cannot be conceived of apart from the power of Satan and of the principalities of iniquity. When our Lord deals with the destruction of Satan's power, it is the language of judgment he uses to express the victory. 'Now is the judgment of this world: now shall the prince of this world be cast out'

(Jn. 12:31). This verse furnishes us with what is perhaps the clearest parallel to Romans 6:7, and indicates that, in overcoming the realm and reign of this world, there is judgment executed. And our Lord's word is corroborative of the doctrine more fully unfolded in Paul, that the death of Christ is that by which this judgment is fulfilled, for Jesus proceeds: 'And I, if I be lifted up from the earth, will draw all men to myself' (vs. 32), a reference to the kind of death he should die (cf. vs. 33 and John 3:14; 8:28).[1]

We are compelled to reach the conclusion that it is by virtue of our having died with Christ, and our being raised with him in his resurrection from the dead, that the decisive breach with sin in its power, control, and defilement has been wrought, and that the reason for this is that Christ in his death and resurrection broke the power of sin, triumphed over the god of this world, the prince of darkness, executed judgment upon the world and its ruler, and by that victory delivered all those who were united to him from the power of darkness, and translated them into his own kingdom. So intimate is the union between Christ and his people, that they were partakers with him in all these triumphal achievements, and therefore died to sin, rose with Christ in the power of his resurrection, and have their fruit unto holiness, and the end everlasting life. As the death and resurrection are central in the whole process of redemptive accomplishment, so are they central in that by which sanctification itself is wrought in the hearts and lives of God's people.

The second question with which we are concerned in this connection is: When did believers die with Christ to sin, and rise with him to newness of life? It might appear unnecessary to ask this question because, if they died with Christ and rose with him in his resurrection, the time can only be when Christ himself died and rose again. And since Christ himself died once for all and, having risen from the dead, dies no more, it would appear necessary to restrict our death to sin and entrance upon newness of life (after the likeness of Jesus' resurrection) to the historic past where Jesus died and rose from the dead. There is the tendency to posit such a severe restriction because it appears to guard and support

[1] For further treatment of this subject cf. the present writer, *The Epistle to the Romans*, Vol. I (Grand Rapids: Eerdmans Pub. Co., 1959), pp. 277-284.

the interests of objectivity, which on all accounts must be maintained in connection with the death and resurrection of Christ. But there are other considerations which must not be discarded. It is to be noted that Paul, in one of the passages where this making alive with Christ is so prominent, speaks of the same persons as being dead in trespasses and sins, as having at one time walked according to the course of this world, as having conducted their life aforetime in the lusts of the flesh, doing the will of the flesh and of the mind, and says that they were children of wrath even as others (Eph. 2:1–4). And not only so—he says that it was when they were dead in trespasses that they were made alive together with Christ (vs. 5). Furthermore, it is too apparent to need demonstration, that the historic events of Calvary and the resurrection from Joseph's tomb do not register the changes which are continuously being wrought when the people of God are translated from the power of darkness into Christ's kingdom of life, liberty, and peace.

We are thus faced with the tension arising from the demands of the past historical, on the one hand, and the demands of the ethico-religious, on the other. And we cannot tone down the considerations which weigh in both directions.

If we think of the starting point of Paul's argument in Romans 6, namely, 'we died to sin,' it is obvious that he is dealing with the believer's actual death to sin. This follows for several reasons. (1) He is giving this as the reason why we no longer live in sin, and why it is both absurd and impossible to plead the argument of licence, 'Let us continue in sin that grace may abound.' The radical cleavage with the power and defilement of sin is conceived of as having taken place, and is instituted by the contrast between death to sin and living in sin. (2) The apostle appeals to the significance of baptism to support his thesis that the persons in view no longer live in sin. 'Or do ye not know that as many of us as were baptized into Christ Jesus were baptized into his death?' (vs. 3). He is, therefore, dealing with that new life which is represented, signified, and sealed by baptism. Hence it is vital and spiritual union with Christ that must be in view, a union that results in walking in newness of life after the pattern and in the power of Jesus' own resurrection (vss. 4, 5). (3) Death to sin is correlative with, if not interpreted in terms of, the crucifixion of the old man, the destruction of the body of sin, and deliverance from the reigning power of sin (vss. 6, 7). It is, therefore, the new man in Christ Jesus who is contemplated as having died to sin. (4) Those in view are not under law but under grace (vs. 14), and the exhortations directed to them are those appropriate to such as have been emancipated from the dominion of sin—sin shall not have the dominion, therefore they are to reckon themselves to be dead to sin and alive to God (vs. 11).

These reasons place beyond question the conclusion that the persons are regarded as the actual partakers of the virtue of Christ's death and resurrection. Examination of the other passages in which this same teaching appears (2 Cor. 5:14, 15; Eph. 2:1–6; Col. 3:1–3; 1 Pet. 4:1–4) will show the same result. So we must conclude that death to sin and newness of life refer to events which occur in the life history of the believer.

Are we, therefore, to suppose that the death of the believer with Christ, and the rising again with him, have *exclusive* reference to what takes place within the sphere of the effectual operations of grace in the heart and life of the believer? There are reasons for refusing to grant this inference. (1) We found already that it is impossible to dissociate the death and resurrection of Christ from his identification with those on whose behalf he died and rose again. To make a disjunction here is to rob the death and resurrection of Christ of meaning or purpose; it would make an abstraction impossible in divine conception as well as human. (2) Those on whose behalf Christ died and rose again were chosen in him before the foundation of the world. They were, therefore, in him when he died and rose again, and it is impossible to dissociate them from the death and resurrection of him in whom they were. (3) The apostle constantly interweaves the most explicit references to the death and resurrection of Christ as once-for-all historic events with the teaching respecting actual, experiential death to sin on the part of the believer. His arguments for the decisive and irrevocable breach with sin, and translation to new life, are bound up with the once-for-allness of Jesus' death. 'For in that he died, he died to sin once for all' (vs. 10). This sustained introduction of the once-for-all past historical in a context that clearly deals with what occurs actually and practically in the life-history of individuals makes inevitable the interpretation that the past historical conditions the continuously existential, not simply as laying the basis for it, and as providing the analogy in the realm of the past historical for what continues to occur in the realm of our experience, but conditions the latter for the reason that something occurred in the past historical which makes necessary what is realized and exemplified in the actual life-history of these same persons.

It is necessary to stress both aspects, the past historical and the experiential in their distinctness, on the one hand, and in their inter-dependence, on the other. The experiential must not be allowed to obscure the once-for-all historical, nor the once-for-all historical so to overshadow our thinking that we fail to give proper emphasis to the way in which its meaning and efficacy come to realization in the practical life of the believer. In other words, due emphasis must fall upon the objective and subjective in our dying and rising again with Christ in his death to sin and living again to God. It is only in this way that we can avoid the tendency to deny the vicarious significance of that which Christ wrought once-for-all in the realm of history to be as concrete and real as any other historical event.

The principle, or *modus operandi,* illustrated in this instance, as it bears upon the question of sanctification, is not essentially different from that which we find elsewhere in connection with the categories which define for us the atonement itself. Christ expiated the sins of his people in the offering of himself once for all—he purged our sins and sat down at the right hand of the Majesty on high (cf. Heb. 1:3). But sins are not actually forgiven until there is repentance and faith. Christ propitiated the wrath of God once for all when he died on the tree. But until we are savingly united to Christ we are children of wrath, even as others. We are reconciled to God by the death of Christ, and reconciliation is an accomplished work, but we are not at peace with God until we are justified. Admittedly it is difficult to define the precise relations of the past historical to the continuously operative in these cases. To put it more accurately, it is difficult to determine how the finished action of Christ in the past relates itself to those who are contemplated in that action prior to the time when that past action takes effect in their life history. But this difficulty in no way interferes with the distinction between the finished work and its actual application. Any added difficulty there may be in connection with our present topic arises, not from what is intrinsic to the subject, but from our unfamiliarity with this aspect of our relation to the death and resurrection of Christ.

Christ was identified with sin when he died, and for that reason alone did he die upon the accursed tree. But, because it was *he* who died, he died to sin—he destroyed its power, executed judgment upon it, and rose triumphant as the Lord of righteousness and life. He established thus for men the realm of life. And since his people were in him when he wrought victory and executed judgment, they also must be conceived of, in some mysterious manner that betokens the marvel of divine conception, wisdom, reckoning, and grace, yet really in terms of a divine constitution, as having died to sin also, and as having been raised up to newness of life. It is this fact that is basic and central. The mysteriousness of it must not be allowed to impair or tone down the reality of it in God's reckoning, and in the actual constitution established by him in the union of his people with Christ. It is basic and central, because only by virtue of what did happen in the past and finished historical, does it come to pass in the sphere of the practical and existential, that we actually come into possession of our identification with Christ when *he* died to sin and lived unto God.

We see, therefore, that the decisive and definitive breach with sin that occurs at the inception of Christian life is one necessitated by the fact that the death of Christ was decisive and definitive. It is just because we cannot allow for any reversal or repetition of Christ's death on the tree that we cannot allow for any compromise on the doctrine that every believer has died to sin and no longer lives under its dominion. Sin no longer lords it over him. To equivocate here is to assail the definitiveness of Christ's death. Likewise the decisive and definitive entrance upon newness of life in the case of every believer is required by the fact that the resurrection of Christ was decisive and definitive. As we cannot allow for any reversal or repetition of the resurrection, so we cannot allow for any compromise on the doctrine that every believer is a new man, that the old man has been crucified, that the body of sin has been destroyed, and that, as a new man in Christ Jesus, he serves God in the newness which is none other than that of the Holy Spirit of whom he has become the habitation and his body the temple.

23

Progressive Sanctification

It might appear from the emphasis which is placed in the New Testament upon the definitive breach with sin and the newness of life in the Spirit which union with Christ entails, that no place remains for a process of mortification and sanctification by which sin is more and more put to death and conformity to holiness progressively attained. Romans 6 is the passage in which more than any other the accent falls upon the decisive deliverance from the power and defilement of sin. But it is in that same Epistle that the apostle delineates for us the conflict that ensues for the believer by reason of indwelling sin. And it is significant that he should have to bring against himself such indictments as 'I am carnal, sold under sin' (7:14); 'I find another law in my members, warring against the law of my mind, and bringing me into captivity to the law of sin which is in my members. O wretched man that I am!' (7:23, 24); 'I myself . . . with the flesh serve the law of sin' (7:25). Even in Romans 6 we find repeated exhortations which imply, to say the least, the need for constant vigilance against the encroachments of sin.

No New Testament writer is more insistent upon the definitive character of the believer's sanctification than is the apostle John. So sweeping are John's terms that we have the greatest difficulty in reconciling them with the teaching of the New Testament elsewhere and with the obvious facts of Christian experience. 'Every one who is born of God does not commit sin; for his seed remaineth in him: and he cannot sin, because he is born of God' (1 John 3:9). 'Whosoever abideth in him sinneth not: whosoever sinneth hath not seen him, neither known him' (1 John 3:6). Yet John in that same epistle says, 'If we say that we have no sin, we deceive ourselves, and the truth is not in us' (1 John 1:8). He does not regard the believer as sinlessly perfect, for he sets forth the consolation for the believer when he sins—'we have an advocate with the Father, Jesus Christ the righteous' (1 John 2:1). And for John there is the self-purifying aspect of the believer's life: 'Every one that hath this hope in him purifieth himself even as he is pure' (1 John 3:3).

When we take account of the sin which still inheres in the believer, and of the fact that he has not yet attained to the goal appointed for him, the condition of the believer in this life is not one of a static *status quo*. There is abundant evidence to show that it is one of progression, a progression both negative and positive in character; it embraces both mortification and sanctification.

In reference to mortification there are two passages in the New Testament which are particularly striking because of the contexts in which they appear. 'But if by the Spirit ye put to death the deeds of the body, ye shall live' (Rom. 8:13). 'Put to death, therefore, the members which are upon the earth, fornication, uncleanness, passion, evil lust, and the covetousness which is idolatry' (Col. 3:5). These two passages are the more instructive because they occur in contexts in which the once-for-all death to sin, and the translation thereby to the realm of new life in Christ, are in the forefront. In Romans 6 the accent falls upon this definitive transition, and the pivotal consideration is 'ye died to sin'. But in Romans 8:13 the apostle addresses believers and clearly intimates that their own agency is to be enlisted in putting to death the deeds of the body, a duty made all the more remarkable since he had already said that the body of sin had been destroyed (Rom. 6:6). This activity is one that can be exercised only in the strength and grace of the Holy Spirit, and of that Paul takes account when he says, 'by the Spirit'. But it is an activity in which they as believers are to be engaged, and it consists in nothing less violent than that of putting to death. The context of Colossians 3:5 contains the same reflection upon the once-for-all death to sin by the death of Christ. 'If ye died with Christ from the rudiments of the world, why as living in the world do you subject yourselves to ordinances?' (Col. 2:20). 'For ye died, and your life is hid with Christ in

God' (Col. 3:3). The exhortation, 'Put to death, therefore, the members which are upon the earth', is one that arises from the categorical propositions which precede. It is clear, as in Romans 8:13, that the activity of the believer is enlisted in this process. The implication is, therefore, to the effect that, notwithstanding the definitive death to sin alluded to in Colossians 2:20; 3:3, the believer is not so delivered from sin in its lust and defilement but that he needs to be actively engaged in the business of the slaughterhouse with reference to his own sins. And just as the language used in reference to the definitive death to sin is that of passivity—ye died to sin, ye died with Christ, ye were put to death to the law (Rom. 6:2; Col. 2:20; Rom. 7:4)—so now the terms are those of activity on the part of the believer himself. The exhortation of 2 Corinthians 7:1—'having therefore these promises, beloved, let us cleanse ourselves from all filthiness of flesh and spirit, perfecting holiness in the fear of God'—is to the same effect. The assumption is that there is defilement of flesh and spirit and that we ourselves are to be actively engaged in cleansing ourselves from that defilement, just as on the more positive side we are to perfect holiness in the fear of God.

This mortifying and cleansing process is concerned with sin and defilement still adhering to the believer, and it contemplates as its aim the removal of all defilement of flesh and spirit. Nothing less than the complete eradication of this sinfulness is compatible with the destination of the believer, namely, conformity to the image of God's Son. He was holy, harmless, undefiled, and separate from sinners, and they must be like him. It is not only to the image of Christ that they are to be conformed, but also to that of the Father. Jesus himself said, 'Ye shall be perfect as your heavenly Father is perfect' (Matt. 5:48). And it is the Father of whom John is speaking when he says, 'Not yet hath it been made manifest what we shall be. We know that when it shall be manifested, we shall be like him, because we shall see him as he is' (1 John 3:2). We shall be like the Father. It is no wonder that, when John's thought is absorbed in this hope, he should immediately focus attention upon the implications of this hope as they bear upon our sinfulness. He adds immediately: 'And every one who has this hope in him [the Father] purifieth himself even as he is pure' (1 John 3:3). The demand for eradication, and therefore for the mortification which contributes to that eradication, inheres in the nature of the salvation enjoyed and the goal to which it is directed.

It is not only the cleansing from sin, however, that sanctification as process involves. The eradication of sin would not of itself constitute the goal. It is eloquent of something more positive, that Paul should have added in 2 Corinthians 7:1 the words, 'perfecting holiness in the fear of God'. Perhaps the most expressive term used in the New Testament to indicate the progressive change that is directed to, and terminates in conformity to holiness as the epitome of divine perfection, if not the sum of God's perfections, is that used by Paul on two occasions: 'Be not conformed to this world, but be ye transformed by the renewing of your mind' (Rom. 12:2). 'But we all with unveiled face beholding the glory of the Lord are being transformed unto the same image from glory to glory' (2 Cor. 3:18). It is this same term that is used with reference to Jesus' transfiguration (Matt. 17:2; Mark 9:3). Since the goal of the whole redemptive process, as it has respect to the people of God, is conformity to the image of Christ as the firstborn among many brethren, no passage in Scripture defines for us specifically the method of progressive sanctification more than 2 Corinthians 3:18. Whether the thought is that we reflect the glory of the Lord Christ, or that we behold his glory, both thoughts are implied. If we reflect his glory it is because we behold it after the pattern of John's declaration, 'We beheld his glory, glory as of the only-begotten from the Father, full of grace and truth' (John 1:14), and in beholding, are being more and more transformed into his likeness. The eyes of heart and mind become so fixed upon him as the effulgence of the Father's glory and the express image of his being (cf. Heb. 1:3), and therefore upon him in his matchless glory, that we more and more take on the characters of his image from one degree of similitude to another, until finally we are completely transfigured. It is a law of our psychology that we become like that in which our interests and ambitions are absorbed, and that law is not suspended in this case. But the apostle here reminds us that natural factors are not the secret of this transformation; it is from the Spirit of the Lord that this transformation proceeds. Even if we render this expression 'from the Lord of the Spirit', as may well be proper, the allusion to the Holy Spirit is not eliminated, and harks back to verses

6 and 8 where the quickening power and effective ministry of the Holy Spirit are instanced as marking the pre-eminence of the new covenant. If Paul speaks here of 'the Lord of the Spirit', he is reflecting even more strikingly upon the way in which the Holy Spirit works in the interests of glorifying Christ, and of bringing to perfection the goal of the redemptive process. And we are reminded of our Lord's own words, 'When he the Spirit of truth is come, he will guide you into all the truth: for he will not speak from himself, but whatsoever things he hears those he will speak . . . He shall glorify me, because he will take of mine and show them to you' (John 16:13, 14).

The progressiveness in its more positive character is set forth in a great variety of ways. Paul prayed that the love of the Philippians might 'abound more and more in knowledge and in all discernment' (Phil. 1:9). Peter speaks of believers as growing, by the sincere milk of the Word, unto salvation (1 Pet. 2:2), salvation being understood as salvation consummated and ready to be revealed in the last time (cf. 1:5). And he also exhorts his readers to 'grow in the grace and the knowledge of our Lord and Saviour Jesus Christ' (2 Pet. 3:18). Perhaps no one passage offers more instruction than Ephesians 4:12–16, and particularly when related to the teaching of the Epistle as a whole. The accent falls clearly upon the necessity of growth, and growth as crystallized in knowledge and love. The offices specified in verse 11 are directed to the perfecting of the saints, and to the building up of the body of Christ, 'until we all come unto the unity of the faith and of the knowledge of the Son of God unto a perfect man, unto the measure of the stature of the fulness of Christ, that we be no longer babes, tossed and carried about with every wind of doctrine in the craft of men' (vss. 13, 14). The corresponding exhortation is that believers, 'speaking the truth in love, may grow up into him in all things, who is the head, even Christ' (vs. 15). The law of growth applies, therefore, in the realm of Christian life. God is pleased to work through process, and to fail to take account of this principle in the sanctification of the people of God is to frustrate both the wisdom and the grace of God. The child who acts as a man is a monstrosity; the man who acts as a child is a tragedy. If this is true in nature, how much more in Christian behaviour. There are babes in Christ; there are young men, and there are old men. And what monstrosities and tragedies have marred the witness of the church by failure to take account of the law of growth!

This process is exemplified particularly in knowledge and love. The prominence given to knowledge and to the enlightenment of the understanding (cf. Eph. 1:17, 18; 4:13–15; 2 Pet. 3:18), as the knowledge and understanding of the truth, enforces the lesson that it is in proportion to this increase that there can be the increase of the fruit of the Spirit in love, joy, and peace. The complementation is illustrated in Paul's prayer for the Philippian believers, that their love might abound more and more in knowledge and in all discernment, and by his injunction in the Ephesian Epistle that we are to speak the truth in love. As John reminds us, 'God is love, and he who abides in love abides in God, and God abides in him' (1 John 4:16). But love is not a static emotion; it must increase and abound more and more (cf. Phil. 1:9; 1 Thess. 3:12; 4:10). And love is fed by the increasing apprehension of the glory of him who is love, and of him in whom the love of God is manifested.

This progression has respect, not only to the individual, but also to the church in its unity and solidarity as the body of Christ. In reality the growth of the individual does not take place except in the fellowship of the church as the fellowship of the Spirit. Believers have never existed as independent units. In God's eternal counsel they were chosen in Christ (Eph. 1:4); in the accomplishment of their redemption they were in Christ (2 Cor. 5:14, 15; Eph. 1:7); in the application of redemption they are ushered into the fellowship of Christ (1 Cor. 1:9). And sanctification itself is a process that moves to a consummation which will not be realized for the individual until the whole body of Christ is complete and presented in its totality faultless and without blemish. This points up the necessity of cultivating and promoting the sanctification of the whole body, and the practical implications for responsibility, privilege, and opportunity become apparent.

If the individual is indifferent to the sanctification of others, and does not seek to promote their growth in grace, love, faith, knowledge, obedience, and holiness, this interferes with his own sanctification in at least two respects. (1) His lack of concern for others is itself a vice that gnaws at the root of spiritual growth. If we are not concerned with, or vigilant in respect of the fruit of the Spirit in others, then it is because we do not burn with holy zeal for the honour of Christ himself. All shortcoming and sin in us dishonour Christ, and a believer betrays the coldness of his love to Christ when he fails to bemoan the defects of those who are members of Christ's body. (2) His indifference to the interests of others means the absence of the ministry which he should have afforded others. This absence results in the impoverishment of these others to the extent of his failure, and this impoverishment reacts upon himself, because these others are not able to minister to him to the full extent of the support, encouragement, instruction, edification, and exhortation which they owe to him.

We see, therefore, the endless respects in which interaction and inter-communication within the fellowship of the saints are brought to bear upon the progressive sanctification of the people of God. 'If one member suffers, all the other members suffer with it; and if one member is honoured, all the others rejoice with it' (1 Cor. 12:26). The truth of our inter-dependence within the solidarity of the body of Christ exposes the peril and contradiction of exclusive absorption in our own individual sanctification. How eloquent of the virtue which is the antonym of independency and aloofness are the words of the apostle: 'And he [Christ] gave some apostles, and some prophets, and some evangelists, and some pastors and teachers, for the perfecting of the saints unto the work of the ministry, unto the edifying of the body of Christ; until we all come in the unity of the faith and of the knowledge of the Son of God, unto a perfect man, unto the measure of the stature of the fulness of Christ'! (Eph. 4:11–13; cf. Rom. 12:4ff.; 1 Cor. 12:12ff.; Col. 2:19).

This fellowship in growth requires us to take account of the expression just quoted, 'the measure of the stature of the fulness of Christ'. This expression concerns not only the goal of the sanctifying process; it is also germane to the process itself. Nothing in the New Testament defines for us that in which the process consists more characteristically than the impartation and reception of the fulness of Christ. What is the fulness of Christ?

We may begin with Colossians 1:19: 'It pleased the Father that all the fulness should take up its abode in him'. This text has been interpreted ontologically, and thus 'all the fulness' has been regarded as reflecting upon the fulness that belongs to Christ essentially as the eternal Son.

There are good reasons for disputing this interpretation, and for regarding the reference as economic, that is, to the fulness that dwells in Christ in his redemptive and mediatorial identity. The reasons are the following. (1) It is distinctly of a messianically conditioned and economic relationship that verse 18 speaks, when Christ is said to be the 'head of the body, the church'. (2) The expression 'first begotten from the dead' is not an ontological designation, but one that belongs to Christ by virtue of the historical event of his resurrection. Therefore it is a pre-eminence accruing to him from this historical event, and not that intrinsic to his eternal Sonship and Deity, a pre-eminence, furthermore, stated expressly to be the designed result of his being the first begotten from the dead. (3) Verse 19 enunciates a causal relation to the pre-eminence achieved. It is because it pleased the Father that all the fulness should come to dwell in Christ, that this pre-eminence belongs to him. It is indeed true that such pre-eminence could not be accorded him unless he were intrinsically competent for its possession and exercise, that is, unless the fulness of Deity were essentially his. But it is more in accord with the contextual emphasis upon the economic, to regard verse 19 likewise as referring to the *investiture* in virtue of which the pre-eminence is constituted. (4) If verse 19 were interpreted ontologically, we should encounter a grave theological difficulty, which we have no need or warrant to create. It is not by the will of the Father that the fulness of Deity dwells in the Son. Deity is essentially and self-existently his. For these reasons the fulness of which Colossians 1:19 speaks must be interpreted as the fulness bestowed in Christ's messianic identity in the economy of salvation. Colossians 2:9 should not be regarded as incompatible with this conclusion. For, though the latter text refers to the fulness of Godhood that belongs to Christ essentially as eternal Son, the chief interest of the apostle is to assert that this fulness dwells in him in his incarnate state, and is not in the least curtailed by his bodily identity as the Word made flesh. That the fulness of Deity is Christ's essentially does not interfere with the fulness he comes to possess for the execution of messianic office.

The fulness that has come to dwell in Christ may thus be properly construed as the plenitude of life, of grace, of truth, of wisdom, of knowledge, of goodness, of mercy, of righteousness, of power. This concept provides us with a ready explanation of Pauline texts about which so much dispute has arisen, and it is one that is pivotal in the doctrine of sanctification.

We may now turn to Ephesians 1:23: 'And gave him to be head over all things to the church, which is his body, the fulness of him who filleth all in all.' The first question is the force of the term here rendered 'filleth'. Is it to be interpreted actively or passively? If the latter view is adopted, then of Christ it is said that he is being filled, and 'all in all' would mean that he is being filled throughout or thoroughly, giving intensity to the thought of being filled. The thought would be that he continues to be filled with that which the fulness as applied to him denotes. There is a question as to the propriety of this view. Can the filling of Christ be regarded as a process? Does not the fulness have its permanent abode in him? 'It pleased the Father that all the fulness should come to dwell in him' (Col. 1:19). This suggests, to say the least, a finished impartation. If we adopt the active meaning, then of Christ it is said that he fills all in all. 'All in all' could have cosmic reference: Christ is head over all things to the church (Eph. 1:22) and he fills all things (Eph. 4:10). But 'all in all' could refer simply to the church. He fills the church throughout or thoroughly. On the exact force of the term in question it is difficult to be dogmatic.

Of greater significance is the question: What is the antecedent of the term 'the fulness'? Is it Christ, referred to in verse 22, or the church?

To regard Christ as the antecedent is scarcely a tenable position for several reasons. (1) Syntactically, it is harsh to go back to verse 22 for the antecedent of 'the fulness' and, for that reason, this construction should not be resorted to unless any other view would offer insuperable difficulty. (2) If Christ himself is 'the fulness', then, in view of what follows, he would have to be the fulness of another person who is conceived of as filling all in all. This would have to be God the Father. But this would offer a concept alien to New Testament thought, and to that of Paul in particular. Christ is never represented as the fulness of the Father. In him dwells the fulness of Godhood, but he is not spoken of as the fulness of another person of the Godhead. (3) The person of whom Christ would be the fulness would, on this position, have to be regarded as filling all in all. According to Paul, however, it is Christ who fills all in all, whether 'all in all' refers to the cosmos or to the church. In this same Epistle this is expressly predicated of Christ (Eph. 4:10) and it would be exegetically indefensible to apply this notion to any other than to Christ. For these reasons, especially the second and third, the interpretation in question will have to be rejected, and the only alternative is to regard the church as 'the fulness'. The close antecedence of 'the church, which is his body' makes this the natural construction, and it should not be contested unless compelling considerations demand another interpretation. Such considerations do not exist.

If the church as the body of Christ is 'the fulness', then it is the fulness of Christ. How can the church be such? It would be counter to New Testament teaching, and to that of Paul in particular, to suppose that the church fills Christ. On the contrary it is out of his fulness we all receive (John 1:16). All the fulness has its abode in him (Col. 1:19; 2:9), and it is to the measure of the stature of the fulness of Christ that the church in due time attains (Eph. 4:13). Fulness could, however, be understood in the sense of that which completes, the complement (cf. Matt. 9:16; Mark 2:21). Christ in his economic capacity and offices may never be thought of apart from those united to him. He is the head of the body, the church, and, as a head does not exist as the head apart from the body, so Christ and the church are always complementary the one to the other. Since the headship of Christ to the church is so prominent in this passage, it would be appropriate to reflect on this notion of complementation by the use of the term 'fulness'.

'Fulness' can also denote that which is the receptacle of something. In this Epistle this meaning appears on two occasions (3:19; 4:13), and the only meaning that is appropriate in these instances is that the church is filled with the plenitude that is in Christ. The thought is that of John 1:16: 'out of his fulness have all we received'. When believers are conceived of as 'filled unto all the fulness of God' (Eph. 3:19), the thought is surely that of communication to them of the fulness that is in God. And when they attain to 'the stature of the fulness of Christ' (Eph. 4:13), this stature is that of being filled with the grace and virtue, truth and wisdom, righteousness and holiness of which Christ is the embodiment. This communication is the only way of being conformed to the image of him who is the firstborn among many brethren. So, in respect of

Ephesians 1:23, the analogy of Paul's teaching would point to the conclusion that the church is the fulness of Christ, because to the church as the body of Christ is being imparted the fulness that is in Christ. The church is the recipient of that fulness of righteousness, wisdom, knowledge, power, grace, goodness, patience, love, truth, and mercy, which has its permanent abode in Christ, and abides in him in terms of an economy that has no relevance apart from the purpose and realization of this same communication. This fulness believers do not receive as discrete individuals, but in the unity and fellowship of the church as the body of Christ.

The process, therefore, that progressive sanctification involves is one directed to conformity to the image of God's Son, a conformity attained not through external imitative assimilation, but through an impartation of the fulness of grace in Christ, an impartation which flows through a living organism that subsists and acts on an immensely higher plane than any form of organic or animate life with which we are acquainted in our earthly existence. As this applies to our responsibility and privilege, it means that in progressive sanctification the basic consideration is that we must recognize increasingly the implications of union and communion with Christ, and of communication from him. There is no need of ours, no exigency arising from the high calling of God in Christ Jesus, no demand flowing from membership in his body, and no office which we are called upon to discharge in the service of Christ and the church, that is not supplied out of the fulness that resides in Christ. It is an affront to Christ, as the one in whom dwells all the fulness, to doubt the sufficiency of his grace for the discharge of every demand which the goal of sanctification entails. And as we think of the goal of conformity to the image of Christ as the firstbegotten, and the stature of his fulness, it is only the fulness of Christ that can generate hope and confidence of ultimate achievement.

24

The Pattern of Sanctification

No aspect of the doctrine of sanctification confronts us with the sanctity and seriousness of our subject more forcefully than the question of the pattern. For pattern is concerned with that to which the people of God are to be conformed and, after all, nothing enters more constitutively into the definition than the norm after which sanctification, either as definitive act or as process, is accomplished.

The primary consideration in this connection is that God himself is the pattern. Sanctification has respect to holiness. The Old Testament as well as the New lays stress upon this fact. 'For I am the Lord your God: sanctify yourselves therefore, and be ye holy; for I am holy. . . . For I am the Lord that brought you up out of the land of Egypt, to be your God: ye shall therefore be holy, for I am holy' (Lev. 11:44, 45). It is summed up again in Leviticus 19:2: 'Ye shall be holy; for I the Lord your God am holy.' So the reason why sanctification has respect to holiness is that God himself is holy. Peter, in accord with this Old Testament witness and with express appeal to it, writes: 'As he who has called you is holy, so be ye also holy in all manner of life, because it is written, Be ye holy, for I am holy' (1 Pet. 1:15, 16). Our Lord himself enunciated the same principle when he said to his disciples: 'Ye shall therefore be perfect as your heavenly Father is perfect' (Matt. 5:48). It is worthy of note how this governing principle is introduced by our Lord: it is appealed to in order to enforce a very concrete and practical duty. The disciples are being exhorted to bestow lovingkindness upon their enemies, and the reason is that God himself is kind to the unthankful and to the evil. They are to follow the example of their heavenly

Father and thus show themselves to be sons of the Father who is in heaven. So we are thus provided with a concrete example of what is involved in being perfect as God is perfect.

Our proper concern with the law of God as the criterion of right and wrong, or with the revealed will of God as the norm of what is well-pleasing to God, or even with conformity to the image of Christ, must not prevent us from appreciating what underlies all of these other aspects, and gives them validity and sanction, namely, that likeness to God is the ultimate pattern of sanctification. The reason why God himself is the pattern should be obvious: man is made in the image of God and nothing less than the image of God can define the restoration which redemption contemplates. Initial and definitive sanctification consists in being created anew after God in knowledge, righteousness, and holiness of the truth (Eph. 4:24; Col. 3:10).

When we say, as Scripture plainly asserts, that God himself is the pattern, we must not overlook the distinction which must be guarded. There is a total discrepancy between God as God and man as man, between God as Creator and man as creature, between God as sovereign and man as dependent. So it must not be thought that likeness to God is absolute. There is a sense in which to aspire after likeness to God is the epitome of iniquity. This again illustrates how fine is the line of demarcation between iniquity and holiness at the point of divergence. Strange as it may seem, the recognition that there is no likeness to God, in respect of that which he uniquely is, is the presupposition of the principle with which we are now concerned, namely, that likeness to God is the ultimate and primary pattern in sanctification. And it is very likely that the genius of the allegation with which the tempter first seduced Eve, 'Ye shall be as God knowing good and evil', consisted in confusing the false and the true in reference to likeness with God. In view, therefore, of the distinction which must be jealously guarded, revelation defining the respects in which likeness to God is the pattern is indispensable. Otherwise we should be in hopeless confusion respecting the ultimate principle regulative of our sanctification.

The necessity of revelation defining the respects in which likeness to God prescribes the norm of sanctification, shows how consonant with the ultimate principle are the other considerations, that the law of God, the revealed will of God, and the example of our Lord are the criteria and patterns according to which sanctification proceeds. The law of God is the transcript of God's perfection; it is God's perfection coming to expression for the regulation of thought and conduct consonant with his holiness. As thus defined, the law of God guards the distinction of which we have spoken, because the law of God is the revealed will of God for us; it regulates our thought and behaviour in ways consonant with his perfection. And this is why every depreciation of the law of God as the pattern in terms of which sanctification is fashioned invariably leads to the adoption of patterns which impinge upon the unique prerogatives of God in the transcendent and inimitable glory that belongs to him. There is one lawgiver. This belongs to the uniqueness in respect of which the attempt to be like God is blasphemy, and shows that whenever we do not appreciate the limitations prescribed by law, it is because we have failed to guard the differentiation that is correlative with the demand for likeness.

The Scripture speaks of the law of God as spiritual. This means that it is of divine origin and character, and more specifically, that it is derived from the Holy Spirit, is validated by his authority, and bespeaks his character. The law is also spoken of as holy, just, and good. These are attributes which express what God is; and to characterize the law as holy, just, and good is but to claim in the most explicit way possible that the law is of God and bears the imprint of his character as holy, just, and good. Thus every lack of conformity to the law of God is lack of conformity to God's likeness, and all conformity to the law is but conformity to that pattern which is the primary and ultimate pattern of sanctification.

When the apostle says: 'Be not conformed to this world, but be ye transformed by the renewal of your mind, that ye may prove what is the will of God, the good, the acceptable, and the perfect' (Rom. 12:2), he defines for us the pattern in terms of the will of God. But what is of importance is to note how he characterizes this will. He does not describe it simply as good, and acceptable, and perfect, but as that which is 'the good and the acceptable and the perfect'. The will of God is that which for us is the epitome of the good, the well-pleasing, and the perfect. It is that which defines the zenith of good, acceptable, and perfect. And such characterizations would be impossible if it were not the case that the will of God for us reflects that which God is, as alone ultimately good and perfect.

The supreme revelation of what God is and of his will for us, the supreme exhibition of that pattern which is the exemplar of sanctification, is the Lord Jesus Christ himself. He is the effulgence of the Father's glory and the express image of his being; he is the image of the invisible God. 'No man hath seen God at any time: God only begotten who is in the bosom of the Father, he hath revealed him' (John 1:18). He who hath seen him hath seen the Father (cf. John 14:9). In flesh, which is identical with ours as to its nature, the holiness of God, as it is reflected in and impressed upon man, comes to perfect expression and illustration. In no other way could God's holiness, as relevant to our responsibility and as exemplifying the pattern to which the saints of God are to be conformed, be so effectively revealed. This is why, in the concrete and practical, the example of our Lord is invested with incomparable significance, and our Lord himself could say, 'I have given you an example that ye should do as I have done to you' (John 13:15). Again, he says, 'Whosoever would be first among you, let him be servant of all: for even the Son of man came not to be ministered unto but to minister, and to give his life a ransom for many' (Mark 10:44, 45; cf. Matt. 20:27, 28). And the apostles could enjoin to the same effect: 'For hereunto were ye called: because Christ also suffered for you, leaving you an example, that ye should follow his steps' (1 Pet. 2:21); 'Let this mind be in you which was also in Christ Jesus' (Phil. 2:5).

Such appeals to Christ's example set forth some important lessons.

1. The example of Christ is adduced by our Lord himself and by his apostles, to enforce the elementary duties of humble service to others, unselfish considerateness for others, patient endurance of suffering, and Christian liberality (cf. 2 Cor. 8:7–9). It is not by way of abstract generalization that the example of our Lord is pleaded; his example is brought to bear upon the concrete details of practical life.

2. Perhaps the most striking feature of these passages is that the climactic events of Jesus' messianic accomplishment are adduced to enforce the elementary duties of our high vocation. This fact shows that the most transcendent truths of the gospel, the accomplishments which lay at the

centre of Jesus' messianic commission and commitment, bear directly upon the pattern by which the believer's life in its concrete, practical details is to be governed and regulated. We have a distorted conception of the relation of doctrine to life if we think that the most transcendent truths of the faith are impractical in their bearing upon the most menial tasks of our vocation.

3. We find in these passages the differentiation which is parallel to the differentiation we found already in respect of likeness to God. It is striking indeed that the supreme and incomparable actions of our Lord should be appealed to as providing us with examples after which our dispositions and actions are to be patterned. But it lies on the face of these texts that the actions which induce in us conformity to his example are not actions which we are represented as likewise performing. Our Lord could appeal to the fact that he gave his life a ransom for many as the supreme example of ministry to others. But there is no suggestion that the example is to be followed by giving our lives a ransom for many. Peter can say that Christ gave us an example that we should follow his steps, but in that context he forbids us to think that we participate with Jesus in bearing our sins. Oh, no! He says: 'who his own self bare our sins in his own body upon the tree, that we, having died to sins, might live unto righteousness; by whose stripes ye were healed' (1 Pet. 2:24). Paul can say, 'Let this mind be in you which was also in Christ Jesus', and make appeal in that connection to the successive stages of our Lord's humiliation. But it is just as clear that he is not enjoining upon us actions which reproduce or repeat or copy the transcendent actions of which our Lord was the subject. Of him alone could it be said, 'who, being in the form of God, thought it not robbery to be equal with God, but made himself of no reputation, taking the form of a servant' (Phil. 2:6, 7).

4. It is, however, the uniqueness of our Lord's accomplishment, arising from the uniqueness of his person, the uniqueness of his commission, and the uniqueness of the task performed, that invests his example with supreme relevance. His commission and task were such as only God manifest in the flesh could perform. But since his example bears upon us in the realm of our attitude and performance as mere men called into the fellowship of God's Son, the example of Christ brings to expression the primary and ultimate pattern by which the sanctification of the

saints is regulated and brought to fruition. The example of Christ has peculiar relevance to us, because it was in the flesh he gave us an example. It was as truly human he manifested himself. But he was also divine. And so his example does not fall short one whit of what we have found to be ultimate and primary. He is the image of the invisible God and in him dwells the fulness of Godhead bodily.

Thus the process of sanctification can be described in its richest meaning as transformation into the image of Christ. The goal of the Father's predestination is conformity to the image of the Son, that he might be the firstborn among many brethren, and the whole redemptive process subserves the achievement of this goal. Sanctification as one aspect of that process must, in the nature of the case, be patterned after the image, conformity to which is the final end. There is no incompatibility between likeness to Christ and likeness to the Father for, as noted, Christ is the image of the Father. And John can define the consummation of the sanctifying process as likeness to the Father when he says: 'we know that if it shall be manifested, we shall be like him, for we shall see him as he is' (I John 3:2). It is of the Father that John is speaking in this context, and so it is likeness to the Father he has in view. Seeing the Father as he is does not refer to physical sight, but to the fulness and clearness of the knowledge of the Father that will follow upon understanding undimmed by sin, and the revelation of the full splendour of the Father's glory. Believers will then know even as they are known. Every cloud of sin will have been dispelled and to the full extent of their finite capacity they will be irradiated by the glory of the Father. This irradiation will be, in the finite realm, the perfect reflection of God's glory, and that is why the people of God will be fully conformed to the image of Christ. It is with the glory of the Father that the Son of God incarnate is himself glorified, and when believers are also glorified with that glory there must be the conformity by which the Son is the firstborn among many brethren.

When we think of sanctification as being patterned after the image of Christ, we must ask the question: How does it take place? As we think of definitive sanctification, we found already that this basically consists in union with Christ in his death and resurrection. And that simply means that we have been conformed to his death and resurrection. We died with him and we rose with him. Nothing could be more significant in this connection than the apostle's word: 'For if we have become grown together in the likeness of his death, we shall be also in the likeness of his resurrection' (Rom. 6:5). For here the term 'likeness' points to the conception with which we are now concerned, namely, pattern. So the inception of sanctification demands conformity to, or patterning after, that which is central in the redemptive accomplishment of the incarnate Son, namely, his death and resurrection.

Though it is this conformity that constitutes definitive sanctification, we are not by any means to think that this conformity does not also bear upon progressive sanctification. To a large extent the progress of sanctification is dependent upon the increasing understanding and appropriation of the implications of that identification with Christ in his death and resurrection. Nothing is more relevant to progressive sanctification than the reckoning of ourselves to be dead to sin and alive to God through Jesus Christ (cf. Rom. 6:11). And when Paul contemplates the prize of the high calling of God in Christ Jesus and the hope of the resurrection, nothing is more characteristic of his present preoccupation than to know Christ 'and the power of his resurrection, and the fellowship of his sufferings, being made conformable to his death' (Phil. 3:10). It is as we have fellowship in Christ's sufferings, and are conformed to his death, that we may entertain the assurance of resurrection to life, and reach forth for the prize of the high calling of God.

But there is much more involved in the way by which this conformity takes place than the realization of the implications of union with Christ in his death and resurrection. Paul elsewhere speaks of being transformed into the image of Christ, from glory to glory, and he tells us of the way in which this transformation takes place—'beholding as in a glass the glory of the Lord' (2 Cor. 3:18). It is possible that this means 'reflecting' the glory of the Lord. But on either interpretation the import is that, as we come into intelligent, believing, and adoring encounter with the glory of Christ, we take on the characters which belong to him. We must remember, of course, that supernatural agency is at work in this process. But the means by which this work of grace is wrought are clearly indicated. The glory of Christ is portrayed and exhibited to us in the pages of Scripture. The Holy Spirit illumines our minds and quickens our hearts to behold the glory; he takes of the things of Christ and shows them to us. He thus glorifies Christ. The responses in us are adoration, love, obedience, and communion. His glory fills our minds, captivates our hearts, constrains our wills. Our whole being is rendered captive to him and to his glory. In ways appropriate to each aspect of our personality and to each detail of demand arising for us, we are transformed more and more so that the fashion of this present world is displaced by conformity to him who captivates faith, love, and hope. That Christ should be focal in thought and affection does no prejudice or dishonour to the Father and Spirit. It is in the face of Christ that the glory of God is resplendent. He is the effulgence of the Father's glory. It is the prerogative of the Spirit to glorify Christ. Hence, when Christ is truly honoured, the other persons of the Godhead are likewise honoured.

This process of conformation to the image of Christ does not take place by quiescent passivity on our part. It is only by concentrated application to the data of revelation that we come into this encounter with the glory of the Lord. And all the energies of our being are enlisted in the exercise of adoration, love, obedience, and fellowship.

25

The Goal of Sanctification

THE goal of sanctification is to be understood in two senses. There is firstly, the chief end to be promoted by it, and secondly, the attainment to which it is directed and in which it finds its terminus.

1. The chief end is the glory of God (cf. Eph. 1:6, 12, 14; Phil. 1:11). As we entertain the hope of our own glorification, this chief end should be uppermost in our objective and hope. If we think that the glory of God interferes in any way with the glory that belongs to our own glorification, it is because we have a distorted view of that which will be constitutive of our own glorification, namely, the glory that will redound to God in the consummation of the sanctifying process, and the vindication that will be accorded in the manifestation of his glory. Sometimes we have difficulty with the thought of the judgment that will be executed with reference to believers at the judgment seat of Christ, when God will bring every work into judgment with every secret thing, whether it be good or evil. We wonder how the exposure of sins will comport with the bliss of resurrection to life. This difficulty only arises when we have restricted our thought to our own bliss and have overlooked the demands of the glory of God. When we give the priority to the claims of God's glory, then we appreciate the fact that the prerequisite to our bliss is the vindication of the glory of God. And the glory of God requires that there be perfect adjudication of all things, that the whole panorama of history will be finally adjudicated with perfect equity and truth. God 'will judge the world with righteousness, and the people with his truth' (Psalm 96:13). How could the people of God contemplate with delight an eternity that would leave anything at

loose ends? The adjudication that God will render with reference to their sins is not one that will fill them with dismay, but one that will only enhance in their esteem the marvels of redeeming grace, as it will also serve to exhibit the perfect justice of God in the provisions of his saving mercy. When sin is exposed in its true proportions and gravity, it is then that the glory of redemptive grace will be fully exhibited and the joy of the saints will reach its zenith. The bliss of heaven is not constituted by forgetting sin, but by glorying in the redemption that washed from sin and made us white in the blood of the Lamb.

When we think of the glory of God as the chief end in the goal of sanctification, we must appreciate the extent to which God will be glorified in the glorification of his people. There is no limitation to the glory that will redound to God from the completion of the sanctifying process. God will be glorified in all his works. The damnation of the reprobate will redound to the glory of God, and no speck of stain will attach to God's action. It will redound to the glory of his justice and power. But in the glorification of the people of God, the whole sum of the divine perfections will be manifested as in no other handiwork of his. We must say this, because it is only in relation to the redemption of the elect that the incarnation of the Son has meaning. The glorification of the elect is really one with the final glorification of him who himself is the embodiment of the glory of God. So when his glory will be revealed, the people of God will also be manifested with him in glory. But the revelation of Christ's glory is surely the supreme exhibition of the glory of God.

This great truth, that the glorification of the saints has not only as its chief end the glory of God, but is really constituted by the exhibition and vindication of the glory of God, is illustrated by the word of the apostle when he says that 'we rejoice in hope of the glory of God' (Rom. 5:2). There is good reason for believing that 'the glory of God' refers to God's own glory (possessive genitive; *cf.* John 11:4; Rom. 1:23; 15:7; 1 Cor. 10:31; 2 Cor. 4:6, 15; Phil. 1:11; 2:11; 1 Tim. 1:11; Tit. 2:13; Rev. 21:11, 23), and not to the glory that comes from God and is bestowed upon us (cf. Rom. 2:7, 10; 8:18, 21; 9:23b; 1 Cor. 2:7; 15:43; 2 Cor. 3:18b; 4:17; Col. 1:27; 3:4; Heb. 2:10). So when Paul says, 'We rejoice in hope of the glory of God', he represents the eschatological finale of the believer's hope as hope of the manifestation of God's own glory (cf. 1 Thess. 2:12; 1 Pet. 5:10). This is simply to say that the theocentric interest of the believer is paramount in the hope which constitutes the completion of the redemptive process.

If we ask the question: How can this chief end be related to sanctification?, the answer is at hand. It is only as the believer is wholly sanctified that he will be able to contain the full manifestation of the glory of God, and it is the full manifestation of the glory of God that will itself bring with it the glorification of the believer. These are correlative the one with the other.

2. The second sense in which the goal of sanctification is to be understood is the attainment in which it finds its terminus. This is the glorification of the believer and of the whole body of the elect. It is noteworthy how seldom the term 'glorify' (δοξάζω) is used with reference to the people of God (cf. Rom. 8:17, 30). This term is almost uniformly used of glorifying God or Christ. What is of particular significance in the glorification of the people of God is the relation it sustains to the glorification of Christ himself. In Rom. 8:17, believers and Christ are said to be glorified together, and in Rom. 8:29, 30 it is apparent that the glorification spoken of in verse 20 is the realization of the predestinating purpose spoken of in verse 29, namely, conformity to the image of God's Son, that he might be the firstborn among many brethren. These two texts, therefore (Rom. 8:17; 8:29, 30), both indicate the inseparable conjunction and community that exists between Christ and believers in respect of what is the final phase of Christ's exaltation and glorification, and the glorification of the elect. The title 'firstborn' or 'firstbegotten' (πρωτότοκος) refers to priority and pre-eminence and points to the supereminence that belongs to Christ. But it is supereminence among brethren, and therefore the supereminence involved has no meaning except in that relation. Hence, though there can be no underestimation of the pre-eminence belonging to the Son as the firstbegotten, yet the interdependence is just as necessary. The glory bestowed upon the redeemed is derived from the relation they sustain to the 'firstborn'. But the specific character involved in being the 'firstborn' is derived from the relation he sustains to the redeemed in that capacity. Hence they must be glorified *together*.

The glorification of the elect is, by implication, said to consist in conformity to the image of the *Son*. The marvel of the destination is hereby brought to our attention in a way that is unique. For the title 'Son' has reference to Christ as the only-begotten (Rom. 8:3, 32), and the eternal sonship is in view. The conformity cannot, of course, have in view conformity to him in that capacity or relation. The conformity includes conformity to the likeness of the body of Christ's glory (Phil. 3:21), and must, therefore, be conceived of as conformity to the image of the Son incarnate. But the glorified Christ does not cease to be the eternal Son. Hence conformity to his image as incarnate and glorified is conformity to the image of him who is the eternal and only-begotten Son. This is the highest end conceivable for created beings, the highest end conceivable not only by men but also by God himself. God himself could not contemplate or determine a higher destiny for his creatures.

We must not overlook, however, the succeeding clause—'that he might be the firstborn among many brethren.' This specifies the final aim of the conformity spoken of. We might well ask: What can be more ultimate than conformity of the sons of God to the image of the only-begotten and firstborn? If such a question has any appeal by way of objection, it is because our orientation is anthropocentric, rather than Christocentric and theocentric. There is a final end that is more ultimate than the glorification of the people of God. It is the pre-eminence of Christ, and that pre-eminence vindicated and exemplified in the final phase of his glorification. 'Firstborn' reflects on the *priority* and *supremacy* of Christ (cf. Col. 1:15, 18; Heb. 1:6; Rev. 1:5). The glory of God is always supreme and ultimate. And the supreme glory of God is manifested in the glorifying of the Son. Did not Jesus say, 'Now is the Son of man glorified, and God is glorified in him; if God is glorified in him, God will also glorify him in himself, and will straightway glorify him' (John 13:31, 32; cf. 14:13; 16:14; 17:1, 4, 5)?

But the glory for the people of God is only enhanced by the emphasis placed upon the pre-eminence of Christ. For it is *among many brethren* that Christ is the firstborn. That they should be classified as brethren brings to the thought of glorification with Christ the deepest mystery of community. The fraternal relationship is subsumed under the ultimate aim of the predestinating decree. This means that the *pre-eminence* of the Son as the firstborn carries with it the correlative *eminence* of the children of God. The unique dignity of the Son enhances the dignity bestowed upon the many sons who are to be brought to glory. 'Both he that sanctifieth and they who are sanctified are all of one: for which cause he is not ashamed to call them brethren' (Heb. 2:11).

We thus see how, in the final realization of the goal of sanctification, there is exemplified and vindicated to the fullest extent, an extent that staggers our thought by reason of its stupendous reality, the truth inscribed upon the whole process of redemption, from its inception in the electing grace of the Father (cf. Eph. 1:4; Rom. 8:29) to its consummation in the adoption (cf. Rom. 8:23; Eph. 1:5), that Christ in all his offices as Redeemer is never to be conceived of apart from the church, and the church is not to be conceived of apart from Christ. There is correlativity in election, there is correlativity in redemption once for all accomplished, there is correlativity in the mediatorial ministry which Christ continues to exercise at the right hand of the Father, and there is correlativity in the consummation, when Christ will come the second time without sin for those that look for him unto salvation. This is the goal of sanctification; this is the hope it enshrines, and thereby its demands upon us are invested with sanctions of surpassing glory.

SELECT BIBLIOGRAPHY ON SANCTIFICATION
John Ball, *The Power of Godliness* (London 1657); G. C. Berkouwer, *Faith and Sanctification* (E. T. Grand Rapids 1952); John Calvin, *Institutes* (iii.vi.ff); R. S. Candlish, *The Christian's Sacrifice and Service of Praise* (London 1860); John Downame, *The Christian Warfare* (London 1634); James Fraser, *A Treatise on Sanctification* (revised edition, London 1898); George Gritter, *The Quest for Holiness* (Grand Rapids 1955); Adolf Köberle, *The Quest for Holiness* (Augsburg, 1930); Walter Marshall, *The Gospel Mystery of Sanctification* (London 1692); John Owen, *The Grace and Duty of Being Spiritually Minded* (London 1681, *Works* VII, 261ff Goold Edition); J. C. Ryle, *Holiness: Its Nature, Hindrances, Difficulties, and Roots* (London 1879); R. S. Wallace, *Calvin's Doctrine of the Christian Life* (London 1959).

VI

IV

26

The Nature and Unity of the Church[1]

ANY inquiry as to what the New Testament means by the church (ἐκκλησία) cannot be biblically conducted without taking into account the Old Testament background and preparation. Our Lord and his apostles constantly appealed to the Old Testament for support and confirmation of their teaching, and not only so, but also used language derived from the Old Testament as the medium for conveying some of their most significant statements. The term for 'church' occurs frequently in the Greek version with which the New Testament writers were familiar and from which they quote. To suppose that the frequent use of the term in the Septuagint did not exercise a decisive influence upon the New Testament writers would be contrary to all analogy.

The Hebrew term corresponding to the Greek term is קהל, and this Hebrew term is regularly, though not uniformly, rendered by ἐκκλησία. The first instance in the Septuagint of ἐκκλησία is Deuteronomy 4:10. The Hebrew does not have the corresponding noun in this instance, though it does have the verb, and the latter means 'to assemble' or 'summon an assembly'.

Perhaps the most pivotal passages in the Old Testament are Deuteronomy 9:10; 10:4; 18:16, which speak of 'the day of the assembly' (יום קהל = ἡμέρα ἐκκλησίας). The assembly is the covenant people of God gathered before him (cf. Exod. 19:5–25; 1 Kings 8:14, 22, 55, 65; 1 Chron. 13:2, 4; 28:8; 29:1, 10, 20; 2 Chron. 6:3, 12, 13; 7:8). It is this concept of assembly summoned before God as God's 'own posses-

[1] This chapter and the one which follows were lectures delivered at the Leicester Ministers Conference, July, 1964.

321

sion from among all peoples . . . a kingdom of priests, and a holy nation' (Exod. 19:5, 6), 'the people which I formed for myself, that they might set forth my praise' (Isa. 43:21; cf. Hos. 1:6, 9; 2:1). It is precisely these same terms that Peter takes over when he describes the church, but does not use the term: 'But ye are an elect race, a royal priesthood, a holy nation, a people for God's own possession, that ye may show forth the excellencies of him who called you out of darkness into his marvellous light: who in time past were no people, but are now the people of God: who had not obtained mercy, but now have obtained mercy' (1 Pet. 2:9, 10). We have also the most express identification in the words of Stephen (Acts 7:38), when he says of Moses: 'This is he who was in the church in the wilderness with the angel that spake to him in the mount Sinai, and with our fathers: who received living oracles to give unto us'.

The assembly of God's people was not a passing phase of Israel's history; it was not ephemeral. The references above cited make plain that it was a permanent feature of Israel's identity (cf. Psalm 22:22, 25; 35:18; 40:9; 89:5; 107:32; 149:1; Joel 2:16; Mic. 2:5). The tabernacle was the focus of the assembly and of the worship. Exod. 29:42–46 is the one passage that enunciates more than any other what the tabernacle signified, and epitomizes what were the central features of the covenant relation. God meets with his people and speaks to them. He dwells among his people. Both are signified and certified by the Shekinah glory. God is their God. We cannot but see the expression here of what is central in the covenant blessing throughout its whole history, and coming to its consummation in the new covenant, 'I will be your God, and ye shall be my people' (cf. Rev. 21:3).

It is this same basic conception that obtains in the messianic passages and we can have no doubt that these determine the direction in which we are to seek the meaning of the most significant statement of our Lord himself (Matt. 16:18). I am thinking particularly of Psalm 22:22, 25; 'I will declare thy name unto my brethren: in the midst of the assembly will I praise thee' (קהל = ἐκκλησία); 'Of thee cometh my praise in the great assembly' (קהל רב = ἐκκλησίᾳ μεγάλῃ); Psalm 40:9, 10: 'I have proclaimed glad tidings of righteousness in the great assembly (קהל רב = ἐκκλησίᾳ μεγάλῃ) . . . I have not hid thy righteousness within my heart; I have declared thy faithfulness and thy salvation; I have not concealed thy lovingkindness and thy truth from the great assembly' (לקהל רב = ἀπὸ συναγωγῆς πολλῆς).

Passing on to the New Testament usage respecting the church, it becomes apparent that the notion of assembly or congregation is in the forefront. There is the non-ecclesiastical use in Acts 19:32, 39, 40, where this meaning is obvious. In the sacred use there are the frequent instances of particularization such as the church in Jerusalem (Acts 8:1; 11:22), at Antioch (Acts 11:26; 14:27; 15:3), at Ephesus (Acts 20:17, 28), at Cenchrea (Rom. 16:1), at Corinth (1 Cor. 1:2), in Laodicea (Col. 4:16), in Thessalonica (1 Thess. 1:1), and those mentioned in Rev. 2:1, 8, 12, 18; 3:1, 7, 14. In accordance with this particularization we have manifold references to the churches. There are the churches in Cilicia (Acts 15:41), the churches of Galatia (1 Cor. 16:1; Gal. 1:2), the churches of Asia (1 Cor. 16:19), the churches of Macedonia (2 Cor. 8:1), the churches of Judaea (Gal. 1:22; 1 Thess. 2:14), and the seven churches in Asia (Rev. 1:4, 20). Not only so, but Paul can speak inclusively in the plural and speak of 'all the churches of the Gentiles' (Rom. 16:4), 'all the churches of Christ' (Rom. 16:16), 'the churches of God' (1 Cor. 11:16; 2 Thess. 1:4), 'all the churches of the saints' (1 Cor. 14:33). The particularization becomes most accentuated where Paul speaks of the church in a house (Rom. 16:5; 1 Cor. 16:19; Col. 4:15; Phm. 2). Here, therefore, is plurality, and all that is comprised in the church of God, denotatively considered, can be spoken of as the churches of God, or of Christ, or of the saints.

But now we must also take account of the inclusive use of the word 'church' in the New Testament. No passage is more significant than Matt. 16:18. The generic use here is apparent, but is confirmed by the contextual considerations. One particular, localized assembly could not measure up to the rôle assigned to Peter, and the stewardship of the kingdom of heaven, in terms of which the administration of the affairs of the church is defined. When Jesus speaks of 'my church', he is thinking of those gathered and knit together after the pattern provided by the Old Testament as the people for his possession, as the community which he is to constitute, and which stands in a relation to him comparable to the congregation of the Lord in the Old Testament.

The other instance (Matt. 18:17) is particularly interesting in this connection, because there is particularization. It shows that in Jesus' own teaching we find the particular and inclusive uses of the term.

Paul, as we found, speaks of particular churches and uses the plural quite frequently. But Paul uses the singular in the inclusive sense. When we are introduced to Paul we are told that 'he laid waste the church' (Acts 8:3), and he uses similar terms in his own confessions. 'I persecuted the church of God' (1 Cor. 15:9; cf. Gal. 1:13; Phil. 3:6). We see already in this use that there is a universalizing, so that unity as well as plurality applies to the church of God and of Christ. This is also strikingly illustrated in Acts 9:31. For, although we read of the churches of Judaea (Gal. 1:22), here we read that 'the church throughout all Judaea and Galilee and Samaria had peace, being edified'. Similar use appears in 1 Cor. 12:28 (cf. 1 Cor. 10:32).

There is difference of judgment on the question: Which is more basic and determinative, the general or the particular? K. L. Schmidt, for example, contends that 'the Church is not a great community made up of an accumulation of small communities, but is truly present in its wholeness in every company of believers, however small. The proper translation in those verses [1 Cor. 1:2; 2 Cor. 1:1] is not "the Corinthian Congregation"—taking its place beside the Roman, etc.—but "the Congregation, Church, gathering, as it is in Corinth". When it is said that in such a gathering any one is despised (1 Cor. 6:4), that people come together (1 Cor. 11:18; cf. 14:23 and Acts 14:27), that women must keep silence (1 Cor. 14:34), or that it must not be burdened (1 Tim. 5:16), it is not the local congregation, but the Church as a whole, that is in view' (*Bible Key Words,* 1951, II, p. 10). It may not be necessary to state the alternatives with such sharp contrast, and the evidence will not always fit into the formula which Schmidt proposes (cf. 1 Thess. 1:1; 2 Thess. 1:1, where Paul speaks of the church of the Thessalonians, and where 'the whole church' means the whole congregation in one place— Acts 15:22; 1 Cor. 14:23; possibly Rom. 16:23). While, however, we may not fail to take account of the corporate unity which the inclusive use of the word 'church' implies, yet, on the other hand, and with equal emphasis, we must recognize that, wherever believers are gathered together in accordance with Christ's institution and in his name, there is the church of God, and to that church of God belong all the functions, prerogatives, and promises which God has accorded to the church. Where two or three are gathered together in Jesus' name, he is in the midst of them (cf. Matt. 18:20 in relation to the preceding context respecting discipline, supplication, intercession). The localized assembly is the body of which Christ is the head. And thus we must speak, not only of the church universal, but of the churches of God throughout the world; that is to say, of the plurality of the church of God. The local church is 'the church of the living God, the pillar and ground of the truth' (1 Tim. 3:15); it is 'the fulness of him that filleth all in all' (Eph. 1:23).

It is in the Epistles to the Ephesians and Colossians that the inclusiveness and oneness come to fullest expression. It is easy to conclude that here the church is viewed transcendentally as the whole body of the elect in all ages, and is to be equated with what has been called the church invisible. This would appear to be the necessary concept in Eph. 5:25, 26. On this view the church as a visible, organized entity, after the pattern of the pervasive usage elsewhere in the New Testament, would not be contemplated or, at least, would not be the governing idea. There are reasons for calling in question this interpretation.

1. The first instance (Eph. 1:22, 23) is sufficient to warn us against this facile solution. When the Father is said to have given Christ to be head over all things to the church, this refers to the investiture that took place on Christ's exaltation, to Christ's mediatorial lordship as the exalted, ascended God-man. It is not something that antedates his mediatorial exaltation.

2. The church is here said to be Christ's body. We are bound to think of Matthew 16:18 where Christ speaks of his church as that to be built and administered in the way stated in the context.

3. The church is said to be subject unto Christ. In the context there must be a concreteness that is parallel to that which is enjoined, namely, that in like manner wives should be subject to their husbands. The exhortation would be bereft of its strongest appeal if the analogy is something that belongs simply to the invisible and transcendental realm.

4. When Paul says that he fills up the things that are lacking of the afflictions of Christ in his flesh 'on behalf of his body, which is the

church', he is again thinking of the benefits that accrue to the church in the concrete existence of the existential.

It would be, therefore, far too abstract to find in these two Epistles reference to the church viewed transcendentally and invisibly. It is the church, exemplified in the saints and faithful brethren in Ephesus and Colosse, which Christ loved and of which he is the head.

This does not mean that the generic, the inclusive, the ecumenical does not reach its highest expression in these two Epistles. And not only so, but in these Epistles the eschatological outreach is conspicuous (cf. Eph. 2:7; 3:21; 5:27). What is to be emphasized is that in these Epistles where the universal and eschatological motifs are so much in prominence, we must not conceive of the church as anything other, on the broadest scale, than that which the church in Corinth or the church in Judaea is.

At this point it may be most appropriate to focus some attention on the questions pertaining to the church as visible. The church may not be defined as an entity wholly invisible to human perception and observation. What needs to be observed is that, whether the church is viewed as the broader communion of the saints or as the unit or assembly of believers in a home or town or city, it is always a visible observable entity. The spiritual facts which constitute persons members of the church, though invisible, nevertheless find expression in what is observable. The people of God do come together, in accordance with Christ's institution and prescription, for purposes of collective worship and testimony, for the administration of divinely instituted ordinances, for mutual edification, and for the exercise of government and discipline. Hence visible association and organization are necessary to the church. There are institutions to be administered and government exercised. But this administration is executed by men. In view of the infirmity and fallibility belonging to men, we are faced with the anomaly that the visible entity which is called the church may comprise within its membership those who do not truly belong to the body of Christ. In view of this, it has been customary to define the church, viewed from its visible aspect, in terms merely of profession, and thus to allow for the discrepancy between the church ideally considered and the church realistically considered. This allows for a definition that is embracive enough to include those who are not really members of Christ's body. This, I submit, is an error, and contrary to what we find in Scripture.

When Paul writes to the church in Corinth, his salutation is to be noted: 'Paul, called to be an apostle of Christ Jesus through the will of God, and Sosthenes our brother, to the church of God which is at Corinth, to them who are sanctified in Christ Jesus, called to be saints' (1 Cor. 1:1, 2). The apposition is obvious. When Paul addressed the church, he did not construe the church in such terms as would allow for the inclusion of those persons who might have borne the Christian name, and had been admitted to the privileges of the church, but who were not sanctified in Christ Jesus and called to be saints. This is all the more significant in view of the disciplinary provisions of Chapter 5. (Paul recognized that there was old leaven which needed to be purged out. But he does not address the church as a community to be defined in terms of new leaven and old leaven.) Other salutations are to the same effect (cf. Rom. 1:7; 2 Cor. 1:1; Eph. 1:1; Phil. 1:1; Col. 1:2; 1 Thess. 1:1; 2 Thess. 1:1. The last two are particularly relevant).

This is an all-important distinction, namely, that between what a situation may existentially be by reason of the sin, hypocrisy, and infirmity of men, on the one hand, and the terms in which the church is to be defined, on the other. For only if we apply the latter can we maintain the character of that to which the promises belong, indeed, maintain the primary idea in terms of which the church is to be defined, the covenant people of God. Only thus understood can we use Peter's terms (1 Pet. 2:9, 10). Only thus can we entertain Christ's promises: 'The gates of hell shall not prevail against it', and 'Where two or three are gathered in my name, there am I in the midst of them.' Only thus can we conceive of the church as the body of Christ. Only thus can we think of the church as Christ's bride (Eph. 5:25–32).

We must now pay some attention to the church as the body of Christ. It is necessary at the outset to note that the body of Christ refers frequently in the New Testament to the physical body crucified, laid in the tomb, and raised on the third day (Matt. 26:12; 27:58, 59; Mark 15:43; Luke 23:52, 55; 24:3, 23; John 2:21; 20:12; Rom. 7:4; Col. 1:22; Heb. 10:10; 1 Pet. 2:24). In addition to these, there are those references which appear in the teaching regarding the Lord's supper

(Matt. 26:26; Mark 14:22; Luke 22:19; 1 Cor. 10:16; 11:24). That 1 Corinthians 10:16 refers to the physical body is apparent from the parallel: 'communion of the blood of Christ' and 'communion of the body of Christ'. There is a reasonable question as to 'body' in 1 Cor. 10:17: 'because one bread (loaf), we the many are one body'. Since the preceding verse speaks of participating in the body of Christ offered for us, this could mean that, as we partake of the one loaf at the supper, this symbolizes participation of the one body of Christ, the body given for us in the offering of Christ. But this is not the most acceptable interpretation. (1) The body of Christ in verse 16 is clearly enough the one body of Christ, and 'communion of the body' does itself sufficiently express the oneness of the body of which believers partake in the supper. (2) The clause in question in verse 17 does not conveniently express the thought of *partaking* of the one body. It reads: 'We, the many, are one body'. There is a distinct difference, even discrepancy. If we partake of one body, we are not the body of which we partake. Hence we may conclude that in verse 17 Paul refers to believers as 'one body', and that this is symbolically represented by the one loaf (cf. Rom. 12:5).

It is true that Paul here does not say that we are the body of Christ. But since in 1 Cor. 12:27 he makes this identification—'but ye are the body of Christ and members in particular'—it would not be reasonable to think otherwise in 1 Cor. 10:17. Besides, it is only as one body in Christ, or as the body of Christ, that believers are one body.

This passage is rather unique in that it brings the two denotations of the term 'body' into such close juxtaposition. The closest parallel is Col. 1:18, 22. But the juxtaposition is not nearly as close or as striking as in 1 Cor. 10:16, 17. We can scarcely escape the inference that there is a close relationship between the two distinct denotations and concepts. It is because we are partakers of Christ's body that we are one body in him. It is because we are the beneficiaries of the offering of the body of Christ once for all, because he bore our sins in his own body upon the tree, that we are constituted the body of Christ. It is because representatively, and by mysterious identification with Christ in his death and resurrection, yea, even in his ascension to the heavenlies (Eph. 2:4-7), and thus identification with him in that which he accomplished in his own body, that we are one body in him. Indeed, it is because he was obedient unto death, even the death of the cross, that he is head over all things to his body the church.

This relationship might seem to lend support to a notion given currency in various forms that the church is the extension of the incarnation, and that the church sustains a very intimate relationship to the incarnate Christ. In the words of E. L. Mascall: 'Becoming a Christian means being re-created by being incorporated into the glorified manhood of the ascended Christ' (*Christ, the Christian and the Church*, 1946, p. 78). This means for Mascall that without loss of personal identity we are 'incorporated into the concrete human nature of another man' (*ibid.*, p. 93), 'established in *corpore Christi*, given an ontological union with, and participation in, his glorified human nature, so that all that he possesses in it becomes ours' (*ibid.*, p. 94). L. S. Thornton appears to express a similar idea when he says that 'by membership in the mystical body we are incorporated into the One Man. For the Body stands for the whole Man and is identical with him in one aspect of the divine-human organism' (*The Common Life in the Body of Christ*, 1950, p. 314). Perhaps the crassest statement of this position is that of John A. T. Robinson, to the effect that the church is the glorified body of the risen Lord, 'the risen organism of Christ's person in all its concrete reality . . . as concrete and as singular as the body of the Incarnation' (*The Body*, 1952, p. 51). If the church is Christ's glorified body, the continuity of Christ's resurrected body with the body of his flesh and the body crucified on the cross would demand the same kind of identification with Christ's body in his humiliation. The absurdity is apparent. We need but go over the passages already cited, which refer to the body of Christ's flesh as offered on the accursed tree, to see how impossible the hypothesis would be shown to be. The mere fact that the church is not yet glorified demonstrates the discrepancy between the church and the glorified humanity of Jesus (cf. Rom. 8:17–23; Phil. 3:20, 21).

It is surely demanded by the analogy of Scripture to infer that in the proposition, 'the church is the body of Christ', we have figurative language. Christ does not speak of the church as his body. But he does use another figure closely related to this concept. It is that of the vine and the branches, and no one would attempt to literalize the proposition, 'I am the vine: ye are the branches' (cf. also Matt. 16:18).

It is a principle never to be forgotten that analogy is not identity.

(The literal fact on which the concept is based is the organic unity of the physical body. This is clear from Rom. 12:4, 5; 1 Cor. 12:12–27.)

After we have recognized the figurative force, it must be acknowledged that the relationship which the figure of the human body illustrates is very difficult to define. To say that the language is figurative does not of itself provide us with any positive lines of thought. The following positions should be maintained:

1. Christ and the church are complementary. We cannot think of a body without a head, or a head without a body. Christ is the head of the body (Col. 1:18). Thornton expresses this graphically when he says: 'The Church apart from Christ would be like an empty wine-cup. Christ without the Church would be like wine which, for lack of a wine-cup, no one could drink' (*ibid*, p. 310). In like manner Christ's cosmic sovereignty as head over all is his only in relation to the church. He is head over all to his body, the church (cf. Eph. 1:22, 23). The same thought is more fully expressed in Col. 1:18, 19: 'And he is the head of the body, the church: who is the beginning, the firstborn from the dead, in order that he might be pre-eminent in all things, because it pleased the Father that in him all the fulness should dwell'. Also in Colossians 2:9, 10: 'In him dwells all the fulness of Godhead bodily, and ye are complete in him, who is the head of all principality and power' (authority). Christ's mediatorial dominion is ecclesially conditioned and his headship over the church is conditioned by universal dominion.

2. The figure of the body implies an organic relationship that exists on an infinitely higher plane than anything with which we are acquainted in our phenomenal experience. A supra-personal collective, such as we have in the institution of the state, does not exemplify this organic character, and falls far short of what obtains in the mystical body of Christ.

3. The church as the body derives all its life from Christ the head. It is here that the passages in Ephesians are particularly significant (Eph. 1:23; 3:19; 4:13–16). Much dispute has arisen in connection with the last clause of 1:23, 'the fulness of him that filleth all in all'. It has even been proposed that this term 'fulness' here does not refer to the church, but to Christ, and finds its antecedent in the personal pronouns in verses 22,

23a, which in turn refer to Christ in verse 20, a view which exegetically is untenable, if not monstrous. As referring to the church it could mean 'complement'. The church, as noted earlier, is always complementary to Christ. But the other passages in Ephesians and Colossians indicate that the meaning is that the church is the receptacle of the fulness, and in this sense is being filled with him who himself fills all things, or, possibly, is himself being filled all in all. This is the meaning of 3:19: 'in order that ye might be filled unto all the fulness of God'; of 4:13: 'until we all come in the unity of the faith and of the knowledge of the Son of God, unto a perfect man, unto the measure of the stature of the fulness of Christ'; and of Col. 2:10: 'and ye are complete in him, who is the head of all principality and authority', properly rendered also, 'ye are filled in him' or 'ye are in the condition of having been filled by him'.

The church is the fulness of Christ in that the fulness that resides in him, the fulness of grace and truth (cf. John 1:14), 'the treasures of wisdom and knowledge' (Col. 2:3), the fulness of life (cf. John 5:26), the fulness of power (cf. Matt. 28:18), is being communicated to the church. It is not without relevance that the figure of the vine and the branches in the teaching of Jesus, recorded only by John (John 15), conveys precisely this truth of utter dependence and communication of life, and that in terms of 'fulness' it is John who expresses this precise concept when he says: 'because out of his fulness we all received and grace for grace' (John 1:16).

More recently L. S. Thornton has presented this viewpoint and he has done so effectively. 'In the primary sense', he says, 'the Church is the fulness, because the mystical body is like a vessel into which the fulness of Christ is poured. He fills it with himself' (*ibid.*, p. 310). There is no contradiction between the thought of completeness or fulness in Christ and the necessity of being filled more and more (cf. Eph. 1:23; Col. 2:10, on the one hand, and Eph. 3:19; 4:13 on the other). This is but the paradox arising from the imperfection that still inheres in the church, and that waits for the consummation as the day when it will be finally eliminated (cf. Thornton: *ibid.*, pp. 307ff.).

4. The body of Christ is a unit, and all the members are united to the head and to one another. It is, of course, necessary to take account of the different perspectives in Romans and 1 Corinthians, on the one hand,

and in Ephesians and Colossians, on the other. The headship of Christ is not enunciated in the former, whereas this is the leading emphasis in the latter. We must keep both perspectives in view in this topic of unity.

There are numerous passages which expressly appeal to the oneness of the body, but it is not necessary to discuss them in detail (cf. Rom. 12:4, 5; 1 Cor. 6:16; 10:17; 12:12, 13, 20; Eph. 2:15; 4:4; Col. 3:15). We should bear in mind what we have already found to be the concept of the church, and we may not attempt to escape from the implications of this oneness, and the obligation incident to it, by taking refuge in the notion of the invisible church. When Paul says to the church at Rome, 'we, the many, are one body in Christ, and members one of another', he is thinking most concretely, and enforcing the exhortation that each member in the church is to think soberly as God has distributed to each a measure of faith, and that each is to exercise his gift or gifts in the practical, day-to-day life of the community of believers. Or again, when to the church at Corinth Paul says, 'we the many are one body', he is directing this truth to the schismatic discrimination practised at Corinth in the celebration of the Lord's supper, and to the correction of the same. Although in 1 Corinthians 12:12, 13 the accent falls on the harmony and order to be maintained in the exercise of the various gifts, in recognition of the truth set forth in Romans 12:3–6 that all of these gifts are exercised by the one Holy Spirit, yet we cannot dissociate this emphasis upon oneness from the divisive attitudes and practices so severely condemned in the first chapter (1 Cor. 1:10–17). It should be noted that here the situation was one of schism and strife (vv. 10, 11). The contradiction of this disunity is exposed by the questions: 'Is Christ divided? Was Paul crucified for you, or were ye baptized in the name of Paul?' (v. 13). In a word, the unity of the body of Christ, is not a tenet that may be relegated to the transcendental realm of invisible, spiritual relationship, but a truth that governs, regulates, and conditions the behaviour of the people of God in that communal, covenant relationship which they sustain to Christ in the institute of the church.

But this same unity pertains to the church in its most inclusive and universal denotation. In the Epistle to the Ephesians the catholicity of the church comes to its fullest expression and, as we found, there is the eschatological outreach (2:7; 3:21). Hence, to maintain that the unity belonging to the church does not entail ecumenical embodiment, is to deny the catholicity of the church of Christ. If the church is catholic, then unity is catholic.

It is well to bear in mind what is the undergirding truth. Why is the church one? First of all, it is that Christ is one. 'Is Christ divided?' is Paul's protestation. And he adds later: 'For as the body is one, and hath many members, and all the members of the body, being many, are one body, even so is Christ' (1 Cor. 12:12). Here, I take it, Paul in this brief clause, 'even so is Christ', brings together the church and Christ, and says in effect 'Christ is one, and so the church is one'.

It is not only the oneness of Christ, but also the oneness of the Spirit, from whom all the grace by which the church is constituted and equipped proceeds. 'In one Spirit were we all baptized into one body . . . and were all made to drink one Spirit' (1 Cor. 12:13). The intimate dependence of the preceding clause on this one should be noted. The church is one, 'for in one Spirit were we all baptized into one body' (cf. 1 Cor. 12:9, 11; also 6:17).

But this undergirding truth is to be given a further extension; it embraces the Godhead. 'There is one body and one Spirit, even as ye were called in one hope of your calling: one Lord, one faith, one baptism: one God and Father of all, who is over all, and through all, and in all' (Eph. 4:4–6). It is, in a word, the oneness of the Godhead in the particularity of prerogative, function and relation of each person in the economy of salvation that undergirds the oneness of the church, whether the church be viewed in its most restricted denotation as two or three gathered in Jesus' name, or in its most catholic dimensions as comprising all who in every place call upon the name of the Lord Jesus.

When we think thus we are inevitably reminded of Jesus' intercessory prayer, and of the astounding analogy by which he impresses upon us the intimacy of union with himself, as well as enforces the sanction by which the oneness of the church is to be sought: 'Not for these only do I ask, but also for those who believe on me through their word, that they all may be one, as thou, Father, art in me and I in thee, in order that they also may be in us, in order that the world may believe that thou hast sent me. And the glory which thou hast given me I have given to them, in order that they may be one, as we are one. I in them and thou in me, in order that they may be perfected in one, in order that the world may know that thou hast sent me, and hast loved them as thou hast loved me' (John 17:20–23). The sustained emphasis on oneness must be noted. But the analogy in terms of which this oneness is to be effected, and the pattern after which it is to be fashioned, is the transcendent oneness of the Father and the Son.

It is a monstrous travesty to make this prayer of Jesus the plea and the warrant for the kind of affiliation represented by the World Council of Churches. First, John 17:21 must not be divorced from John 17:20. To dissociate the unity for which Jesus prayed from all that is involved in believing on him is to rend asunder what our Lord joined together. And this believing on him is not a faith that can be abstracted from the total witness of the New Testament to the identity of Jesus. Our Lord pointed to this when he said: 'those who believe on me through their word'. If we might even restrict this witness to that of the Gospel in which this word of Jesus is recorded, it is, to say the least, anomalous that this word of Jesus from John's Gospel should be weighted with such significance, when the witness which Jesus bears to himself in this Gospel, and which this Gospel bears to Jesus, should be so largely discarded in defining the confession which forms the basis of the World Council.

But, second, the pattern Jesus provides—'as thou, Father, art in me and I in thee'—makes mockery of any unity not based upon the doctrine of the Father and the Son which the apostolic witness provides.

Third, this unity for which Jesus prayed is the unity to which Jesus himself continued to bear witness through his apostles. The apostolic witness is the teaching of Jesus (cf. Acts 1:1). And the unity urged in this apostolic witness is 'the unity of the Spirit in the bond of peace' (Eph. 4:3). It is to 'stand in one spirit, with one soul striving together for the faith of the gospel' (Phil. 1:27). It is impossible to believe that the radical diversity of belief that exists within this affiliation has any affinity with the kind of unity contemplated in Jesus' prayer and in apostolic witness. 'There is one body and one Spirit, even as ye were called in one hope of your calling' (Eph. 4:4). If we apply the criterion of one hope, the criterion of collective eschatology, do we not have a diversity that strikes at what is focal in the Christian hope? Or again, let us think of Eph. 4:13: 'till we all come in the unity of the faith'.

But while spurious unity is to be condemned, the lack of unity among churches of Christ which profess the faith in its purity is a patent violation of the unity of the body of Christ, and of that unity which the prayer of our Lord requires us to promote. We cannot escape from the implications for us by resorting to the notion of the invisible church. The body of Christ is not an invisible entity, and the prayer of Jesus was directed to the end that the world might believe. The unity prayed for was one that would bear witness to the world, and therefore belonged to the realm of the observable. The implications for visible confession and witness are unavoidable.

It is to be admitted that the fragmentation and lack of co-ordination and solidarity which we find within strictly evangelical and Reformed Churches create a difficult situation, and how this disunity is to be remedied 'in the unity of the Spirit and the bond of peace' is a task not easily accomplished. But what needs to be indicted, and indicted with vehemence, is the complacency so widespread, and the failure to be aware that this is an evil, dishonouring to Christ, destructive of the edification defined by the apostle as 'the increase of the body into the building up of itself in love' (Eph. 4:16), and prejudicial to the evangelistic outreach to the world. If we are once convinced of this evil, the evil of schism in the body of Christ, the evil of disruption in the communion of saints, then we have made great progress. We shall then be constrained to preach the evil, to bring conviction to the hearts of others also, to implore God's grace and wisdom in remedying the evil, and to devise ways and means of healing these ruptures, to the promotion of united witness to the faith of Jesus and the whole counsel of God.

27

The Government of the Church

WHEN we speak of the government of the church we are liable to focus attention upon a particular *form* of government, and to think of the mechanics in terms of which government is conducted. This is not improper and, since there are various forms of church government, it is natural that our minds should entertain that denotation of the term. But it is necessary to think of the simple fact and concept of government before we consider the ways of administering that government. This does not mean that we can ever think of government in abstraction from its exercise, and exercise always takes on concrete form. But we have to begin with the general principle, and to establish the fact and necessity of government before we embark upon the details of administrative execution.

We have already observed how the New Testament concept of the church is based upon, and is continuous with the congregation of Israel, the assembly of the covenant people of God, whose religious life and worship found its centre in the tabernacle as the sanctuary, as God's dwelling place in the midst of Israel, and as the tent of meeting where God met with his people. It is a fact that detailed regulations were given by God for the government of Israel. A great many of these prescriptions could not have any permanent relevance to the church because they pertained to the preparatory and transitory conditions of Israel under the Old Covenant. As regulative of religious life and worship, they could only be regulative as long as the ceremonial institution lasted.

There is, however, one feature of the government of Israel as the people of God that can scarcely have failed to provide a pattern for the government of the church under the New Testament. It is the frequent mention of, and the place occupied by 'the elders' in the life of Israel. It is to be admitted that 'the elders' exercised functions that did not fall strictly into what we would call the *specifically* religious realm. But their functions did pertain to what was specifically religious, and they performed services which will have to be regarded as juridical and jurisdictional in the religious life of Israel (cf. Exod. 3:16, 18; 4:29; 12:21; 17:5, 6; 18:12; 19:7; 24:1; Lev. 4:15; 9:1, 2; Numb. 11:16, 17, 24, 25; Deut. 5:23; 22:15–17; 27:1; Josh. 7:6; 8:33; 1 Kings 8:1, 3; 1 Chron. 21:16; Psalm 107:32; Lam. 5:14; Ezek. 8:1). Their position as representative of the people, and as embodying jurisdictional authority, is attested by the fact that they are closely associated with Moses, with the priests, the Levites, and the judges of Israel. They are sometimes called the elders of the congregation (זִקְנֵי הָעֵדָה—Lev. 4:15; Judg. 21:16). The interesting feature is that in many instances these are called the *presbuteroi*, and in several cases γερουσία, which means the council of the elders. Now I submit that when we come to the New Testament and find the presbyterate as a governing body in the church of Christ, it is contrary to all reasonable supposition that the Old Testament eldership did not exercise a profound influence upon the institution which appears in such unmistakable characters in the New Testament church, especially when we take account of the continuance of this Old Testament pattern in the synagogue of the Jews (cf. Luke 22:66; Acts 22:5 for *presbuterion*).

We must now turn to the New Testament itself. No passage is of greater significance than the word of our Lord to Peter: 'Upon this rock I will build my church . . . I will give unto thee the keys of the kingdom of heaven' (Matt. 16:18, 19). It is not a question that needs to be discussed now: What is the precise relation of the kingdom of heaven to the church? The sequence surely implies that since the building of the church and its indestructibility is the theme in verse 18, verse 19, concerned as it is with administration, cannot have in view something entirely different. This is demonstrated by what is stated to be the consequence, or perchance the function, arising from investiture with the keys, namely, 'whatsoever thou shalt bind on earth shall be bound in heaven *etc.*' The binding and loosing are in the realm of sacred things, of which a prime example is given by Jesus later: 'whose soever sins ye remit, they are remitted to them; and whose soever sins ye retain, they are retained' (John 20:23). The binding and loosing must refer to some kind of ministry that falls within the province of the church. Thus the keys of the kingdom of heaven must also pertain to that ministry.

The keys represent stewardship, and this is government; it is administration. This administration is to be performed by men. It is scarcely necessary to argue that Peter on this occasion acted in his confession as the spokesman of the disciples, and in receiving the investiture, received such as representing the disciples. If Peter alone was given possession of the keys, there would be contradiction between this passage and John 20:21–23. In the latter Jesus says: 'Peace be unto you: as the Father hath sent me, even so send I you. And when he had said this he breathed on them and said to them, Receive ye the Holy Ghost. Whose soever sins ye remit, they are remitted unto them: whose soever sins ye retain, they are retained.' No exercise of the power of the keys, no act of binding and loosing in terms of Matt. 16:18, 19, could be more basic or representative than the remission or non-remission of sins. Nothing certified Jesus' authority as the Son of man more clearly than his authority to forgive sins. Likewise, in the exercise of the keys, nothing could be more symptomatic of its involvements than remission of sins. But all the disciples are given that prerogative.

Of similar import in respect of government executed by men is Matt. 18:17, 18. The accent in this text as it pertains to the church falls on the function the church performs in the constraint it brings to bear upon an offending brother unto his repentance and, failing repentance, the judgment to be entertained on the part of the person sinned against. There is, therefore, a decisive rôle assigned to the church in adjudication. Nothing is expressly stated in this instance respecting binding and loosing. But we can hardly suppress the application. The refusal to hear the church, to respect and accede to its judgment, or at least to its counsel, places upon the offended brother the necessity of regarding the offender as outside the bond of fellowship, 'as the heathen man and the publican'.

In this case the church comes into view in the exercise of discipline. So unavoidably in this case we have judicial discipline. The church means plurality, and thus the jurisdiction involves administration by a body. The church in this case need not be the whole congregation. According to the Old Testament pattern the whole congregation is represented as present and acting when the elders act on its behalf (cf. Exod. 12:3, 21; Num. 35:12, 24; Josh. 20:4). They are really identified with the congregation.

This fact of government vested in the church, and in men delegated to discharge the same, is all the more remarkable because of the context in which this institution is enunciated and authorized. Jesus said: 'I will build'. He is the architect and the builder, and the church is viewed as a completed edifice. But in striking contrast: 'I will give thee the keys'. Then again there is the contrast between 'my church' and 'the keys of the kingdom of heaven'. It is not Peter's kingdom. It is the rule and domain of God, and so rulership and possession as of God enhance the dignity and responsibility of those acting as stewards.

This appears perhaps more forcefully in connection with the figure of the body. The headship of Christ is not overtly intimated in Romans 12:8; 1 Corinthians 12:28. But the analogy of what is so explicitly stressed in Ephesians and Colossians must be applied, that when the church is viewed as the body of Christ, and when, viewed from that aspect, rulership (Rom. 12:8) and governments (1 Cor. 12:28) are considered to be gifts which are exercised for the perfecting of the church, the headship of Christ must never be overlooked. In Ephesians 4:4–16, the hegemony of Christ is expressed in various ways. We read: 'There is one Lord', 'he that descended is the same also that ascended far above all the heavens, in order that he might fill all things', 'the measure of the stature of the fulness of Christ', 'that we might grow unto him in all things, who is the head, even Christ'. But it is just in the heart of this sustained emphasis on Christ's supremacy that we have perhaps the most eloquent enumeration of the offices assigned to men: 'And he gave some apostles, and some prophets, and some evangelists, and some pastors and teachers, unto the perfecting of the saints for the work of the ministry, unto the building up of the body of Christ'.

In these passages, therefore, we have the hegemony and headship in direct relation to the ministry and, more particularly for our present interest, to the government exercised by men. The headship of Christ is not suspended or curtailed by the authority vested in men, nor is the government executed by men prejudicial to the headship of Christ. In fact it is the abiding headship of Christ that gives sanction and validity to human instrumentality. From his exalted glory he gave some apostles, some prophets, some evangelists, some pastors and teachers. The two aspects are correlative.

All-important inferences are to be appreciated. Preferably the case should be stated as the implications:

1. The government exercised by men must always be conducted in accordance with the institution and will of Christ. It is a complete travesty of all order and authority in the church of Christ for the governmental affairs of the church to be arranged and conducted without constant reference to that revelation in which alone does Christ make known to us his will for the regulation of that which stands in no less intimate relation to him than *his* body, *his* church, the church for which he gave himself, that he might present it as the church glorious, holy and without blemish. We act presumptuously, and take false refuge from our failure, when we so concentrate upon the eschatological realization of Ephesians 5:25–27 that we do not bring the various facets of its teaching to bear upon the jealousy for Christ's honour and will with which we seek to conduct the government of the church. This is just saying that Ephesians 4:11–16, in respect of the implications for good government, sustains the closer relation to Ephesians 5:25–27 even in its eschatological consummation.

2. The headship of Christ is ecumenical. It extends to the whole church. Here is unity in government that is indisputable. Schism is unthinkable. Severance from the head is to be outside the church, to be cut off from the body. However much diversity there may be and is, it all must come under the unity which the headship of Christ demands. To use another figure: however great the dimensions of the pyramid, it all tapers off into the apex, and this apex is Christ. Whatever may be the implications for the delegated government instituted by Christ, it cannot be doubted that what is fontal in the sphere of jurisdiction is characterized by the ecumenical principle. Calvin's quotation from Cyprian is eloquent of this: 'The church is one, which is spread abroad far and wide into a multitude by an increase of fruitfulness. As there are

many rays of the sun but one light, and many branches of a tree but one strong trunk grounded in its tenacious root, and since from one spring flow many streams, although a goodly number seem outpoured from their bounty and superabundance, still, at the source unity abides' (*Inst.* IV, ii, 6, E. T. by F. L. Battles, 1950, Vol. II, p. 1047).

3. The apostolate had unique authority in the New Testament institution. I do not say supreme authority, for this belongs to Christ as the head of the Church, and to the Holy Spirit as Christ's vicar in the church, as the other paraclete who was promised to lead the disciples into all the truth, and take of the things of Christ and show them unto the disciples. Among our contemporaries, no one has done service in bringing the apostolic institution into proper focus, comparable to that of Herman N. Ridderbos in his three monographs: *The Coming of the Kingdom*, *When the Time had Fully Come*, and *The Authority of the New Testament Scriptures*. Ridderbos properly speaks of the apostolic institution as 'the canonicity which Jesus Christ Himself conferred on His apostles' (*When the Time had Fully Come*, Grand Rapids, 1957, p. 87). The unique authority of the apostles finds its original certification prior to the momentous utterance of Jesus at Caesarea Philippi (Matt. 16:18, 19). We find it in the sending forth of the twelve and even of the seventy. But this institution is patent in Matthew 16:18, 19; John 20:21–23; John 14–17 (especially 14:26; 15:26, 27; 16:7–15; 17:11, 12, 14–18); Acts 1:1, 2, 8, 15–26; 1 Corinthians 15:1–3; Ephesians 2:20; 2 Thessalonians 3:12–14; Hebrews 2:3, 4; Jude 3. The particular interest for us at present is the way in which this institution exemplifies the ecumenical principle in government. If there is the canonicity of the apostolate by delegation from Christ, and by inspiration of the Holy Spirit, there can be no question but it is a universal and perpetual canonicity as far as the church is concerned (cf. Ridderbos: *The Authority of the New Testament Scriptures*, 1963, p. 27). Thus no less than in respect of the headship of Christ do we have here also the principle of unity. The government of the church is one under the auspices and direction of apostolic witness. What apostolic instruction and proclamation binds on earth is bound in heaven. There is continued and applied the word of Christ: 'He that heareth you heareth me, and he that rejecteth you rejecteth me; and he that rejecteth me rejecteth him that sent me' (Luke 10:16).

It may not be disputed then that there is a descending hierarchy in the church of God. At the top is the sole hierarchy of Christ. Next we have that of the apostles. There is no hierarchy in the apostles. There is plurality and parity, and both features are of the greatest significance. Only in the head of the church is there singularity of rule. Whenever we descend to apostolic rule we have plurality and corresponding parity.

4. The presbyterate is the form of government for the church of Christ. There are two considerations that have to be borne in mind. First, there was an institution intermediate between the apostolate and the presbyterate. This is exemplified in Timothy and Titus (cf. 1 Tim. 1:3, 4, 18; 3:14, 15; 4:11–5:1; 5:7, 9, 21, 22; 6:13, 14, 20; 2 Tim. 1:6, 13, 14; 2:2, 14; 3:14; 4:1, 2, 5; Titus 1:5, 13). Whether Timothy and Titus should be called technically evangelists in the sense of Ephesians 4:11 (cf. 2 Tim. 4:5 where Paul enjoins Timothy to do the work of an evangelist) is a question. As we survey the charges given in the passages cited, both Timothy and Titus appear to act as delegates of the apostle, but not without due approbation and ordination by the church (cf. 1 Tim. 4:14). Next to the apostolate they do exercise functions and prerogatives that are of a more embracive character than those belonging to the bishops and elders in the various churches. The second consideration of importance is that elders were ordained in the various churches concurrently with the ministry of the apostles. Most striking in this respect is Acts 14:23, where, referring to such places as Antioch, Iconium, and Lystra, we read 'that when they had ordained them elders in every church, and had prayed with fasting, they commended them to the Lord on whom they believed.' Thus, as soon as the churches were established, elders were appointed. And so we find the eldership to be the local governing body in each church (cf. Acts 11:30; 15:2–23; 16:4; 20:17; 21:18; Phil. 1:1; Tit. 1:5; James 5:14). The authority of the apostolate lies behind this institution, and in no way does the concurrent exercise of rule introduce discrepancy. Rule by elders is the apostolic institution for the government of the local congregation, and this involves the principles of plurality and parity. The inference is inescapable that this is a permanent provision for the government of the churches. Since the apostolate is not permanent, and since there is in the

New Testament no other provision for the government of the local congregation, we must conclude that the council of elders is the only abiding institution for the government of the church of Christ according to the New Testament.

Here emerges the great question: How does this principle of rule by elders relate itself to the unity of the body of Christ? As we found in earlier studies, the oneness of the church of Christ is incontrovertible, and this oneness should find expression in every phase of the life and activity of the church as church. Taking the figure of the body, no member of the body acts but as a member of the whole, and no action can be outside this unity. So in the body of Christ.

We also found that, in respect of government, there is the most embracive oneness in the headship of Christ, and the church in all aspects of government is subject to the hegemony of Christ. Here there is supremacy and finality of jurisdiction. Again, in the descending hierarchy we have, by Christ's own appointment, apostolic canonicity and, subordinately to the headship of Christ, this hegemony is as embracive as is Christ's own. So we have here also corporate government exercised directly while the apostles lived, and through the inspired Scripture after their departure.

Are we to suppose that in the government of the church now and ever since the decease of the apostles, corporate government no longer exists? Are we to suppose that every unit of the church of Christ exists governmentally in complete independence of all other units, and directs its affairs under the supervision of no other hierarchy than the supreme headship of Christ and the delegated canonicity of the apostles? If the answer is in the affirmative, we must recognize the complete change that took place with the death of the apostles. It is to be admitted that persuasive argument could be advanced in support of the thesis that, since no corporate overseership could be equated with that of Christ and of his apostles by delegation from him, no other corporate supervision is instituted or allowed. But this resolution of the question is not to be adopted for the following reasons.

1. It is contrary to the unity that belongs to the church to suppose that since the death of the apostles the solidarity has been terminated. In all respects of fellowship, of faith, of witness, the oneness exists. It is

contrary to all analogy to suppose that, at the point of government, this is suspended.

2. The unity of the body must come to expression in every phase of the church's activity. If we think in terms of *koinōnia*, whether the idea is that of fellowship or participation, in either case independency violates the principle of interdependence and mutual exchange which the fellowship involves.

3. The keys, though given to, and administered by the apostolate in a primary and pre-eminent sense, are yet exercised by the institution of Christ and the apostles. This is concretely illustrated in Matthew 18:17, 18; 1 Cor. 5:5. But we should remember that the investiture (Matt. 16:19) applied to the church in its broadest and most inclusive denotation.

4. In the body of Christ the organic connection is such, that if one member suffers the whole body suffers. Are we to suppose that there is no redress that can be made by the whole body, when maladministration in one member of the churches of Christ imperils the health of the whole body? Surely the intimacy of relationship is such that not only is correction a mercy and blessing, but an obligation.

5. We may not discount the example of the Jerusalem council (Acts 15). The church at Antioch conferred with the apostles and elders at Jerusalem, and they determined the question in debate, not only for the church at Antioch, but for all the churches (Acts 16:4). It is all the more striking that the church should have resorted to such deliberation, and to this method of resolving an issue, since it was the era of special revelation (cf. the difference between this method and that exemplified in the case of Cornelius and the admission of the Gentiles—Acts 10). There is provided for us a pattern of consultation and adjudication that cannot be neglected in the permanent government of the church.

6. The only permanent institution for government is the eldership, the *presbuterion*. In some way or other, this institution is the means whereby corporate government is to be effected. We should keep in mind that the gifts Christ bestows are for the good, for the edification of the whole body. It is consonant with this ecumenical extension of the relevance of gifts that the gifts for rule, as well as those for other phases of ministry, should be brought to bear upon the edification of the whole church, as well as upon the local congregation.

28

The Form of Government[1]

WHEN we examine the New Testament there needs to be no question of the fact that those invested with the gift and function of government are called elders. Titus was left in Crete that he might set in order the things that were lacking and 'ordain elders in every city' (Titus 1:5). From Miletus Paul sent to Ephesus and called thither the elders of the church (Acts 20:17). Peter writes to exhort the elders, as undershepherds under the archshepherd, to shepherd the flock of God (1 Pet. 5:1, 2). That these elders ruled the church is apparent. The elders whom Titus was to ordain in Crete were also called bishops and stewards of God (Tit. 1:7). In his charge to the elders at Ephesus Paul says, 'Take heed to yourselves and to all the flock over which the Holy Spirit hath made you overseers (bishops)' (Acts 20:28). And 1 Timothy 5:17 makes clear that all elders ruled, though there is the further differentiation that some ruled better than others, and some, in addition to ruling, laboured in the word and doctrine.

There are certain observations to be elicited from these passages and others of kindred character.

1. *Plurality*. This feature lies on the face of the evidence. Titus was enjoined to ordain *elders* in every city. He was not instructed to ordain an elder or bishop in every city. Paul called to Miletus the elders of the church and charged them, as a plurality, to shepherd the flock of God. The writer of the Epistle to the Hebrews writes, 'Remember them that have the rule over you' (Heb. 13:7). This emphasis upon plurality

[1] The following is part of a published lecture *The Presbyterian Form of Church Government*, Evangelical Presbyterian Fellowship, 1958.

indicates the jealousy with which the New Testament guards against government by one man. The New Testament institution is not, as we have seen, a pure democracy. Neither is it an autocracy. It is the simple truth that singularity has no place in the government of Christ's church. In every case the singularity exemplified in diocesan episcopacy, whether it be in the most extreme form of the papacy, or in the most restricted application of local diocesan bishops, is a patent deviation from, indeed presumptuous contradiction of, the institution of Christ. Plurality is written in the boldest letters in the pages of the New Testament, and singularity bears the hallmark of despite to Christ's institution.

It is not for us to question the institution of Christ even when we are unable to discover the reasons for it. But in this instance it is not difficult to see the wisdom and grace of the head of the church. Plurality is a safeguard against the arrogance and tyranny to which man has the most characteristic proclivity. And plurality in this sphere always differentiates the singularity that belongs to Christ and to him alone. It is no wonder that failure to adhere to the plurality that must be maintained in the government of the church has, by logical steps, resulted in what on all accounts is the greatest travesty ever witnessed in the history of Christendom, namely, the pretensions and blasphemies of the Roman see.

This plurality must be practised in every sphere of jurisdiction. Titus was not only to ordain elders, but elders in every city. This is the most distinctive feature of Paul's charge in this connection. Every locality had its own elders. It was not a case of itinerant elders exercising jurisdiction over a large area. We see how rigidly the principle of plurality was maintained, and this provision of plurality in every town accentuates the perversion to which singularity in government has subjected the institution of the New Testament.

2. *Parity.* The principle of parity is co-ordinate with that of plurality. Strictly speaking there can be no plurality if there is not parity. For if one is in the least degree above the others, then, in respect of that hegemony, there is no longer plurality. Plurality applies to all government of the church, and there must therefore be parity in the plurality. There is not the slightest evidence in the New Testament that among the elders there was any hierarchy; the elders exercise government in unison, and on a parity with one another.

This principle has oftentimes suffered eclipse within the presbyterian fold. It has come to expression within presbyterian churches by the entertaining of the notion that to the minister of the Word belongs priority or pre-eminence in the government of the church. It is true that the minister as a teaching elder has his own distinctive function in the preaching and teaching of the Word. He labours in the Word and doctrine. It is natural and proper that his knowledge and experience should be given due respect in the deliberations which must be undertaken by the elders in the exercise of the government of the church. But it cannot be too strongly emphasised that, in respect of ruling, the minister of the Word is on a parity with all the others who are designated elders. When this is discarded, then there ensues that type of clerical hierarchism which has reached its logical outcome in what is known as hierarchical episcopacy, and it is the first step in the abandonment of the institution of Christ. Ministers of the word in presbyterian denominations are not immune to the vice of autocracy, and they are too ready to grasp at an authority that does not belong to them. This evil, which has marred the witness of churches professing presbyterian government, only illustrates the need for constant vigilance, lest the elementary principles of presbyterian government be violated and desecrated. It is not only by erroneous theory that presbytery is prejudiced, but also by practice which subtly annuls the theory professed.

3. The Episcopacy. It is so obvious that those exercising the ruling function in the New Testament are sometimes called elders, and at other times bishops, that no elaborate argument is necessary to establish the identity. In Acts 20:17 we read that Paul sent from Miletus to Ephesus, and called the *elders* of the church. At verse 28 we have the charge given to these elders: 'Take heed to yourselves and to all the flock in which the Holy Spirit hath made you bishops.' Again in Titus 1:5 we read: 'For this cause left I thee in Crete . . . that thou mightest ordain elders in every city.' Then Paul proceeds to give some of the qualifications, and states the reason why these qualifications must be possessed by those ordained to this office—'For a bishop must be blameless, as the steward of God' (Tit. 1:7). It would be senseless to state this reason if the bishop referred to a different office or function. Hence when Paul says to Timothy, 'Faithful is the saying, if any one desires the office of a bishop

347

(the episcopacy) he desires a good work' (1 Tim. 3:1), he cannot have in mind any other office than is in view in Titus 1:7, where the person designated a bishop has already been identified in Titus 1:5 as an elder.

The term 'elder' is not itself indicative or definitive of function; the term 'bishop' is, and refers expressly to the oversight, supervision, or rulership which defines the function of the elder, in the institution of government.

We must, therefore, recognize that in the New Testament the term 'bishop' is identical in respect of office and function with that of elder, and must not be associated in the remotest way with the hierarchical denotation or connotation that has come to be attached to it in the course of history. The New Testament institution is presbyterial; it is also episcopal. And these are identical. The principles already enunciated —plurality and parity—apply without any qualification to what the New Testament means by episcopacy.

4. Local Government. We have found that the kind of government set forth in the New Testament is that of a plurality of elders or bishops exercising oversight on a parity with one another. It is all-important to take account of the fact that it is on the local level that this must, first of all, be applied. It is in the local assembly, or congregation of God's people, that the ordinances of Christ's appointment for his church are regularly administered. The importance of the local congregation is therefore paramount and it is in the local congregation that the presbyterian principle must first be exemplified. If it is not preserved and practised at this point, it is not in operation at all. If and when it so happens that a particular congregation of God's people is not able, for reasons of geographical isolation, or for reasons of loyalty to the whole counsel of God, to establish a broader fellowship with other congregations of like faith and practice, that congregation must not consider itself pre-empted from discharging all the rights and prerogatives, as well as duties, of presbytery. In the New Testament the *presbuterion* is simply the elders gathered together for the discharge of those functions of government devolving upon them, and no prerogative of presbytery is denied them when acting in that capacity. The presbyterian principle begins at the level of the particular flock or congregation, and if, for good reasons, it does not extend further than one congregation, we are not to deem it unpresbyterian. To be concrete, to that local presbytery belong all the functions that Christ has accorded to presbytery.

5. *Ecumenical Government.* While it is all-important to maintain and promote presbyterian government on the level of the local congregation, and to recognize all the rights and prerogatives belonging to this *presbuterion*, yet it is also necessary to appreciate the broader fellowship that obtains in the church of Christ. In the presbyterian tradition this has come to expression in the gradation of courts of jurisdiction. This is a reasonable and proper way of giving expression to the unity of the church of Christ. It should be recognized that there is much in the form of organization and procedure adopted in presbyterian churches that cannot plead the authority of the New Testament. And the reason why certain forms of organization and procedure have been adopted and practised, which cannot plead the prescription or warrant of Scripture itself, is simply the recognition that there are some circumstances concerning the worship of God and government of the church which are to be ordered by the light of nature and Christian prudence, in accord with the general principles of the Word of God. Much in the actual polity of the church falls into this category and we must guard against the notion that differences in the form of organization, and particularly in mode of procedure, necessarily violate the biblical principles of presbyterian government. There is much room for variety, and the church of Christ is always under the necessity of devising and adopting better forms of procedure and organization than those which tradition may have established.

But the main consideration at this point is that the unity of government exemplified in the gradation of courts of jurisdiction is a principle which belongs to the form of government which the New Testament sets forth. In the history of the church several facts have been appealed to in support of this principle of inclusive or expansive jurisdiction. The example of the Jerusalem council recorded in Acts 15 has been adduced, and that not without warrant. Apostolic example has the force of divine prescription. And the church at Antioch, in connection with the dissension that arose concerning circumcision, deemed it proper to send Paul and Barnabas and others to Jerusalem to confer with the apostles and elders about this question. The apostles and elders came together to consider this matter. The decrees that were issued by the council were regarded as having regulative force throughout the whole church. For we read that Paul and Silas on Paul's second missionary journey, as they went through the cities, 'delivered them the decrees for to keep, that were ordained of the apostles and elders which were at Jerusalem' (Acts 16:4).

The consideration, however, that should be deemed primary and basic in this connection is the unity and community of the church as the body of Christ. The local congregation is indeed the church of Christ, but so are all the assemblies of God's people. The unity that belongs to the body of Christ must come to expression in government, as well as in the other functions which are properly those of the church. That each congregation should be entirely independent in its government is incompatible with the oneness of the body of Christ. 'There is one body and one Spirit, even as ye were called in one hope of your calling: one Lord, one faith, one baptism: one God and Father of all, who is above all, and through all, and in all' (Eph. 4:4–6). The co-ordination and subordination exemplified in presbyterian churches are the expression in the sphere of government of this unity. In any case, there must be some way of bringing this unity to expression. And the only feasible way is that the whole church should be governed by a *presbuterion* that will be as widely representative as the church itself. All that is absolutely essential in terms of the New Testament is that government be as inclusive as the whole body. The particular ways of applying this ecumenity of government are but the expedients of Christian prudence in accord with the general principles of the word.

29

Arguments against Term Eldership[1]

THE question being discussed in this brief article is whether ruling elders, in being elected and ordained, may be elected and ordained to the office for a limited and specified period of time, or whether election and ordination should have in view permanent tenure and exercise of the office. The position being taken by the present writer is the latter, namely, that the idea of being ordained to office for a limited period of time is without warrant from the New Testament, and is contrary to the implications of election and ordination.

In taking this position, it is necessary at the outset to make clear what it does not involve. It does not mean that a ruling elder may not be removed from office. Of course an elder may be deposed from office for false doctrine or immorality. And even though he may not be guilty of error or immorality, he may be relieved of his office for other reasons. For example, he may prove to be destitute of the requisite gifts and, in such an event, it would be a travesty of the order instituted by Christ for him to continue to retain the office and presume to exercise its functions. The elder in such a case may resign and his resignation should be accepted. Or he may simply be divested of his office by the proper action of the session. What the procedure would be in this latter case is not our interest at the present time. Again, when an elder ceases to be able to exercise the functions of the office, he should no longer retain the

[1] Published in *The Presbyterian Guardian*, February 15, 1955, when the revision of the Form of Government of The Orthodox Presbyterian Church was under consideration. The author was a member of the revision committee.

office. This inability may arise from infirmity, or the elder in question may have to move from the locality in which the congregation that elected him resides, so that he is no longer able to discharge the duties. It is not feasible for the elder to retain his office in these circumstances— we may not separate the office from its functions. Ordination to permanent tenure of the office, therefore, does not in the least degree interfere with the duty of resignation from office when that is necessary, nor with the right and duty of removal from office when the circumstances require it. The question in debate is something quite different.

It is true that the practice of ordaining ruling elders for a limited period has a long history in Reformed Churches. Many interesting facts could be brought to light if that history were to be traced. But now we are concerned to discover what may be elicited from the Scripture on the question.

In support of the position adopted in this article, it will have to be said, first of all, that there is no *overt* warrant from the New Testament for what we may call 'term eldership'. There is no intimation in the relevant passages that the elders in question were ordained to the office for a specified term. This is a consideration that must not lightly be dismissed. While it does not, of itself, conclusively determine the question, yet it is necessary to take account of this absence of explicit warrant for term eldership. We must bear in mind that there are two ways in which the Scripture reveals to us God's will, namely, what is expressly set down in Scripture, and what by good and necessary consequence may be deduced from Scripture. We are now concerned with the former, and we are affirming at the outset that, in respect of express warrant, there is no evidence to support the idea of term eldership.

It could well be argued, however, that, though there is no express warrant for term eldership, yet there is no evidence against it, and the New Testament leaves the matter an open question; it is a matter on which the New Testament does not legislate. It is this position that the present writer controverts. While the New Testament does not *expressly* legislate against term eldership, there are considerations which fall into the category of good and necessary inference, and which militate against the propriety of this practice. These considerations are derived from the implications which underlie or inhere in the acts of electing and ordaining to this office, implications which are incompatible with the idea of term eldership.

It is quite obvious that the qualifications for eldership are well defined in the New Testament (1 Tim. 3:1–7; Titus 1:5–9; cf. Acts 20:28–35). The qualifications are of a high order, and they imply that the person possessing them is endowed with them by the Holy Spirit and by Christ the head of the church. The implication is that the person thus qualified is invested with these gifts and graces to the end that he may serve the church of Christ in that capacity for which these endowments fit him. There are diversities of gifts in the church of God, and the gifts possessed dictate the function or functions which each person is to perform in the unity of the whole body. Now the gifts for eldership are not of a temporary character. If a person possesses them, the implication is that he permanently possesses them. Sadly enough he may through unfaithfulness lose them. But when a man possesses them we must proceed upon the assumption that he is going to prove faithful, and we may not entertain any suspicion to the effect that he is going to prove unfaithful. The simple fact is that when a man possesses certain endowments which qualify him for eldership, we must proceed on the assumption that they are abiding, and permanently qualify him for the discharge of the functions of the office.

When the congregation elects a man to the office of elder, and when the session ordains him to the office, both the congregation and the session must be convinced that he is possessed of these qualifications. When they act otherwise they violate the New Testament institution. But this judgment on the part of congregation and session involves more than the conviction that he is possessed of these qualifications; it is also judgment to the effect that, by reason of the gifts with which he is endowed, Christ the head of the church, and the Holy Spirit who dwells in the church, are calling this man to the exercise of this sacred office. In other words, the congregation and session ought to recognize themselves as merely the instruments through which the call of Christ and of his Spirit comes to effect. The Church is acting *ministerially* in doing the will of Christ. The word of Paul to the elders of Ephesus is surely relevant to this fact: 'Take heed to yourselves and to all the flock, in which the Holy Spirit hath made you bishops, to shepherd the church of God, which he hath purchased with his own blood' (Acts 20:28).

When these two facts are co-ordinated, namely, the permanency of the gifts which qualify for the office, and the judgment of the church that Christ is calling this man to the exercise of the office, it seems to me quite inconsistent with all that is implicit in the judgment and action of the church, for the person in question to be ordained and installed in the office for a limited term. In the absence of any express warrant for term eldership it is, to say the least, most precarious to assume that ordination for a limited term is legitimate. When we duly assess the weight of the consideration that the gifts which qualify for the office are the gifts of Christ, and therefore in effect the call of Christ and of his Spirit to the exercise of these gifts, when we bear in mind that the possession of these gifts is not temporary but abiding, and that the gifts increase in fruitfulness and effectiveness with their exercise, the most conclusive warrant for ordination to temporary office would have to be provided in order to justify that kind of ordination. It is precisely that conclusive warrant that is lacking. It is in this light that the absence of express warrant takes on the greatest significance. Only conclusive warrant can offset the cogency of these considerations with which we have been dealing.

Finally, there is the argument that pertains to the unity of the office of ruling. In respect of ruling in the church of God, the ruling elder and the teaching elder are on complete parity. When the teaching elder is ordained, he is ordained to rule as well as to teach, and his ruling function is just as permanent as is his teaching function. In the Orthodox Presbyterian Church there is no provision for term ordination of teaching elders, nor has it ever been proposed, as far as I am aware. Term ordination for ruling elders has been proposed and contended for. There is surely some inconsistency here. To say the least, consistency would appear to demand that, if term eldership is approved and provided for in our Form of Government in the case of ruling elders, the same should be approved and provided for in the case of teaching elders.

It will perhaps help to point up the anomaly of term eldership when we think of the same type of ordination in the case of teaching elders. No doubt the reason why the latter has not been seriously proposed is that it appears incompatible with the calling which teaching eldership implies, that is, the call to the gospel ministry. Exactly so! When the call to ruling eldership is properly weighed, and its implications properly evaluated, we should have the same sense of incompatibility in thinking of term eldership in the case of ruling elders.

The most important consideration of all in this connection is that term eldership for ruling elders draws a line of cleavage between ruling elders and teaching elders in respect of that one function which is common to both, and in terms of which both are on complete parity. The teaching elder is ordained to permanent tenure of the ruling office, the ruling elder would not be if the practice of term eldership is adopted. Here is a line of distinction which tends to institute a sharp cleavage between the ruling elder and the teaching elder in respect of that one thing where it is necessary to preserve unity and complete parity. One cannot but feel that the practice of term eldership for ruling elders is but a hangover of an unwholesome clericalism which has failed to recognize the basic unity of the office of elder and, particularly, the complete parity of all elders in the matter of government.

If it should be argued that the minister is called to a life work, and makes labour in the Word and doctrine his exclusive, full-time employment, whereas the ruling elder does not, there are these things to be said:

1. Granted that the minister gives all his time to this task, and the elder does not, it by no means follows that the elder need not be regarded as called to the permanent discharge of the office of ruling. He may not devote all his time to it, but there is absolutely no evidence that he is not called to it as a permanent office. Full-time and part-time has absolutely nothing to do with the question of the permanency of the call to office.

2. 1 Tim. 5:17, 18 indicates that the ruling elder is to be remuneratively rewarded for his labour in ruling. The call to part-time remunerative labour has as much claim to permanence as full-time remunerative labour.

3. Even ruling elders may devote all their time to the ruling and pastoral duties, and be remunerated accordingly. The labourer is worthy of his hire.

PRACTICAL CONSIDERATIONS AGAINST TERM ELDERSHIP

1. It tends to create in the minds of the people the notion of trial periods. That should have no place whatsoever in the election of elders.

2. It tends to develop such a notion in the minds of elders themselves, and therefore a decreased sense of responsibility and office.

3. It interferes with the continuity, and therefore with the sense of responsibility, as also with the stability of the office.

4. It may occasion the removal of good elders as well as bad ones.

5. It may minister to party division and strife.

6. It is rather liable to give the impression of representative government and of democracy. Presbyterianism is not democratic.

7. It tends to promote the idea that the eldership should be passed around.

In conclusion there is no sound practical argument that may be advanced that cannot be offset by a multiplicity of practical arguments on the other side.

30

Office in the Church[1]

With reference to service in the church of Christ it is customary to employ the word 'office' to designate the position pertaining to the exercise of certain functions. In Reformed Churches it is common to speak of the office of the minister, the office of the elder, and the office of the deacon. In the New Testament the term can properly be used in the translation of certain words (cf. Luke 1:9; Rom. 11:13; 1 Tim. 3:1; Heb. 7:5). But there is no one term that denotes 'office' in the sense in which it has become current in the church. Hence, when we seek to discover the New Testament conception of 'office' in the church, we cannot proceed by determining the definition of the term that corresponds to our word 'office'. There is no such term, and our inquiry is complicated by that fact. The only course we can pursue is to find out what the New Testament teaches respecting persons endowed with particular gifts, and discharging the corresponding functions in virtue of which they are set apart and distinguished from others by certain designations indicative of the specific functions performed. It lies on the face of the New Testament that there are such persons and designations (cf. 1 Cor. 12:27–30; Eph. 4:11, 12). These passages, and others to similar

---

[1] This unpublished study was written in 1970 as work which the author prepared as a member of a committee of the Reformed Ecumenical Synod. In submitting this study for the consideration of his colleagues on the committee he wrote: 'I have decisive views on the matter concerned with women, namely, that women are not eligible for what falls into the category of office. The argument in support I could have appended to my study. But that was not my assignment.' This was probably the last written work which John Murray contributed as a committee-member of the R.E.S.

effect, are basic to our inquiry. But they do not of themselves answer our question as to what constitutes 'office' in the permanent ministry and government of the church of Christ. This is so for two reasons:

First, in these enumerations there are functions, and persons exercising them, which no longer obtain in the church of Christ. This is apparent in the case of apostles and prophets, and it is questionable if 'evangelists' (Eph. 4:11) are to be equated with those who *now* carry on the work of evangelism. Second, differentiation would have to be found in the list of functions given in 1 Corinthians 12:27–30 (cf. Rom. 12:6–8). It is obvious that apostles held a position that can properly be denoted 'office' in our use of the term. The same holds true of pastors, of those who rule (Rom. 12:8; 1 Cor. 12:28), and of the diaconate (Rom. 12:7). But this can scarcely be said of some of the other gifts mentioned as, for example, miracles, gifts of healing, speaking in tongues (1 Cor. 12:28), giving and showing mercy (Rom. 12:8). The gifts differ (Rom. 12:6; 1 Cor. 12:4–6), therefore, not only in respect of the functions concerned, but also in respect of the status involved, and thus we are provided with an index to differentiation beyond that of function to what we may properly call office. For office there must be the corresponding gift, but not all gifts bestowed by the Spirit and necessarily exercised within the unity of the body of Christ and for its edification, invest the participants with office in the sense in which this applies to apostles, prophets, pastors, rulers in the church, and the diaconate.

It is not necessary at this stage of inquiry to discuss or attempt to resolve all questions that arise in connection with the passages referred to, for example, the precise character of 'evangelists' (Eph. 4:11), and whether the expression 'pastors and teachers' refers to the same persons or to different persons. Suffice it to recognize that in the New Testament there is the evidence to establish the existence in the apostolic church of certain persons endowed with gifts which not only called for exercise but which qualified the persons possessing them for an office, with the connotation which we attach to the term. Though not all of these offices are permanent in the church of Christ, some of them undoubtedly are, and by examining these our inquiry can be advanced.

There is copious evidence to establish the presbyterial office, and, since it is apparent that presbyters and bishops refer in New Testament usage to the same persons (cf. Acts 20:17, 28; Tit. 1:5, 7; 1 Tim. 3:1), this office can be designated also as episcopal, without the least hierarchical denotation or connotation that has come to be attached to it in the course of history. Paul and Barnabas on their missionary journey through south Galatia 'ordained elders' in every church. Titus was left in Crete, Paul tells us, that he might 'ordain elders in every city' (Tit. 1:5). From Miletus Paul called for 'the elders of the church' at Ephesus (Acts 20:17), and later reminded them of their responsibilities as bishops (Acts 20;28). James' exhortation (James 5:14) is based on the assumption that there were elders in the church in whom were vested special responsibilities and prerogatives. And Peter found it appropriate to direct exhortation to the elders very similar to that of Paul at Miletus (1 Pet. 5:1–3). These references are of themselves sufficient to prove that eldership was a common feature in the life and organization of the churches, even when the apostles and their official delegates were still alive and active.

The duties devolving upon elders are easily elicited from these and other passages.

1. They were to act as shepherds of the church of God (Acts 20:28; 1 Pet. 5:2).

2. They exercised oversight (Acts 20:28). This is the specific reason for the designation 'bishops'.

3. Implicit in oversight, or at least correlative with it, is rule or government (1 Tim. 3:5; 5:17; 1 Pet. 5:3; cf. Heb. 13:7). Since this is an integral function of the office, we are compelled to identify the ruling of Romans 12:8 and the government of 1 Corinthians 12:28 with this office; in the regular administration of the church it would not be possible to think of two distinct governing agencies.

4. The elder is the steward of God (Tit. 1:7), a function indicative of entrustment with what belongs to God. The foregoing duties focus attention upon the care exercised over the saints as the church of God. Stewardship focuses thought upon the care to be exercised in the administration of God's property.

5. The elder is to exhort and teach in the discharge of his duties as shepherd, overseer, ruler, and steward (1 Tim. 3:2; Tit. 1:9). As will presently appear, there is differentiation in respect of endowment with,

and exercise of, the teaching gift. But all elders exhort in sound doctrine and refute gainsayers as occasion demands.

The differentiation alluded to above appears in 1 Tim. 5:17 and is concerned particularly with labour in word and doctrine. 'Word and doctrine' may properly be construed as preaching and teaching. Though it is necessary for all elders to hold fast the faithful word, so as to be able to exhort in sound doctrine and refute gainsayers, though all must be competent to teach, yet not all labour in preaching and teaching. On the other hand, there are those who do. They devote themselves to these activities. Whether there is differentiation between elders labouring in preaching, and those labouring in teaching, so that two distinct functions are contemplated, it is difficult if not impossible to say. But it would not be justifiable to insist that there is such differentiation. Those concerned may well, if not more reasonably, be conceived of as labouring in both word and doctrine. But in any case those labouring in word and doctrine are classified as elders who, in addition to ruling, devote themselves to the preaching and teaching of the Word of God and, are thus in a special way accounted worthy of the compensation which their labour warrants (cf. vs. 18).

It is now appropriate to relate what has been found regarding this episcopal, presbyterial office, to the 'pastors and teachers' of Eph. 4:11. Elders are shepherds of the flock; they are to 'shepherd the church of God' (Acts 20:28) and 'the flock of God' (1 Pet. 5:2; cf. vss. 3, 4). It is the same term 'shepherd' that appears in Eph. 4:11. Since Paul penned the latter, it would be necessary for us to infer that he has in view the same function which he enjoined upon the elders from Ephesus. And so the conclusion is that the pastors (shepherds) of Eph. 4:11 are those designated in Acts 20:17, 28 as elders and bishops. In a word, the evidence would require the conclusion that the pastors are elders of the church of God. The same doubt would arise with reference to 'pastors and teachers' in Eph. 4:11 as arises in 1 Tim. 5:17 with reference to 'labour in word and doctrine'. There may be two groups differentiated from each other. But, as in 1 Tim. 5:17, we may not insist that two groups are in view; those concerned may well, if not more reasonably, be regarded as exercising both functions, namely, shepherding and teaching. Furthermore, in terms of the evidence, we would have no right to differentiate the teaching of Eph. 4:11 from the labour in teaching of 1 Tim. 5:17. Thus the 'pastors and teachers' should be identified with the elders who 'labour in word and doctrine'. These considerations point, therefore, to the conclusion that two functions belong to the episcopal, presbyterial office, namely, government of the church and ministry of the Word. All elders exercise rule in the church of God, but some, in virtue of their gifts and calling, labour in preaching and teaching. It may be that those in the latter category may be divided into two classes, the one particularly devoted to preaching, the other to teaching. But, in that event, both classes are elders with the distinguishing function of *labour* in the ministry of the Word of God.

It is sufficiently clear, from the intimations given in the New Testament, that elders were appointed or ordained to and put in charge of the office on the recognition of their possessing the necessary qualifications. Paul and Barnabas appointed elders in every church (Acts 14:23). Titus was instructed by Paul to appoint elders in every city (Tit. 1:5). Timothy and Titus were instructed as to the qualifications required for the office (1 Tim. 3:1-7; Tit. 1:6-9). We have good reason to assume that Timothy, like Titus, had the authority and responsibility to appoint elders. There must have been in the churches an acknowledgment and recognition of those set apart to the office, and of this we have distinct indications (cf. Heb. 13:7; James 5:14; 1 Pet. 5:1).

The fact of appointment being thus established, the question arises: What was the appointing agency in the absence of apostles and associates? It would be reasonable to expect that, with the passing of what was temporary, the right and duty of appointment would be vested in the governing agency in the church of God, namely, the eldership. There are considerations in support of this presumption. The elders are overseers who take care of the church and act as shepherds of the flock. To the eldership is assigned the ministry of the Word. In the discharge of these responsibilities, no action could be of greater concern than to ensure that the government of the church and the ministry of the Word should be conducted by competent and faithful men (cf. 2 Tim. 2:2).

We have also a datum of more express relevance to our question. Paul refers to the presbytery and to its action in laying hands upon Timothy (1 Tim. 4:14). The presbytery can be none other than a body of presbyters (elders). If the elders, acting as a unit and in unison, performed such a function in reference to Timothy, how much more would this type of action apply to the appointment of others to augment their number and strengthen their ministry.

In this reference to the laying on of hands of the presbytery we are provided with evidence that the laying on of hands was an element, if not the constitutive act, in investiture. The laying on of hands had significance in other connections, in the imparting of grace, blessing, and gift (cf. Matt. 9:18; 19:13; Mark 6:5; 7:32; 8:23; Luke 13:13; Acts 8:17; 9:12, 17; 13:3; 19:6; 1 Tim. 5:22). As symbolic of impartation, it is altogether consonant with what is involved in appointment to office or to the discharge of a particular function belonging to that office. Confirmation is derived from what was done in the case of the seven. They were selected by the congregation and when brought before the apostles they prayed and 'laid their hands on them' (Acts 6:6). Likewise, when Paul and Barnabas were set apart for a missionary undertaking, the prophets and teachers at Antioch 'fasted and prayed and laid their hands on them' (Acts 13:3). The practice of laying on hands is of such a character that the reference to this action on the part of the presbytery (1 Tim. 4:14), and the laying on of hands in the appointment of the seven (Acts 6:6), create the strongest presumption that 'the presbytery', in the ordination of elders, laid on hands as the consummating act in appointment to office.

It is necessary now to reflect on the question of the position occupied by the eldership in the administration of the church. There are, in particular, three passages that bear significantly on this question (Acts 20:17, 28; Phil. 1:1; 1 Pet. 5:1). When Paul called for the elders of the church at Ephesus to come to Miletus, and then gave them the solemn charge of Acts 20:28 (cf. also vss. 29–32), it is implied that the elders exercised the most responsible functions in the church at Ephesus. There could not be any other office in the church there with priority in respect of jurisdiction. In a word, the eldership held the highest position in shepherding and overseeing the church. The same conclusion can be derived from Phil. 1:1. Paul addresses the saints at Philippi and then adds: 'with the bishops and deacons'. The bishops and deacons, we must infer, comprised those who were differentiated by office, and the absence of any other designation would imply that there were no others to be thus differentiated. Bishops are mentioned first, and for this reason as well as others they are given the priority. When Peter directs exhortation to the elders (1 Pet. 5:1) and classifies himself with them, the implication is apparent: of those differentiated in virtue of office, elders had a unique position as those who shepherded the flock of God. This unique place and the responsibility involved is underlined by the reminder that they are under-shepherds and that Christ is the Chief Shepherd, to whom they must give account, and from whom they will receive their reward.

The New Testament evidence, therefore, shows conclusively that the office of elder (bishop) was firmly established in the church, that this office provided for the government of the church and the ministry of the Word in both preaching and teaching, that in the regular and permanent care of the church there was no other office exercising higher authority and responsibility, that it was an office certified to the church and accorded public recognition by investiture in the acts of prayer and the laying on of hands, and that by its very nature and the purposes served it is a permanent institution in the church of Christ.

When we inquire as to what constitutes office in the permanent institution of the New Testament, it is to the eldership that we must look as that which *par excellence*, and by way of eminence, exemplifies what office is. No other institution in the organization of the church is comparable in regard to dignity, function, and responsibility.

Eldership is not, however, the sole office. No passage illustrates this fact more than Philippians 1:1. With the bishops are linked the deacons. Hence, the term 'deacon' is used in this instance in a distinctly specific sense in contrast with the more generic sense of 'servant' in which it frequently occurs in the New Testament (cf., e.g. John 12:26; Rom. 13:4; 1 Cor. 3:5; 2 Cor. 6:4; 11:23; Eph. 3:7; 1 Thess. 3:28; 1 Tim. 4:6). The differentiation implicit in the text makes this specialized use obvious. This distinction is similarly apparent in the cognate abstract noun (*diakonia*). It may not have the specialized sense of 'deaconship' although in Romans 12:7 the context would indicate that this application is most likely. It is clear that the verb is used in the specific sense of 'serving as deacon' in 1 Timothy 3:10, 13. The infrequency of the application of the term and of its cognates to a distinct office in no way interferes with the specialized denotation in Philippians 1:1. The same holds true in 1 Timothy 3:8, 12. In this passage 'deacons' are again closely linked with bishops. The close sequence in which direction as to their qualifications occurs, with the directions respecting the qualifications of bishops, as well as the introductory words, 'likewise the deacons', make this co-ordination apparent.

The difference between elders and deacons needs no argument. To deacons are not assigned the duties devolving upon elders, and the qualifications are correspondingly different. The qualities required are, however, of a high order and some of them are similar to those of elders (cf. 1 Tim. 3:2, 4, 12). Perhaps most notable is the requirement that they hold 'the mystery of the faith with a pure conscience' (1 Tim. 3:9).

It has sometimes been thought that the office of deacon took its origin in the appointment of the seven (Acts 6:1–6). The seven were not called deacons and some of them performed functions that do not fall within the province of deacons (cf. Acts 6:8–15; 8:5–40.) There is not sufficient warrant, therefore, to identify the seven with the deacons who appear later on in the development of the church's organization nor is it apparent that the diaconate took its origin from the appointment of the seven. Nevertheless it is probable that the appointment of the seven, and more particularly the principle that led to their appointment (Acts 6:2), provided the pattern for the erection of the diaconate as a distinct office, and also for the kind of service rendered by the diaconate in and for the church. There is not much evidence in the New Testament bearing upon the functions belonging to the diaconal office. It is more by way of inference that we construe this office as concerned with the administration of affairs that do not come within the province of elders. Ministry to the poor in material things is an important function of the church (cf. Rom. 15:25, 26; Gal. 2:10). It is reasonable to infer that to the deacons is committed this ministry, and other activities of a similar character in the sphere of mercy.

These two offices are permanent in the church of Christ, and they are the only offices that can be demonstrated to be in that category. It may be that the office of evangelist is permanent (Eph. 4:11). On the other hand, however, it may be in the same category as apostle and prophet, and may refer to men like Timothy and Titus who were given special authority and responsibility as delegates of the apostles (cf. 2 Tim. 4:5). If the term, as used in the New Testament (Acts 21:8; Eph. 4:11; 2 Tim. 4:5), designates a special, temporary office, this in no way prejudices the work of evangelism that is permanent in the church of Christ. The persons specially set apart for, and appointed to this work would necessarily, in accord with analogy, be exercising an office in the ministry of the Word (cf. 1 Tim. 5:17) and could be classified with elders who labour in the Word. But in view of the specific character of their work as in many cases itinerant and unconfined, it is admittedly difficult to subsume their activity under the 'pastors and teachers' of Eph. 4:11, or the elders who 'labour in the word' of 1 Tim. 5:17. It would appear, therefore, that here is a moot question on which we are compelled to be indecisive. We should be prepared to allow for a distinct office of 'evangelist' without equating it with the specialized office to which the term is possibly applied in the three instances in which it occurs in the New Testament.

31

The Sacraments

The word 'sacrament' is not strictly a biblical term. But it has come to designate certain ordinances of New Testament institution. In the Reformed Churches it is used to denote two ordinances and only two. Why? These are two ordinances which are unique in that they are characterized by a combination of features that is not duplicated in any other ordinance of the New Testament. And since they are unique in this respect, it is convenient to adopt a distinguishing designation. The distinct features provide us with the definition. What are these?

There is the definition of Augustine: 'The word is added to the element and it becomes a sacrament', and that of Lombard: 'The sacrament is the visible form of invisible grace'. These definitions contain important features. But they are not inclusive enough. So we must specify more particularly.

1. Ordinances instituted directly by Christ himself. The Lord's supper was instituted on the night in which he was being betrayed, and baptism on the eve of his ascension. With respect to the latter, it is necessary to distinguish between the baptism of John and that performed by Jesus' disciples, on the one hand, and that instituted by Jesus after his resurrection, on the other: John's baptism, like his ministry, was anticipatory, transitional, and preparatory.

2. They are ordinances in which material elements and visible signs are used, in baptism water and washing with water, in the Lord's supper bread and wine and the oral participation of these.

3. These elements and the use made of them are signs of spiritual blessing

—visible forms of invisible grace. Only as bearing that significance, do the elements and actions have meaning. The meaning of baptism is expressed in the word of institution and that of the Lord's supper likewise.

4. They are seals, certifications, confirmations to us of the grace they signify (cf. Gen. 17:9–11; Rom. 4:11).

5. They are to be observed perpetually in the church of Christ (Matt. 28:19; 1 Cor. 11:26). Hence they apply to all circumstances and conditions.

It is apparent that only baptism and the Lord's supper belong to the category defined by this combination. For example, Christ instituted the office of apostle, and the apostles as a group formed the apostolate. But the apostolate does not possess the other features.

EFFICACY

There are several observations:

1. The efficacy does not reside in the elements, nor in the actions, nor in the character of the person administering them, but only in the blessing of Christ and the working of his Spirit in those who possess the grace signified and sealed:

2. Since they are signs and seals, they presuppose the existence of the blessings they represent, and therefore are not to be conceived of as the means of establishing or constituting the relationship signified. Hence the grace symbolized is conveyed apart from their use. They are not themselves the means of salvation, or of the union with Christ by which the state of salvation is effected.

3. They are means of grace and convey blessing. Here a distinction must be drawn between baptism and the Lord's supper. Baptism is a means of grace and conveys blessing, because it is the certification to us of God's grace and in the acceptance of that certification we rely upon God's faithfulness, bear witness to his grace, and thereby strengthen our faith. Blessing always accrues to us from obedient and grateful observance of a divine ordinance. This also applies to the Lord's supper. But in the latter there is more. In the Lord's supper that signified is increased and cultivated, namely, communion with Christ and participation of the virtue accruing from his body and blood. The Lord's supper represents

that which is continuously being wrought. We partake of Christ's body and blood through the means of the ordinance.

We thus see that the accent falls on the faithfulness of God, and the efficacy resides in the response we yield to that faithfulness. In other words, the blessing flows to us in the degree in which we appropriate by faith the witness that God bears to his own faithfulness in the sacraments. They are condescensions to our weakness. He adds to the promise the visible sign, so that by two things, promise and sacrament, we may have full assurance of faith. Promise and sacrament are in this respect parallel to promise and covenant.

NECESSITY

We must distinguish between the necessity of precept and that of means. The necessity of means is maintained by sacerdotalist Churches, that baptism, in particular, is indispensable to salvation. The error of this position is apparent from the nature of the sacraments. They are signs and seals of grace. They are added for the purpose of certifying God's faithfulness to the grace and promise of the gospel. A seal presupposes the existence of that which has been certified, and is not the way of bringing into existence. But though denying the necessity of means this should not be taken as depreciating in any way the obligation to observe the sacraments. They are institutions of Christ and are to be observed in obedience to him. They belong to that which Jesus enjoined—'teaching them to observe all things whatsoever I have commanded you' (Matt. 28:20). Disregard of the sacraments is disobedience to Christ, offers dishonour to his grace, and brings to us and to the church spiritual impoverishment. The person possessing the qualifications for observance, and neglecting the duty and privilege, excludes himself from the blessing which observance in faith and obedience imparts. It is significant that Peter said: 'Repent and be baptised each one of you in the name of Jesus Christ' (Acts 2:38), and Paul: 'As often as ye eat this bread and drink the cup, ye do show forth the Lord's death, until he come' (1 Cor. 11:26). We must keep in view that salvation is more than its inception. And the sacraments are means through which we are to grow unto the salvation perfected in the last time.

It is easy to give way to a spurious kind of spirituality, and regard the sacraments as tending to externalism and ritualism, and not necessary to the highest form of devotion. We must beware of substituting spurious sentiment for obedience.

What is necessary to their administration?
1. The elements.
2. The actions.
3. Intention—of doing what Christ commanded.

The Roman Catholic Church thinks that validity depends on the official standing of the administrator.

Christ has established institutions that promote order and decorum. He has appointed officers for the preaching of the Word and the administration of the sacraments. To depart from this order is a violation of Christ's institution. But if the sacraments are administered in seriousness and with the intent of observing the institution of Christ, yet in violation of this order, we may not say they are invalid.

32

Baptism[1]

BAPTISM is the ordinance instituted by Christ on the eve of his ascension (Matt. 28:19). The word of institution does itself teach a great deal respecting the ordinance, and these features provide the starting point for our study.

THE PLACE OF BAPTISM

The word of institution shows that it belongs to the task of making disciples. A disciple is one who follows a master. In this case the master is Christ, and discipleship involves, therefore, total commitment and allegiance. The sequence is significant. 'All authority in heaven and in earth has been committed unto me' (v. 18). So the discipleship is commensurate with the absolute lordship of Christ. The baptized person recognizes and professes the lordship of Christ.

When we turn to other passages we find something that is correlative. It is that by baptism we become members of the church or, at least, register our membership. I am thinking of Acts 2:38, 41, 47. 'Repent, and be baptized each one of you, in the name of Jesus Christ.' 'Those who had received his word were baptized, and there were added in that day about three thousand souls.' 'And the Lord was adding daily unto them those who were being saved.'

Here it is necessary to correct an error that is widespread, that only those who go to the Lord's table are members of the church, that merely baptized persons are not making a profession. This is a pernicious underestimate of the meaning of baptism. It so happens that most of us have

[1] For fuller treatment see the author's *Christian Baptism*, 1952 and reprinted 1970 (The Presbyterian and Reformed Publishing Company).

been baptized in infancy. But the same holds true for those baptized in infancy. Unless we have repudiated our infant baptism we *are* professing.

There are certain consequences:

1. Baptized persons are under the discipline of the church and therefore subject to censure in the event of delinquency.

2. When reckoned to be members of the church, this presses home upon the church itself the responsibility for nurture.

'Baptism is a sacrament of the New Testament, ordained by Jesus Christ, not only for the solemn admission of the party baptized into the visible church, but also to be unto him a sign and seal of the covenant of grace, of his ingrafting into Christ, of regeneration, of remission of sins, and of his giving up unto God through Jesus Christ, to walk in newness of life' (*Westminster Confession*, XXVIII). Our Catechism, too, should have advised us of this.

IMPORT

Though the washing of regeneration and the sprinkling of the blood of Christ are signified by baptism (cf. John 3:5; 1 Cor. 6:11; Col. 2:11, 12; Titus 3:5; Acts 2:38; 22:16; 1 Pet. 3:21), yet the more explicit references indicate that, central to the import is union with Christ (cf. Rom. 6:3–6; 1 Cor. 12:13; Gal. 3:27, 28; Col. 2:11, 12). The word of institution points us to this. For baptism into the name means baptism into union with, and discipleship of, the three persons of the Godhead.

It is Jesus' own witness that the union with himself embraces the other persons of the Godhead. The terms in which this witness is expressed are really staggering. We read: 'If one loves me he will keep my word, and my Father will love him, and we will come unto him and make our abode with him' (John 14:23). 'Not for these only do I ask, but also for those who believe on me through their word, in order that they all may be one, as thou, Father art in me and I in thee, in order that they also may be in us, in order that the world may believe that thou hast sent me. And the glory thou hast given me I have given to them, in order that they may be one, as we are one; I in them and thou in me, that they be perfected in one' (John 17:20–23). This is the union with the Father. But the same applies to the Holy Spirit in the distinctive way that belongs to him. 'And I will pray the Father' etc. (John 14:16, 17).

In the institution of baptism, all of this is implicit in the words, 'baptizing them into the name' (Matt. 28:19). The name stands for the person in the fulness of his revealed character. That it is the one name indicates that all three persons conjointly claim our devotion in the distinguishing relations each person sustains to us in the economy of salvation.

There is also the pattern of Numbers 6:24–27. In baptism there is the seal of God's ownership.

MODE

The argument of Baptists that immersion is the only valid mode is based on the allegations that the Greek terms mean immersion, and that certain passages (Rom. 6:3–6; Col. 2:11, 12) indicate that the burial of Christ in the earth, and his emergence, provide the pattern. The fallacy of the second resides in an arbitrary selection of certain aspects of Paul's teaching on our union with Christ. It is true that believers are united with Christ in his burial and resurrection, and it is also true that immersion in, and emergence from the water appear to represent and symbolize this phase of union with Christ. But the union signified by baptism includes more than union with him in his burial and resurrection. It signifies union with him in his *death* and *crucifixion*. The burial must not be equated with either. Paul in Romans 6 speaks of being baptized into Jesus' *death* (v. 3), of being *planted together* with him in the likeness of his death (v. 5), and of being *crucified* with him (v. 6; cf. Gal. 2:20). It is apparent that immersion and emergence do not resemble these. But they are as germane to union with Christ as burial and resurrection. In the Baptist argument, therefore, the burial and resurrection are accorded the exclusive relevance in the plea for symbolism.

Other passages likewise prove the arbitrariness of preoccupation with the analogy of burial and resurrection. Paul also writes: 'For as many of you as were baptized into Christ did put on Christ' (Gal. 3:27). It would be as legitimate to argue for the mode of baptism from this passage as from Romans 6:4. But the figure here is that of putting on a garment, to which immersion bears no resemblance. In 1 Cor. 12:13 the figure is that of making up one body, which is foreign by way of analogy to immersion. The fact is that baptism signifies union with Christ in the whole range of his ministry, and other aspects are as integral as burial and resurrection. It is prejudicial to the completeness of the union signified to limit the symbolism to any one phase of Christ's redemptive accomplishment.

It is not possible in the space available to set forth the evidence bearing upon the meaning of the terms which denote baptism. Suffice it to say that there are numerous instances in which the action denoted does not imply immersion and which prove that baptism does not *mean* immersion (cf. Lev. 14:6, 51; Matt. 15:2; Mark 7:2–5; Luke 11:38; 1 Cor. 10:2; Heb. 9:10–23). The Greek term $\beta\alpha\pi\tau\acute{\iota}\zeta\omega$ indicates a certain effect, without prescribing the precise mode by which this effect is secured. Hence the ordinance is properly administered by sprinkling or affusion.

SUBJECTS

There is no issue of principle between Baptists and non-Baptists respecting the conditions necessary for the baptism of adults. It is true that there has been in some cases a difference of viewpoint, or at least of emphasis, on the question of the prerogatives belonging to the church in the admission of candidates for baptism. But this difference can exist among Baptists and among non-Baptists. So the line of demarcation should not be drawn in these terms. The injunctions of Peter on the day of Pentecost, and the practice followed on that occasion, make it clear that repentance, the faith of the gospel, and the reception of the Word, are the conditions upon which baptism was administered (Acts 2:38, 41, 42, 44). Other instances corroborate this as apostolic practice (Acts 8:34, 35, 36, 38; 10:34–47; 16:14, 15, 31–33). The only question that properly arises is: What criteria does the church apply in its judgment? The classic Reformed position is that it is not the prerogative of the church, or of those who in the name of the church administer baptism, to determine whether those seeking baptism truly and sincerely repent and believe. It is the duty of the church to propound the conditions and insist that only those complying with them are eligible in the sight of God. And the church must assist candidates to examine themselves. But the church accepts for baptism those who make an intelligent and uncontradicted confession of faith: any other position errs either on the side of presumption or looseness.

The crucial issue concerns the baptism of infants, and on this Baptists offer vigorous dissent. The argument in support of infant baptism is based upon the essential unity and continuity of the covenant grace administered to Abraham, unfolded in the Mosaic and Davidic covenants, and attaining to its highest fruition in the new covenant. The new covenant is the administration of grace that brings to fulfilment the promise given to Abraham: 'In thy seed shall all the nations of the earth be blessed' (Gen. 22:18). It is the blessing of Abraham that comes upon the Gentiles through Christ (Gal. 3:14). Abraham is the father of all believers, and they are Abraham's seed and heirs according to promise (Rom. 4:16–18; Gal. 3:7–9). The promises fulfilled in Christ were given to Abraham with covenantal confirmation. So it is proper and necessary to say that the new covenant is the fulfilment and unfolding of the Abrahamic covenant (cf. Gal. 3:15–17). The same unity and continuity are intimated when the covenant people of God are likened to one olive tree with several branches, all of which grow from one root and stock, and form one organism (Rom. 11:16–24).

The covenant made with Abraham included the infant seed, and was signified and sealed by circumcision administered by divine command (Gen. 17:9–14). That circumcision is the sign of the covenant in its deepest spiritual significance is demonstrated by the fact that it is called the covenant (Gen. 17:10; cf. Acts 7:8) and therefore identified as taken (cf. Gen. 17:11) with the covenant in the highest reaches of its meaning (cf. Gen. 17:7; Exod. 19:5, 6; Deut. 7:6; 14:2; 30:6; Jer. 4:4; Rom. 4:11; Col. 2:11, 12). Since the infant seed of the faithful were embraced in the covenant relation, and there is no indication that this feature of covenant administration has been abrogated under the new covenant, the conclusion derived from the unity and continuity of covenant grace is that the same privilege belongs to the infant seed of believers under the new covenant. In addition, there is the evidence showing the continuance of this principle (Matt. 19:13, 14; Acts 2:38, 39; 16:15, 33, 34; 1 Cor. 1:16; 1 Cor. 7:14; Eph. 6:1, 4; Col. 3:20, 21). These considerations are the ground for the propriety and validity of infant baptism.

The basis upon which baptism is dispensed to infants is, therefore, this divine institution. The promise of the covenant is to believers and their children. The abuses often attendant upon the baptism of infants should not be pleaded as objections to the ordinance itself. It is necessary that the church should exercise care and vigilance to prevent these abuses. Parents eligible to receive baptism for their offspring are only such as are faithful in their confession and in the discharge of their covenant obligations. Those who do not give evidence of the union with Christ which baptism signifies cannot claim the grace and promise extended in this institution (cf. Ps. 103:17, 18).

EFFICACY

As a rite instituted by Christ, baptism is not to be identified with the grace signified and sealed. This is apparent from the terms of institution (Matt. 28:19), and from the nature of baptism as seal. The existence of the grace sealed is presupposed in the giving of the seal. The tenet of baptismal regeneration reverses the order inherent in the definition which Scripture provides. The efficacy resides entirely in the pledge of God's faithfulness. God not only brings men and women into union with Christ as the embodiment of covenant grace at the zenith of its realization, he not only gives exceeding great and precious promises that are yea and amen in Christ, but he seals this union and confirms these promises by an ordinance that portrays to our senses the certainty of his grace. Depreciation of baptism insults the wisdom and grace of God and, more particularly, his faithfulness. He confirms to us the bond of union with himself by adding the seal of baptism, to the end that we may be more firmly established in the faith of his covenant grace.

BIBLIOGRAPHY

J. Calvin, *Institutes*, IV, xiv–xvi; R. Wilson, *Infant Baptism a Scriptural Service*, etc. (1848); P. Ch. Marcel, *The Biblical Doctrine of Infant Baptism* (1953); O. Cullman, *Baptism in the New Testament* (1950); J. Jeremias, *Infant Baptism in the First Four Centuries* (1962).

33

The Lord's Supper

THERE are two memorial ordinances in the New Testament, and there are only two, the Lord's supper and the Lord's day. The one celebrates the Lord's death, the other his resurrection. It is most significant that this should be the case. These are the pivotal events of redemption. The Lord's day is ever recurrent and the Lord's supper should be frequently administered. 'As often as ye eat this bread' (1 Cor. 11:26).

SEAL

In dealing with the Lord's supper it is well to start with our Lord's word: 'This cup is the new covenant in my blood, which is shed for you' (Luke 22:20; cf. Matt. 26:28; Mark 14:24). In the history of revelation there were several covenants. Covenant is a sovereign administration of grace or of command, divine in origin, revelation, confirmation, and fulfilment. At the centre from Abraham onwards is the promise: 'I will be your God' etc. Covenant is not to be equated with promise; it is confirmatory and similar to an oath. It is the oath—certified confirmation of promise. Redemptive revelation took the form of covenant. So implicit in redemption is the confirmation which covenant always involves.

The covenant associated with the coming and blood-shedding of Christ is the new covenant. There is much that is new, unique, and transcendent, and all of this is involved in the uniqueness of him who is its mediator and surety. Indeed, it is involved in the unprecedented fact that Christ is given to be the covenant. He embodies in himself all of the grace and faithfulness that covenant, at the zenith of its revelation and

376

realization, involves. But we must not so emphasize the newness that we overlook the covenantal character of Christ's institution. And when Jesus says, 'the new covenant in my blood', he means that all that covenant represents as oath-certified confirmation, and covenant at the zenith of realization, comes to men in his shed blood. The new covenant in the richness, fulness, and perpetuity of its grace, blessing, and promise comes to us in the blood of Christ. If we have the sprinkling of the blood and are cleansed thereby, then the new covenant in all that its newness implies, and in all the certification that covenant involves, is ours.

But Jesus on this occasion was speaking of the cup in the Lord's supper. We might think that there is an anticlimax, that the grandeur of the concept, 'the new covenant in my blood', is now curtailed. Oh, it is precisely the grandeur of the conception that enhances the significance of the Lord's supper! All that the new covenant in Jesus' blood means is represented and sealed in the Lord's supper. The confirmatory character of covenant is transferred to the cup. This is what the cup bespeaks. And when we partake of the cup in faith, it is the Lord's own certification to us that all that the new covenant in his blood involves is ours. It is the seal of his grace and faithfulness.

COMMEMORATION

This do in remembrance of me (Luke 22:19; cf. 1 Cor. 11:24, 25). The showing forth of the Lord's death (1 Cor. 11:26) is to be placed in the same category. This applies to both the bread and the wine.

1. *Remembrance.*—'This do in my remembrance.' That the remembrance of Jesus' death is focal cannot be questioned. Whether we take the briefest form, 'This is my body' or the longer forms, 'This is my body which is given for you', 'This is my body which is for you', the allusion to the bearing of sin in his body upon the tree cannot be suppressed. And the references to the blood are to the shedding of blood in the giving of his life. The proclaiming of the death is explicit (1 Cor. 11:26). That there should be a perpetual commemoration of Jesus' death by his own express institution is the most emphatic witness to the significance Jesus attached, and likewise the apostles, to the death on the cross in the redemption accomplished, and in the perpetual application of it. It is not simply a recollection that the death took place, and not

simply a remembrance of its focal place in the accomplishment of redemption. It is celebration. It is an event in which we glory (cf. Gal. 6:14).

2. *The Form*—'in my remembrance.' How jealously is excluded any notion of repetition. There is no affinity to the offering of sacrifice or even to the re-presentation of the sacrifice. This is a subterfuge. For we have to ask: when was the presentation? And then ask: if re-presentation, is this not repetition?

But 'my remembrance' conveys two thoughts. (a) His death must never be dissociated from his person. It is remembrance of him as dying and as being dead (cf. Acts 2:24; Heb. 2:9; Rev. 1:17, 18). (b) It is the Lord we are remembering. So frequently, believers become so introspective, that preoccupation with themselves excludes preoccupation with Christ.

COMMUNION

The text particularly relevant is 1 Cor. 10:16, 17. Several observations: 1. 'The cup of blessing' is most probably to be understood as the cup over which the blessing is asked; that 'which we bless' defines the cup of blessing. The plural points to the participation of all in the blessing invoked, and points to the communion of all in each element.

2. The communion of the blood of Christ has no reference to physical partaking of the literal blood. The disciples participated in all that is communicated. But Jesus' blood had not been shed. So what is meant by communion of the blood is what the disciples enjoyed, and therefore a virtue proceeding from the shed blood that had not yet taken place, but a virtue nevertheless that went backward by way of anticipation, as well as forward by way of realization. But though physical participation is not intended, we must not rule out, or depreciate, the reference to the literal blood of Jesus. It is to the shedding of blood as equivalent to the giving of life that reference is made. And communion of the blood means that we are partakers of all that Jesus accomplished and procured by the shedding of his blood and the giving of his life. The participation signified by the cup in the Lord's supper is the participation of nothing less than of all that Jesus' blood secured—redemption in all the reaches of its grace and power.

3. 'The bread which we break.' The same thought applies as to the blessing of the cup. In the breaking all should participate.

4. 'Communion of the body of Christ.' Again no physical eating of the literal body! Jesus' body is in heaven and it is not omnipresent. But reference is made to the physical body, to the body upon the tree in which Jesus bore our sins, the body in which he was buried, in which he arose and ascended to heaven. The same principle applies as applies to the blood, that, although there is no physical eating of the literal body, yet the participation signified is nothing less than of all that Jesus, by bearing sin in his own body on the tree, accomplished and secured. We must bear in mind, also, that all of the virtue accruing from Jesus' death resides in Christ as exalted and glorified. But he is glorified in the body in which he suffered. We may never think of him apart from the body. Hence communion with the body of Christ, or communion of the body of Christ, includes the glorified body, more accurately, communion with him in respect of his glorified body. The virtue proceeding from him is a virtue that proceeds from him as the God-man, and to him in this identity belongs his glorified body. Thus the body performs a function indispensable to the communion of which the Lord's supper is a seal and a means of communication.

5. The communion of the saints. 'We, the many, are one bread, one body, for we all partake of the one bread.' Communal actions are mentioned earlier. But now the unity in one body is the theme. The symbolism of one loaf is essential to the ordinance.

ANTICIPATION

'Until he come.' In the Lord's supper there is the outreach of hope. Christ is truly present in the supper, but in a different way from that in which he will become present. When he comes, he will be bodily, physically, and visibly present. Then there will be no further need of symbols and signs.

OBSERVANCE

I Cor. 11:26 is an index to the necessity of recurrent and unceasing observance. But Acts 2:42 is one of the most instructive passages in the New Testament. 'The breaking of the bread' must refer to the Lord's supper. Although this term (κλάσις) occurs only once elsewhere (Luke 24:35) of Jesus' breaking of bread with the two who had been on the way to Emmaus, yet the corresponding verb occurs frequently with reference to the Lord's supper (Matt. 26:26; Mark 14:22; Luke 22:19; Acts 20:7; 1 Cor. 10:16), and the context indicates that the breaking of the bread belonged specifically to religious exercise—the apostles' doctrine and fellowship and the prayers. Acts 2:46 indicates that the breaking of bread from house to house refers to ordinary eating. It was from house to house, and is interpreted as receiving their food with gladness and singleness of heart. The co-ordination in Acts 2:42 implies that the supper was an integral part of the worship of the early church, practised by those who had received the Word, were baptized, and were added to the disciples (cf. vs. 41).

34

Restricted Communion

WHATEVER position we may take on the question at issue, we cannot, on any scriptural basis, get away from the notion of restricted communion. The Lord's supper is not for all indiscriminately as the gospel is. The Lord's supper is chiefly commemoration and communion. It is for those who discern the Lord's body, who can commemorate his death in faith and love. And since the supper is also Communion it is obviously for those who commune with Christ and with one another in the unity of the body which is the church. There can be no communion without union and therefore the central qualification for participation is union with Christ. The Lord's supper is for those who are his.

It is part of the whole counsel of God that those conditions be clearly and insistently set forth, to the end that those who are eligible partake and those who are not refrain. This is just saying that preaching on this question is directed to ensuring that what is registered in the forum of each individual's conscience should correspond with what is true in the forum of the divine judgment.

It is also apparent that God has instituted government in his church to the end that purity may be maintained and order and decorum observed. It is the responsibility of those in whom this government is vested to ensure that those admitted to membership in the church fulfil those requirements of credible and intelligent profession which are the criteria by which those in whom government is vested are to judge. We say that the session must require an intelligent and credible confession of faith in Christ as Saviour and Lord. It may happen, and it sometimes does, that those who are truly united to Christ and who, therefore, in

381

the forum of the divine judgment as well as in the forum of conscience are eligible to partake are, nevertheless, excluded by the session and that quite properly because they are not able to make the requisite confession of faith. A session is not able in some mystical fashion to examine the heart and God does not give special revelation respecting those who are his. The session must act upon the basis of credibility and observable data. This discrepancy and apparent injustice arise from the infirmity inseparable from the limitations under which God himself has placed those who govern in the church. It is regrettable that the person concerned is not able to make the necessary confession but we *may not say* that, in the absence of this confession, it is regrettable that the session excluded the person concerned. If we say so then we are reflecting upon the divine institution which men are under obligation to observe. We must, therefore, recognize this limitation that governs the administration of the Lord's supper.

Furthermore the session is under obligation to exclude from the Lord's supper those who are guilty of such overt sin as requires exclusion. This applies even to those who have made the requisite confession and may be truly united to Christ, until such time as they give evidence of repentance and reformation. To deny this necessity is to waive completely the demands of discipline.

The question is whether the session is under obligation to apply this same principle to those who are not members of the congregation but desire to partake of the Lord's supper with the congregation. Or must the session leave that question entirely to the conscience of those who may be in that category?

It must be admitted that if the session exercises supervision to the extent of requiring all who partake to receive from the session permission to do so, then, on occasion at least, some person may be excluded who is qualified to partake and to whom the session would be very glad to grant the privilege. But the question is not to be settled on the basis of that contingency. A person who is thus deprived is not caused to stumble by that exclusion provided it is made plain, as should be the case, what the reason is for this exclusion. That person if sensitive to the demands of purity should only appreciate the reason for this on their exclusion on that particular occasion.

It seems utterly unreasonable to leave the matter entirely to the conscience of the person concerned, when this is not done and should not be done in the case of the members of the congregation. There are the following considerations:

1. *The Purity of the Church.* It is the obligation of the session to ensure to the utmost of its prerogative that only those eligible to partake should partake. It is not exercising this prerogative unless it exercises its supervision over all who participate. This is applicable in two respects, first as it applies to the individual and second as it applies to the body of Christ. In the first case there may be a person present who is not a member of any church, who is indeed a notorious character but who for one or several erroneous and unworthy reasons wishes to participate. This person's conscience is grievously perverted, his motives are unworthy, his conception of the sacrament is distorted, and if he, or she, partakes the person is committing a sin against Christ and the institution of the Church. It is to perform a great service to that person to prevent him or her from that unworthy act, to preserve him or her from sacrilege of the worst sort. Perhaps this is well known to the session; it knows of the violence that will be perpetuated. Are we to say that all that may be done in that case is simply the persuasive warning that may be given in the fencing of the table? Surely not! But in the second case the session must preserve to the utmost of its ability, the body of Christ from this desecration. Why did Paul enjoin upon the church in Corinth that the incestuous person was to be put away and delivered unto Satan for the destruction of the flesh that the spirit might be saved in the day of the Lord Jesus? One reason he mentions is that a little leaven leaveneth the whole lump (1 Cor. 5:5, 6). Now this has reference to a person who was a member of the church and on whom the sentence of excommunication could be pronounced and its implications put into effect. But are we to suppose that no such discipline can be exercised over those who are outside the particular communion of the congregation but who wish, nevertheless, to enjoy the privilege of that communion on a particular occasion? Surely the considerations which the apostle pleads in this case are not completely suspended on a particular occasion simply because that person does not happen to be a member of that congregation.

2. *The Unity of the Church.* This principle has respect to the unity that

belongs to the denomination and to the whole church of Christ throughout the world.

In respect to the first, a person may be under discipline by another congregation of the denomination. That person would be prevented from participating in his own congregation. What means would be used is another question. But it is obvious that it would be a travesty of discipline to permit that person to sit at the Lord's table. If he goes to another congregation is the session of the congregation inhibited from exercising the same kind of exclusion as is exercised by the session under whose jurisdiction the person is? You can see the desecration that would be committed if the session of the one church is to leave the matter entirely to the conscience of the person when the session of the church to which he belongs does not do that but exercises other means of prevention. He simply must respect the discipline exercised by other congregations of his denomination.

But it is not only the denomination we have to take into account. We must also take into account the whole church and we must be as jealous for the discipline exercised by other bodies as well as our own denomination. How is this going to be done? It can only be done if some supervision is exercised by the session to ensure as far as possible that such desecrations do not occur. Even then it is possible that mistakes will occur. Of course there is no perfect application in this world of any principle. But are we to abandon a principle simply because in particular cases due to human infirmity there are errors and aberrations which are inconsistent with the principle? If that were the case then we should have to abandon all the principles of the biblical ethic.

In conclusion, the person who on a particular occasion wishes to communicate is in the category of being within. He is among you and you are extending to him the most intimate fellowship that is afforded in this world. 'Do not ye judge them that are within? . . . Put away from among yourselves that wicked person' (1 Cor. 5:13).

VII

35

The Interadventual Period
and the Advent: Matthew 24 and 25[1]

THE discourse is in answer to the disciples' question: 'When shall these things be, and what will be the sign of thy coming and of the consummation of the age?' (Matt. 24:3; cf. Mark 13:4; Luke 21:7), and this question was provoked by the statement of Jesus: 'See ye not all these things? Verily I say unto you, there shall not be left here stone upon stone that will not be thrown down' (Matt. 24:2; cf. Mark 13:2; Luke 21:6). In view of the terms of the parallel verses in Mark and Luke—'when will these things be, and what will be the sign when all these things shall come to pass' (Mark 13:4)—we should most probably regard the disciples as thinking of the destruction of the temple and the coming (παρουσία) as coincident, and the sign, in their esteem, would be the sign of all three events specified in Matthew 24:3—destruction of the temple, the coming, and the consummation of the age. But whatever conception had been entertained by the disciples, it is necessary for us to keep in mind the distinct elements specified, and recognize that the subsequent discourse is concerned, not only with the destruction of the temple, but also with the advent and consummation of the age. In other words, the terms of Matthew 24:3 dictate a perspective as extensive as the advent of Christ and the consummation of the age, and we are not surprised, therefore, that at Matthew 24:14 we find such a statement as 'then shall the end come' (καὶ τότε ἥξει τὸ τέλος), and at verses 27, 37, 39 express mention of 'the coming of the Son of man' (ἡ παρουσία τοῦ Υἱοῦ τοῦ ἀνθρώπου).

The discourse has its distinct divisions. In verses 4–14 Jesus deals with

1 An address given at a School of Theology convened in London in September, 1968.

387

certain outstanding features of the interadventual period. We are reminded at verse 6 that the end is not immediately, that the activity of deceivers, and reports of wars and rumours of wars, are not to be regarded as portents of an imminent consummation (cf. Luke 19:11); and at verses 7, 8 that wars, famines, and earthquakes are but the beginning of sorrows (ὠδίνων). At verse 14 the more auspicious aspect of interadventual history is promised, the worldwide preaching of the gospel for a witness to all the nations, in accord with our Lord's post-resurrection commissions (Matt. 28:18–20; Luke 24:46, 47), a reminder again of the extended period that the events of interadventual history require for their fulfilment. However, this section of the discourse brings us to what is surely of the same purport as 'the consummation of the age' in the question of the disciples (vs. 3), namely, 'the end'—'then shall the end come'. So we are compelled to construe verses 4–14 as, in brief outline, a forecast of interadventual history.

Verses 15–28 comprise another section of the discourse. This section cannot be a continuation, because verse 14 had brought us up to the end. It must be, to some extent, recapitulation. Our Lord forecasts to the disciples certain additional features of the period that had been delineated in verses 4–14, and gives the warnings and exhortations appropriate to the events involved. Here we have a principle that must be applied in the interpretation of prophecy. Delineation of the eschatological drama is not always continuously progressive; it is often recapitulatory. But recapitulation is not repetition.

In verse 15 it is not as apparent as it is in Luke 21:20 that Jesus is dealing with the destruction of Jerusalem. In the latter the reference is explicit: 'When ye see Jerusalem encompassed by armies, then know ye that its desolation has drawn nigh'. The warnings and exhortations are given in verses 16–20. Verse 21 describes the tribulation involved. Verses 23, 24 deal with deceivers and are similar to verses 5 and 11. Verses 23–26 provide the reason for the emphasis in verse 27, and verse 27 gives the reason why we are to give no credence to the pretensions mentioned in verses 23–26. Verse 27 deals obviously with the advent. It gives no information, however, respecting the chronological position or sequence. All we have in this verse is characterization in respect of its public, visible character. It will be so public and universal that, when it occurs, no one will or can be in any doubt. Hence the error of deceivers who will say: 'Behold, he is in the desert' or 'Behold, he is in the secret places' (vs. 26). This public unconcealable character is illustrated by a phenomenon observable in nature, namely, that wherever there is a carcase, there are the vultures. So will it be at Christ's coming (vs. 28). For verse 28 cf. Job 39:30—'Where the slain are, there is she'. It is not necessary to resort to any such application as, wherever sinners are, there the judgments of God are.

When we come to verse 29, we encounter some difficulty. For 'the tribulation of those days' might appear to refer to the 'great tribulation' of verse 21 which is associated particularly with the desolation of Jerusalem. And we ask: How could it be said that, immediately after 70 A.D., the events specified in verses 29–31 took place? More especially, how could verses 30 and 31 be regarded as taking place in immediate sequence with the destruction of Jerusalem? Verse 30, for several reasons to be adduced later, surely refers to the advent in glory, and the sign of the Son of man to the sign of the coming of Christ and of the consummation of the age in the disciples' question (vs. 3). The parallel passage in Luke 21:24 helps us to resolve the difficulty. Luke includes an observation in Jesus' discourse not included in Matthew's account, and it belongs to what precedes Matthew 24:29, and must therefore be inserted. The observation given in Luke 21:24 is that 'Jerusalem will be trodden down by the Gentiles until the times of the Gentiles are fulfilled.' So, in view of this element, it is apparent that our Lord's delineation extended far beyond the destruction of Jerusalem and the events immediately associated with it. Hence the period 'those days', in Matthew 24:29, must be regarded as the days that extend to the threshold of what is specified in verses 29–31. But, apart from Luke 21:24, it would be reasonable, even on the basis of Matthew's own account, to take the expression 'the tribulation of those days' inclusively and not restrictively. 'Those days' could properly be taken to mean the days preceding that of which Jesus now proceeds to speak, the days depicted already in verses 4–14, and 'the tribulation' not exclusively the 'great tribulation' of verse 21, but the tribulation which, according to the earlier part of the discourse, is represented as characterizing the interadventual period as a whole.

We must deal, however, in more detail with the question: To what do verses 29–31 refer? I submit that the various considerations belonging to the passage itself, and derived from the analogy of New Testament teaching, point to one identification, namely, the advent of Christ in glory and its accompaniments. The reasons are as follows:

1. 'The sign of the Son of man in heaven' (vs. 30) is surely the sign spoken of in the question of the disciples. In a different context the sign might be something else. But to ignore the index provided by the question to which the discourse is the answer is exegetically untenable. In verse 3, however, the sign is that of the advent and of the consummation of the age, the denotation of which is put beyond question by the usage of the New Testament.

2. The terms of verse 30, that all the tribes of the earth 'will see the Son of man coming upon the clouds of heaven with great power and glory' (or 'with power and great glory') are terms that are quite definitely those of the second advent in the terminology of the New Testament (cf. Matt. 16:27; Mark 8:38; Matt. 25:31; Acts 1:9–11; 1 Thess. 4:17; 2 Thess. 1:7; Rev. 1:7). This is not to say that such an expression as 'see the Son of man', or even 'see the Son of man coming', could not apply to a more proximate coming by a different mode and for another purpose. The point is simply that the whole expression can reasonably be taken to specify no other event than the one which the language of the New Testament would indicate, namely, the advent in glory. Again we have to keep in view the reference to the advent in the disciples' question. Even in Matthew 26:64, the 'coming upon the clouds of heaven' may not be regarded as a proximate coming, but as the advent of glory. Jesus, in that instance, brings his exaltation to the right hand of power, and the final advent, into conjunction. The exaltation was in the immediate future (a few weeks) and for this reason Jesus could say 'from now on'. The two events are so bound up with each other that they can be thus juxtaposed in prophetic perspective, in what is exemplified elsewhere and has been called foreshortening.

3. There is another index for the identification of the event specified in verse 30. Luke 21:25–28 is parallel to Matthew 24:29–31. Now in Luke 21:28 we read: 'When these things begin to come to pass, brace yourselves up, and lift up your heads, because your redemption is nigh at hand'. This word 'redemption' (ἀπολύτρωσις), when used with refer-

ence to the future, has a distinctly eschatological connotation, the final redemption, the consummation of the redemptive process (cf. Rom. 8:23; 1 Cor. 1:30; Eph. 1:14; 4:30). Hence analogy would again point to the eschatological complex of events.

4. There is ample allusion to the sound of the trumpet and to the ministry of angels elsewhere in the New Testament, in connection with Christ's advent (cf. 1 Cor. 15:52; 1 Thess. 4:16). Hence verse 31 can most readily be taken to refer to the gathering of the elect at the resurrection.

If these verses refer to the advent of Christ in glory, the question naturally arises as to the events of verse 29 and their relation to the advent as the focal event of the whole passage. If we regard these occurrences as commotions and upheavals in the physical cosmos, how are we to reconcile such visible events with the uniform teaching of our Lord respecting the suddenness and unexpectedness of his advent? The answer is that the advent has its concomitants. There is to be the cosmic renovation (cf. Rom. 8:18–23; 2 Pet. 3:10–13). The cosmic commotions of verse 29 are consonant with the descriptions given elsewhere respecting the great change that will take place in the cosmos. These commotions are an integral part of the complex of events focused in Christ's advent. They can be said to constitute the *entourage* of the advent, and are so intimately bound up with it that their incidence in no way contradicts the teaching that no man knows the day nor the hour of our Lord's coming.

Verses 32, 33 are obviously intended to inculcate the lesson to be derived from the events foretold in verse 29–31. The cosmic upheavals will fill men with consternation (cf. Luke 21:25, 26). Believers are not to be filled with horror (cf. Luke 21:28). When they see these things, they are to know that the hour has come. To use the language of Luke 21:31, they are to know that the kingdom of God is nigh. The parable of the fig tree is given simply for the purpose of illustrating and enforcing the expectancy and rejoicing that the events, so terrifying to unbelievers, should evoke in believers.

THIS GENERATION

We arrive now at verse 34. It has been the occasion for more controversy than any other verse in the discourse. Ostensibly the expression 'this generation' would suggest the generation then living, the period, commonly designated 'generation', in which Jesus spoke these words. And the question would then arise: Did all the things spoken of in the preceding context actually occur? It has been suggested that the term (γενεά) does not mean generation, but race, and that Jesus referred simply to the fact that Israel as a people would not cease until all the things foretold would come to pass. This, it has been claimed, would eliminate all apparent discrepancy. But I submit that this interpretation of 'generation' is wholly untenable, for the reasons that will now be adduced:

1. In the LXX the term (γενεά) most frequently occurs as the translation of the Hebrew דּוֹר. It often occurs in the plural in such expressions as 'unto your generations', 'unto their generations', 'unto perpetual generations', and these unmistakably refer to successive generations. The time reference is apparent. The sense is also apparent in such expressions as the third, fourth, and fifth generation (Gen. 9:12; Exod. 34:7; cf. Gen. 6:9; 7:1 where Noah is said to be 'perfect in his generations' and 'righteous in this generation'). The expression εἰς γενεὰν καὶ γενεὰν is very frequent, and means 'from generation to generation' (cf. ἕως γενεᾶς καὶ γενεᾶς = to all generations). The expression 'a perpetual statute (law) unto your generations' is very frequent. In the singular 'this generation' occurs seldom (cf. Gen. 7:1; Psalm 12:7). But there are many instances of the singular where the meaning 'generation' is apparent (cf. Numb. 32:13; Deut. 29:22; 32:5; Judg. 2:10; Job 8:8; Psalm 14:5; 22:30; 48:13; 71:18; Eccl. 1:4).

Apparently, the only instance in which γενεά is used to translate עַם (people) is Leviticus 20:18—'Both of them shall be cut off from the midst of their people'. But even here the text of the LXX is not certain, and probably ἐκ τοῦ γένους αὐτῶν is the correct reading rather than ἐκ τῆς γενεᾶς αὐτῶν.

2. If race or people were intended in Matthew 24:34, one wonders why γένος rather than γενεά had not been used. γένος would have conveyed the thought without any ambiguity. γένος means kind, family, descent, offspring, or nation, and is used in the sense of race or nation in Mark 7:26; Acts 4:36; 7:19; 13:26 (in the sense of stock); 18:2, 24; 2 Corinthians 11:26; Galatians 1:14; Philippians 3:5; 1 Peter 2:9. At least, in

several of these instances, this meaning is apparent, and in the others the meaning is closely related. In the LXX, furthermore, γένος is frequently the rendering of the Hebrew עַם (cf. Gen. 11:6; 17:14; 34:16; Isa. 22:4; 42:6; 43:20).

3. In most instances in the New Testament the term occurs in the expression we find in the text concerned (Matt. 24:34; cf. Mark 13:30; Luke 21:32). There are two considerations determining the meaning. (i) Matthew 23:36: 'All these things will come upon this generation.' In the context Jesus is upbraiding the Jews of his own time; they had filled up the measure of their fathers; upon them would come all the righteous blood shed upon the earth. In the succeeding context there is the lament over Jerusalem and the pronouncement of its abandonment. Surely verse 36, therefore, refers to the generation then living—they had filled to the brim the cup of indignation, and the judgment is executed. (ii) The meaning is clearly that of the living generation, or the generations in succession to one another, in numerous passages (Matt. 1:17; Luke 1:48, 50; Acts 13:36; 14:16; 15:21; Eph. 3:5; Col. 1:26).

Usage in both Testaments requires, therefore, that 'generation' in Matthew 24:34 be understood in the sense of the living generation. How, then, are we to resolve the question posed by the events specified in the preceding context, especially in verses 29–31, which did not occur in the generation of which our Lord spoke? There are several observations that appear to resolve the apparent discrepancy.

1. Apart from verses 29–31 there are events mentioned in the preceding part of the discourse which *obviously* were not intended by our Lord to fall within the scope of the generation specified as 'this generation'. There is 'the end' of verse 14. And unless we place upon this term a meaning alien to its use elsewhere, when used as an eschatological designation, we must regard it as synonymous with 'the consummation of the age', namely, the end of this age in contrast with the age to come. Then there is the explicit reference to the second advent in verse 27. Again there is the period of the dispersion of Israel into all nations subsequent to the destruction of Jerusalem, and the treading down of the same by the Gentiles until the times of the Gentiles should be fulfilled (Luke 21:24). Furthermore, in Luke 21:31 there is mention of the eschatological kingdom of God. We are thus advised that, in the intent

of our Lord, and, therefore, in the understanding he intended for the disciples, not every event specified in the preceding part of the discourse came within the scope of the 'all things' predicted as occurring in that generation. And so we are required to give to the 'all things' a more restricted denotation, and there should be no more difficulty in excluding the advent complex of events of verses 29–31 than there is in excluding the other events of verses 14, 27 and Luke 21:24, 31.

2. It is reasonable to suppose that in Matthew 24:34 (cf. Mark 13:30; Luke 21:32) Jesus is answering the first part of the disciples' question, that pertaining to the destruction of the temple: 'When will these things be?' Our Lord is making a sharp distinction, in regard to eventuation, between the destruction of the temple and his advent, that is to say, between the two elements of the question asked by the disciples. This is the force of the contrast in verses 34 and 36. We must not fail to appreciate the sequence and the antithesis—'this generation shall not pass until all these things be accomplished . . . but of that day and hour no one knows . . . but the Father only.' Of particular significance is the contrast between what he knew and foretold (vss. 34, 35) and what he did not know (vs. 36). In interpreting verse 34 it is a capital error to overlook the sequence of verse 36 and to fail to construe verse 34 accordingly. This would have made clear to the disciples the distinction between the destruction of Jerusalem and correlative events on the more proximate horizon, on the one hand, and the day of his advent, on the other. The disciples would have been prepared for this because repeatedly, in the earlier part of the discourse, Jesus had made clear the distinction between what was on the more immediate horizon and what was not (vss. 6, 8, 26, 27; Luke 21:24).

3. If it were maintained that verse 36 means simply that, although all things specified would occur in the current generation, yet the particular hour or day was unknown to men, angels, and himself, this interpretation of verse 36 is untenable for several reasons. (1) 'That day' has obtained, in the usage of the New Testament, a well-defined eschatological denotation to designate the day of the Lord, the last day (cf. Matt. 7:22; Luke 10:12; 21:34; 2 Thess. 1:10; 2 Tim. 1:12, 18; 4:8). So much is this the case, that the expression 'the day' has taken on a distinctly technical meaning (cf. Rom. 13:12; 1 Cor. 3:13; 1 Thess. 5:4;

Heb. 10:25; 2 Pet. 1:19). (2) Our Lord in this discourse warns repeatedly that his coming would be unknown and would happen unexpectedly (cf. vss. 39, 42, 44, 50), and in Matt. 25:13 he uses the same expression as in 24:36, namely, 'ye do not know the day nor the hour'. (3) The identity of 'that day and hour' (vs. 36) is placed beyond question by verses 37–39. That Jesus was speaking of his advent in verse 36 is clearly indicated by the close connection at the beginning of verse 37: 'For as (ὥσπερ γάρ) the days of Noah were'. He institutes a parallel to establish and enforce what is said to be unknown in verse 36. But in verse 37 it is 'the advent of the Son of man' that is in view, as also in verse 39. If he were not speaking of the day and hour of his advent in verse 36, then the ὥσπερ γάρ of verse 37 would lose its relevance. (4) The fallacy of the interpretation being refuted is demonstrated by the impossibility, on any interpretation of verse 34, of confining the events to occur in the living generation to a day or hour. So the interpretation defeats itself.

THE COMING JUDGMENT

In verse 27, as noted earlier, it is the public, visible, unmistakable character of the advent that is emphasized. In verses 37–39 it is the sudden and unexpected feature that is in view—'they did not know until the flood came and took them all away: so will be the advent of the Son of man.'

Verses 40, 41 deal with the separation that takes place at the advent. The immediate sequence is indicated by 'then' (τότε). We know from other passages that there will be the separation of just and unjust (cf. Matt. 25:32; 1 Thess. 4:15–17), and there is neither need nor warrant to load this passage with notions of a secret rapture. This separation occurs at the advent, as is clear from the explicit reference to the advent in verses 37 and 39; and in verse 27 we are advised that 'the advent of the Son of man', the same designation as we find in verses 37 and 39, will be as public and visible as the lightning shining from east to west.

Then we have a series of parallels to enforce the various lessons to be learned from the certainty and character of the advent. The first is that of the householder (vss. 42–44), and the lessons are watchfulness and preparedness. The consideration demanding these is that the day and hour are unknown—'Watch therefore, because ye do not know on what day your Lord comes'; 'Be ye also ready, for in an hour that ye think not the Son of man comes' (vss. 42, 44).

The second is that of the faithful and wise servant (vss. 45–51) and the lesson is that of faithfulness and the reward of unfaithfulness. The same consideration, that we know not the day nor the hour of the Lord's coming, is implied in verse 50.

The third parable is that of the ten virgins (Matt. 25:1–13). The lesson is the need for preparedness and the same exhortation is given as in verse 42—'Watch therefore, because ye know not the day nor the hour' (vs. 13).

The fourth parable is that of the talents. The lessons are diligence and faithfulness (Matt. 25:14–30) and the parable ends with the same warning of retribution that we find earlier at 24:51—'there shall be the weeping and the gnashing of the teeth' (vs. 30).

There appears to be a parallelism in these four parables, between the first and third, and the second and fourth.

We thus arrive at Matthew 25:31: 'When the Son of man shall come in his glory and all the angels with him, then he will sit on the throne of his glory.' There is nothing to suggest that our Lord had made a transition to a new phase of eschatological eventuation. At Matthew 24:37–41 he dealt with his advent and with the resultant separation. The intervening parables inculcated the relevant and necessary attitudes, with particular emphasis upon the fact that the day of the advent is unknown. And there is no transition apparent or even possible. The terms of 25:31 are distinctly reminiscent of what we find in the earlier passages respecting the advent: 'When the Son of man shall come in his glory and all the angels with him, then he will sit upon the throne of his glory' (cf. 24:27, 30, 31, 37, 39, 44). And we cannot overlook the terms of our Lord's statements elsewhere (cf. Rom, 2:6–16; 2 Thess. 1:6–11; Acts 17:31).

This passage (25:31–46) is the most extended teaching of our Lord respecting the judgment he will execute at his coming, and it deserves the closest examination. In verse 32 we read: 'And before him will be gathered all the nations, and he will separate them from one another'. It has been claimed that this judgment is that of nations as nations, and not that of individuals. The expression 'all the nations' or its equivalent occurs frequently in the teaching of our Lord and elsewhere in the New

Testament. It means all peoples, people of all nations. Some examples will show this:

Matthew 28:19: 'Go ye therefore and disciple all the nations, baptizing them in the name of the Father and of the Son and of the Holy Spirit'. It is obvious that this cannot refer to nations collectively and in the aggregate. Neither discipling, nor baptism, nor teaching can be conducted in this way, and in apostolic history there is no example of this kind of activity. But the expression 'all the nations' is the same as in Matthew 25:32.

Luke 24:47: 'And that repentance and remission of sins should be preached in his name unto all the nations'. Repentance is not preached to nations in the aggregate nor is remission dispensed in that manner.

Mark 11:17: 'My house shall be called a house of prayer for all the nations'. The thought of nations in their corporate aggregate would produce absurdity. (Cf. to the same or similar effect Acts 15:17; Rom. 1:5; Rom. 16:26; Gal. 3:8; Eph. 3:8; 2 Tim. 4:17; Rev. 14:8). In some of these instances the accent falls upon Gentile nations. But the same relevance applies even when 'all the nations' has this more restricted reference, namely, that it is not Gentile peoples in the aggregate that are in view. 'All the nations' in Matthew 24:32 is surely to be taken to mean all people, without any differentiation of race or language or colour.

Furthermore, although the portrayal of the judgment in this passage is unique in the teaching of our Lord, and in the New Testament as a whole, in respect of form, the doctrine is the same as that set forth in other instances from the lips of Jesus, and in numerous other New Testament passages (cf. Matt. 12:36; 16:27; Mark 8:38; John 12:48; Acts 17:31; Rom. 2:6–16; 1 Cor. 4:5; 1 Cor. 3:12–15; 2 Cor. 5:10; 1 Thess. 5:3–10; 2 Thess. 1:6–10; Rev. 20:11–15).

Any question that might arise from the criteria applied in this passage, namely, deeds of mercy and the absence of such, is a question that is not peculiar to this passage. Works good and evil are frequently set forth in judgment passages as the criteria in accord with which judgment will be dispensed (cf. Matt. 16:27; Rom. 2:6–16; 2 Cor. 5:10; Rev. 20:13, 14). We must not forget that the judgment that will be executed by the Son of man (cf. John 5:27; Acts 17:31) is God's final adjudication of all history and everything, good and evil, must be adjudicated. God will leave nothing at loose ends (cf. Eccl. 12:14). As far as the wicked are concerned, their evil works and the absence of good works must, in the nature of the case, receive their retributive award. It is a mistake to think that the only sin that merits damnation is the sin of unbelief of the gospel. For those who have heard the gospel this will be the crowning sin (cf. John 3:19). But it is not the only sin. As for those without the gospel, they 'sinned without law and will perish without law' (Rom. 2:12). Those righteous by the faith of Christ will be saved from the penalty due to sin. But in their case it must not be thought that works, such as deeds of mercy, will have no bearing upon the judgment meted out. Good works are the fruit and evidence of faith, and as *such* will be adjudicated. Again, good works will be rewarded in the degrees of glory bestowed (cf. 1 Cor. 3:8, 14, 15). Our Lord himself bespoke this principle (Mark 9:41).

It is important, however, to observe that in Matthew 25:31–46 the good deeds, and the absence of them, in the respective cases are adduced as indications of attitudes to Christ. 'Ye did it unto me' (vs. 40); 'ye did it not to me' (vs. 45). So, after all, in this passage it is the relation to Christ that is ultimate, and, in the last analysis, the criterion. The majesty claimed for himself at this final assize is patent in many other respects. The Son of man comes in his glory; all the angels come with him; he sits on the throne of his glory; before *him* are gathered all the nations; he separates them from one another and assigns to each eternal destiny. It is the *King* who pronounces the verdict, and regal majesty is thereby applied. But in no respect is the majesty of his person and office more pronounced than in the criterion of the final verdict—'ye have done it unto me'; 'ye did it not to me'. What blasphemy this would be for angel or archangel or for mere man. Jesus claims for himself what could be only because of his divine identity as Son of God and final judge in his identity as the Son of man.

CONCLUDING OBSERVATIONS

1. The discourse, as to structure, is recapitulatory to a considerable extent. It is not, therefore, continuously progressive. We are repeatedly brought to the advent and informed of its various features, concomitants, and consequences (vss. 14, 29–31, 37–41; 25:31–46). We should expect,

for this reason, that revelation respecting the future would in other cases follow this pattern. At least we should be alert to the propriety of this structure in predictive prophecy.

2. The discourse advises us that interadventual history is characterized by tribulation, turmoil, strife, perplexity, wars and rumours of wars. Contemporaneous with this, however, is the universal expansion of the ministry of the gospel, and although the effects are not explicitly mentioned, yet by implication we see the worldwide expansion of the Kingdom of God. The elect are finally to be gathered from the ends of the earth (Matt. 24:31).

3. Events are predicted which, in the nature of the case, would require a period of time to elapse. On more than one occasion the impression is conveyed of a rather extended period of time. 'The end is not yet' (24:6); 'all these things are the beginning of sorrows' (24:8); 'this gospel of the kingdom will be preached in the whole earth for a witness to all the nations' (24:14); 'they (this people) shall be carried captive unto all the nations, and Jerusalem shall be trodden down by the Gentiles until the times of the Gentiles will be fulfilled' (Luke 21:24). At the same time the disciples are exhorted in the strongest terms to watch and wait for the Lord's coming (24:42, 44, 48, 50; 25:13). This teaches us the compatibility of two things that might seem incompatible, and which to many are incompatible, namely, the conviction that well-defined events requiring the lapse of time for their fulfilment must take place before the Lord comes, and at the same time the watching by disciples for his advent. Too often it is maintained that to posit the necessity of pre-adventual events is inconsistent with the watching and expectancy the Scripture enjoins. But this discourse, as well as other passages, shows the opposite to be the case. The disciples were distinctly advised of events that would transpire prior to the advent, that the end was not immediately, and yet they were just as explicitly exhorted to watch because they knew not the day nor the hour of the advent. So conviction on the basis of the former was to go hand in hand with obedience to the latter. What was not incompatible for the early disciples cannot be incompatible for us.

It is true, of course, that some of the events predicted to occur prior to the advent have transpired, and we are to that extent in a different historical context. But if we are convinced that other pre-adventual events have not yet occurred and must occur, this conviction is not incompatible with watching for and hastening unto the coming of the Lord. There is in the New Testament a doctrine of imminence to the effect that 'the end of all things is at hand' (1 Pet. 4:7), that 'the night is far spent and the day is at hand' (Rom. 13:12). But it is the imminence of eschatological perspective, the imminence of the next and final event in the objective accomplishment of the redemptive plan of God. This is an imminence compatible with the elapse of millennia, not the imminence of immediate, temporal proximity. It is the imminence that constrains expectancy. 'We, according to his promise, look for new heavens and a new earth, wherein dwelleth righteousness' (2 Pet. 3:13; cf. Rom. 8:23, 24; 2 Cor. 5:1–4; Phil. 3:20, 21; Rev. 22:12, 20).

36

The Last Things[1]

THE INTERMEDIATE STATE

IN the formation of man at the beginning God used material called 'dust from the ground'. From the outset, therefore, man was body. The body is not an appendage or accident, nor is it the prison-house of the spirit. Any disparaging conception of the body springs from pagan and anti-biblical sources and has no affinity with biblical thought (cf. Gen. 2:7; 3:19; I Cor. 6:19). The separation of body and spirit, the dissolution of the unity of the integral elements of man's personality, is abnormal and evil; it is the wages of sin. Certain corollaries follow:

1. The body, as created, was inherently good.
2. Body and spirit are not antithetical to each other; there is no natural or necessary conflict between these two diverse elements in man's being.
3. Man is not naturally mortal; death is not the debt of nature but the wages of sin.

The intermediate state is that condition which is the result of death. It may be called intermediate simply and only because it is temporary, and it is such both for just and unjust. The integrity of personality is to be reconstituted at the resurrection from the dead of just and unjust. Hence the intermediate state designates the condition that exists between the event of death and the resurrection.

The Scripture does not reveal to us a great deal respecting this state, because the biblical revelation is largely concerned with life in the body,

[1] From a report on Eschatology submitted by a committee appointed by the Second Reformed Ecumenical Synod to the Third Synod which met in Grand Rapids in 1963. All that follows was written by John Murray.

and the shadow falls upon the disembodied state. But there is sufficient revelation for the comfort of believers and for warning to the impenitent.

The disembodied state is not the final state. Neither bliss nor woe can be complete until the integrity of personal life is restored by resurrection. Yet Scripture offers no evidence that there will be a reversal of moral and spiritual conditions during the intermediate state. Men are to be judged at the last according to the things done in the body (cf. Matt. 25:34–46; Luke 16:25; 2 Cor. 5:10; Heb. 9:27). The ultimate state of bliss or woe is therefore sealed by the event of death. The Scripture offers no hope of the extension of gospel opportunities beyond the sphere of this life for those who die impenitent. And it offers no threat or warning to those who depart this life in faith, that their relation to Christ may be reversed in the life to come. Those who fall asleep in Jesus are dead in Christ and all such God will bring with him (cf. 1 Thess. 4:13–18; 2 Cor. 5:6, 8; Phil. 1:21, 23). Though the bliss of the saints and the woe of the wicked are not complete in the intermediate state, yet the consummation of bliss is irreversibly reserved for the saints and the consummation of woe for the wicked. The bliss enjoyed in the one case, and the woe endured in the other, in the intermediate state, is to the full measure of the capacity of disembodied spirits.

The Scripture represents the disembodied state as one of full consciousness. Man is spirit and, though man's spirit is separated from the natural and normal relationship, it nevertheless continues to exist and to be active in its own distinct identity as the spirit of the person. There is no warrant in Scripture for the notion of soul-sleep or of semi-consciousness in the intermediate state. For the saints who have departed this life, it is represented as presence with Christ, a presence highly to be desired in contrast with life in this world (Phil. 1:23; 2 Cor. 5:6–8; cf. Luke 2:29, 30; 16:25) and therefore a presence which secures greater joy and closer communion with the exalted Lord. Such enhancement is not compatible with a reduced state of consciousness; it requires, rather, an intensification of knowledge and activity. For the wicked it is a state, not of semi-conscious stupor, but of conscious endurance of unmitigated torment (Luke 16:23–28; cf. Jude 7). Those expressions in Scripture which might appear to support the notion of sleep do not reflect upon the psychological condition of the disembodied spirit but upon the phenomenal aspect of death. The person is no longer active in this sphere of life and activity, and therefore with reference to this life has fallen asleep.

The question of the places of abode of the departed spirits in reference to the final abodes of the just and unjust is not one that needs to be pressed with any ardour. The saints who have departed this life are now with Christ, and he is at the right hand of God in the exercise of his mediatorial kingship and sovereignty. This implies the highest bliss conceivable or possible for disembodied spirits who are waiting for the liberty of the glory of the children of God to be dispensed at the resurrection. But there must be some change in the habitation of the people of God when the consummation of bliss will be administered and the new heavens and the new earth will be ushered in. As for the wicked who have departed this life they suffer unrelieved torment commensurate with their capacity as disembodied spirits. This they endure in the place of woe. But what precisely is the relation of the place of woe in which they now suffer to the final place of woe, the Scripture does not appear to settle for us. It must not, however, be taken for granted that they are two distinct abodes. What the Scripture calls *gehenna*, and which it designates as the final place of retribution, is an abode of unembodied evil spirits and may therefore also be the abode of disembodied reprobate men. The Scripture does not clearly indicate that *hades*, as the place of woe, is distinct from *gehenna* and the place of everlasting punishment prepared for the devil and his angels (Matt. 25:41, 46).

THE ADVENT OF CHRIST

The advent of Christ is the pivotal event of collective eschatology. It consists in the bodily, public, visible return to this earth of the exalted Lord and Saviour Jesus Christ, when he will appear in the clouds of heaven with great power and glory (Matt. 24:30; 26:64; Mark 13:26; 14:62; Luke 21:27; Rev. 1:7), and 'descend from heaven with a shout, with the voice of the archangel and with the trumpet of God' (1 Thess. 4:16; cf. 1 Cor. 15:52). This manifestation of the great God and our Saviour Jesus Christ is 'the blessed hope' (Titus 2:13), and constitutes the cardinal event of eschatological faith and expectation. Diversity of viewpoint respecting the relation of other events to the advent of the

Lord in visible glory should never be allowed to obscure the centrality for faith and hope of the advent itself, nor should this diversity be construed as interfering with the place which the advent occupies in all true, Christian hope. The coming of Christ in great power and glory is the common property of all faith which is biblically conditioned.

The terms used to designate this event are varied. The most common is *parousia*. Though this term of itself can mean 'presence' when used of Christ's coming in glory, it is the thought of *becoming* present, rather than of *being* present, that is distinctly in prominence. When the disciples asked Jesus the question: 'What will be the sign of thy *parousia?*' (Matt. 24:3), it is apparent that the meaning is 'advent'. It would be inappropriate to speak of the sign of 'presence'. It would readily be seen that in Matt. 24:37, 39 the idea of advent suits the emphasis placed upon suddenness in these passages, and it would be awkward to impose the meaning 'presence' upon numerous other passages (cf. Matt. 24:27; 1 Cor. 15:23; 1 Thess. 3:13; 4:15; 2 Thess. 2:8; 2 Peter 3:4). The thought of advent is furthermore appropriate in all the instances, even though in a few the idea of presence would be suitable.

There is no evidence to support the notion of a secret *parousia*. It is upon the public character that the accent falls in Matt. 24:27. When Christ comes there can be no deception because there will be no concealment. Although in other passages other features of the *parousia* are stressed, there is no retraction of the feature so clearly affirmed in this passage (cf. Matt. 24:37, 39; 2 Thess. 2:8; 2 Peter 3:4).

Two other terms, *apokalupsis* and *epiphaneia*, are not to be construed as referring to a different event. They mean, respectively, 'revelation' and 'manifestation', and therefore both emphasize the visible character of the coming of Christ, the feature which is prominent also in the term *parousia*. The identification of the *revelation* and the *parousia* is apparent when Matt. 24:37:39 is compared with Luke 17:26–30. The comparisons instituted in both passages are to the same effect. In Matt. 24:39 the term used is 'the *parousia* of the Son of man', whereas in Luke 17:30 this same event is called 'the day when the Son of man is revealed'. It would be arbitrary to regard the *revelation* as something different from 'the day when the Son of man is revealed'. In other passages the identification is equally evident (cf. 1 Cor. 1:7; 2 Thess. 1:7; 1 Peter 1:7, 13; 4:13). In view of the stress placed upon the public character of the *parousia*, it would not be possible to regard the *epiphany* as the manifestation of a precedent secret coming. Hence, in 2 Thessalonians 2:8, 'the *epiphany* of his *parousia*' would have to be constructed as the *epiphany* which consists in his *parousia*, or as the glorious manifestation which the *parousia* will demonstrate (cf. Titus 2:13), but, in any case, not the making manifest of what will be antecedently a fact (cf. 1 Tim. 6:14; 2 Tim. 4:1, 8).

That other terms, such as 'the day of the Lord', 'the end', 'the end of the age', designate the same event or are brought into conjunction with the *parousia*, is a thesis that can be established by a great deal of evidence. A few examples may be given.

There should be no doubt that in 2 Peter 3:4 the *parousia* mentioned is the same as that referred to already as the advent of Christ. In verse 10 Peter is giving emphatic affirmation of the certainty of that which the scoffers called in question (vs. 4). But the term used is 'the day of the Lord', indicating that this is but a variant expression for the same event. There would be a *non sequitur* in Peter's argument if this were not the case.

In 1 Corinthians 1:7, 8 there are three eschatological terms, 'the revelation', 'the end', and 'the day of our Lord Jesus'. Believers are represented as waiting for the revelation of the Lord; it is the goal of their expectation. The force of verse 8 is not that Christ will confirm them to the end as well as to the revelation, but states what Christ will do until that event for which they are waiting. And 'the end' is here used to designate that terminus of expectation. Furthermore, 'blameless in the day of our Lord Jesus' stands in apposition to 'confirm you unto the end' or, at least, defines that in which the confirmation will consist, and harks back to that which in verse 7 is stated to be the goal of expectation. Thus all three terms specify that event which is the goal of hope and the terminus of confirmation, namely, the advent of Christ, beyond which there will be no further place for expectation, nor need for the confirmation contemplated. 'Hope that is seen is not hope: for what a man seeth, why doth he yet hope for?' (Rom. 8:24).

In 1 Corinthians 15:24 this conjunction in respect of 'the end' should be borne in mind. But even in this passage the evidence indicates the coincidence of the *parousia* and the *telos*. The chief consideration is that, in verses 54, 55, the victory over death is brought into conjunction with the resurrection of the just, which in turn is at the *parousia* (vs. 24), while in verses 24–26 the bringing to nought of death is at the *telos*. It is not feasible to regard the swallowing up of death in victory (vs. 54), and the destruction of death (vs. 26), as referring to different events.

The advent of Christ is the event that will end this age and usher in the age to come (cf. Matt. 13:39, 40, 49; 24:3; 28:20; Mark 10:30; Luke 16:8; 18:30; 20:34; 35; Eph. 1:21; Titus 2:12, 13), the consummating act of the whole process of redemption (cf. Rom. 8:23), the event that will signalize the cosmic renovation when the creation will be delivered from the bondage of corruption into the liberty of the glory of the children of God (cf. Rom. 8:17–23), and the present order will give place to the new heavens and the new earth (cf. 2 Peter 3:4–14). Of supreme significance will be the exhibition of the glory of God and of his Christ. Then will be finally manifested and vindicated the transcendent honour bestowed upon Christ as the reward of his obedience unto death, even the death of the cross, that he has been given the name that is above every name, and every knee shall bow and tongue confess that he is Lord to the glory of God the Father (cf. Phil. 2:9–11). The subjugation of all enemies, including death the last enemy, will demonstrate the conquest to which the present reign of Christ is directed, and he will deliver over the kingdom to God and the Father, that God may be all in all (cf. 1 Cor. 15:24–28).

THE PRECURSORS OF THE ADVENT

The practice of fixing a date for the coming of the Lord, exemplified in the Montanist movement about 200 A.D., and reappearing in other circles from time to time, has proven itself to be presumptuous, and should have been prevented by the word of our Lord himself: 'But of that day and hour no one knows, neither the angels of heaven, nor the Son, but the Father only' (Matt. 24:36). A position much more common and plausible is the teaching that the Lord's coming is imminent. This tenet would appear to derive support from the repeated injunctions of Jesus to his disciples that they were to watch intently and wait for his advent, because they did not know at what hour he might come (cf. Matt. 24:42–44; 25:13; Luke 12:35–38). In the apostolic church also believers waited and prayed for the Lord's appearing (cf. 1 Thess. 1:10; 2 Peter 3:11, 12; Rev. 22:20).

But the insistence that the advent is imminent is likewise without warrant, and its falsity should have been demonstrated by events. The word 'imminent' means 'just at hand' and cannot properly be used with reference to an event which may be several years removed from the point of time occupied. For all we know the advent may be hundreds of years distant, and it is presumptuous for us to aver that it is imminent. If what is meant by imminent is that the Lord's coming *may* be near at hand, that no well-defined events must occur before the advent, this is not equivalent to saying that it *is* imminent, and the use of the proposition is misleading and improper.

Furthermore, it is not in the best interests of understanding, to use the proposition in question to designate what the New Testament means by the nearness of the advent. There is a sense in which the Lord is at hand (cf. Rom. 13:11, 12; Phil. 4:5; James 5:8; 1 Peter 4:7). But this nearness is compatible with the elapse of nineteen hundred years, and must also be compatible with another long interval in our calendar. In our usage the proposition is not calculated to express this New Testament concept of nearness.

There is no doubt that Jesus enjoined watching and waiting, that the New Testament believers followed this injunction, and that it is a mark of faith and love to long for Christ's advent in glory. The Reformed Church has enshrined this attitude of mind in its confession. 'As Christ would have us to be certainly persuaded that there shall be a day of judgment, both to deter all men from sin; and for the greater consolation of the godly in their adversity: so will he have that day unknown to men, that they may shake off all carnal security, and be always watchful, because they know not at what hour the Lord will come; and may ever be prepared to say, Come Lord Jesus, come quickly, Amen' (*The Westminster Confession of Faith*, Chapter XXXIII, iii).

It must, however, be recognized that the watching and waiting enjoined by our Lord is not inconsistent with conviction respecting the necessity of intervening events. Jesus taught his disciples to watch for his coming, and at the same time delineated the history of the interadventual period. He predicted the occurrence of events which required the lapse of time, warned them that the end was not yet, and that the tribulations specified were the beginning of travails (cf. Matt. 24:4–14; Luke 19:11). The watching for his advent must, therefore, have been compatible with the conviction that these events would transpire prior to his coming. Hence watching does not require belief in the *imminent* return.

The disciples asked Jesus for the sign of his coming (Matt. 24:3). And Jesus did answer to this extent: 'Then shall appear the sign of the Son of man in heaven' (Matt. 24:30). The sign, however, is the immediate portent of his advent, and is so bound up with it, that we shall not be able to forecast beforehand the time of his appearing. The sign is but part of the *entourage* of the coming itself.

The precursors of the advent are those happenings which must precede Jesus' coming.

1. *The world-wide preaching of the gospel* is one of these (Matt. 24:14). This word of our Lord does not imply that all nations will be converted, nor that all people will at all times have the witness of the gospel borne to them. But it does mean world-wide extension of the gospel witness and of the kingdom of God. There is in the New Testament evidence of the rapidity with which this prediction, and the apostolic commission corresponding to it (Matt. 28:18–20), were being carried into effect (cf. Col. 1:6, 23). And since the gospel always registers its triumphs and brings forth fruit (2 Cor. 2:14–17; Col. 1:86), the world-wide witness means the world-wide extension of the church.

The context in which Jesus gave the promise imparts to it added significance. He had shown that the interadventual period would be cast in tribulation, persecution, wars and rumours of wars (Matt. 24:4–26). But concurrently with these distressing features of world history, the gospel would follow its onward course and secure its triumphs. In this connection it is all-important to bear in mind the significance of Pentecost, and the sending of the Holy Spirit in the fulness of his power and the world-wide operations of his grace. Jesus had promised that the Holy Spirit would convict the world of sin, of righteousness, and of judgment (John 16:8–11). In the witness borne to the gospel it is by the power and demonstration of the Spirit that the Word is effectual, and it is his prerogative to take of the things of Christ and show them unto men (cf. 1 Cor. 2:4, 5; 1 Thess. 1:5, 6; John 16:14). Pentecost is correlative with Jesus' promise that the gospel will be preached for a witness to all the nations, and, while Pentecost was an event, it was an event with abiding significance for the extension of Christ's Kingdom.

When Christ's promise will have attained the degree of fulfilment necessary for his advent, it is impossible for us to determine.

2. *The Conversion of Israel* is another precursor of the advent. While the middle wall of partition between Jew and Gentile has been broken down (cf. Eph. 2:13–22; Col. 2:13–14), so that in respect of the privileges of the gospel there is now no longer Jew nor Gentile, male nor female, bond nor free, but Christ is all and in all (cf. Gal. 3:28; Col. 3:11), it does not follow that Israel as an ethnic entity ceases to exist, nor that God has ceased to reckon with Israel in its distinguishing identity as a people who are the seed of Abraham according to the flesh. To what purpose would have been Paul's concern for Israel in Romans 9–11 if the distinguishing identity of Israel had been obliterated and God's purpose with reference to Israel had not been within his purview? In Romans 9–11 it should be apparent that ethnic Israel is in view, for Paul speaks of his 'kinsmen according to the flesh' (Rom. 9:3), and Israel is contrasted with the Gentiles (cf. Rom. 11:11, 12). In this Epistle, and in relation to the subject of interest, the most relevant passages are Romans 11:12, 15, 26–32. The interpretation of these passages herewith presented is that Paul envisions a restoration of Israel as a people to God's covenant favour and blessing. In Romans 11:15 this viewpoint appears inescapable. The casting away of Israel (*apobolē*) is the rejection of Israel as a people collectively (cf. Matt. 21:43). The rhetorical question which follows implies that there is to be a reception of them again (*proslēmpsis*), a restoration of that from which they had been rejected. But the same collective aspect must apply to the restoration; otherwise the contrast would lose its force. The parallelism of verses 12 and 15 provides the index to the meaning of Israel's fulness (*plērōma*) in verse 12. And, in like manner, the statement in verse 26, 'all Israel shall be saved' should be taken as referring to the same event, an interpretation supported by verse 31 to the effect that, by the mercy bestowed upon the Gentiles, Israel also will obtain mercy.

The collective restoration of Israel does not require the conversion at a future date of all Jews any more than did the rejection mean the apostasy and reprobation of every Israelite. But it surely must imply the widespread acceptance of Jesus as Messiah and entrance into the church of Christ. Other passages in the New Testament have the same import (cf. Matt. 23:38, 39; 2 Cor. 3:14–16).

3. A third precursor of the advent is *the revelation of the man of sin* (2 Thess. 2:8–10). It is noteworthy that this disclosure on the part of the apostle was occasioned by the pretension that the day of the Lord had come, or was just at hand (vs. 2). The teaching respecting the precedent apostasy, culminating in the man of sin, is given to correct this misapprehension.

The man of sin, or of lawlessness, is to be distinguished from what the apostle John calls antichrist (1 John 2:18, 22; 4:3; 2 John 7). John speaks of many antichrists. While these antichrists, no doubt, sustain a close relationship to the apostasy and to the man of sin, since all iniquity is organically related and is instigated by Satan, yet the man of sin is a distinct personage who will appear on the scene of this world just prior to the advent of Christ. This is indicated by his appellation, and by the fact that the Lord Jesus will consume him 'by the breath of his mouth', and destroy him 'by the epiphany of his *parousia*' (vs. 8).

While difficulty, and therefore diversity of interpretation, arise in connection with 'the restraint' (vs. 6) and 'the restrainer' (vs. 7), there should not be uncertainty as to the character and location in history of the man of sin—his destruction at the epiphany of Christ's advent indicates the time of his appearing. The terms in which satanic influence is described (vss. 9–11) point to this complex of events as the final manifestation and concentration of the powers of darkness prior to the subjugation which Christ's advent will execute, and which will reach its climax in the destruction of the last enemy, death (1 Cor. 15:26).

THE RESURRECTION

The Scriptures are clear beyond all question that there will be a resurrection of just and unjust (cf. John 5:28, 29; Acts 24:15). The resurrection of the wicked does not receive the same prominence as that of the righteous. The reason for this is that the Scriptures are mainly concerned with the resurrection to life and salvation. The resurrection of Christ is cardinal in the accomplishment of salvation. Though the wicked will be raised by the power of Christ in the exercise of his messianic dominion, yet the resurrection of Christ does not provide the pattern according to which the wicked will be raised from the dead. Christ is 'the firstfruits of those who have fallen asleep' (1 Cor. 15:20; cf. vs. 23), but the wicked are not included in that relationship. The soteric significance of Christ's resurrection makes this impossible, and the characteristics of the resurrection body of unbelievers will not conform to those mentioned by Paul in 1 Cor. 15:42–50. All we can say of the resurrection of the unjust is that they will be raised from the dead, that their disembodied spirits will be reunited with their bodies, that the integrity of personal life will thus be reconstituted, and that the bodies will be endowed with qualities adapted to their eternal abode.

The resurrection of the just in its distinguishing character and result is guaranteed by the resurrection of Christ. 'Christ is risen from the dead, the firstfruits of those who have fallen asleep' (1 Cor. 15:20), and the indwelling of the Spirit of Christ is the added assurance that he that raised up Christ from the dead will also quicken their mortal bodies (Rom. 8:11). Christ by his resurrection has established the realm of the resurrection, a realm pneumatically conditioned and constituted. He is also himself 'life-giving spirit' (1 Cor. 15:45). It is, however, only in behalf of, and in union with, his people that he established this realm and exercises his life-giving energies in it. Just as Jesus' vicarious death would be meaningless apart from those who died with him, so his resurrection, and the sequel of life and power resulting from it, would have no relevance apart from those who will live in him and with him. Failure of resurrection for those who were given to Christ by the Father would mean the defeat of Jesus' commission and commitment. Of all whom the Father has given he will lose nothing, but will raise it up at the last day (John 6:39).

The resurrection body of believers will be like the body which Christ has in his exalted glory (Phil. 3:21). The body that was raised from the tomb on the third day was the same body as was laid in the tomb. But it was endowed with new qualities. So is it with the resurrection of believers. There is unity and continuity. The usage of Scripture with respect to both Christ and believers is noteworthy in this respect. It was not a body that was laid in the tomb of Jesus: it was *he* as respects his body. *He* was buried, *he* lay in the tomb, and *he* rose from the dead. So it is with believers. *They* die and *they* are laid in their graves. At the resurrection *they* will be raised up; *they* will hear Jesus' voice and will come forth. This identification of their persons with what was laid in the grave underlines the continuity. The person buried is the person raised. The difficulty of forming a concrete idea of the resurrection body is no valid objection to the reality. The pronounced difference between the grain sown and the ear that sprouts, appealed to by Paul in 1 Corinthians 15:36–38, illustrates what takes place in the raising of the body that is sown in weakness and dishonour.

When Paul speaks of the 'spiritual body' and says that 'flesh and blood cannot inherit the kingdom of God' (1 Cor. 15:44, 50), we are not to think that the resurrection body ceases to be physical and material in its composition; it will still be 'body' in distinction from 'spirit'. And the statement respecting 'flesh and blood' as not inheriting the kingdom of God must be understood as flesh characterized by the weakness, corruption, and dishonour in which the body is sown (vss. 42, 43). The 'spiritual body' is body 'framed by, filled with, and led by' the Holy Spirit. The preservation of the identity of the body does not interfere with the far-reaching change wrought in the resurrection. All sin-caused defects will be removed, the mortality and corruption resulting from sin will give place to incorruptibleness, honour, glory, and power (1 Cor. 15:42–55). The new body will eradiate glory after the pattern of the body of Christ's glory. It will be perfectly adapted to the state of eternal bliss in the new heavens and the new earth.

Christ redeemed the whole person, and thus the consummation of redemption must involve the redemption of the body (Rom. 8:23; cf. Eph. 1:14). It is in the integrity of personal life, reconstituted by the resurrection, that the saints will enter into and eternally enjoy the inheritance incorruptible, undefiled, and unfading.

It is in the resurrection that the last enemy death will be destroyed. It will be the final act of Christ's reign of conquest. The salvation which is in Christ is one conditioned by this outreach of hope, and therefore one that in its present possession is characterized by groaning for deliverance and waiting for the adoption (Rom. 8:23, 24). But even now there is the exultant thanksgiving in anticipation of the glory to be revealed (1 Cor. 15:57). For when 'this corruptible will put on incorruption and this mortal will put on immortality, then will be brought to pass the saying that is written, Death is swallowed up in victory: O death, where is thy victory? O death, where is thy sting?' (1 Cor. 15:54, 55). Pessimism contradicts the Christian faith because it knows not the believer's hope.

The foregoing doctrine of Scripture is well summarized in the *Larger Catechism* of the Westminster Assembly when it says: 'We are to believe that at the last day there shall be a general resurrection of the dead, both of the just and unjust: when they that are then found alive shall in a moment be changed; and the selfsame bodies of the dead which were laid in the grave, being then again united to their souls for ever, shall be raised up by the power of Christ. The bodies of the just, by the Spirit of Christ, and by virtue of his resurrection as their head, shall be raised in power, spiritual, incorruptible, and made like to his glorious body; and the bodies of the wicked shall be raised up in dishonour by him, as an offended judge' (Q. 87).

THE JUDGMENT

One all-important aspect of eschatology is the fact of judgment, that God will bring every work into judgment, that the whole panorama of history waits for God's final adjudication.

1. The *necessity* of this judgment resides in the truth of God's sovereignty, and that there is no other God but one. It is significant that when the apostle appeals to the fact that we must all be made manifest before the judgment seat of God, he supports this assertion by quoting from Isaiah 45:23 (Rom. 14:10, 11). The refrain of this chapter in Isaiah's prophecy is that God is God and there is none beside him (cf. vss. 5–7, 14, 18, 21, 22), and the import is that the judgment which is the theme of verse 23, just as the salvation of verses 21, 22 and the justification of verses 24, 25, finds its basis and certainty in the fact that God alone is God.

2. The *universality* of the judgment is co-ordinate with its necessity and certainty. There is no more possibility of escape from God's all-inclusive adjudication than there is from his all-pervasive sovereignty. The universality is clearly affirmed in Scripture. Our Lord's own account of the final issues is prefaced by the statement that 'before him will be

gathered all the nations' (Matt. 25:32). The terms Paul uses are unmistakably to this effect when he describes the day of God's righteous judgment. God 'will render to each one according to his works . . . tribulation and anguish upon every soul of man who works the evil . . . but glory and honour and peace to every one who works the good' (Rom. 2:6–10). Besides, the repeated use of the terms 'Jew first, and Greek' advertises, in accord with Paul's usage, the undiscriminating inclusiveness of the judgment. Furthermore, the universality is stressed by verses 12–16, where the two categories within which all mankind may be classified are specified—'without law' and 'in law'. Judgment and its issues have respect to both classes.

Many Christians have encountered difficulty with the thought of judgment being executed with reference to the thoughts, words, and deeds of believers. It is natural for believers to think that such an exposure would be incompatible with the bliss which the redeemed are represented as enjoying at the coming of Christ. There is, however, no ambiguity in the biblical statements. It is of believers Paul speaks when he says: 'We must all be made manifest before the judgment seat of Christ, in order that each one may receive the things done through the body, according to that he hath done, whether good or bad' (2 Cor. 5:10). The same teaching appears in Romans 2:14–16, when Paul closes his delineation of the judgment, as it will affect all classes, by calling it 'the day when God will judge the secrets of men according to my gospel through Christ Jesus' (cf. 1 Cor. 3:10–15; Acts 17:31; Psalm 96:13; 98:9; Eccl. 12:14).

The difficulty entertained on this score arises from prepossession with what is conceived to be our interests and comfort rather than with the claims and vindication of the glory of God. The supreme aim and concern of the people of God is the glory of God, and it is failure to apply and carry into effect this chief end that causes perplexity in connection with the judgment. God will leave nothing at loose ends; everything will be adjudicated with perfect equity. When believers will be fully sanctified, their minds and hearts will perfectly reflect the interests of God's glory, and their consciences will even require the kind of judgment which the Scriptures describe. There will, therefore, be no grief to prejudice the glory of their bliss. Besides, it is against the gravity of their sins that their salvation in Christ will be magnified, and not only the grace but the righteousness of God will be extolled in the consummation of their redemption (cf. Rom. 5:21).

3. The *criteria* of God's final judgment are law and gospel. Those outside the pale of special revelation will be judged by the law of nature. When Paul says that those 'who sinned without law shall also perish without law' (Rom. 2:12), he is referring to those who have 'the work of the law written in their hearts', who are 'a law to themselves' and 'do by nature the things of the law' (vss. 14, 15). They are not entirely without law, and so the term 'without law' refers to specially revealed law. They will not be judged by specially revealed law or by the gospel. But they will be judged by the law they possess and they will also perish.

Those inside the pale of special revelation will be judged by that standard (Rom. 2:12). This does not mean that the natural law will have no relevance to them, but their responsibility will be enhanced by the special revelation bestowed on them. In the case of the ungodly who have rejected the gospel, sin against natural law, specially revealed law, and the gospel, will be the ground of condemnation. By faith in the gospel all sin is remitted, but the rejection of Christ, though it is the chief condemnation, does not abrogate the sins against law naturally or specially revealed.

Judgment will concern, and be executed, in reference to the things done in the body (2 Cor. 5:10). Future destiny will not be determined by what transpires between death and the resurrection. 'It is appointed unto men once to die, and after this, judgment' (Heb. 9:27). This conjunction likewise points to the decisiveness for judgment of that which precedes death. In accord with this emphasis upon bodily existence is the fact that the judgment will succeed the resurrection. As the basis of judgment is life in the integrity of personal life, so the judgment and its issues will be executed only when that integrity is reconstituted by resurrection from the dead.

4. The *agent* of final judgment will be the Lord Jesus Christ. This fact is correlative with the exaltation of Christ. The exaltation bestowed upon him is the highest exaltation conceivable (cf. Eph. 1:20–22; Phil. 2:9; Heb. 1:3; 4:14; 8:1; 1 Peter 3:22) and this exaltation will be

verified and consummated in the judgment of the whole world (cf. Phil. 2:10, 11).

Jesus, in the days of his flesh, affirmed this to be a function he would perform in his messianic capacity as the Son of man (John 5:27; Matt. 25:31, 32) and Paul draws our attention to this same fact in striking terms, when he says that God 'has appointed a day in which he will judge the world in righteousness by the man whom he hath ordained' (Acts 17:31). This cosmic significance of Christ's messianic office and function exemplifies and is consonant with his investiture with all authority in heaven and in earth, and that he is head over all things (cf. Matt. 28:18; Eph. 1:22).

The fact that Jesus will sit upon the throne of judgment will be the consternation of his enemies and the consolation of his people. It is the Saviour of the people of God who will execute judgment, and therefore the transcendent majesty which the throne of judgment involves will not for them entail any suspension of the grace and love which Christ's Saviourhood bespeaks. It is 'the King' who will say to them on his right hand, 'Come, ye blessed of my Father, inherit the kingdom prepared for you from the foundation of the world' (Matt. 25:34).

5. The *result* of the judgment will be the eternal awards of the life that now is, 'everlasting destruction from the presence of the Lord and from the glory of his power' (2 Thess. 1:9) to all the impenitent, and glory, honour, immortality, and eternal life to all who obey the gospel of our Lord Jesus Christ. It will mean the consignment of each to the corresponding destiny. 'These shall go away into everlasting punishment, but the righteous into life eternal' (Matt. 25:46). God's final tribunal is charged with surpassing solemnity, and the church of Christ is unfaithful to her commission, and betrays the testimony of her Lord, when the gravity of these final issues is compromised or suppressed.

Judgment according to works does not contravene salvation by grace. Salvation is by grace through faith. But the faith that is saving bears fruit in good works, and faith without works is dead. Good works are therefore the index to a state of salvation.

The good works of believers will be rewarded (cf. Matt. 10:41, 42; 1 Cor. 3:8, 12–15). This reward does not consist in salvation nor in the eternal life inherited in the world to come. It consists in the degree of glory bestowed in the state of bliss. Glory itself is the gift of grace and secured by the righteousness of Christ (cf. Rom. 5:18–21). But the degrees of glory are proportioned to the faithfulness and labour of the saints.

The church must constantly live and bear its witness in the conviction of the impending judgment. The summons to repentance, faith, and the obedience of the gospel receives its most urgent sanction from the certainty of the account that will be rendered to Christ as judge of all. And the church must also bear witness to the grandeur of the hope which the judgment presents, the manifestation and vindication of the glory of God.